DAILY LIFE OF

WOMEN IN ANCIENT ROME

DAILY LIFE OF

WOMEN IN ANCIENT ROME

SARA ELISE PHANG

The Greenwood Press Daily Life Through History Series

 GREENWOOD™

An Imprint of ABC-CLIO, LLC
Santa Barbara, California • Denver, Colorado

Library of Congress Cataloging-in-Publication Data

Names: Phang, Sara Elise, author.
Title: Daily life of women in ancient Rome / Sara Elise Phang.
Description: Santa Barbara, California : ABC-CLIO, LLC, [2022] |
    Series: The Greenwood press daily life through history series |
    Includes bibliographical references and index.
Identifiers: LCCN 2021054202 (print) | LCCN 2021054203
    (ebook) | ISBN 9781440871689 (hardcover) | ISBN
9781440871696 (ebook)
Subjects: LCSH: Women—Rome—Social conditions. | Women—
    Rome. | Women—History—To 500.
Classification: LCC HQ1136 .P49 2022 (print) | LCC HQ1136
    (ebook) | DDC 305.40937/63—dc23/eng/20211108
LC record available at https://lccn.loc.gov/2021054202
LC ebook record available at https://lccn.loc.gov/2021054203

ISBN: 978-1-4408-7168-9 (print)
        978-1-4408-7169-6 (ebook)

26 25 24 23 22   1 2 3 4 5

This book is also available as an eBook.

Greenwood
An Imprint of ABC-CLIO, LLC

ABC-CLIO, LLC
147 Castilian Drive
Santa Barbara, California 93117
www.abc-clio.com

This book is printed on acid-free paper ∞

Manufactured in the United States of America

CONTENTS

INTRODUCTION

A historian studying women in the Roman world faces a wide and seemingly contradictory range of sources. As seen on the epitaph of a woman named Claudia, from the second century BCE,

> Friend, I have not much to say. Stop and read me. This tomb, which is not pretty, is for a pretty woman. Her parents gave her the name Claudia. She loved her husband in her heart. She bore two sons, of whom she left one above ground. She kept the house and worked with wool. That is all. You may go.

Roman epitaphs often addressed the passer-by directly, as tombs were placed along roads outside the city limits. The ostentatious modesty of Claudia's epitaph is part of the ideology of female *pudicitia* (chastity), discussed in chapter 1. It contrasts dramatically with another memorial, that of the female benefactor Junia Rustica of Cartima in Spain in the late first century CE:

> Junia Rustica, daughter of Decimus, first and perpetual priestess in the town of Cartima, restored the public porticoes that had collapsed due to old age, gave land for a bathhouse, reimbursed the public taxes, set up a bronze statue of Mars in the forum [public square], gave at her own expense porticoes next to the bathhouse on her own land, with a pool and a statue of Cupid, and dedicated them after giving a feast and public shows.

Junia continues by listing the statues of herself and her son that the town of Cartima decreed in her honor and that she graciously paid for. On the other hand, two slave women who worked in a clay brick and tile factory scrawled their names, "Detfri slave of Herennius Sattius" and "Amica slave of Herennius," on the tile and stamped their feet on it, preserving their presence for the ages. The experiences of women in the Roman world ranged from ideas, mostly written by men, about women's ideal behavior (reflected in the epitaph of Claudia) to the power wielded by privileged women such as Junia Rustica, the daughter and wife of local aristocrats, to the barely recorded or unrecorded labor of female domestic servants, textile and craft workers, and agricultural laborers.[1]

This book is about the "daily life" of Roman women in the largest sense of daily life—the larger experiences of life from birth and childhood, through marriage and the family, their economic activities, public roles, pre-Christian religion, and the universal experiences of death and mourning. These are topics in social history, a field that has expanded remarkably in classical history from the 1970s–1980s onward. The casual impression or stereotype of classical Greece and Rome is a society of (to employ an equally stereotypical term) Great Men, such as Pericles and Alcibiades in classical Athens, or Cicero, Caesar, and Augustus in ancient Rome, and of a few canonical male authors, such as Thucydides for classical Greece and Livy and Tacitus for Rome. Frustrated with this narrow definition, female scholars sought to recover a "women's history" of antiquity (exemplified by Sarah Pomeroy's *Goddesses, Whores, Wives, and Slaves* [1975] and by the first edition of Mary R. Lefkowitz and Maureen B. Fant's *Women's Life in Greece and Rome: A Source Book in Translation* [1982], now in its fourth edition [2016]). The field has shifted and broadened to include gender or ideologies *about* masculinity and femininity that shape how men and women think and behave; gender is a wider field than women's history, as it can affect almost any aspect of society. Gender studies are a complex field involving literary and social theory and will not be the main focus of this book, though the influence of contemporary Greco-Roman ideas about women will be discussed.

The study of Roman women was hindered for a long time by two stereotypes fostered by Roman literature. One was of the chaste, dutiful, and submissive daughter and wife (as with Claudia mentioned earlier), subjugated by *patria potestas* (the legal total authority of a father over his children) and by archaic *manus* marriage (which gave a husband similar authority over his wife). This stereotype of patriarchy was attributed by modern scholars to the early Republic (509–376 BCE). The other stereotype, also fostered by Roman literature, is of promiscuous and adulterous women who lived extravagant lives, wearing transparent silk dresses and carried in litters through the teeming city, drinking pearls dissolved in vinegar to show how they could squander their wealth. This stereotype is attributed to the Late Republic (ca. 129–27 BCE) and to the early and middle imperial era (27 BCE–284 CE). We will see that both stereotypes are equally unwarranted. They were the product of a literary culture that emphasized praise and blame (see "Literary Sources"). The reality for Roman women of the Late Republic and Principate lay in the middle.

The corollary of these stereotypes is that Roman women were originally repressed and subservient and gained more freedom and economic and political power in the Late Republic and early Empire. Modern nineteenth- and twentieth-century scholars variously depicted this as emancipation or decadence. The change is probably illusory; there are far more sources available for women's history from the late Roman Republic onward, and especially from the first three centuries of the Roman Empire. Junia Rustica's monument is one of many female benefactors. But Claudia's epitaph emphasizing traditional female virtues also has many imitators. Many kinds of women's behaviors existed simultaneously, and so did general limits on what women could do.

Rome was still a "patriarchal" society in its fundamental social and political structures. Women could not serve in the military or hold political office or military officerships. During the imperial era, the empresses or *Augustae* had no formal political powers, even when they were de facto regents for their children. Women were (as feminist theorists have termed them) objects of exchange between families, transferred in marriage. Marriage was a social arrangement between families, not based on personal preference; it was "for the procreation of children," legitimate children who were the progeny of their father. Male-authored Roman sources show a veritable obsession with adultery not because women's adultery was so frequent, but because their marital fidelity assured the physical and social reproduction of the family, including property transmission from one generation to the next. Stories of promiscuous women fascinated the ancient authors because of the importance of women's *pudicitia*, a term that signifies their fidelity to their husbands and sexual unavailability to any other men as long as they were married. However, as this book shows, women's lives were not restricted to the home or to purely domestic activities.

The focus of this book is on relatively "ordinary" women—including women of the upper classes—and away from "extraordinary" women such as the relatives of aristocratic politicians during the Late Republic or the empresses and women of the imperial family during the Principate. Sometimes anecdotes about the latter category of women are cited to illustrate a point, but the male authors who recorded information about extraordinary women were not objective. They tended to insert such women into a mold of praise or blame, making it uncertain how much we can know reliably about female personages. This book uses documentary sources as well as literary ones; two inscriptions have already been quoted from the *Corpus Inscriptionum Latinarum*, a collection of hundreds of thousands of Latin inscriptions on stone that have been reconstructed, transcribed, and published. Other documentary sources are discussed in this chapter. They are more likely to represent women's own voices and display the agency that women had within the framework of Roman society.

SUMMARY OF CHAPTERS

The first chapter, "Status and Gender," outlines the social structure of the Roman Empire and the nature of *pudicitia*, a virtue that was closely associated with women's social status. As this chapter argues, there was no universal "Roman woman" but many different status and occupational groups of women, whose experiences were highly divergent. Very often we know more about the Roman upper and middle social strata, which are defined in this chapter, and relatively little about the lower strata.

The second chapter, "Birth and Mortality," concerns experiences that *were* universal in the ancient world: the impact of disease and medical practices on demography, the shape of populations and of the course of individual lives through time. Aspects of demography include how many infants are born in an average family, how many of them survive to adulthood, when women and men marry, and how their life expectancy changes with age. The Roman world was a premodern society marked by high mortality rates and an extremely low life expectancy at birth (between twenty and thirty years of age). This low life expectancy is an *average*; it resulted from extremely high infant and child mortality, on a scale that is difficult to imagine today. The causes included malaria, a major killer of children and of pregnant women in the climate and ecological conditions of the ancient Mediterranean, but also other infectious diseases that spread in crowded cities. The high death rate of infants and very small children probably affected how they were cared for; they were not mourned in the same manner as older children or adults.

The third chapter, "Childhood and Education," examines what childhood was like for Roman girls. Some Roman child-rearing practices appear universal to both boys and girls. There is far more evidence for the education of elite boys, who thus were prepared for public careers from which women were excluded. It appears that even upper-stratum girls' education was often truncated in contrast with their male peers because elite girls were expected to marry in their early to mid-teens, leading us into the next chapter, "Marriage."

The chapter "Marriage" differentiates aspects of historical Roman marriage from the patriarchal stereotype of marriage with *manus*, a legal anachronism practiced mainly by the state priesthood. According to Roman law, marriage in the Late Republic and imperial era was a relatively weak relationship, in which the wife still belonged to her father's family; if legally independent, she had separate control of her own property, and in fact husband and wife were forbidden to give each other substantial gifts. This relatively weak legal relationship, however, left Roman women at a disadvantage in inheritance from/to their husbands or their husband's children. Socially, however, women were probably expected to be the junior partners in marriage because they were often much younger than their husbands. Documentary evidence from epitaphs suggests that Roman women's age at first marriage was in the middle to late teens; their husbands might be at least a decade older, and among the elite many men were much older than their wives. A sexual double standard existed; a husband was not required to be faithful to his wife, but *pudicitia* required a wife to be faithful to her husband. The last part of the chapter concerns the public intervention by the emperor Augustus (27 BCE–14 CE) in marriage, creating a complex of laws that promoted the marriages of the upper strata, required remarriage after divorce or widowhood, and punished adultery. Being married and bearing children provided status for women; there appears to be no group of unmarried women, whether nuns or spinsters, but certain groups were not allowed *legal* marriage; they formed de facto marriages that left them vulnerable in law and society.

The fifth chapter, "Dress and Status," concerns the material interface of women with the outside world—how they were dressed.

It explores the material and social constraints of dress in a period when the hand production of thread and cloth made clothing expensive. Certain garments may have been associated with high-status roles. Dress that hid the body was a way of guarding and paradoxically displaying a woman's *pudicitia*. Adornment with clothing, cosmetics, and jewelry conferred an ambiguous form of status; it displayed wealth, but was deplored as frivolous extravagance by male moralists who used it to sexualize women and minimize their importance as economic participants.

The sixth chapter, "Economic Life," examines the economic status and activities of women of the elite and lower strata. Many elite women inherited substantial wealth and under Roman law, despite a doctrine of feminine incapability and legal guardianship of women, became able to manage their property freely. Women were not merely passive consumers; elite women often took the initiative to increase the household net worth. The great majority of women did not enjoy these privileges, and the economic labor of the Empire was supported by them to a degree that is impossible to appreciate from textual sources (where women as domestic wives and mothers are so emphasized even in the lower strata) but can be inferred demographically. At random and through the household cycle, households might have few or no adult men and women had to support them.

Many women were owned and exploited as slaves, the subject of the seventh chapter, "Slavery and Manumission." This chapter sets Roman slavery in context with some contrasts with the nature of New World slavery; Roman slavery was not based on racial difference and had its own internal hierarchy, with wealthy slaves holding positions of authority in the imperial bureaucracy or in elite households. Many relatively privileged slaves were freed and their children merged into Roman society. However, women slaves were doubly stigmatized as women and as slaves; they were less likely to hold positions of authority, were vulnerable to sexual exploitation, and, if they were freed, faced greater legal stigma than men.

"Social Life," the eighth chapter, discusses women's leisure and social activities, mainly in the urban setting of the city of Rome and similar smaller cities and towns. It examines how women made use of the amenities of Roman civilization—public baths, theaters, games and spectacles in the amphitheater, shops, and other public spaces—and how men perceived their social activities.

"Public Life," the ninth chapter, surveys a surprising fact of the Roman world: parts of its smaller cities and towns were actually built by female benefactors, who funded public buildings, temples, baths, theaters, and other infrastructure. Despite women's exclusion from magistracies and town councils and despite a persistent ideal in male authors that women should not intervene in public affairs, women thus played roles in civic life as patronesses and benefactors.

A public role that was acceptable for women was that of priestess or lay participant in religious rituals, the subject of the tenth chapter, "Religious Life," which examines women's religious practices from the Vestal Virgins (elite state priestesses at Rome) to ordinary people's household religion, private divination, and magic. Many traditional Roman religious festivals involved the family, bringing us to the practices surrounding death and remembrance.

The eleventh chapter, "Death and Remembrance," examines women's roles in the rituals surrounding death and funerals, and how women themselves received commemoration. Again, much more is known about the Roman upper strata, in which women might receive public funerals and eulogies. The public funerals resemble those of men; the eulogies seem to have been gendered, focusing on women's *pudicitia* and domestic virtues, as is also the case with women's epitaphs in the lower social strata. Nonetheless, women could exert some control over how they wanted to be remembered, by making wills (the properly made will was a peculiarly Roman obsession) and dictating epitaphs that provided for remembrance-day feasts and memorial foundations.

SOURCES FOR WOMEN'S LIVES

The Roman sources that have survived provide numerous challenges and opportunities for studying women's lives in the ancient world. In the more recent past, such as eighteenth-century England or America, church and public records, medical records, diaries, personal letters, books, and broadsheets (early newspapers) survive; from the nineteenth century, in addition, newspapers or magazines and advertising survive. The Roman Empire lacked public media such as newspapers. Graffiti and inscriptions painted on whitewashed walls at Pompeii show that the Roman world had rudimentary forms of public announcements and advertising. Public records were kept but mostly do not survive (see "Papyri and Tablets"). Carefully edited collections of personal letters do survive, but they were produced by men (see "Literary Sources"). The types of sources from the Roman world are those that were able to survive the millennia: literary texts, copied over the centuries by medieval monks; wax and wooden tablets, preserved by chance at Herculaneum and elsewhere; papyri, documents written on papyrus, surviving in arid conditions in Egypt and the Near East; and inscriptions cut on stone, often surviving because they were reused in newer buildings. Archeological finds can provide a wider range of evidence for the presence and activity of women, especially in areas stereotyped as for men only, such as military camps. However, the interpretation of such finds is difficult, and this book focuses on literary, legal, and documentary texts.

The sources reflect the social and legal constraints that Roman women faced. Men produced nearly all of the literary sources surviving from the Roman world, including histories, biographies, poetry, encyclopedias, collections of letters, and collections of anecdotes. They tended to see women a certain way, discussed at more length in chapter 1. Often these sources attest not so much what women actually did but what men believed about women. To reduce this problem, in this book, we often emphasize documentary sources that were produced or at least authorized by women, including inscriptions, tablets, papyri, and legal cases involving women. Where possible, to make the sources accessible to students, sourcebooks in translation have been cited in addition to the primary sources.

LITERARY SOURCES

Greek and Roman literary sources, including histories, biographies, collections of anecdotes and letters, encyclopedias, poetry, satire, antiquarian works, and medical texts, were almost always written by men of the social elite (defined in chapter 1). These works reflect elite men's education and social biases. Very often they ignore women. When they mention women, they tend to focus on extraordinary, legendary, or notorious women, who are not the subject of this book except when such individuals illustrate a social point. Due to the highly moralistic and rhetorical education of elite men, the literary sources stereotype women as "good" or "bad," discussed in more detail in chapter 1.[2]

ROMAN LITERATURE

Men of the social elite were educated in a common Greco-Roman literary culture, including both classical Greek and Latin literature.

Latin literature first imitated Greek models but quickly developed
its own independent, vigorous character, especially in oratory, history, satire, epigrams, love poetry, novels, and antiquarian and
technical literature. Each genre has its own special conventions that
must be understood when using it as a source for women's history.
First of all, nearly all of these works were written by men; only a
few female authors, such as the poets Sulpicia and Julia Balbilla,
are attested in the Late Republic and early Empire. The creation
and circulation of literature were part of men's public life and private entertainment. Oratory, obviously, had a major part in public
life, in politics and in legal trials, where highly rhetorical speeches
intended to persuade and move the audience were more common
than the modern technical cross-examination. Claims about people
or groups of people in oratory must thus be regarded with caution.
Denouncing individuals and groups of people in moralistic terms
was the orator's stock-in-trade and also influenced history, biography, and collections of historical anecdotes.

Historiography and biography (such as Tacitus's *Annals* and
Histories and Suetonius's *Twelve Caesars*) were written in a different style but often resorted to similar moralistic generalizations, as
in the Senate debate on whether elite women should accompany
Roman governors to their provinces, a debate that may well have
happened but that serves Tacitus's themes. In reading history and
biography, the reader should be on the lookout for structures and
themes that may shape and distort the representations of important characters. Historiography addressed the "public," the idealized political class, as did public-themed poetry, such as Virgil's
Aeneid and Horace's *Carmen Saeculare*. Epitaphs are another genre
of public-facing literature, in that people presented themselves as
they wished to be remembered in accordance with the ideals of
their society.[3]

In private, the genres of satire and epigram were probably
regarded as men's entertainment. The trading of biting depictions of probably fictional individuals and salty quips about sexual behavior may have been a mode of male bonding and need
to be regarded with skepticism as a source of fact. They are more
likely to be a source of ideology, as with Juvenal's *Sixth Satire*,
a denunciation of present-day Roman women. Elegaic poetry,
named for its technical form rather than "mourning" in the modern sense of the term, also poses problems of a different kind,
as it frequently depicts lovers and their mistresses—in a society
where "respectable" (elite) women were married young and not

permitted sexuality outside marriage. The identity of the women in Roman love elegy continues to be debated; they may not have belonged to the elite.

Literary collections of letters are another source, the most famous being Cicero's *Letters to Atticus* (his friend) and *Letters to His Friends* (including family members), written in the 50s and 40s BCE before Cicero's own death in 43, and Pliny the Younger's *Letters*, written from around 100–112 CE. Both collections were heavily edited for public consumption and, because they were intended to showcase Cicero's and Pliny's own prose, do not contain the replies from their correspondents, except for the emperor Trajan's brief replies in Pliny's *Letters*, book X. They are also intended to present Cicero and Pliny in a flattering light. Nonetheless, these collections contain much evidence for social history. Literary diaries also survive, such as the *Meditations* of Marcus Aurelius (emperor 161–80 CE). But many more autobiographies by notable Romans existed than have survived, including the memoirs of the empress Agrippina the Younger, mother of the emperor Nero (54–68 CE).

Finally, technical and antiquarian literature provides important sources for social history. They are not, however, less subjective and ideological. Among the technical authors that provide information about women are medical authors, working in a Greek tradition that dated back to the legendary Hippocrates (or Hippocratic school). Latin literature also featured encyclopedists and collectors of antiquarian material, such as the *Natural History* encyclopedia by Pliny the Elder, Pliny the Younger's uncle, who died in the eruption of Vesuvius in 79 CE; Valerius Maximus's *Memorable Deeds and Sayings*, a collection of moralistic exempla; and Aulus Gellius's *Noctes Atticae* (*Attic Nights*), with much information on religious practices. The Late Republican author Marcus Terentius Varro compiled a massive encyclopedia on religious practices, the *Divine and Human Antiquities*, that has not survived; it is quoted by Christian authors. The early imperial grammarian Verrius Flaccus wrote a text, *On the Meaning of Words*, that also focused on religion, and was abridged by the second-century CE author Sextus Pompeius Festus. Festus in his turn was partially summarized by the eighth-century CE Paulus Diaconus, not to be confused with the jurist Julius Paulus (see "Legal Literature"). The text of Festus and Paulus, edited by Wallace Lindsay, is indicated by its page numbers. Such texts are important sources for religious tradition, such as Roman wedding and funeral customs. Legal texts, though also authored by the Roman elite, are discussed in a separate section.

PAPYRI AND TABLETS

Documentary sources from the sub-elite below the Greco-Roman upper classes are extremely valuable as historical sources because they were less influenced by elite mentalities and education; many documents attest women's activities, some written in their own words. These texts mostly survive by chance and document all aspects of daily life, including many aspects that the Greco-Roman elite paid little attention to.

Surviving documents from the Roman world include papyri, ostraka, and tablets. Papyri, written in ink on papyrus (a type of paper made from papyrus reeds), survive mainly from very arid areas of Roman Egypt and the Near East. Texts written in ink on potsherds (ostraka) also survive from dry areas, and those written or scratched on wooden and wax-covered tablets have been preserved in arid conditions, by carbonizing (as in the eruption of Vesuvius) or by burial in anaerobic, bog-like conditions. These documents include private letters, legal instruments such as marriage contracts and wills, bureaucratic records, shopping lists, writing exercises, and more. They pose problems of reconstruction by modern scholars, as many texts are fragmentary.[4]

Papyri and tablets also pose problems of context: is a document representative of its kind or a one-off? Does it represent empire-wide practices or local culture? From time to time this book will refer to papyri and tablets from Roman Egypt, from where the largest number of documents survive. People in Roman Italy, northwestern Europe, and the Greek East probably made a similar use of documents which have not survived (some documents have been preserved at Herculaneum in southern Italy and at Vindolanda and Carlisle in northern Britain). But local culture may influence documents, as with marriage contracts from Roman Egypt that were influenced by Greek law and custom (after 323 BCE, Egypt was colonized by Greek settlers under the Ptolemaic monarchy). Furthermore, papyri and tablets reflect only the sub-elite that was literate and wanted to record financial transactions and letters. They represent a relatively well-off stratum, not the masses of Roman society, who (both men and women) were probably illiterate.

INSCRIPTIONS

Another form of documentary source is the Latin (or Greek) inscription on stone. Some inscriptions on metal (usually bronze) survive, but metal tended to be melted down and reused. Hundreds of thousands of stone inscriptions survive from around the ancient Mediterranean and northern Europe. Many more have not survived because stone tended also to be reused. The great mass of surviving inscriptions date from the first to the early third centuries CE, representing the so-called epigraphic habit or tendency of people to erect inscriptions to record major events in their lives and communities or commemorate their dead. As with papyri and tablets, many inscriptions are damaged or fragmentary, and most use extensive common abbreviations, posing challenges for reconstruction and expansion.[5]

The content of inscriptions includes funerary epitaphs, an important source of information regarding the family lives and beliefs of the sub-elite: freedmen and freedwomen and their families at Rome, soldiers all over the Empire, inhabitants of relatively small towns and cities. Pre-Christian Latin epitaphs focused more on the lives of the deceased and their relationships than on the afterlife and so are a useful source for social attitudes and even demography (with caution). The more expensive or aspirational tombstones also featured funerary art. In general, tombstone memorials depict the deceased and their family members as they wished to be seen; they attest public-facing values. Public inscriptions recorded the deeds and careers of important Romans, including women as public priestesses and city benefactors. Religious inscriptions attest the beliefs of pre-Christian inhabitants of the Empire, making vows and dedications to numerous gods.

Inscriptions spanned a wide social range but represented the elite down to the moderately well-off sub-elite rather than the poor. An inscription on stone was somewhat expensive and hence failed to represent the multitudes of poorer inhabitants of the Empire. The poor may have fashioned burial monuments out of painted and carved wood that have not survived.

LEGAL LITERATURE

The other great genre of Latin technical literature, though it tends to be studied separately, is Roman law. Because legal writings form such a major source for the social history of Roman women, they require a separate introduction, explaining their preservation, their major concepts, and their assumptions.[6]

The oldest legal work was the Twelve Tables, ca. 450 BCE, memorized by Roman boys studying law in the Late Republic and early Empire. Many of its provisions were out of date. As this shows, the Romans regarded their law not as a merely technical field of endeavor but as an ideological heritage, prescribing social as well as legal roles with rigorous logic (and many exceptions, reflecting the concerns of real life).

Roman men of the upper classes were expected to be well versed in law and able to plead in the courts, serving as advocates for their social peers or clients (social inferiors linked to them by favors and obligations). Accordingly, this social stratum also produced the jurists (*iuris consulti*), men who were not professional "lawyers" in the modern sense (obtaining a degree from an accredited institution, passing a bar examination, and paid by a firm or the government) but wrote treatises and manuals on legal topics and debated legal reasoning among themselves. Their works became regarded as a source of law in itself. Only a few textbooks of Roman law survive more or less intact; Gaius's *Institutes* is the best known.

Statute law, as we would term it, took the form of *leges* (singular *lex*), passed by the citizen assemblies of the Roman Republic, such as the *Lex Voconia* regulating wealthy women's capacity to inherit. Another source of law was the Praetor's Edict, dating from the Late Republic but amended several times during the Principate and finalized during the reign of Hadrian (117–38 CE). The Praetor, an administrator of legal affairs, regulated many aspects of procedure in Roman law. Edicts of the emperors became another source of law, as did the *senatus consulta* or decrees of the Senate, named for the senator who moved them, though most imperial *senatus consulta* in reality originated with the emperors and their legal advisers. The *senatus consultum Orphitianum* of 178 CE permitted Roman citizen mothers to inherit from their children.

Yet another source of law was imperial rescripts (*rescripta*). Inhabitants of the Roman Empire submitted petitions to the emperor, asking for legal advice, and the replies of the emperors (or rather, their legal advisers) are termed rescripts. Rescripts also became regarded as a source of law in themselves, and they are important because they attest real cases involving actual people rather than hypothetical cases or prescriptive rulings. Jurists in their turn commented upon rescripts.

The corpus of legal writing—treatises, commentaries, manuals, *leges*, edicts, *senatus consulta*, and rescripts—grew with the centuries. When the legal advisers of Justinian (emperor 527–65 CE) sought to systematize and streamline this corpus in the 530s, they collected passages from the corpus and arranged them under subject headings in the *Digest*, a kind of *Bartlett's Familiar Quotations* of Roman law, illustrating concepts and principles. Each excerpted passage was labeled with the jurist's name and the title of the original source and in modern publications is identified by chapter, title, section, and subsection numbers.

Justinian's compilators also assembled the *Codex Iustinianus*, a collection of passages from imperial edicts and rescripts. The Digest and the Codex together are termed the *Corpus Iuris Civilis* and cover approximately the period from the Late Republic to Diocletian (emperor 284–305 CE). A modern English translation of the Digest was published by Roman legal scholar Alan Watson, and a more recent translation of the *Codex Iustinianus* by Bruce W. Frier; the translations of the Digest in this book are from the Watson edition.

Specific aspects of Roman law bearing on the family and women's status will be treated in subsequent chapters, but major concepts will be discussed here in brief. The Roman *law of persons* defined and regulated the legal status of individuals. You were either a Roman citizen (*civis Romanus/civis Romana*) or a slave (*servus/ancilla*) or a free foreigner (*peregrinus/a*). Roman citizens had the right to marry (*conubium*) each other; slaves and foreigners did not possess this right. A married couple, their children, and their slaves (assuming a family well-off enough to have slaves) constituted a *familia*, a term that is more expansive than our "family" and is sometimes used to refer to a slave household. The term for a physical house, particularly in a town or city, was *domus* and was also used to refer to the nuclear family (blood relations). Other, larger kinship groups were important in the earlier Republic: the *gens* or "clan," consisting of all persons with the same *nomen* (family name, such as *Porcius* or *Cornelius*), and the agnates, or all relatives in the male line only. Your father and your father's brother, but not your mother, your mother's brother, or your paternal uncle's wife, were your agnates, as were your brothers and sisters, but not your sister's children. Children belonged to the *familia* of their fathers, not their mothers.

The Romans regarded *patria potestas* as a particularly Roman institution: the paterfamilias (father or oldest male ascendant in a family) had in theory absolute authority over his descendants in the male line, thus over his sons and daughters, and his son's children, but not his daughter's children. The paterfamilias owned all of the property in the *familia*; his sons and daughters, being *in potestate* (in his power), had no legal right to own property. In practice, adult sons and daughters were given a *peculium* or "fund" that they could manage and dispose of, though they did not legally possess it. When the paterfamilias died, his sons and daughters became *sui iuris* (legally independent) and able to own property. Each son then became paterfamilias of his own family, but daughters could not be paterfamilias or hold *potestas* over their children. An adult married woman was a materfamilias, "mother of a family," but this role connoted mainly respectable status and expectations for behavior; it did not confer power parallel to the paterfamilias. Daughters, however, once *sui iuris* were able to inherit property and manage it, with certain restrictions that are described in chapter 6.

Roman law existed to stabilize a traditional society, not to accommodate social change. Nonetheless, the large trend was toward an improvement in the legal status of women, particularly with respect to inheritance between mothers and children. Roman law, because it protected property rights, was often more progressive toward women with property than nonlegal literature toward women. Roman law did not protect women without property, and it treated enslaved men and women *as* property.

ROMAN NAMES

An explanation of Roman nomenclature is provided here. A Roman citizen man's name had three parts: the praenomen, the nomen, and the cognomen. The praenomen was limited to a few standard names: Aulus, Decimus, Gaius (or Caius in some spellings), Gnaeus (or Cnaeus), Lucius, Manius, Marcus, Numerius, Publius, Spurius, Tiberius, Titus. The nomen or main name originally was that of the *gens*, the clan the family belonged to, a form of social organization that was obsolete by the Late Republic. The last name or cognomen originally represented some attribute distinguishing a family; for example, Marcus Tullius Cicero's cognomen derived from *cicer*, "chickpea," suggesting some ancestor's cleft nose tip. The cognomen often became fixed and handed down in families, supplemented with an agnomen referring to a personal deed or adoption from another family. A name that shows all of these is Scipio the Younger, with praenomen Publius, nomen Cornelius, cognomen Scipio, and two agnomens, Africanus Aemilianus, adopted from the family of Aemilius Paulus by the son of Scipio

Africanus the Elder. Many famous Romans are referred to by their shorter modern English names, such as Pompey for Gnaeus Pompeius or Trajan for Marcus Ulpius Traianus (emperor 98–117 CE).

Slaves had single names, often Greek or from another local language. Former slaves took the nomen of their owners, using their slave name as a cognomen. Throughout this book, the terms "master" and "mistress" are avoided and "owner" is used instead, except when an ancient author is quoted or paraphrased.

Women originally had only a nomen in feminine form, for example, Cornelia the mother of the Gracchi. A cognomen indicating birth order might be added: Prima (First), Secunda (Second), Tertia (Third), or Maior (Older), and Minor (Younger). This formal naming, which made women rather anonymous, changed and became more individual in the Late Republic and early Empire. Women's cognomina now might be adapted from men's cognomina, taken from the mother's side of the family, or chosen according to preference.

Nonetheless, many Romans had the same name. For example, various Cornelias appear in this book: the most often mentioned is Cornelia the mother of the Gracchi, from the mid-second century BCE. A century later, another Cornelia, the daughter of Quintus Metellus Scipio, married Pompey the Great. In the reign of Domitian (81–96 CE), a Cornelia Cossa was Vestal Virgin. They were probably not related, and the text will distinguish persons whenever possible.

BEYOND THE SOURCES

It should also be stressed that the sources, literary, documentary, and legal, did not cover some aspects of Roman life that were paradoxically too massive in impact to be seen and that awaited the development of modern statistical disciplines. One of these is premodern demography, which had an impact on all aspects of family life and women's lives. Archeological evidence also provides a corrective to the distortions present in literary sources and culturally influenced documents (such as epitaphs). However, the main focus of this book is on textual and not archeological evidence.

NOTES

1. On Claudia, see *ILS* 8403 = *CIL* VI 15346 = Mary R. Lefkowitz and Maureen B. Fant, *Women's Life in Greece and Rome: A Source Book in Translation*, 4th ed. (Baltimore, MD, 2016), no. 48. On Junia Rustica, see *CIL* II

1956 = *ILS* 5512; Emily A. Hemelrijk, *Hidden Lives, Public Personae: Women and Civic Life in the Roman West* (Oxford, 2015), 159; *Women and Society in the Roman World: A Sourcebook of Inscriptions from the Roman West* (Cambridge, 2021), no. 6.6. On Detfri, see *CIL* I 3556a; Amy Richlin, *Arguments with Silence: Writing the History of Roman Women* (Ann Arbor, MI, 2014), 2; Hemelrijk, *Women and Society*, no. 3.109.

2. On method with literary sources, see David S. Potter, *Literary Texts and the Roman Historian* (London, 1999).

3. Tac. *Ann.* 3.33–34.

4. For an introduction to papyri, ostraka, and tablets, see Roger S. Bagnall, *Reading Papyri, Writing Ancient History* (London, 1995).

5. For an introduction to inscriptions, see Alison E. Cooley, *The Cambridge Manual of Latin Epigraphy* (Cambridge, 2012); Arthur E. Gordon, *Illustrated Introduction to Latin Epigraphy* (Berkeley, CA, 1983).

6. On Roman law, see O. F. Robinson, *The Sources of Roman Law: Problems and Methods for Ancient Historians* (London, 1997); David Johnston, *Roman Law in Context* (Cambridge, 1999); a standard textbook still is Barry Nicholas, *An Introduction to Roman Law* (Oxford, 1962).

CHRONOLOGY

60	First Triumvirate formed
58	Cicero's exile
58–50	Caesar's conquest of Gaul
49–45	Caesarian-Pompeian Civil War; Pompeians defeated
49–44	Caesar's dictatorships
44	Caesar assassinated (March 15)
43	Octavian claims consulship
43–42	Triumviral proscriptions
40–41	Perusine War
40	Treaty of Brundisium; Antony marries Octavian's sister Octavia
33	Antony marries Cleopatra
32–31	War of Octavian and Antony
31	Antony defeated at Actium
30	Suicides of Antony and Cleopatra
27 BCE–14 CE	Reign of Augustus
14	Death of Augustus; Rhine and Danube mutiny; Agrippina at the bridge
14–37	Reign of Tiberius
37–41	Reign of Gaius (Caligula)
41–54	Reign of Claudius; Messalina
54–68	Reign of Nero
54–59	De facto reign of Agrippina the Younger
59	Death of Agrippina
66–70	Jewish War
68–69	Reign of Galba
69	Reigns of Otho and Vitellius
	"Year of Four Emperors" civil war
69–79	Reign of Vespasian
79	Eruption of Mount Vesuvius; Pompeii and Herculaneum destroyed

79–81	Reign of Titus
81–96	Reign of Domitian
96–98	Reign of Nerva
98–117	Reign of Trajan
101–6	Dacian Wars
117–38	Reign of Hadrian
138–61	Reign of Antoninus Pius
161–80	Reign of Marcus Aurelius
180–92	Reign of Commodus
193	Reign of Pertinax
	Reign of Didius Julianus
193–211	Reign of Septimius Severus
211–17	Reign of Caracalla
212	Constitutio Antoniniana grants citizenship to all inhabitants of empire
217–18	Reign of Macrinus
218–22	Reign of Elagabalus
222–35	Reign of Alexander Severus
235–84	Third-century crisis
284–305	Reign of Diocletian
306–37	Reign of Constantine I
476	Fall of Roman Empire in West

GLOSSARY

aedile (pl. aediles): A junior magistrate of the Roman state, in charge of markets and public order.

aes **(pl.** *asses***):** A low-value bronze coin.

ancilla **(pl.** *ancillae***):** A slave woman.

censor: The most senior magistrate of the Roman Republic, elected every five years and in charge of administering the census.

census: Enumeration of Roman citizens, held every five years during the Republic.

concubina **(pl.** *concubinae***):** Concubine; woman in a domestic partnership not regarded as marriage.

concubinus: A homosexual partner, usually an adolescent slave.

consul: One of the two chief executive magistrates and commanders in chief of the Roman Republic, elected yearly—a purely honorary position during the Principate.

cult: The worship of a particular deity, including rites and festivals; not a judgmental or derogatory term.

cursus honorum: The typical sequence of magistracies held by a politician during the Republic.

decurion: A town councilor; generally, the status group from which such councilors and magistrates were recruited.

denarius (pl. denarii): A high-value silver coin, worth 4 sesterces.

equestrian: A member of the equestrian order, the second wealthiest status group in the Roman world, with property worth 400,000 or more.

flamen Dialis: The high priest of Jupiter at Rome.

flaminica (pl. *flaminicae*): A public priestess, usually at small city or town level.

flaminica Dialis: The high priestess of Jupiter at Rome, wife of the *flamen Dialis.*

freedman, freedwoman: A former slave.

ius liberorum: Privileges such as additional inheritance rights and liberation from guardianship, granted to women who give birth to three children.

jurist: A legal expert, whose opinions had the force of law; usually of senatorial or equestrian status. Excerpts of jurists' legal writings are collected in the Digest.

Lares: The gods of a Roman household.

Lex Aelia Sentia: A law restricting the manumission of slaves under thirty years of age.

Lex Fufia Caninia: A law restricting the numbers of slaves who could be manumitted in a will.

Lex Julia de adulteriis: Introduced in 18 BCE, a law that penalized adultery committed by Roman citizens; probable application to higher-status citizens.

Lex Julia de maritandis ordinibus: Introduced in 18 BCE and merged with the *Lex Papia Poppaea* of 9 CE; a law that penalized childless and unmarried citizens and promoted marriage and reproduction.

Lex Julia theatralis: An Augustan law that required different social groups to sit in different areas of the theater or amphitheater at Rome.

Lex Junia: A law that permitted an informally manumitted freedman and freedwoman to attain the Roman citizenship if the freedwoman had a baby who lived to one year of age.

Lex Papia Poppaea: A supplement to the *Lex Julia de maritandis ordinibus* of 18 BCE, passed in 9 CE.

liberta (pl. *libertae*): A female freed slave.

libertus (pl. *liberti*): A male freed slave. Granted Roman citizenship, but owed certain services and respect to his former owner (now his *patronus*).

materfamilias: A Roman citizen mother of a family.

matrona: A Roman citizen wife and mother of high social status, probably of senatorial, equestrian, or decurion status.

nutrix: A nurse or wet nurse, usually a slave woman.

ornatrix: A female hairdresser or lady's maid, usually a slave woman.

Parentalia: Holiday honoring the deceased members of a family.

partititve inheritance: The system of Roman inheritance in which paternal property was divided among all living children, both sons and daughters.

paterfamilias: The father or grandfather of a family, with *patria potestas* over all living descendants in the male line of descent.

patria potestas: The legal authority a paterfamilias wielded over his descendants, including the right to possess property.

patrician: Member of elite clans in the early Republic, merged with wealthy plebeians by the late fourth century BCE.

patronus: A patron who provided assistance, favors, and influence on behalf of his clients, usually people of lower status than himself.

pedagogue: A man or woman, usually a slave or freedperson, who accompanied Roman children to and from school and oversaw their behavior.

Penates: Household gods who protected the household food supply; usually worshipped in the same manner as the *Lares*.

plebeian: Member of nonaristocratic clans in the early Republic; wealthy plebian clans merged with patricians by the late fourth century BCE.

praetor: A magistrate just beneath consul in rank, holding military commands or administering law in the city of Rome.

proconsul: A former consul appointed to govern a province.

public priestess: A priestess of the imperial cult or other gods in smaller cities and towns.

pudicitia: "Modesty" or "chastity," the sexual propriety and unavailability of women, particularly freeborn citizen women of higher status.

regina sacrorum: "Queen for sacred matters," the wife of the *rex sacrorum* or "king for sacred matters," a high priest at Rome with no political power.

rescript: A response from the emperor or his legal staff to a citizen who presented him, usually in writing, with a legal problem.

Saliae: Unmarried young women who may have danced in armor.

senator: A member of the Roman senate, the main governing and advisory body of the Roman Republic, still in existence in the Principate.

senatorial order: The status group to which senators and their wives and children belonged; senators were required to have property worth 1,000,000 sesterces or more.

sesterce (abbrev. HS): A high-value silver coin, worth one-fourth of the denarius.

stola: The sleeveless overdress worn by Roman matrons.

stuprum: Sexual immorality, more general than adultery; committed by unmarried women or homosexually.

toga praetexta: The toga worn by Roman citizen boys and girls below puberty and by Roman magistrates; adorned with a purple border.

toga virilis: The plain white toga worn by adult male Roman citizens who were not magistrates.

tunica: The basic garment of men and women in the Roman world; men's tunics were belted above their knees, while women's tunics (dresses) fell at least to their lower calves.

tutela: Guardianship of women or children, restricting their ability to undertake certain financial transactions. A woman could be freed from guardianship by giving birth to three children.

tutor: A guardian, exerting *tutela* over a woman or a child. The guardianship of women was a much less onerous duty than guardianship of children.

Vestal Virgin: One of six high priestesses of Vesta (the goddess of the sacred fire at Rome), consecrated to virginity; if she engaged in sexual activity, she was liable to execution.

1

STATUS AND GENDER

INTRODUCTION: THE STATUS OF WOMEN IN ROMAN SOCIETY

The experiences of women in the Roman world depended greatly on their social status or their location in the Roman social hierarchy. At the top were women of the social elite: in the Republic, the wives and daughters of consuls; and in the Empire, the empresses and other women of the imperial family. In general, this book describes "elite women" as women of the senatorial and equestrian orders. The term "elite" indicates membership in a socially and economically privileged group; it does not imply that elite individuals were morally superior or more talented than non-elite individuals. In the middle were women from moderately well-off families, termed "sub-elite" in this book. At the bottom were slave women (though Roman slavery was itself highly stratified) and the urban and rural poor. Women's experiences also depended on their age and stage in the life course from infancy to old age. This chapter provides a brief historical account of Roman social structure, describes the main status groups in the Late Republic and imperial period, and then discusses status attributes that were peculiar to women.

DEVELOPMENT OF ROMAN SOCIETY

Roman status groups were closely linked with the political roles of the social elite, and status was closely associated with political power. In the traditional Roman Republic, male citizens elected the governing magistrates. The voting assemblies were stratified by wealth, so that the groups (census classes) with the most wealth also had the most political power. The son of a senator was not automatically a senator; he first served in the military and then was elected to the senate. Thereafter, he ran for offices in the traditional cursus honorum: quaestor, aedile, tribune of the plebs, praetor, possible propraetor, consul, possible proconsul, censor. Quaestors were financial officials who assisted the army with logistics; aediles maintained public order and oversaw markets; tribunes, open to plebeian politicians, served as checks on the other magistrates; praetors were first military commanders and later administered law; propraetors and proconsuls were commanders or governors of provinces; and censors, elected every five years, carried out the census or enumeration of citizens. The most powerful magistrates were the two consuls, who gave their names to the year ("in the consulships of X and Y"). Consuls and praetors waged military campaigns that, when victorious, reaped great profits in the form of booty looted from the enemy and captives sold as slaves. Roman aristocrats who won victories gained great prestige and influence, and the wealth that flooded into Rome financed future political campaigns. Ordinary soldiers were eager to serve in the legions that conquered first Italy, then Africa (the conclusion of the Punic Wars), and finally the Hellenistic kingdoms of the Eastern Mediterranean.[1]

To make a long story short, the generals' campaigns raised the ambitions of the political class until the Republic's political institutions broke. Consuls were supposed to return to private life after their year in office or at best serve as proconsul (governor) for a year or two, not be elected consul year after year, as was Gaius Marius, or seize the dictatorship (originally an emergency office), as did Lucius Cornelius Sulla, waging a bloody purge of his opponents in 83–82 BCE. They were not supposed to refuse to lay down their proconsulship, as did Julius Caesar in 49 BCE, beginning the civil war that led to his own dictatorship and assassination in 44 BCE. Caesar's death triggered further civil warfare that abetted the rise of his great-nephew Gaius Julius Caesar Octavianus, better known as Octavian or Augustus, the first Roman emperor.[2]

Augustus had a long reign, from 27 BCE to 14 CE, and established a system in which the emperor or princeps (first citizen) held a number of powers derived from traditional offices. His title *imperator* derived from the hailing of a victorious general as "imperator" by his troops. He was sacrosanct, holding *tribunicia potestas*, derived from the tribunes of the plebs. He usually held the consulship, sharing it with senators whom he favored. He was *pontifex maximus* (chief priest) and also held the powers of the censor, the magistrate elected every five years who carried out the census and inspected the mores of the upper classes. It was probably as censor that Augustus codified the status groups of the Roman Empire in the interests of stabilizing his reign and promoting his legitimacy. He also promulgated the *Leges Juliae*, the Augustan laws on marriage and adultery, which will be discussed in chapter 4 of this volume. Subsequent emperors also took measures to reinforce the status groups of the Empire.[3]

The focus of this book is on Roman social history from ca. 200 BCE to 284 CE, conventionally known as the Late Republic and the Principate (early and middle Empire). Before 200 BCE, the sources are less available and present other difficulties. After 284 CE, the conventional cutoff date for the early and middle imperial period, massive cultural shifts took place that resulted in the period known as Late Antiquity, which was more and more influenced by Christianity. However, Jewish and Christian women's lives will not be covered in this work.

ROMAN STATUS GROUPS

The status groups or social classes of Roman society were termed *ordines* (sing. *ordo*) or "orders" by Latin authors. The concept of the *ordines* has been debated: Were they caste-like, based on birth and legal privileges, and relatively unaffected by wealth, even though the upper *ordines* were wealthy? Or were they more like modern economic classes, determined by wealth, and relatively mobile, allowing people to move between them as they gained or lost assets? Elite Romans thought that freedmen (former slaves) should never ascend to the senatorial or equestrian *ordines*, however much wealth they attained. Elite authors also loved to denounce luxury or conspicuous consumption. However, senators and equestrians needed to maintain a baseline of wealth, and the emperors even gave financial assistance to those members of these *ordines* whose net worth fell below the qualification. It was not impossible, but rare, for a man of lower-status origins to ascend into the equestrian or senatorial *ordines*; more often such ascent took more than one generation to happen. When one looks at persons from the senatorial, equestrian, or decurial *ordines*—the three "upper classes" of Roman society—it is generally safe to assume that they were wealthy and had inherited wealth, usually in the form of land and other real estate but also commercial interests.[4]

In the earlier Republic (ca. 509–367 BCE), patricians and plebeians had been rigid status groups defined by birth (by membership in particular clans or descent groups), but the conflict between patricians and plebeians had been resolved by 367 BCE and they had been permitted to intermarry, forming a more general aristocracy, the *nobilitas* of the middle and Late Republic, similar to the senatorial order of the Empire. To avoid excessive confusion, we will speak of the senatorial order or "senatorials" (a term not used in classical sources) to denote all members of families who produced senators. Senators were assumed to be wealthy, and Augustus had a minimum property requirement for them of 1 million sesterces (HS). It was harder for merely wealthy persons to be admitted to the order and regarded as social equals, as will be seen in the discussion of the various orders in this chapter.

Senatorial Order

The Roman Senate was the chief advisory body of the Roman Republic, advising the consuls, controlling the state treasury, and responsible for diplomacy and public order. It provided continuity in government because the magistrates served for only a year. At the beginning of the Late Roman Republic, ca. 130 BCE, the senate consisted of some three hundred senators. A man of the political elite who was the son of a senator was not automatically a senator; he had to serve in the army, then hold a junior magistracy, and finally be elected to the senate. The senate underwent turmoil in the Late Republic's political crises, swelling to six hundred under the dictator Sulla as he rewarded his followers by promoting them into the senate, and then to one thousand under Julius Caesar and the triumvirs.

In the Empire, Augustus established the senate at six hundred senators, now elected by the senate itself rather than by popular vote. A senator needed to maintain a property qualification of 1 million HS, an extremely large sum by the standards of the ancient economy, and many senators were much wealthier. The wives and children of senators shared their prestige and are termed "senatorial" in this book, though only the sons of senators had a chance of becoming senators themselves, at age twenty-five. Senatorial families comprised no more than a few thousand individuals in an empire of approximately fifty to sixty million souls; they were a highly privileged minority.[5]

Many of our Roman literary authors, such as Cicero, Pliny the Younger, and Tacitus, were senators, as were many jurists (scholarly experts in Roman law rather than "lawyers"). They regarded their social inferiors with a certain snobbery; they socialized freely with equestrians but probably regarded decurion families as small-town and the common people (plebs) as far beneath them. Senatorial and equestrian families tended to intermarry, though a senator's daughter who married an equestrian took the status of her husband.

The senate continued to be an advisory body to the emperors, pass legal decrees termed *senatus consulta* (SC), and provide provincial governors (proconsuls and legates). It also continued to elect members to magistracies that were now mainly honorary (such as the consulship) or served as imperial functionaries.

Senatorial families did not persist for many generations. Sons of senators were not guaranteed advancement beyond the senate, and many families died out after a generation or two. The reason was structural: the emperors did not want powerful aristocratic families to become rivals to their power. So they promoted so-called new men into the senate, equestrians and increasingly notables from outside Italy, beginning with southern Gaul, Spain, and in the second century CE Greece, Asia Minor, and North Africa. Septimius Severus (emperor 193–211 CE), founder of the Severan dynasty, was from a North African family that had been promoted into the senate.

Equestrian Order

To some extent, the division of Roman society into senators and equestrians dates from the Republic, when equestrians (*equites*) originally had been a cavalry force in the Roman army, receiving horses at public expense. By the second century BCE, equestrians were no longer important as cavalry and instead formed a wealthy stratum below senators and their families in wealth and prestige, but frequently intermarrying with senatorial families. Senatorial families and equestrians should not be confused with patricians and plebeians, respectively. The older status divisions of patricians and plebeians had ceased to mean very much; patrician and plebeian families who frequently held office formed a common nobility, though certain magistracies were still reserved for plebeians (the tribunate of the plebs) and certain priesthoods for patricians.

The impact of the turmoil of the last century BCE was the disappearance of many older noble families, victims of the purges under Sulla and Octavian or of simple impoverishment as fortunes changed, and the promotion of many new Italian families into the senatorial and equestrian orders. This discontinuity meant that when Romans of the Late Republic and Empire spoke of Roman tradition, they had little personal connection to it. Roman tradition was an aspiration, promoted by Augustus and by many Latin poets and authors associated with his and his successors' reigns.

Augustus also regularized the equestrian order, requiring *equites* to have property qualifications starting from 400,000 HS to 1 million HS (some were wealthier). The equestrian order furnished many of the Roman Empire's mid-ranking officials and military officers: procurators (financial officials), military tribunes, and prefects (military officers). It was also the stratum of some of the literary and legal authors. An ambitious equestrian might seek the imperial favor of promotion into the senatorial order. Male senatorials and equestrians were a common elite in that they formed a political and bureaucratic status group with privileges, wealth, and a common education that emphasized Greek and Latin literature, oratory, philosophy, and law.

Decurial Order

Below the equestrian order was the social stratum referred to as decurions or *curiales*, though the term *curiales* is best known in later Roman sources. Decurions were the elites of individual towns and cities in Roman Italy and around the Mediterranean. Their average property qualification is not known but may have ranged from 5,000 or more likely 20,000 HS (at the lower end) to 400,000 HS (the equestrian census). Some city charters specified the property qualification for council members, such as 100,000 HS at Comum in North Italy.[6]

The decurion stratum played an important part in municipal civic life. The Roman imperial state did not attempt to govern individual cities and towns directly; it allowed them self-governance as long as they did not resist the imperial power. Cities elected their own magistrates, termed *duoviri* or (in the Greek East) *archons*, who tended to be wealthy local aristocrats who also funded the cities' amenities such as new public buildings (markets, temples), theatrical, athletic, or gladiatorial games, other festivals, public baths, and charitable foundations. The provision of these amenities was sometimes undertaken by women, members of these aristocratic families, recorded in honorific inscriptions. Decurions were also an educated stratum, and some left their cities for the imperial service. As with senatorials and equestrians, decurion families derived most of their wealth from land ownership (or from long-range trade through intermediaries as direct involvement in commerce was regarded as disreputable by the elite).

Sub-Elite

The sub-elite (a modern term) is probably the lowest social stratum in the Roman Empire that is well documented. It was the closest approximation to our term "middle class." It did not represent a single occupation or source of wealth. Many sub-elite families owned some land. Others derived income from commercial activities. Most merchants and traders (whom we know of) were freedmen and freedwomen in Rome and probably other major cities. Many sub-elite individuals were slaves of senatorial or equestrian families or slaves of the emperor's household; these were privileged slaves who could amass wealth. Other freeborn sub-elite men served in the Roman army as soldiers and low-ranking officers. In most of the first century CE, a legionary soldier earned 900 HS a year but could expect donatives and a much larger discharge bonus after twenty years of service. This was a respectable income by the scale of the poor (see section on rural/urban poor in this chapter). The upper boundary of the sub-elite depended not just on wealth, but on education and prestige; a wealthy person in a stigmatized occupation or lacking education might not be considered elite.

Most of the sub-elite probably identified as "Roman" and were citizens, but noncitizen provincial elites must be included in this category; some served as auxiliaries in the Roman army. Many sub-elite persons probably had dual or multiple identities (e.g., "Greek" in the East, Jewish, or Gallic). Many were literate at a basic level; they could read, write, and do arithmetic but were unlikely to have had "higher" literary education. Even if they could not read and write fluently, they knew how to employ a scribe to read and write for them. The sub-elite is the lowest social stratum represented by legal writings and documents; in fact, most of the surviving evidence for the sub-elite is documentary, including documents on wood tablets and papyrus. Latin epitaphs on tombstones and accompanying sculptural reliefs also represent the sub-elite (as they wanted to be seen for posterity).

Rural/Urban Poor

The rural and urban poor (living at subsistence level) was undoubtedly the largest stratum of the Roman Empire but the least well documented. The upper orders regarded the poor mainly as a social problem and spoke of them with contempt, though some literary authors romanticized the simple peasant's life. We cannot assume that the poor were literate, or informed about Roman law, or that they were Roman citizens (in Italy before 89 BCE, and in the Empire until 212 CE, when the emperor Caracalla bestowed the citizenship on the whole empire), or that they spoke Latin or Greek. Their lives are studied mainly through archeology and will not be the focus of this book. The exception are slaves because Roman law and ideology did concern itself extensively with slaves as the property of the wealthy.

Slaves

Slavery in the Roman Republic and Empire was not racially based; slaves were not viewed as belonging to a distinct race or as physically distinct from free persons. They were the victims of ill fortune, enslaved as prisoners of war, as the captives of bandits, pirates, and slave traders, picked up as abandoned children, or born of slave mothers. In the Late Republic, Rome's conquests of the Mediterranean brought large numbers of enslaved Carthaginians, Greeks, and Gauls to Italy. In the Empire, conquests added Germans, Britons, Jews (taken captive in the Jewish War of 66–70 CE), and Dacians, but an increasing number of slaves were born into slavery.

As this history shows, slaves in the Roman world were not a uniform group. Some were highly educated Greeks who were bought by Roman aristocrats as secretaries and as tutors for their children. These educated slaves were promoted in the imperial administration, particularly finance, because if they committed fraud or theft, they were liable to torture and capital punishment. Many slaves managed commercial enterprises for the wealthy (for the same reason). Such privileged slaves were able to save their own money (though not legally possessing it) and could purchase their manumission and that of their slave spouses and children. Such freedmen and freedwomen are represented in many Latin epitaphs from and near the city of Rome.[7]

Less privileged slaves were servants in aristocratic houses, entertainers, and prostitutes. The least fortunate ones were those who worked on agricultural large estates in the countryside, toiling to produce the Empire's main crops (wheat, wine, and oil). The great majority of slaves probably were never manumitted; they died in slavery, perhaps after relatively short lives (migrants to Italy faced endemic diseases such as malaria).

Peregrines

The focus of this book is on Roman Italy and the Latin- and Greek-speaking areas/strata of the Mediterranean. Beyond these areas or below them, regional or local languages and cultures persisted: in the north and west, Celtic; in North Africa, Punic and other languages; and in Judaea, Syria and Palestine, Hebrew and Aramaic. To the Romans, these native peoples who may not have spoken Latin or Greek were *peregrini* or foreigners. Roman law did not apply to noncitizens. These peregrine societies often adopted social and legal influences from their Greek and Roman colonizers, and vice versa, but identifying these is beyond the scope of this book.

This book ought thus perhaps to be called *Daily Life of Women in the Romanized World*. "Romanization" is the process by which non-Roman peoples acquired the use of Latin and other "Roman" cultural practices, adopted an urban lifestyle in cities laid out along Roman lines, and became citizens of the Empire. It is now a controversial term, which some archeologists and historians argue has colonialist connotations. It does not imply that such a cultural conversion was imposed by the Romans, or that it was total and universal, or that its aim was benevolent (challenged by imperial authors themselves). Women in Latin inscriptions and tablets who have Latin names, who make use of Roman law or participate in municipal public life, may have had other identities and cultural practices that manifested in other areas of their lives. They may have spoken other languages in addition to Latin and Greek, particularly in Britain, Gaul, Spain, North Africa, Egypt, and the Near East. Studying the local cultures of the Roman world often requires quite different linguistic competences (Ancient Near Eastern languages and literatures are usually studied in a different university department than Classical languages and literature) and is often intensely local, based on archeology. Many of the people of the local cultures were also rural and poor.

WOMEN AND ROMAN SOCIETY

Women themselves formed an ambiguous status group within Roman society; they do not seem to be an order, except for *matronae*, discussed in section "Women's Sexual Status." Excluded from many aspects of male life, women were in certain senses "outsiders within," as Christian Laes terms children in Roman society.[8]

Women of the senatorial and equestrian orders represented this privileged stratum but were excluded from political and military offices and other male roles. Though the right to vote was no longer significant outside municipal elections, women were still excluded from public office and from representing others in legal cases, a major feature of elite male public life. Marriages of senatorial women with fellow senatorial men were aimed at preserving or increasing the property of the family and their membership in the order; equestrian marriages had similar motivations. Women's normative behavior (emphasizing sexual fidelity within marriage) maintained family honor even before the state stepped in to enforce women's behavior with the Augustan laws on marriage and adultery (18 BCE; 9 CE). However, as we will see, senatorial and equestrian women could own property in their own right and wielded influence as patrons.

Women of the sub-elite are attested in documents and inscriptions. Here divergences from the ideals prescribed by the Roman elite and Roman law are apparent, though epitaphs also show that many women (or those who commemorated them) aspired to elite ideals concerning women's roles. Lower-status women, below the sub-elite, are doubly invisible; economic necessities probably demanded that they carry out men's work when the men of the family were sick, deceased, or too young to work. Slave women, as we will see, faced a double level of oppression: as slaves and as women, performing "feminine" occupations and liable to sexual exploitation.

In the Empire, no woman could reign as empress in her own right. Mothers could govern behind the throne for young emperors, as Agrippina the Younger was said to have done for young Nero (emperor 54–68 CE) and later the empress Galla Placidia for her son Valentinian III (425–55). However, the empress or Augusta commanded great wealth and personal influence, as did other women from the upper social strata, acting as patrons of cities and towns. Much of women's social power came from their husbands and fathers as wealth and social status that were inherited or attained by marriage. In the early Empire, governors' and officers' wives and families began to accompany them to the frontiers. Officers' wives might lead in a crisis, as did Agrippina the elder, wife of Germanicus, a nephew of the emperor Tiberius (14–37 CE), but Tacitus depicts the women escaping the Varian disaster as a hindrance to the retreating troops (more about these anecdotes will be related in chapter 9).

Elite women had public roles, especially as priestesses and benefactors. Roman women are attested owning land, buying and selling, making loans, and making wills. They were able to inherit wealth in their own right, to possess and increase it, and to bequeath it to their descendants, thus helping to perpetuate the upper orders' economic dominance. Women who bore children perpetuated their families; the Augustan marriage legislation awarded legal privileges to women who had three or more children. Below the elite, families probably depended more upon women as sources of labor or as wage earners in partnership with the men of the family or in their stead.

As this sketch suggests, women were not a homogenous group. There are some signs that they were regarded as a social group. The *Lex Julia theatralis* of the emperor Augustus (Suet. *Aug.* 44.2–3) assigned different seating in the theater to status groups, senators being permitted to sit in the front rows, equestrian men just behind them, occupying the first fourteen rows; lower-status men were relegated to seating further back; and women were required to sit in the rearmost rows (at the top, where it was hard to see the stage). Only exceptionally privileged women, such as the Vestal Virgins and other public priestesses, and in the imperial era the empresses, were permitted to sit in the front. Other evidence, however, suggests that women of the senatorial, equestrian, and decurial orders were termed *matronae* and accorded greater respect. But respect for all women was closely tied up with their sexual behavior.[9]

WOMEN'S SEXUAL STATUS

A status which was (mostly) peculiar to women was their sexual reputation, denoted by such terms as *pudor* (modesty) or *pudicitia* or *castitas* (chastity). Contrary to modern popular impressions that Roman women were sexually promiscuous and that the idealization of chastity was a Christian innovation, Roman authors exalted *pudicitia* as a female virtue. Valerius Maximus, writing in the early Empire, invokes *Pudicitia* (a divine personification): "Whence should I invoke you, Chastity, chief buttress of men and women alike?" Seneca the Elder, a rhetorician, emphasizes the importance of women's reputation for chastity: "For a woman, in fact, the one glory is chastity; so she must take care to be chaste—and to be seen to be chaste." A woman, particularly a woman of the upper orders, was subjected to constant scrutiny as to the reality of her *pudicitia*, which may be better translated as "reputation for sexual unavailability."[10]

Pudicitia is best understood as women's virginity before marriage and sexual fidelity within marriage, rather than virginity or chastity per se, which Roman society had few roles for. With the exception of the Vestal Virgins, all women were expected to marry, and other priestesses were married or widowed women, not virgins. Married women furthermore were expected to have sexual intercourse with their husbands in order to produce legitimate children, perpetuating the family. However, they were sexually unavailable to other men lest they produce "adulterated" children (the Roman etymology for *adulterium*, adultery).

The sexual reputation of women was a marker of their status within a traditionally agrarian patriarchal society that depended on the legitimate transmission of property from fathers to children (not just to sons, as will be seen). As such, *pudicitia* was a virtue above all for women of the propertied upper orders. Its praise and related praise—such as congratulating a man that his wife has produced children resembling their father—are conventional. These forms of praise do not mean that an elite woman's *pudicitia* was actually in question or conversely that she was of unusual virtue compared with her peers. Praising the *pudicitia* of a matron and her production of children who resembled their father celebrated the reproduction of the family and social elite for the next generation. This ideal trickled down to the sub-elite, where it appears in many women's epitaphs.[11]

This brings us to a term for Roman women of high status, the *matrona*. A *matrona* is a married woman, but not all married women were *matronae*. The mid-second century CE grammarian Aulus Gellius thought that *matronae* were married women but not necessarily mothers, whereas a materfamilias (pl. *matres familiarum*) was a mother of a family. The title "materfamilias" donates a female head of household as well as a mother of children. The term *matrona* signifies a married woman of higher social standing, of the upper orders (senatorial, equestrian, and decurion), though no definite or legal definition exists. As we will see, *matronae* were believed to wear the *stola*, a long overdress over the long tunic dress worn by Roman women. A *matrona* was expected to display exemplary *pudicitia* and modesty. In turn, she was traditionally treated with deference: according to Festus, magistrates could not move aside *matronae* in public, and Valerius Maximus states that a man serving a court summons was "not permitted to touch a *matrona* with his body, so that the *stola* should be kept inviolate from the touch of an alien hand." Though they were not restricted to the home as with women in classical Athens and many other Greek city-states, concern to protect *pudicitia* governed how elite Roman women appeared in public. In honorific and funerary statues, they typically appear swathed in cloth, one such statue type actually being named *Pudicitia* by scholars.[12]

The intersection of sexual reputation with social status renders it unclear whether women of the lower strata were still supposed to display *pudicitia*. Whether the Augustan marriage legislation extended all the way down the social scale is discussed in chapter 4. At the time of the Decemvir Appius Claudius's sexual pursuit of the plebeian girl Verginia ca. 450 BCE, women of free birth were expected to have *pudicitia* and, as a consequence, to be protected from rape; slaves were not protected. This was also true at the time that Livy recounted the Verginia legend, at the beginning of the imperial era. Later in the imperial period, the status of free-born impoverished people declined, and the status of lower-class women with respect to *pudicitia* is less clear.[13]

Certain groups of lower-status women were definitely excluded from *pudicitia*. They included slave women (*ancillae*), female prostitutes, female brothel managers, and female stage performers. All these were defined as sexually available and lacking an honorable sexual reputation. But there was a large group of lower-status women not in these stigmatized categories whose sexual reputation is unclear. To this group may have belonged the mistresses who appear in Roman love poetry and the women whom Ovid assured his readers that it was safe to court in his satirical *Art of Love*. Freedwomen (*libertae*) may have had an ambiguous sexual reputation, as is described in chapter 7.

Pudicitia ensured a sexual double standard. Women were expected to be virgins until their first marriage and faithful to their husbands, or face family retribution or (with the Augustan marriage laws) divorce and prosecution for adultery. Men were not required to be sexually faithful to their wives; they would be liable for adultery only if they seduced other elite men's wives. Elite men were permitted to have sexual activity with the groups of women to whom *pudicitia* did not apply, especially slaves, prostitutes, entertainers, and probably freedwomen. An elite man could also have sexual activity with male prostitutes or slaves as long as he penetrated them. The analogue of female *pudicitia* that applied to Roman men was freedom from sexual (anal) penetration, from being the "bottom" or passive partner in homosexual intercourse. This sexual role was considered effeminate, suitable for a woman or a slave. Taking the "active" role as penetrator in homosexual intercourse was consistent with elite masculinity.[14]

Roman culture's emphasis on women's *pudicitia* and production of legitimate children meant that male authors often accused women of sexual impropriety when the women were regarded as disruptive or transgressive in other ways. Most notoriously, the famous legal orator and politician Cicero slandered the sexual reputation of the wealthy noblewoman Clodia because she was the legal opponent of his defendant Caelius. The empress Messalina, wife of the emperor Claudius (41–54 CE), supported the attempted coup of a rival aristocrat, Silius, and is said to have married him, dissolving her union with the elderly and disabled Claudius; a generation later, the satirical poet Juvenal depicted Messalina as a common prostitute. This work of Juvenal's, the Sixth Satire, depicts many activities of Roman women in the most negative possible light. *Daily Life of Women in Ancient Rome* emphasizes documentary texts produced by and for women and does not rely on male-authored misogynistic or prurient literary texts. But satire is not written in a vacuum; Roman women were still excluded from many aspects of male public life. As we will see in further chapters, concern for *pudicitia* may have shaped many of Roman women's behaviors.

WOMEN'S DOMESTIC VIRTUES

Closely related to *pudicitia* was the ideology that women's rightful place was in the home, displaying domestic virtues of piety (toward the household gods, discussed in chapter 10), thriftiness, and hard work, exemplified by *lanificium* (woolworking). These virtues are praised in many women's epitaphs and funeral eulogies. Woolworking meant spinning and weaving in a historical era when fabric production was entirely manual, using hand spindles and looms; even the spinning wheel had not yet been invented. Spinning and weaving were highly time-consuming tasks. It was understood that the married woman who remained devoted to domestic tasks would spend less time outside the home and therefore be at lesser risk for committing adultery; praise of a woman's domestic virtues was thus also implied praise of her *pudicitia*.[15]

Elite male authors associated this ideal domestic virtue with the distant past and the virtuous Romans of the early Republic; it is exemplified by Livy's Lucretia, who was always to be found at home spinning wool. Lucretia's husband ill-fatedly boasted that his wife was the most virtuous of women, inspiring Sextus Tarquinius, the son of Rome's last king Tarquinius Superbus (534–510 BCE), to go with his friends to look her over:

> Lucretia was discovered very differently employed from the daughters-in-law of the king. These they had seen at a luxurious banquet, whiling away the time with their young friends; but Lucretia, though it was late at night, was busily engaged upon her wool, while her slave women toiled about her in the lamplight as she sat in the hall of her house. The prize of this contest in womanly virtues fell to Lucretia. (Livy 1.57.9–1.58.10)

Sextus Tarquinius then raped Lucretia, who committed suicide rather than live with the disgrace to her female honor, declaring "never in future shall any unchaste (*impudica*) woman live through the example of Lucretia."[16]

In depictions of ideal matronal behavior, the authors often set these women in the past, many centuries ago. This domestic ethic conflicted with how Roman elite women actually lived. Many elite households were very wealthy, owning dozens or hundreds of slaves, many of whom were personal servants. The *matrona* of a senatorial or equestrian family supervised these slaves rather than carry out most domestic labor herself. She had slave women to spin and weave for her (even Lucretia is depicted with slave women helping her). If she did any spinning and weaving, it was to earn the credit of being a traditional Roman wife. Nor was she secluded from the outside world. Elite houses were not private realms separated from larger society; men of the upper strata conducted their public and private business and social life within the home, and their wives might be present and expected to socialize (while maintaining their sexual reputation). Women also attended public events such as festivals, the theater, and the amphitheater (only Greek-style athletic competitions, where male athletes competed in the nude, were off-limits to women). Elite women also carried out major economic transactions, including the purchase and sale of land and major loans. They used intermediaries (male slaves or freedmen), but so did elite Roman men who wished to avoid association with commerce. Women of the upper orders even took on conspicuous public roles as priestesses and benefactors, though mainly at the level of smaller cities.

Below the elite, Roman women were also, out of sheer economic necessity, not confined to domestic life, though the sub-elite women represented by Latin epitaphs also aspired to the domestic ideal as a mark of higher social status. These aspirations obscure how many women worked in commerce, in shops, and in agricultural production. Many working women were slaves and freedwomen, at least in Roman Italy.

CONCLUSION

As we will see in the next chapters, the status and role of women through their life course was profoundly affected by the ancient world's high mortality rate and corresponding high fertility rate. The experiences of women were also profoundly affected by their social status. Legal status might vary with the life course, as women became inheritors from their parents and were granted privileges for bearing children (discussed in chapter 4).

NOTES

1. On the traditional Republic, see Andrew W. Lintott, *The Constitution of the Roman Republic* (Oxford, 1999); on the Republican Roman war machine, see William V. Harris, *War and Imperialism in Republican Rome, 327–70 B.C.* (Oxford, 1979); for a more general introduction, see Nathan Rosenstein, "Republican Rome," in *War and Society in the Ancient and Medieval Worlds: Asia, the Mediterranean, Europe, and Mesoamerica* (Washington, DC, 1999), ed. Kurt Raaflaub and Nathan Rosenstein, 193–216.

2. On the Late Republic, see Arthur Keaveney, *The Army in the Roman Revolution* (London, 2007); and Richard Alston, *Rome's Revolution: Death of the Republic and Birth of the Empire* (Oxford, 2015).

3. On the Principate's political and military changes, see J. B. Campbell, *The Emperor and the Roman Army, 31 B.C.–A.D. 235* (Oxford, 1984); on Augustus's reign and ideology, see Paul Zanker, *The Power of Images in the Age of Augustus*, trans. Alan Shapiro (Ann Arbor, MI, 1988); and Beth Severy, *Augustus and the Family at the Birth of the Roman Empire* (London, 2003).

4. That the *ordines* were not determined by wealth and the elite despised and ignored commerce is represented by M. I. Finley's *The Ancient Economy*

(Berkeley, CA, 1973); Peter Garnsey and Richard Saller, *The Roman Empire: Economy, Society, and Culture* (Berkeley, CA, 1987). Recent scholarship's emphasis on a more commercial economy is summarized in *The Cambridge Economic History of the Greco-Roman World* (Cambridge, 2007), ed. Walter Scheidel, Ian Morris, and Richard Saller. As we will see, elite women engaged in commerce at a remove for other reasons.

5. On the imperial senate, see Richard J. A. Talbert, *The Senate of Imperial Rome* (Princeton, NJ, 1984).

6. Emily A. Hemelrijk, *Hidden Lives, Public Personae: Women and Civic Life in the Roman West* (Oxford, 2015), 17; *Matrona Docta: Educated Women in the Roman Elite from Cornelia to Julia Domna* (London, 1999), 25.

7. On slavery, see Keith R. Bradley, *Slavery and Society at Rome* (Cambridge, 1994); Sandra R. Joshel, *Slavery in the Roman World* (Cambridge, 2010).

8. Christian Laes, *Children in the Roman Empire: Outsiders Within* (Cambridge, 2011); on women, general works are Sarah B. Pomeroy, *Goddesses, Whores, Wives, and Slaves: Women in Classical Antiquity* (London, 1975); Eva Cantarella, *Pandora's Daughters: The Role and Status of Women in Greek and Roman Antiquity*, trans. Maureen B. Fant (Baltimore, MD, 1987); and more recently, Eve D'Ambra, *Roman Women* (Cambridge, 2007); Sharon L. James and Sheila Dillon, eds, *A Companion to Women in the Ancient World* (Malden, MA, 2012). For emphasis on methodological problems, see Suzanne Dixon's *Reading Roman Women: Sources, Genres, and Real Life* (London, 2001). For emphasis on the life course, see Laura K. McClure, *Women in Classical Antiquity: From Birth to Death* (Hoboken, NJ, 2019). On empresses and women of the imperial family, Mary T. Boatwright's *Imperial Women of Rome: Power, Gender, Context* (Oxford, 2021).

9. Hemelrijk, *Hidden Lives*, 208–10; Elizabeth Rawson, "*Discrimina ordinum*: The *Lex Julia theatralis*," *Papers of the British School at Rome* 55 (1987), 83–114. Women acting as a group appear most frequently in depictions of Roman religion and will be discussed in chapter 10.

10. Valerius Maximus 6.1.pr.; Seneca *Controversiae* 2.7.9; scrutiny, Kyle Harper, *From Shame to Sin: The Christian Transformation of Sexual Morality in Late Antiquity* (Cambridge, MA, 2013), 41–42; on *pudicitia*, see Rebecca Langlands, *Sexual Morality in Ancient Rome* (Cambridge, 2006); McClure, *Women in Classical Antiquity*, 194–96.

11. On agrarian patriarchal societies' idealization of female virginity and chastity, see Susan R. Mattern, *The Slow Moon Climbs: The Science, History, and Meaning of Menopause* (Princeton, NJ, 2019), 162–63. Roman society was unusual in practicing partitive inheritance (this book, chapter 6) and permitting property to devolve to women through inheritance rather than solely through dowry (this book, chapter 4). Epitaphs: Emily A. Hemelrijk, *Women and Society in the Roman World: A Sourcebook of Inscriptions from the Roman West* (Cambridge, 2021), e.g., no. 1.1, 7, 10, 32, 45.

12. On *matronae*, see Hemelrijk, *Matrona Docta*, 12–14; Amy Richlin, "Carrying water in a sieve: Class and the body in Roman women's religion," in

Women and Goddess Traditions (Minneapolis, 1997), ed. Karen King, 330–74; *Arguments with Silence: Writing the History of Roman Women* (Ann Arbor, MI, 2014), 197–240, at 218–21; on elite chastity, see 221–22, 231–32. On materfamilias, see Gellius *Noctes Atticae* 18.6.8; Richard P. Saller, "*Pater familias, mater familias,* and the gendered semantics of the Roman household," *Classical Philology* 94.2 (1999), 182–97. *Stola:* Festus 112L. Inviolate: Festus 142L; Valerius Maximus 2.1.5. On statues, Glenys Davies, "Honorific vs. funerary statues of women: Essentially the same or fundamentally different?" in *Women and the Roman City in the Latin West* (Leiden, 2013), ed. Emily A. Hemelrijk and Greg Woolf, 174–99.

13. For the story of Verginia, see Livy 3.44–47.

14. On homosexual acts, see Craig A. Williams, *Roman Homosexuality,* 2nd ed. (Oxford, 2010).

15. On *lanificium,* see Jo-Ann Shelton, *The Women of Pliny's* Letters (London, 2013), 94–95; Dixon, *Reading,* 56. Epitaphs and a fuller bibliography are found in chapters 5 and 6.

16. Quotes: Livy 1.57.9; 1.58.10.

2

BIRTH AND MORTALITY

INTRODUCTION

The life course of women in the Roman world (focusing on the Mediterranean region and Latin-speaking areas) begins first with infancy, including their prospects before and during birth, the acceptance of female infants into Roman families, and the precarious life of infants and small children (under five years) under the conditions of high mortality in the ancient world. A third of all infants probably died before their first birthday, and about half of all children born died before their tenth birthday. Many features of Roman infancy and small childhood, such as how infants were fed and cared for and how they were mourned, appear to be adaptations to this high rate of mortality.

Modern demography (the study of how populations change over time, including birth, marriage, migration, and death rates) enjoys access to statistical records; in the seventeenth and eighteenth centuries in England, church parishes kept registers of baptisms, marriages, and burials. No such direct source survives from the classical world. The Romans of the Republic conducted a census every five years, enumerating the citizens for purposes of voting, taxation, and military service, but it probably focused on adult male citizens and only total numbers survive (much debated by scholars). Formal declarations of births are preserved only by chance. The house-to-house census in Roman Egypt, held every fourteen years, listed all persons living in a household by gender, age, and relationship, and many of these records on papyrus were preserved by the dry climate, enabling the reconstruction of the demographics of Roman Egypt. Other evidence, such as Roman legal commentaries, Latin epitaphs, and skeletal evidence, has also been marshaled as evidence.[1]

To set the demography of the Roman world in perspective, modern developed nations (Europe, Israel, the United States and Canada, and increasingly Latin America, some North African and Middle Eastern nations, and East Asia) have passed through the so-called demographic transition. Before that (ca. 1800), populations were marked by high mortality and high fertility; the average life expectancy at birth (LEB) was low, and women on average bore many children, many of whom did not survive, dying from common diseases such as dysentery or measles. The demographic transition is associated with the growth of urban, industrial economies, where women increasingly became educated and participated in the workforce and produced fewer children, more of whom survived; advances in medicine, public health, and sanitation greatly decreased infant and child mortality from disease. In Western Europe and North America, the demographic transition stretches roughly from the construction of public sewers in major cities around 1850 to the mass vaccination programs of the 1950s onward and introduction of hormonal contraceptives in the 1960s. In such a modern family, the couple married relatively late in their lives, after completing advanced education, and had on average one or two children (below replacement rate). Women were not expected to die from complications of pregnancy and childbirth, and infants and small children from infectious diseases. Premature and multiple births were still associated with higher mortality. Aside from rare diseases such as cancer, fatal accidents such as car crashes, gun accidents, and drowning were the most frequent causes of children's deaths in the United States under normal epidemiological conditions, but these were relatively rare. Families were routinely touched by death only later in the life course, typically when a husband and wife reached middle age and confronted the aging and death of their own parents at advanced ages. Average LEB ranged between seventy and eighty. In contrast, as section "Roman Demography: Mortality and Fertility" shows, the demographic profile of the ancient Roman world was very different.[2]

ROMAN DEMOGRAPHY: MORTALITY AND FERTILITY

The Roman Empire's relatively high level of urban and economic development is stressed in recent scholarship: long-distance trade, banking, roads, shipping, the spread of cities and "classical" urban infrastructure, with aqueducts, public baths, and amphitheaters. The paradox is that these stereotypical features of civilization coexisted with a very high mortality rate and corresponding high fertility rate, constraining women's lives, as will be seen. Due to this high fertility rate and migration, the population of Roman Italy grew at a slow rate during the Late Republic and Empire.[3]

The census documents from Roman Egypt, subjected to rigorous statistical analysis, suggest that the average LEB was in the low twenties; allowing for local variation, historians suggest that the average LEB in the Roman Empire was between twenty and thirty years of age, an extremely low figure. To put it in perspective, the average LEB in some Sub-Saharan African nations today is around fifty, whereas that of Japan is over eighty. An average LEB of twenty or thirty reflects extremely high infant and childhood mortality rates; it does not mean that people age abnormally fast, becoming elderly in appearance by age twenty or thirty. In the Roman world, half of all children ever born might die before they reached ten, but a man or woman surviving to age twenty might (depending on the local environment) live another twenty-five to thirty years. The Roman idea of old age was not too different from ours, regarding people of fifty or sixty as elderly. Service in the imperial Roman army, which was extended by Augustus to twenty to twenty-five years for legionaries and twenty-six to twenty-eight years for auxiliaries and sailors, assumed this expectation of life; imperial soldiers were probably recruited around age twenty and discharged just before old age.[4]

MALARIA: MAJOR KILLER OF MOTHERS AND CHILDREN

On the other hand, the overall expectation of health was probably much lower than in modern high-income nations. This section discusses malaria, which severely impacts children and pregnant women and which varies greatly with geography. Mosquitoes, which carry malaria and other diseases, are often listed as the world's deadliest animal, ahead of big cats, sharks, and humans.

As will be seen, the risks of infant and child mortality from disease varied greatly with the local ecology, whether our hypothetical female child was born on the west coast of central Italy, in a highland mountain town, in the city of Rome or lesser large cities, or in the Fayum Depression and Delta of Roman Egypt. Such drastic geographic variation in mortality is a feature of societies before the demographic transition and still undergoing it. In particular, malaria, which is highly variable by region, marked the regional demography of nineteenth-century England, Italy, and the United States, afflicting the English Fenlands, Italy's Maremma, and the Mississippi Delta and Low Country of the southeastern United States.[5]

Malaria is caused by the microscopic protozoan *Plasmodium*, which *Anopheles* mosquitoes harbor in their salivary glands and transfer to humans when they bite them and ingest their blood. In the human body, *Plasmodium* first migrates to the liver, where it proliferates; then it infects red blood cells, consuming their hemoglobin (oxygen-carrying protein) and multiplying until the red blood cells burst, releasing further *Plasmodium* parasites to infect more red blood cells. The proliferation cycle of *Plasmodium* causes the periodic fever of malaria, in which high fever, chills, profuse sweating, and exhaustion repeat every two or three days. As a result of malaria's assault on red blood cells, the patient becomes severely anemic and weak. Malaria sufferers also become chemically attractive to mosquitoes, which bite them and consume the parasite with their blood. The parasite then reproduces sexually within the mosquito and starts its life cycle afresh. Two antimalarial drugs with herbal sources, quinine (derived from cinchona bark, and its modern analogues) and artemisinin, were not known in the ancient Mediterranean.

Of the species of *Plasmodium*, only *P. falciparum* and *P. vivax* are discussed here. *Plasmodium vivax* is a less severe illness, termed "benign tertian fever" in modern literature, though its effects are highly debilitating and a patient in premodern disease conditions might well succumb to other illnesses. *Plasmodium falciparum* is the more lethal species, causing "malignant tertian fever," though its cycle of fever, chills, and sweating is less marked and the fever may be continuous. *Plasmodium falciparum* infects vital organs such as the liver, kidneys, placenta of pregnant women, and brain, where it is termed cerebral malaria and causes delirium, coma, and death.

How do we know that malaria ravaged the ancient Mediterranean? Medical authors such as Galen describe the periodic fevers, which they designated as tertian, quartan (every three days), and quotidian (no clear pattern). For decades the evidence was indirect, pointing to pathological changes in Roman-era skeletal remains that are caused by severe anemia. In these changes, cranial bone becomes more fragile and porous due to its invasion by bone marrow to compensate for the anemia; these changes also occur in the bone of the eye sockets. Such pathological changes are common in skeletons from the Roman Mediterranean, but archeologists differed over the causes; malaria is an obvious cause of anemia, but so are thalassemias (see later in this section) and other infections, as well as malnutrition and an iron-poor diet. The lower social strata in the Roman world had a mostly vegetarian diet, the largest sources of calories being bread, olive oil, wine, and legumes; meat, a prestige food, was eaten only occasionally. People who lived near the sea also consumed fish and other marine foods. The "Mediterranean diet" is advocated for health today because many Americans have cardiovascular disease associated with an animal-based diet heavy in meat and dairy products, but it assumes access to protein and vitamin and mineral supplements. A diet based on whole grains without meat or supplementation is low in iron and may block iron absorption.[6]

This nearly vegetarian diet may have been particularly unhealthy for pregnant women and their infants in the Roman world, certainly among the poor. It is not known whether women had lesser access to meat and were expected to eat less than men, but passages by Greek moralistic authors suggest that this was so. In general, women's energy needs, though smaller than men's, are increased during pregnancy, and repeated pregnancies on a low-protein diet prove to be unhealthy. Maternal anemia itself (even without placental malaria) can deprive the fetus of oxygen and nutrition, causing premature labor, risking the mother's and infant's lives in labor, and producing low-birth-weight infants with anemia and less resistance to diseases such as malaria. Found in Roman burial sites, perinatal infant skeletons (the result of stillbirths or of death soon after birth) are on average unusually small.[7]

Since *Plasmodium* cannot complete its reproduction inside mosquitoes at colder temperatures, malaria is a disease of the summer months. Strong evidence for malaria and other infectious diseases associated with hot weather (waterborne diseases; see section "Maternal and Infant Mortality") was provided by statistical studies of Christian epitaphs from third- to fifth-century CE Rome. These epitaphs, thousands of which survive, specify the date of death by month, day, and even hour—marking the entry of the deceased person into the blessed afterlife. They show a marked peak in the death rate from July to September, the so-called dog days when classical authors associated the rising of the Dog Star (Sirius) with deadly fevers. Children's epitaphs in this group also show the July–September peak in death rate; elderly people tended also to die in winter, presumably from respiratory illnesses. The Roman poet Horace writes that parents "become pale with fear for their children" in hot summer weather.[8]

Direct evidence of malaria in the Roman world has been provided recently by studies of ancient DNA, identifying *Plasmodium* DNA in a child's skeletal remains from a cemetery from Late Antiquity at Lugnano in Italy and other molecules associated with *Plasmodium* in mummy remains from Roman Egypt. Furthermore, the genome of humans living in the Mediterranean has adapted to endemic malaria, being selected for hereditary anemias (another cause of the aforementioned bone defects). These anemias, termed thalassemias, are genetic recessive traits; if two carrier parents (each with one copy of the thalassemia gene) marry, they may have a child with both genes who manifests full-blown thalassemia and is likely to die young. The carriers, however, benefit because they are less likely to contract malaria, as with sickle-cell anemia in Sub-Saharan African populations. Two forms of thalassemia, alpha-thalassemia and beta-thalassemia, are most common in malarial regions; alpha-thalassemia is more common in Africa and the Middle East and often causes the death of infants before birth. Beta-thalassemia is common in Greece and areas settled by Greeks, and children with it may survive birth but are severely anemic. Southern Italy and Sicily were colonized by Greeks ca. 500 BCE, and the Romans brought many Greek slaves to Italy in the last two centuries BCE.[9]

Comparative evidence from medieval and early modern Italy (through the 1800s), assuming that the ecology was not markedly different, also suggests that malaria was endemic in the Roman period. But recent studies of climate in the ancient Mediterranean suggest that the incidence of malaria (and other diseases associated with hot weather) may have been higher than in medieval and modern times. According to recent scientific studies based on the evidence of glacier ice cores, tree rings, and other data sources, the climate of the Roman Empire was somewhat warmer and more humid than in centuries before or after it (the early modern period in Europe was markedly colder, and malaria plagued Italy even then). This so-called Roman Climate Optimum or Warm Period was marked by steady solar activity and lack of volcanic activity, which causes global cooling (the eruption of Mount Vesuvius in 79 CE had no long-term effect). It seems probable that this warmer climate and greater availability of water promoted the spread of falciparum malaria.[10]

The urbanization of Roman Italy, unintentionally producing more marshland and wet areas, may even have promoted the spread of malaria. The *Anopheles* mosquito, carrier of malaria, lays its eggs in water, typically swamps, marshes, or small pools formed by rain or floods. Habitats for *Anopheles* larvae were increased by Roman-era deforestation in which upland forests were logged to provide timber for houses, heating, and shipbuilding. This deforestation resulted in erosion. Mediterranean soil is not very thick or water-absorbent and was washed downstream from the deforested hills by winter rain and into streams and rivers by the infrequent-but-heavy summer rains. This silt settled out in lowland areas, making rivers more prone to flooding and silting up harbors, creating large marshy areas especially on the west coast of central Italy (Tuscany and Campagna, ancient Etruria and Campania). The Tiber river became prone to flooding, inundating the streets of Rome with sewage-laden muddy water (Rome's sewers emptied into the Tiber). Rome's aqueducts, public fountains, and public baths allowed clean water to overflow into the streets, maintaining wet conditions suitable for mosquito larvae; the city also had irrigated gardens and ornamental lakes and ponds that provided breeding habitats for *Anopheles* mosquitoes. Elite houses had courtyards with pools to catch and store rainwater. Furthermore, the spread of malaria was assisted by population growth. The huge size of the population of the city of Rome (about 750,000 during the reign of Augustus, 1 million in the late first and early second centuries CE) made malaria and other infectious diseases "hyperendemic," persisting because so many people were infected and able to transmit the disease. Other large cities also harbored similar endemic diseases.[11]

Thus, the disease environment varied widely with region— large cities and lowland areas, such as the west coast of Italy, were deadly for their inhabitants, while smaller towns in highland areas, with less standing water and being too cold in winter for mosquitoes to survive, boasted healthier inhabitants. Unfortunately, no one in ancient times connected the biting mosquitoes with illness. They believed that the foul odors (*miasmata* in Greek) of rotting waste, marshy areas, and stagnant water caused disease directly, a belief that persisted through the centuries of the Black Death (from 1348 to 1666 and beyond) in Europe. Greek medical writers and the Roman architectural writer Vitruvius observed that low-lying, marshy areas were unhealthy and highland ones more salubrious. Pliny the Younger, writing at the start of the second century CE, remarked that the mountain town of Tifernum Tiberinum was extremely healthy, so much so that none of his slaves had died during his stay at his villa there, and that the town had many older people, "grandfathers and great-grandfathers," whose lore was useful to their descendants. Within lowland areas, the wealthy coped by building their homes on hills or headlands. In Rome, the rich built houses upon its seven hills, while the poorer inhabitants dwelt in slums on the Tiber floodplain. The wealthy also built their palatial homes along the river, though, and all were exposed to waterborne and airborne diseases.[12]

To return to the life course of women, infant mortality may have begun even before birth because of *P. falciparum* and other infectious diseases. Falciparum malaria often infects pregnant women; mosquitoes are more prone to bite pregnant women, who exhale more carbon dioxide (attractive to mosquitoes) and have a higher metabolic rate. The *Plasmodium* parasite infects the placenta, attaching to and clogging its small blood vessels and depriving the fetus of oxygen and nutrients from the mother. Accordingly, *P. falciparum* is a major cause of miscarriages and stillbirths where it is endemic today—above all Sub-Saharan Africa, and to a lesser extent tropical Latin America and South and Southeast Asia. Under premodern conditions, such miscarriages and premature births were also dangerous for the mother, risking death from hemorrhages. Mothers with placental malaria whose infants survived to birth might give birth to low-birth-weight infants, anemic and at greater risk of infection with malaria and other diseases. Other infectious diseases, such as brucellosis, transmitted from sheep and goats (common livestock in Roman Italy) via unpasteurized milk, and viruses also cause spontaneous abortions and fetal malformations. As the next section relates, even normal childbirth was a dangerous event for mothers and infants, and babies and small children faced death from many other infectious diseases.[13]

MATERNAL AND INFANT MORTALITY

Childbirth is highly dangerous for both the mother and the fetus under premodern conditions, resembling conditions in many impoverished modern nations where women die from exhaustion, hemorrhages, and infection and their infants may die from birth defects or oxygen deprivation during delivery. In such nations, infectious diseases are a major cause of what medical personnel term "perinatal mortality"—the high rate of miscarriages, still-birth, and low-birth-weight infants who fail to survive. This peri-natal mortality means that it may be impossible to ever determine the rate of abortion in ancient Greece and Rome, which male Latin authors treat sensationally, blaming women for aborting their fetuses in order to retain their youthful beauty and hide pregnan-cies resulting from adultery. Latin uses the same verb and noun (*aborior, -iri; abortus*) for spontaneous miscarriage or stillbirth and deliberate abortion. In any case, mechanical abortion (inserting devices into the womb) led to deadly infections without antisepsis, and herbal abortifacients were also dangerous.[14]

In early modern Europe from about 1750 to 1850, the greater cause of maternal mortality in or after childbirth appears to have been uterine infection (puerperal fever), spread by physicians who had begun using forceps to turn malpositioned infants (e.g., breech births) but who still had no knowledge of antisepsis. In this period, many women attended "lying-in" maternity hospitals where puer-peral infection spread from one patient to another. Ancient Roman women were attended by midwives, who must have practiced on a smaller scale and thus were less likely to spread disease. It was rare for male physicians to attend women undergoing childbirth; the high value on female modesty was probably a reason. Greco-Roman obstetrics rarely used forceps, so that Roman midwives were unlikely to directly reposition infants in the womb, perform-ing only external manipulation; this may have caused less infec-tion but probably led to more deaths of women from exhaustion or hemorrhage, unable to deliver their infants. Delivery complications were especially likely among the poorer strata. Many women mar-ried in their early or mid-teens, whose puberty had been delayed by malnutrition or disease, may have had narrow hips unable to deliver children successfully, as was tragically shown by the skel-etal remains of a victim of the eruption of Mount Vesuvius in 79 CE. This young woman, approximately sixteen, was seven months pregnant; the archeologists of the Herculaneum skeletons com-mented that if she had not died in the eruption, she would prob-ably have died in childbirth. Though it was known in antiquity, a "cesarean section" was undertaken to save the infant only when a pregnant woman was dying or already dead (it is a myth that

Julius Caesar was born this way, as his mother was still alive in his lifetime).[15]

However, women of the elite and sub-elite were not spared the risks of pregnancy and childbirth. As we have seen, in cities they shared the same disease environment. Among them was Julius Caesar's daughter Julia, married to Pompey in 59 BCE, who had a miscarriage in 55 and died in 54 from the premature delivery of a child who also died. Cicero's daughter Tullia had a miscarriage during her marriage to Marcus Cornelius Dolabella; she died from complications of childbirth after bearing a son in 45 BCE, who also died. Pliny the Younger's wife Calpurnia also suffered a miscarriage. Inscriptions attest women who died in childbirth, such as twenty-one-year-old Veturia Grata, who bore her husband three children and died during the premature birth of the fourth; another Veturia was married at eleven, dying at twenty-seven; her epitaph reads, "After six deliveries, I died. Just one child survived." The public priestess and mother Rubria Festa, aged thirty-six, had given birth to ten children and died after the delivery of her tenth; her husband considered her fortunate that "she left behind five surviving children in good health."[16]

After birth, children faced the choice of their elders to raise or to expose (abandon) them, with or without the intent of infanticide. In literary sources, exposure was a choice of impoverished parents who could not afford to feed a child or a response to birth defects, which were regarded with superstition. The academic controversy over exposure, its reality, and its demographic impact has still not settled. Overall, infant mortality probably greatly exceeded the incidence of exposure or infanticide. The practice of exposure, however, spawned legends of rulers and cultural heroes who were exposed as infants, from Sargon of Akkad and Moses to King Oedipus and Romulus and Remus, and became a plot device in classical literature. Slave traders were believed to collect exposed infants, rearing them as slaves, and in Greek and Roman comedies, the reunion of the slave child with his or her birth family (like Oliver Twist or "orphans of high degree" in British literature) provided a happy ending. Whether any children in documentary sources can be identified as exposed is uncertain. It has been suggested that female children were more often exposed, based on a papyrus letter from 1 BCE in which a husband writes to his pregnant wife, "If you bear a boy, keep it; if it is a girl, throw it out." But "missing females"—a demographic shortage of women, seen today in cultures with a strong preference for male children which practice gender-specific abortion—are difficult to prove given the general bias of ancient sources in favor of males.[17]

The practice of exposure, however, was legally and socially significant because exposed children were picked up by slave traders (and probably by ordinary people) and raised as slaves. As we will see in chapter 7, the high price of adolescent and adult slaves in the Roman world made rearing slave children a practical strategy for owners, if they could raise them through the period of high infant and child mortality.

Even if a child survived birth and escaped exposure, she was less likely to survive in the Roman world's disease environment. A child who survived birth and was accepted into the family could still die in its first year, whether shortly after birth or at weaning. Falciparum malaria also preferentially infects infants and small children; adults who remain in a malarious environment tend to acquire some immunity. The Greco-Roman medical writers considered tertian fever principally a disease of children. Children (and adults) were exposed to airborne diseases, which remained in circulation due to the sheer size and overcrowding of the city of Rome and other urban centers. Of these, tuberculosis is best attested. Tuberculosis is a disease of poverty and overcrowding; it spread in Western large cities in the eighteenth and nineteenth centuries, when the population of London reached 1,000,000 around 1800. There is skeletal and ancient DNA evidence for tuberculosis being widespread in the Roman Empire, along with malaria; the two may appear together, weakening the immune system. Viral diseases such as measles, mumps, and influenza may have existed but are difficult to identify in medical writings; in any case, viral diseases evolve rapidly and are less likely to have been identical in ancient times. The polio virus appears to have been ancient, its resulting deformities attested in art.[18]

Besides malaria and respiratory diseases, infants and children died from waterborne diseases; the medical writer Celsus remarks that children frequently fell sick due to diarrheal diseases. The cause of these diseases was the relative lack of sanitation of Roman cities, despite the presence of aqueducts and sewers. Roman aqueducts provided necessary fresh and relatively clean water, conveyed from hill springs well outside the city and covered for most of their routes. These aqueducts fed public fountains and public baths and even flushed public toilets associated with other major amenities such as the arena, theaters, and baths. The Romans also built sewers, starting with the very ancient Cloaca Maxima, to drain the lower elevations of the city, particularly the Forum and other marketplaces. These sewers were mainly storm drains, carrying off excess water from rain, runoff, and the outflow of the fountains and baths. They were not designed as sanitary sewers serving every dwelling. Many private houses had no running water, and their latrines were not connected to the sewers. People fetched water from the public fountains, a point of possible contamination, and emptied chamber pots into the drains or streets. Enterprising people cleaned out the latrines in private homes and sold the waste as fertilizer to market farmers outside Rome, introducing fecal contamination into the food supply. The streets were frequently clogged with filthy mud from the Tiber's floods; when a young Vespasian (the future emperor) was in charge of keeping the streets clean, the emperor Gaius Caligula humiliated him by filling his toga with mud from the streets. It is possible to reconstruct a very dirty and unhealthy city from Latin satirists who liked such themes. But even when water and urban amenities appeared to be clean, disease bacteria might be present—the germ theory of disease awaited the late nineteenth century for its discovery.[19]

SOCIAL RESPONSES TO INFANT MORTALITY

Several Roman infant-rearing practices appear to be social responses to high infant mortality and may have made it more severe: newborn infants were not immediately named, and those that died were not buried with the same level of ritual as older persons; infants who survived were often turned over to wet nurses, distancing the parents from their children. First of all, neonatal infants were not named for their first week of life; girl babies were given names on their eighth day of life, boys on their ninth. This seems to reflect the assumption that the newborn might die soon after birth; it was not yet fully part of the family. It was also in this interim period that newborns were exposed.

The Roman name-day ceremony is described by antiquarian authors. The family held a vigil all night, the men of the family wielding farming implements to drive away evil spirits; in the morning, the mother's brother arrived and hailed the infant by its name, making offerings to the gods and congratulating the parents. The mother's sister performed a ritual to "open the eyes" of the infant, moistening its eyelids and mouth with her saliva. The infant was adorned with protective amulets and was brought outside to display its existence to Jupiter, god of the heavens; the family took auspices, the sighting of birds as a form of divination; sighting woodpeckers and sparrows was regarded as lucky. Then the family held a ritual feast. These customs signaled that the infant was incorporated into the family; as we will see later in the discussion of the *ius liberorum* (privilege of children), the name-day also marked a child's legal existence. Such rituals may not always have been carried out.[20]

Even after they were named, Roman infants who died often did not receive full ritual mourning or the same type of funeral as grown persons. As chapter 11 describes, Roman ritual mourning was a cumbersome tradition in which the family of the deceased person became ritually impure until after the funeral, when they underwent a cleansing ritual with "fire and water." Given the scale of infant mortality, mourning them on an adult scale would have brought Roman society to a halt. Infants often did not receive formal grave memorials; of the hundreds of thousands of Latin epitaphs surviving from the Roman Empire, very few commemorate infants or indeed very young children, even though in demographic terms, infants and small children comprised the largest number of deaths in any given year (without an epidemic). Individual touching epitaphs for infants and very young children do exist. The standard form of disposal of the body was cremation in the Late Republic and early Empire; Pliny the Elder (writing in the mid-first century CE) states that infants "who have not yet cut their teeth" are not cremated. Archeological evidence shows that infant bodies were often inhumed (buried) in urns or amphorae on the edges of cemeteries. Tombs, whether holding ashes or bodies, were required by law to be located outside cities and towns, more because of the ritual pollution from dead bodies than from concern for public health, though "practical considerations" such as the foulness of mass graves within cities played a role. But infant bodies are sometimes found interred within buildings in cities and towns, even within military camps; it is possible that their bodies, being still marginal to society, were not considered polluting.[21]

Parents also put a distance between themselves and their infants by employing wet nurses rather than following maternal nursing. Whether all families who could afford it practiced wet nursing is uncertain; maternal nursing was regarded as more virtuous and praised by philosophical authors, and the poorest could not afford a wet nurse's services. Mothers may have wished to avoid bonding with infants who might die from common diseases. However, the other reason for wet-nursing was the pressure of the high-mortality demographic regime of the ancient world, requiring equally high fertility from women. To keep the population stable, a Roman woman needed to give birth to five or six children in her lifetime—possibly more in high-disease areas—all of whom would not live to reproduce. Lactation is a suppressor of fertility; wet nurses themselves were required to abstain from sexual intercourse, lest they get pregnant and their milk dry up. By choosing wet-nursing over maternal nursing, Roman women ensured that they could reproduce again as soon as possible. It is uncertain whether families display "birth spacing"—the separation of children by two or three years or more, reflecting long-term maternal nursing and frequently used as a family-planning strategy in societies without effective contraception. To be sure, sending an infant to a wet nurse (sometimes outside the home) was not equivalent to exposing it; many wet nurses (*nutrix*, pl. *nutrices*) were beloved by their charges, who maintained a bond well after the period of nursing was over.[22]

Yet another belief attests an attempt, however irrational, to rationalize infant mortality: the belief that witches snatched infants away from their cradles. Witches (*strigae*) were believed to be the spirits of mothers who had lost their children; *lamiae* were vampire-like beings who were women who had died before they could marry and bear children. In Petronius's *Satyrica*, a character relates the story of a baby who was abducted by witches, who left behind a dummy made of straw.[23]

INFANT CARE AND MEDICINE

The Roman infant also needed to survive the advice and attentions of Greek doctors. "Pediatrics" as a subdiscipline of medicine is a modern creation; the normative patient of Greek medical theory is an adult able to follow the advised regimen. Greek doctors emphasized restoration of the balance of humors through diet, exercise, bleeding, purges, and fasting, the latter three as likely to harm the patients as help them. Women, in particular, were described by Greek and Roman medical authors as constitutionally moist, with an excess of blood and phlegm that was best relieved through menstruation or bleeding; medical treatment was likely to cause anemia, as well as infection at bleeding sites and injury from caustic poultices. Infants were also characterized as moist, and in general medical authors (all of whom were male) seem to express frustration with them as alien creatures. Female doctors, healers, and midwives (discussed in occupations of women, section "Lower-Status Women's Occupations: Urban," may have been more empathetic).[24]

Latin funerary inscription on marble, Roman, 1st–2nd century CE. Lollia Genialis was commemorated by her mother Lollia Sameramis (the name suggests non-Roman, possibly slave, origins). The mother terms herself infelicissima mater (most unfortunate mother); though the age of Lollia Genialis is not stated, it is probable that she was a young child. (The Metropolitan Museum of Art)

Greek and Roman physicians' advice on the care of infants was often more harmful than helpful. The postpartum mother's initial milk, colostrum, is rich in antibodies that protect the newborn infant from infection. Ancient doctors advised against letting newborns suckle the first milk because it seemed too thick and indigestible, and advised feeding the infant on honey water (which might be contaminated with bacteria) for the first few days. The next most vulnerable time for infants, after the neonatal period, was weaning, which often came very early; medical authors recommended weaning onto gruel or porridge, which provided little protein, deprived the infant of the antibodies and vitamins in human milk, and could possibly be contaminated with pathogens. Recommended weaning foods included bread crumbs soaked in honey, sweet wine, mead, milk, and thin gruel. This advice, if followed, boded ill for the children of the elite.[25]

Folk remedies probably had much wider distribution. Some folk remedies are listed by the Roman agricultural writer Cato the Elder and in Pliny the Elder's *Natural History* and suggest the helplessness of Roman parents against the illnesses of infants. Pliny recommends, "A viper's brain tied on with a piece of his skin helps dentition. The largest teeth of serpents have the same effect. The dung of a raven attached with wool as an amulet cures babies' coughs." Amulets for children survive in archeological finds and were intended to protect them from natural and supernatural ills. There was a cult of *Febris* (fever) in Rome and a cult of *Mephitis* (swamp stench) that were probably attempts to propitiate the deadly deities. "Cult" is the technical term for ritual worship paid to a pre-Christian deity; it does not have the social significance of "cult" in modern society.[26]

All social strata seem to be affected equally by the disease environment of Rome. Even though they could afford better food, dwelt on hills away from the mosquitoes, and often left the city of Rome during the summer, the upper orders do not seem to display greater longevity. We hear relatively little about child mortality from elite authors; they probably regarded the raising of small children as women's and slaves' work. Three elite mothers became legendary for their fecundity, but these anecdotes show that they also lost many of their children, presumably to disease. In the mid-second century BCE, Cornelia, a daughter of Scipio Africanus and mother of the tribunes Tiberius and Gaius Gracchus, gave birth to twelve children during her marriage to Tiberius Gracchus senior; only three of the children survived to adulthood, the tribunes and a daughter. Agrippina the Elder, a granddaughter of Augustus, married Germanicus, a nephew of the emperor Tiberius (14–37 CE), and had eight children, of whom six survived childhood. A century later, Faustina the Younger, the wife of Marcus Aurelius (161–80 CE), had fourteen children, of whom only a daughter and a son, the future emperor Commodus (180–93 CE), outlived Marcus. The orator Marcus Cornelius Fronto, a friend of the young Marcus Aurelius, writes of his own five children and one grandson who died.[27]

Nonetheless ordinary people of Rome and Italy—and around the Mediterranean—do seem to have regarded their infants and small children with affection and to have mourned them when they died. The number of Latin epitaphs for infants and small children is not proportionate to their probable death rate, but it is still culturally significant. Funerary monuments illustrate aspirations for children, even young ones, and attest the sentiments that they died untimely. It is possible that more freedmen and freedwomen (former slaves, usually purchasing their freedom or granted it in an owner's will) valued their children, born in liberty and symbolic of their family's future, and mourned them more intensely.

The (male) children of Roman senators were pressured to emulate the military and political careers of illustrious ancestors, not a prospect while the children were still small. Once children reach the age of eight or ten, they become more visible in the sources, though older male children are more visible than female children, the subject of chapter 3.[28]

CONCLUSION

As will be shown in subsequent chapters of the book, the impact of high mortality rates on the Roman family and marriage was far-reaching. High mortality shaped families, meaning that girls might have relatively few surviving siblings and might lose a father or a mother while they were still young. The expectations of high fertility thrust women into marriage at a young age, in their early to mid-teens (depending on social status), even before the advent of the Augustan marriage legislation coerced elite men and women to marry and reproduce. These laws will be discussed in more detail in chapter 4. They were motivated by the perception of Augustus and his advisers that Roman men (probably limited to senators and equestrians) were not marrying or having children. Moralists often attacked childlessness, more often blaming women for not bearing children for trivial reasons such as wanting to retain their youthful appearance. These views reflect a society that put a very high value on fertility because of the pressure of high mortality. Many "childless" married women might have had miscarriages or stillbirths or young children who died. Those women fortunate enough to inherit wealth from their fathers and to survive the gauntlet of repeated pregnancies earned legal privileges and were able to manage their own economic affairs, described in chapter 6. But, as with other premodern societies, death and mourning were never far away, the topic of the funerary customs described in chapter 11.

NOTES

1. On the census and population of Italy, the arguments from P. A. Brunt, *Italian Manpower, 225 B.C.–A.D. 14*, 2nd ed. (Oxford, 1987), onward are reviewed by Saskia Hin, *The Demography of Roman Italy: Population Dynamics in an Ancient Conquest Society (201 BCE–14 CE)* (Cambridge, 2013), 1–7, 261–97. On Egyptian census declarations, see Roger S. Bagnall and Bruce W. Frier, *The Demography of Roman Egypt* (Cambridge, 2006). Other sources are reviewed by Tim G. Parkin, *Demography and Roman Society* (Baltimore, MD, 1992); Walter Schiedel, "Roman

age structure: Evidence and models," *JRS* 91 (2001), 1–26; Hin, *Demography*, 101–9. An introduction to Roman demography is Parkin, *Demography*; Richard P. Saller, *Patriarchy, Property, and Death in the Roman Family* (Cambridge, 1994), 9–69; for more recent overview, see Walter Scheidel, "Demography," in *The Cambridge Economic History of the Greco-Roman World* (Cambridge, 2007), ed. Walter Scheidel, Ian Morris, and Richard Saller, 38–86.

2. For an introduction to the transition, see Paul Morland, *The Human Tide: How Population Shaped the Modern World* (New York, 2019); also Oxford University's *Our World in Data*, https://ourworldindata.org/. On modern child mortality, including teenagers, see Rebecca M. Cunningham, Maureen A. Walton, and Patrick M. Carter, "The major causes of death in children and adolescents in the United States," *New England Journal of Medicine* 379 (2018), 2468–75; for children under five, drowning was the most frequent cause of death. The demographic impact of the COVID-19 pandemic is still unclear.

3. Scheidel, "Demography," 45; Hin, *Demography* focuses on the late Republic at a level of detail not discussed in this chapter.

4. For life expectancy at birth, see Parkin, *Demography*, 79–80; Saller, *Patriarchy*, 12–25; Bagnall and Frier, *Demography*, 90, 109; Scheidel, "Age structure," 12; "Demography," 39; Hin, *Demography*, 102–9; Christian Laes, *Children in the Roman Empire: Outsiders Within* (Cambridge, 2011), 23–30. On demography of the Roman army, see Walter Scheidel, "The demography of the Roman imperial army," in *Measuring Sex, Age, and Death in the Roman Empire* (Portsmouth, RI, 1996), ed. Walter Scheidel, 93–138.

5. On early modern Italy and England, see Robert Sallares, *Malaria and Rome: A History of Malaria in Ancient Italy* (Oxford, 2002), 151–67; on the United States, see Timothy C. Winegard, *The Mosquito: A Human History of Our Deadliest Predator* (New York, 2019).

6. For details regarding bone changes termed "porotic hyperostosis," see M. Grmek, *Diseases in the Ancient Greek World* (Baltimore, MD, 1989), 245–83; Parkin, *Demography*, 41–58; Robert Sallares, Abigal Bouwman, and Cecilia Anderung, "The spread of malaria to southern Europe in antiquity," *Medical History* 48 (2004), 311–28; Alessandra Sperduti, Luca Bondioli, Oliver E. Craig, Tracy Prowse, and Peter Garnsey, "Bones, teeth, and history," in *The Science of Roman History: Biology, Climate, and the Future of the Past* (Princeton, 2018), ed. Walter Scheidel, 123–73. On diet, see P. Garnsey, *Food and Society in Classical Antiquity* (Cambridge, 1999), 20–1; Sallares, "Ecology," in Scheidel et al., *Economic History*, 15–37, at 34; Kyle Harper, *The Fate of Rome: Climate, Disease, and the End of an Empire* (Princeton, 2017), 78–79; more optimistically, see W. Jongman, "The early Roman empire: Consumption," in Scheidel et al., *Economic History*, 592–618. A wider range of health also appears in the Herculaneum skeletons, who died in the volcanic disaster, not of disease; see Ray Laurence, "Health and the life course at Herculaneum and Pompeii," in *Health in Antiquity* (London, 2005), ed. Helen King, 83–96.

7. Moralists, e.g., Xenophon *Oeconomicus* 7.5–6; Peter Garnsey, *Food and Society in Classical Antiquity* (Cambridge, 1999), 103, 108–9. On vegetarian diet, see ibid., 39. On the impact of maternal anemia in modern societies, see R. J. Stoltzfus, L. Mullany, and R. E. Black, "Iron deficiency anaemia," in *Comparative Quantification of Health Risks: Global and Regional Burden of Disease Attributable to Selected Major Risk Factors* (Geneva, 2004), ed. Majid Ezzati et al., 163–209. Anemia should not be confused with "chlorosis" in Greek medical authors; see Helen King, *Hippocrates' Woman: Reading the Female Body in Ancient Greece* (London, 2002), 188–204. On small infant skeletons, see Nathan Pilkington, "Growing up Roman: Infant mortality and reproductive development," *Journal of Interdisciplinary History* 44.1 (2013), 1–35.

8. On epitaphs, see Walter Scheidel, "Libitina's bitter gains: Seasonal mortality and endemic disease in the ancient city of Rome," *Ancient Society* 25 (1994), 151–75; Brent D. Shaw, "Seasons of death: Aspects of mortality in imperial Rome," *JRS* 86 (1996), 100–138. On parents, Horace, *Epistles* 1.7.5-9.

9. For direct evidence, see Sallares et al., "The spread of malaria"; in general, on ancient DNA and other approaches to osteoarcheology, see Sperduti et al., "Bones." On the mutations, see D. P. Kwiatkowski, "How malaria has affected the human genome and what human genetics can tell us about malaria," *American Journal of Human Genetics* 77 (2005), 171–92.

10. On climate, see Sallares, *Malaria*, 101–3; for more current research, Hin, *Demography*, 74–85; Harper, *Fate of Rome*, 39–58.

11. For *Anopheles* habitats, deforestation, and alluviation, see Schiedel, "Age structure," 18–19; Sallares, *Malaria*, 67–72, 103–8; J. D. Hughes, *Environmental Problems of the Greeks and Romans: Ecology in the Ancient Mediterranean* (Baltimore, MD, 2014); for standing water and flooding, see Sallares, *Malaria*, 109–10, 214, 228–29; Hin, *Demography*, 79–85; for regional hyperendemic disease, see Sallares, *Malaria*, 201–34 (Rome); Scheidel, "Demography," 78; Hin, *Demography*, 92–3, 125.

12. On *miasmata*, see F. Borca, "Towns and marshes in the ancient world," in *Death and Disease in the Ancient City* (London, 2000), ed. Valerie M. Hope and Eireann Marshall, 74–84; Mark Bradley, ed., *Rome, Pollution and Propriety: Dirt, Disease, and Hygiene in the Eternal City from Antiquity to Modernity* (Cambridge, 2012); Ann Olga Koloski-Ostrow, *The Archaeology of Sanitation in Roman Italy: Toilets, Sewers, and Water Systems* (Chapel Hill, NC, 2015). *Anopheles* mosquitoes are weak fliers and do not fly upward; Sallares, *Malaria*, 96, 98; on unhealthy locations, see Vitruvius *On Architecture* 1.4.12; on healthy locations such as Tifernum Tiberinum, see Plin. *Ep.* 5.6.2–3; the 1882 map of malaria in Italy (Sallares, *Malaria*, 237) is basically one of low elevation.

13. On placental malaria, see Sallares, *Malaria*, 125–26; on maternal mortality in general, see Hin, *Demography*, 128–29.

14. On literary depictions of abortion, see Suzanne Dixon, *Reading Roman Women: Sources, Genres, and Real Life* (London, 2001), 56–65; Ovid *Amores* 2.13–14; Aulus Gellius *Noctes Atticae* 12.1.18.

15. On early modern deaths, see I. Loudon, "Deaths in childbed from the eighteenth century to 1935," *Medical History* 30.1 (1986), 1–41; on Roman midwives, see Ralph Jackson, *Doctors and Diseases in the Roman Empire* (London, 1988), 86–88; more skeptically, see King, *Hippocrates' Woman*; on pregnant victim, see Valerie M. Hope, *Roman Death: The Dying and the Dead in Ancient Rome* (London, 2009), 45; on late puberty, around age fourteen, see Hin, Demography, 151–2; Pilkington, "Growing up Roman," 32; e.g., Soranus *Gynecology* 1.20; Gaius *Institutes* 1.96.

16. Julia, Plut. *Pompey* 53; Calpurnia, Plin. *Ep.* 8.10–11; Tullia, Cic. *Att.* 12.15; Cic. *Fam.* 4.5.1, 4–6; Jo-Ann Shelton, *As the Romans Did: A Source Book in Roman Social History* (Oxford, 1988), nos. 111–12, 286; inscriptions, *CIL* V 28753; *CIL* III 3572; *L'Année Epigraphique* 1995, 1793; Laes, *Children*, 51–54. For more text of epitaphs, see Laes, *Children*, 53–54; cf. Beryl Rawson, *Children and Childhood in Roman Italy* (Oxford, 2003), 96–97, 103; Jo-Ann Shelton, *The Women of Pliny's* Letters (London, 2013), 126–27; Emily A. Hemelrijk, *Women and Society in the Roman World: A Sourcebook of Inscriptions from the Roman West* (Cambridge, 2021), no. 1.51–53, 5.32.

17. On exposure, see William V. Harris, "Child-exposure in the Roman empire," *JRS* 84 (1994), 1–22; Parkin, *Demography*, 95–100; Rawson, *Children*, 116–18; Hope, *Roman Death*, 138; Hin, *Demography*, 134–47; "throw it out," *P. Oxy.* 744 = Shelton, no. 31 = Mary R. Lefkowitz and Maureen B. Fant, *Women's Life in Greece and Rome: A Source Book in Translation*, 4th ed. (Baltimore, MD, 2016), no. 295.

18. On malaria, a disease of children, see Sallares, *Malaria*, 125; Scheidel, "Libitina's bitter gains," 162; Shaw, "Seasons of death," 118; on tuberculosis, see Harper, *Fate of Rome*, 89–91; on other diseases, see Scheidel, "Age structure," 8–10; Rawson, *Children*, 115–16; on the thought that malaria may by comorbid with other diseases, see Sallares, *Malaria*, 127–28, 136.

19. On diarrheal diseases, see Celsus *On Medicine.* 2.8.30; on general disease, see Laes, *Children*, 39–44; on sanitation, see Alex Scobie, "Slums, sanitation, and mortality in the Roman world," *Klio* 68 (1986), 399–433; Hughes, *Environmental Problems*, 176–78; Koloski-Ostrow, *Archaeology of Sanitation*, 49, 82–83; Harper, *Fate of Rome*, 80–81, 83, 85; on flooding, see Sallares, *Malaria*, n. 11 earlier; Vespasian, Suet. *Vespasian* 5.3; on satirists, see Koloski-Ostrow, 104–11; Emily Gowers, "The anatomy of Rome: From Capitol to Cloaca," *JRS* 85 (1995), 23–32; Neville Morley, "The salubriousness of the Roman city," in King, *Health in Antiquity*, 192–204.

20. On rites, see Rawson, *Children*, 112–16; Laes, *Children*, 66–68.

21. On infant care, see Veronique Dasen, "Childbirth and infancy in Greek and Roman antiquity," in *A Companion to Families in the Greek and Roman Worlds* (Malden, MA, 2010), ed. B. Rawson, 291–314; on naming, see 304; on death rituals, see Valerie M. Hope, "Contempt and respect: The treatment of the corpse in ancient Rome," in Hope and Marshall, *Death and Disease*, 104–27; John Bodel, "Dealing with the dead: Undertakers, executioners, and potters' fields in ancient Rome," in Hope and Marshall,

Death and Disease, 128–51; on infant burials, see Cic. *Tusculan Disputationes* 1.39.194; Plin. *Natural History* 7.72; Juvenal 15.138–40; Fulgentius 7; J. Pearce, "Infants, cemeteries, and communities in the Roman provinces," in *TRAC 2000: Proceedings of the Tenth Annual Theoretical Roman Archaeology Conference*, ed. Gwyn Davies, Andrew Gardner, and Kris Lockyear (London, 2001), 125–42; Rawson, *Children*, 341–43; on marginal status, see Dasen, "Childbirth," 304–6; on Isola Sacra, see Hope, *Roman Death*, 158; on military camps, see Penelope Allison, *People and Spaces in Roman Military Bases* (Cambridge, 2013), 261–65; on individual epitaphs, see, e.g., Hemelrijk, *Women and Society*, no. 1.58–64.

22. On wet-nursing, see, in general, Rawson, *Children*, 124–26; Laes, *Children*, 69–77; Dasen, "Childbirth," 307–9; on fertility and demography, see Parkin, *Demography*, 88–90, 94–95; Bagnall and Frier, *Demography*, 135–59; Hin, *Demography*, 195–9; Scheidel, "Demography," 41; Sabine Huebner, *The Family in Roman Egypt: A Comparative Approach to Intergenerational Solidarity and Conflict* (Cambridge, 2015). To maintain population stability, women might have to bear as many as six to nine children in extremely high-mortality areas, Sallares, *Malaria*, 127.

23. Laes, *Children*, 68. On witches, Petronius *Satyrica* 63.

24. On women in medical authors, see Jackson, *Doctors*, 86–104; for a more in-depth study, see King, *Hippocrates' Woman*; on infants in medical authors, see Dasen, "Childbirth," 293–94.

25. Soranus *Gynecology* 2.17–18, 46–47; Galen *Hygiene* 31; Jackson, *Doctors*, 102–3; on porridge, see Garnsey, *Food*, 52–53, 106–7; on foods, see Laes, *Children*, 73; on honey, see Dasen, "Childbirth," 303.

26. Quoted in Plin. *Natural History* 30.137. On folk remedies for malaria, see Sallares, *Malaria*, 53–54, 134.

27. Elite left the city in summer; see Sallares, *Malaria*, 228, 279–80; on no greater longevity, see Walter Scheidel, "Emperors, aristocrats, and the Grim Reaper: Towards a demographic profile of the Roman elite," *Classical Quarterly* 49.1 (1999), 254–81; On Cornelia, Agrippina, and Faustina, see Susan Treggiari, *Roman Marriage: Iusti Coniuges from the Time of Cicero to the Time of Ulpian* (Oxford, 1991), 403–5; Parkin, *Demography*, 94, 114; Harper, *Fate of Rome*, 74; Cornelia, Plin. *Natural History* 7.13.57; Plut. *Moralia* 312; Plut. *Tiberius Gracchus* 1.4–5; Sen. *Moralia* 16.3; Agrippina, Suet. *Gaius* 7; Quintilian *Institutio Oratoria* 6.pr. 2–11; Fronto *Letters* 1.12; Hope, *Roman Death*, 139.

28. On funerary commemoration of children, see Hope, *Roman Death*, 139; the number of children's epitaphs is not proportionate to their mortality rate, see Keith Hopkins, "On the probable age structure of the Roman population," *Population Studies* 20.2 (1966), 245–65; Parkin, *Demography*, 6.

3

CHILDHOOD AND EDUCATION

INTRODUCTION

Pliny the Younger's *Letters* preserve the eulogy of a young girl named Minicia Marcella, the daughter of Minicius Fundanus.

> She had not yet reached the age of fourteen, and yet she combined the wisdom of an elderly woman and dignity of a matron with the sweetness and modesty of youth and innocence. She would cling to her father's neck, and embrace us, his friends, with modest affection; she loved her nurses, her attendants and her teachers, each one for the service given her; she applied herself intelligently to her books and was moderate and restrained in her play. She bore her last illness with patient resignation and, indeed, with courage; she obeyed her doctors' orders, cheered her sister and father, and by sheer force of will carried on after her physical strength had failed her. This will-power remained with her to the end, and neither the length of her illness nor fear of death could break it.

Belonging to an aristocratic family in northern Italy, Minicia was, according to Pliny, thirteen years old; a surviving Latin epitaph records her as twelve years, eleven months, and seven days old (such elaborate precision is usual in Roman epitaphs). Pliny does not record the disease that she faced so bravely and that killed her. He mentions that she was soon to be married:

> She was already engaged to marry a distinguished young man, the day for the wedding was fixed, and we had received our invitations. Such joy, and now such sorrow! No words can express my grief when I heard [her father Minicius] Fundanus giving his own orders . . . for the money he had intended for clothing, pearls and jewels [for her wedding] to be spent on incense, ointment and spices [for her funeral pyre].

Pliny's words suggest that Roman girls were thought to transition directly from childhood to marriage at puberty (which, as we will see in chapter 4, was true for girls of senatorial or equestrian families but perhaps not for the sub-elite). The eulogy of Minicia raises other problems. Pliny is addressing her father, Minicius Fundanus, who was a believer in Stoicism, an ancient philosophy that stressed the pursuit of virtue and the maintenance of equanimity and self-control in the face of adversity. Pliny thus praises Minicius Fundanus by eulogizing his daughter's self-control when faced with severe illness and death. Minicia's eulogy in general emphasizes mature qualities in a child: she plays very little, and applies herself to her studies (elite girls, as we will see, were usually tutored privately). She displays "the wisdom (*prudentia*) of an elderly woman and the dignity (*gravitas*) of a matron." Were Roman children, both boys and girls, expected to behave like miniature grown-ups?[1]

Elaborate epitaphs and tomb monuments survive that eulogize young boys in a similar manner for displaying adult skills, such as the aspiring eleven-year-old poet Quintus Sulpicius Maximus, who won a prize in a major poetry competition at Rome in 94 CE, or the thirteen-year-old orator in training Valerius Pudens, or the six-year-old scholar Lucius Titius Valerius. Such boy "prodigies" were depicted in adult togas which they would not yet have worn and holding the scrolls and making the conventional gestures of orators. These eulogies and that of Minicia Marcella suggest how differently boys and girls were raised, and illustrate their parents' different aspirations for them. A eulogy for an elite boy of the same age as Minicia might have dwelled on his precocious talent at poetry or oratory, and might have emphasized the loss of his future public career as an orator, a military officer, or a politician. Despite her application to her studies, if she had not died prematurely, Minicia was destined to be a wife and mother. We cannot assume that Roman girls' experience of childhood was the same as that of boys.[2]

The study of premodern childhood (before the nineteenth and twentieth centuries) is one of history's more difficult and controversial subjects, as the sources are dominated by adult, male concerns and tend to ignore children, let alone girls. What is knowable about childhood in premodern Europe seems particularly alienating: extremely high infant and child mortality rates, to which adult contemporaries seemed indifferent, paying relatively little attention to infants and small children. Other attitudes that have greatly changed in recent history include attitudes toward child labor, corporal punishment of children, and sexual exploitation of children. Some European historians took an evolutionary approach toward the history of childhood, arguing that childhood as we know it did not exist in premodern societies and that childhood as a protected phase of human life, reserved for education and shielded from sexuality and economic necessities, is a modern invention. This approach promoted a backlash with historians showing that parental love and protection of their children existed even in ancient and medieval societies. However, the evolutionary approach is useful, as it suggests that the experience of childhood in Roman society was probably highly stratified. As this chapter will show, the children of elite parents were indeed cherished and protected, but they were differentiated from the children of the poor and slave children—the majority of children—who lacked such protections, had to work from an early age, and were subjected to sexual exploitation. In turn, it is possible that girls of the elite classes were raised more strictly than boys.[3]

GENDER AND LIFE STAGES

Looking for girls in accounts of Roman childhood is a frustrating exercise. Overwhelmingly, ancient sources' depictions of children and childhood focus on boys and, because of the highly gendered nature of Roman society, it cannot be assumed that generic children included both boys and girls. In some past or traditional cultures boys and girls are not strongly differentiated till puberty, when children are initiated into distinct male and female gender roles. Even in modern societies, gender differentiation may undergo abrupt shifts; in the first decades of the twentieth century, pink was considered an appropriate color for small boys and light blue for girls, the colors reversing later in the century.

Roman infants, who were customarily swaddled, may not have been strongly gender differentiated. Female babies were named on

the eighth day of life, and male babies on the ninth; a Greek physi-
cian recommended that female infants be swaddled more loosely at
the hips, to encourage the development of a feminine body shape
with wider hips, but otherwise infants were treated alike. For those
children who survived infancy, boys and girls began to be differentiated in dress, upbringing, and education. A *puer* (pl. *pueri*) was a
boy, a *puella* (pl. *puellae*) a girl (*puer* was also used to address adult
male slaves, and *puellae* was slang for sexually available women).
Only very small children are denoted generically as *infantes* (sing.
infans), literally those unable to speak. In law the jurists emphasized that a generic male term such as *filius* (son) also includes
females, and if a Roman father died intestate, his estate was equally
divided among his sons and daughters. But, as we have seen in
chapter 1, Roman society was in many ways more misogynistic
than Roman law.[4]

Suggesting gender non-differentiation is the evidence that before
puberty, both boys and girls wore the *toga praetexta*, which had a
purple border. The *toga praetexta* was worn only by Roman magistrates and by freeborn children; it marked the children from slaves,
as will be seen. The toga was hard to keep on the body and not
suited to active children; freeborn children may have worn it only
as formal dress, and there are very few visual depictions of girls
wearing the *toga praetexta*. Under the toga or without it, boys and
girls were dressed differently. Boys wore short tunics, belted to
the knee. Girls wore long tunics, the same length as adult wom-
en's tunics, implying that girls engaged in less physical activity or
were expected to display greater decorum. Girls do not seem to
have worn their hair down; long, unbound hair was an age marker
(indicating an unmarried girl) in other premodern societies such as
medieval Europe. Roman girls may have worn their hair in simple
buns or braids that were tied up on the head.[5]

Roman children come into sharper focus when they are past
infancy and small childhood, probably influenced by classical the-
ories of life stages. In Greek and Latin literary authors, there are
elaborate chronological definitions of life stages, from infancy to
old age, typically using periods such as seven years and focused on
males. *Infantia* (infancy) is the period from zero to seven years of
age, *pueritia* (boyhood) age seven to fourteen, adolescence fourteen
to twenty-one, young manhood twenty-one to twenty-eight, and
so on. These stages corresponded to expectations for elite men's
education and careers; education could take until age twenty-one
(though it was not formalized by ages, years, and tracks) and holding political office could begin in young manhood; a man could not

become a Roman sena-
tor until age twenty-
five. In contrast, the life
stages of women were
not defined, but would
probably also include
infantia (zero to seven
years) and girlhood
(seven to fourteen years),
followed at once and
notionally by married
womanhood, even if not
all women (as we will
see) were married at age
fourteen. In Roman law,
girls could be married
at twelve. Because all
women were expected
to marry, the sexually
mature but unmarried
young woman (*adulta
virgo*) occupied a fleeting
place in Roman society,
except for the Vestal Virgins, female priestesses
recruited at age six to ten
who were required to be
virgin and unmarried for
thirty years. The absence
of an *adulescens* phase for
Roman women suggests
that their education was

Portrait bust of a young girl, from Rome,
Italy, ca. 250–275 CE. The girl is three or
four years old and identified as female by
her dress, despite her cropped hair. Other
sculptures of young girls show long hair
worn pinned up, but visual representations
of young girls are relatively rare, despite
the high mortality rate of all young children. (Purchase from the J. H. Wade Fund,
The Cleveland Museum of Art)

briefer, discussed in section "Education of Girls." It also suggests
that elite girls, once married, were expected to grow up "at once,"
managing households and raising children (though, as we will see,
they were not primary caregivers of small children).[6]

Babies and small children died in great numbers with little social
recognition. Tombstones and elaborate monuments were usually
erected for older children, aged seven to fourteen, when adult aspirations for them became more definite. In contrast, infants (under
two) are vastly under-commemorated; in disproportion to the high
infant mortality rate, their epitaphs are few. Infant burials however
have been often overlooked by archeologists; infant bones degrade

more quickly in the earth and are more fragile; their burials were, as has been seen, often in marginal sites on the edges of cemeteries or even within or under the eaves of houses. Children from two to seven were more likely to be commemorated than babies, but were still considered *infantes* by Roman social norms, not yet full persons in the eyes of the law.[7]

Whether or not young children were expected to behave like adults probably varied greatly with social status. By the early Empire, classical sculptors were aware that children do not look like miniature adults; their portraits are sculpted with different facial and bodily proportions, with larger foreheads, smaller noses and chins, larger heads, and shorter limbs. Children were depicted at play on the elaborately carved sarcophagi (stone caskets) that became the fashion among the wealthy in the second century CE and later. These depict children through their life course. After about age seven, more adult behavior seems expected from, for one, boys of the upper orders and princes of the imperial family, who were destined for power and prestige. The imperial princes often took up public roles as the emperors' prospective heirs from a young age. They could deliver orations on public occasions. As we have seen, epitaphs extol boy poets and orators who won prizes in competitions. The eulogy of Minicia Marcella suggests that a parallel ideal applied to elite girls, expected to display "the *gravitas* of a *matrona*" from an early age, in keeping with their future social status. Minicia is praised for application to her studies and for rarely playing.[8]

At the other end of the social scale, slave children and freeborn poor children were expected to work from an early age, as young as five to seven years old, when children performed light agricultural and household tasks. A slave child in a wealthy household sometimes filled an ambiguous role termed *delicium*, "darling" or "pet," was treated like a pet animal as much as a beloved child and was often eroticized and subjected to sexual abuse. The question of child labor is discussed in section "Slave Children and Other Vulnerable Children" of this chapter.[9]

MOTHERS AND OTHER CAREGIVERS

The parents of Roman elite children seem to have been less involved in the daily care of young children, leaving their care to nurses (*nutrices*) and pedagogues (*paedagogi*). Such handing of children to servant caregivers was common in premodern European elite families, down through the pre–World War II period in

England. Evolutionary historians of the family have suggested that premodern parenting's hands-off style was an adaptation to high infant and child mortality: parents would grieve less for young children whom they rarely saw. It is especially difficult to judge these practices in Roman families, since elite male authors focus relatively little on children. When children are mentioned, the parents do seem to regard them with affection. The Roman family may have evolved from relative indifference to children, regarded merely as continuators of the family name, to greater affection for children as individuals, associated with greater emphasis on the conjugal household. In this view, the Principate deterred aristocratic males from traditional pursuit of fame and glory through political and military achievement; men turned to their families for emotional satisfaction. However, other scholars have refuted this evolutionary history of the Roman family, pointing to instances of direct parental involvement with their young children (usually sons) from early times.[10]

Such anecdotes indicate that ideal elite parents should teach their children how to behave as future members of the same elite, establishing role models for them. Roman mothers in particular were expected to educate their children in correct moral behavior, probably by telling them the stories or *exempla* of past Romans (often legendary) that we have seen in chapter 1. In Tacitus's *Dialogue on Orators*, the interlocutor Messalla (a man) blames the decline of oratory on "the laziness of our young men, the carelessness of parents, the ignorance of teachers, and the decay of the old-fashioned virtue" and contrasts the parenting provided by great Roman mothers of the past:

> In the good old days, every man's son . . . was brought up not in the bedroom of a slave nurse, but in his mother's lap, and at her knee. And that mother could have no higher praise than that she managed the house and devoted herself to her children . . . It was in this spirit, we are told, that Cornelia, the mother of the Gracchi, directed their upbringing, Aurelia that of [Julius] Caesar, Atia of Augustus: thus it was that these mothers trained their princely children.

The dialogue continues by blaming present-day elite Roman mothers for turning their children over to slave caregivers, causing the children to acquire "servile" and lower-class characteristics, taking them in with their slave nurse's milk. Virtuous women of the past, such as the wife of Cato the Elder or Cornelia the mother of the reformist politicians Tiberius and Gaius Gracchus, nursed their infants themselves. Closer in time was Cnaeus Julius Agricola's mother, Julia Procilla, who raised him after his father's death. Tacitus implies that serious-minded elite women knew enough about the public deeds of their male relatives and ancestors to impart this knowledge to their sons. But the portrayal of present-day idle women in order to praise exemplary women of the past is typical of Latin rhetoric and fails to illuminate what women actually did.[11]

Parenting responsibilities might be undertaken by grandmothers or aunts if mothers were not available. In Pliny's *Letters*, Ummidia Quadratilla, a wealthy older woman of a senatorial family, was responsible for raising her grandson and granddaughter. Though Pliny disapproves of Ummidia's own moral character, she subjected her grandson to appropriate discipline, urging him to go and study and not permitting him to watch the pantomime shows that she loved (these shows by live actors had a bawdy reputation). Pliny says nothing about the granddaughter.[12]

In the *Consolatio ad Helviam*, Seneca the Younger urges his mother Helvia to take up the responsibility of educating and forming the character of her granddaughter Novatilla (his niece), who may have been in late childhood, soon to marry:

> Now is the time to order her character, now is the time to shape it; instruction that is stamped upon the plastic years leaves a deeper mark. Let her become accustomed to your conversation, let her be molded to your pleasure; you will give her much even if you give her nothing but your example.

The tone is admonitory. The verb form of "Let her . . ." is frequently used for commands and laws in Latin, though it is less stern than Cato's advice to an estate owner on managing his *vilica* (housekeeper, a slave woman): "Let her fear you."[13]

In practice, child-rearing by slave and freedperson servants was too well established to go away, and slave/freed nurses might themselves be quite strict with their charges, as Augustine relates of the elderly nurse of his mother Monica and her sisters:

> She was strict about disciplining them with a devoted firmness, and with sober caution when it came to teaching them. She would not allow them to drink even water, even if they were burning with thirst, outside the family mealtimes when they had enough to drink: she was taking precautions against bad habits and added this sensible advice, "Now it is water that you are drinking, because you are not

able to drink wine. But once you get married and are mistresses over store rooms and larders, water will lose its appeal, but the habit of drinking will remain strong."

The context may be particular to Augustine's North African and Christian family in the fourth century CE, but we will see that a stereotype of women was that they liked to drink wine, leading to other misbehavior, and that of old Roman husbands punished wives severely for drinking wine. The nurse in Augustine's anecdote would not even permit her charges to satisfy their thirst with water, lest it lead them to drinking wine. It is possible that Roman girls were brought up more strictly than boys, because of the need to guard girls' *pudicitia* (discussed in chapter 1 and in section "Vulnerability of Children: Freeborn versus Slave") and because girls were seen as the future moral educators of their own children.[14]

Roman elite children did accompany their parents at dinner (where they were seated rather than reclining at table), and in public on festival and other special occasions. On these occasions, the children were probably required to be on their best behavior, representing the continuity of the family to society at large. Pliny's description of Minicia, quoted at the start of this chapter, suggests awareness of her winning personality because she was permitted to socialize with her father's friends on such occasions (before her illness). But the daily care of children was still the responsibility of nurses and pedagogues.

An infant or small child's primary caregiver was their *nutrix* or wet nurse. Many Roman elite mothers did not breastfeed their own infants, choosing instead to use wet nurses, women who had recently been pregnant and nursed their employers' children besides or instead of their own (the nurses might have sent their own infants to other wet nurses, or their own infants had died). This practice was controversial, Roman moralists idealizing mothers of the past who nursed their own children. *Nutrices* were of low social status, freedwomen or slaves, though poor freeborn women are possible. The *nutrix* was the main daily caregiver for infants and small children, and might still be a caregiver of older children, who regarded their nurses with affection. Wet nurses were among the caregivers whom Roman owners were permitted to manumit, for reasons of affection, below the legal age of thirty. Wealthy Romans might reward their former nurses substantially; Pliny the Younger gave his old *nutrix* a farm worth

100,000 sesterces (HS; though she appears to have lived in town and employed an estate manager).[15]

Wet-nursing was also practiced below the upper orders. Sub-elite Roman families also appear to have employed wet nurses, attested in contracts from Roman Egypt. Probably because slave women were often wet nurses, maternal nursing had acquired a stigma as slaves' work. In a papyrus from the early Empire, a father or mother (part of the document is missing) says to his or her son-in-law, "I beg you, let the baby have a wet nurse. I will not allow my daughter to nurse her own child." In wealthy households, the infants of slave women were also wet-nursed, in order to free the slave women for their daily tasks; the slave infants were sent to the countryside to be raised, where they had a greater chance of survival than in the crowded, disease-prone cities. However, women of the lower social strata probably nursed their own children because they could not afford wet nurses.[16]

Older elite children (out of *infantia*) were cared for by a pedagogue (Greek *paidagogos*, Latin *paedagogus*), a male slave or freedman who accompanied children in public, typically taking them to and from school and supervising them in other public places. The pedagogue's tasks were to assure the children's safety and teach them how to behave in public. He accordingly might be strict, resembling the stereotype of a governess in a nineteenth-century English or American elite family. His role was also to protect elite children from kidnapping by slave traders and from sexual molestation. Though a pedagogue was not mainly a teacher, he may have coached his protégés with their lessons, which involved much rote memorization. Girls may have had female pedagogues; some are attested in epitaphs, though they also needed male attendants to provide security. A less wealthy family might have one pedagogue for several children, both boys and girls. Valerius Maximus tells of a father, Pontius Aufidianus, who killed his daughter and her pedagogue when he caught them having an affair; the anecdote resembles other gruesome stories about the punishment of *impudicitia* (cf. Lucretia and Verginia, cited in chapter 1). However, the relative absence of pedagogues for girls in inscriptions suggests that girls of the upper orders were taught privately at home rather than attending school.[17]

IMPACT OF MORTALITY ON FAMILY LIFE

Children themselves must have noticed the deaths of their brothers and sisters from common diseases. The mortality rate was such that a third of all infants died in their first year, and approximately half of all children died before they were ten years old. As a result, effective family size (the number of children alive at any one time, rather than all the children that were ever born) was often small, leading the Roman political class to believe that families were not reproducing adequately and motivating Augustus's famous *Leges Juliae* on marriage (discussed in chapter 4). Though Cornelia, the mother of the Gracchi, gave birth to twelve children, only three survived to adulthood, Tiberius and Gaius Gracchus and a sister. Large families, stereotypically farm families, were a phenomenon of the late nineteenth and early twentieth centuries in England and North America, reflecting the demographic transition's improved hygiene and medical practices that caused infant and child mortality to decline well before the fertility rate also began to drop.[18]

Roman families were also often disrupted and recombined by the frequent death and divorce of fathers and mothers. A high proportion of Roman children lost their fathers at a relatively young age because of the age gap in Roman marriage: fathers were significantly older than mothers. Prudent fathers appointed *tutores*, guardians, in their wills to look after their children's financial interests; a suitable *tutor* might be a male relative or a trusted friend, and the law safeguarded the wards (*pupilli*) of *tutores* against malfeasance by the *tutores*. However, a child did not usually live with their *tutor*; if their mother remarried, as was likely, the child would live with the new family. Because of these shifting arrangements, slave or freedperson caregivers were often the people who provided the most continuity of care.[19]

Remarriage was common in Roman families. As we will see in chapter 4, the Augustan marriage legislation required widowed or divorced spouses to remarry (others) until a woman had either given birth to three children or both men and women were elderly (sixty for men, fifty for women). Custody of children was interpreted differently than in modern English and American society, where the mother is the presumed caregiver and usually receives custody, and where it is possible for fathers to evade providing care. In cases of divorce or death of a Roman mother, her children lived with their father, who had custody as the paterfamilias or head of a family. His children were in his *potestas* and legally belonged to his *familia*. If the father remarried, a stepmother and her children might compete for the father's affections with the children of his previous marriage. Surviving grandmothers or aunts might also help raise children who had lost their mothers.[20]

A family bereft of its father was in a more precarious situation. If a father died, or if he divorced and was proven to be an unsuitable caregiver (based on immorality, criminality, etc.), his children might live with their mother, but the financial situation of such a mother and her children was precarious. She might need to remarry for financial reasons, even before the Augustan marriage laws. Furthermore, a widowed mother was also not the legal guardian (*tutor*) of her underaged children and could not authorize financial decisions on their behalf. She depended on the *tutor* appointed by her husband to guard her children's interests. If no parent survived, a child might be taken into another household as an *alumnus/a*, a fosterling, indicating their dependent status rather than formal adoption.[21]

EDUCATION OF GIRLS

Rome had no public school system or institutional private schools and no ideal that all members of society should be literate or reach a certain educational standard. We call the lowest level of available school "primary" for convenience, since it taught only reading, writing, and arithmetic, but its lack of structure meant that its students were within an age range (on average seven to fourteen) and left when they had mastered the skills, not when they had completed a number of years. Primary school was held in public places, such as forums and arcades, with only benches for the pupils, who were equipped at their own expense with slates or wax tablets and with lamps on dark winter mornings. Primary education was funded by the students' parents, who paid small sums to the schoolmaster (*ludimagister*); accordingly, a schoolmaster was a poor and relatively low-status man.[22]

Literary authors emphasized the tedium and brutality of primary school. Primary school was tedious because it emphasized rote learning, progressing from reciting the alphabet to reciting nonsense combinations of letters and syllables and finally words and sentences. Children who were learning the alphabet were termed "abecedarians." An excerpt from a primary schoolbook, dating from Late Antiquity, takes the reader through an elite boy's daily life, including getting up in the morning and going to school attended by his pedagogue. Arithmetic was also taught by rote learning. The *ludimagister* was also proverbial for beating his students (mostly boys). Girls are offhand mentioned by Latin authors as attending primary school. Livy depicts the plebeian girl Verginia as attending school, where she was ogled by the evil Decemvir Appius Claudius, who sent his slave to kidnap and enslave her (450 BCE). This anecdote is more likely to reflect the assumptions of Livy's own times (the beginning of the Principate) that girls might attend primary school than the prevalence of school in a far earlier period with even more illiteracy.[23]

"Secondary" education taught by a *grammaticus* (grammarian) focused on learning Greek and Latin literature, often by rote. The *grammaticus* was more highly respected and better paid than the *ludimagister*. Instead of teaching merely basic skills, he was regarded as conveying culture, conferring a degree of cultivation that gave its learners a step up into the social elite. An educated gentleman was expected to be familiar with Greek and Latin literature and literary allusions. Girls are not recorded as attending lessons with *grammatici*; they may have received private tutoring at this stage, out of concern for their sexual propriety. A female teacher of literature was preferable; the epitaph of a female grammarian named Volusia Tertullina, dead at forty-three, survives from Caesarea in Mauretania.[24]

Postsecondary education trained youths in oratory and rhetoric, including related liberal arts such as philosophy, music, and architecture. They did not necessarily leave home to study these subjects, though studying at Athens was prestigious. There was still no rigid age tracking and program; students acquired these skills at different ages and rates, as seen with the boy "prodigies" in poetry and oratory. Teachers of rhetoric were publicly funded and honored; training in rhetoric and oratory was a fundamental skill for the Roman political elite, for oratory was used in political activity, in law courts, and as a social performance. Training in oratory was not regarded as appropriate for women, who could not hold political office or represent others in law courts. Hortensia, an elite woman of the Late Republic, was famous for defending the right of Roman matrons not to be taxed. She was believed to have acquired her skills from her father Quintus Hortensius, a famous orator. Oratory in the courts was regarded as incompatible with women's modesty, as in the case of Carfania, a woman also of the Late Republic who (in the eyes of the male jurists) disgraced herself by pursuing many vexatious lawsuits in person.[25]

For men, literary and rhetorical education was strongly associated with high social status. A man of the upper orders would seem ignorant and vulgar if he did not have a literary and rhetorical education and only knew how to read, write, and do arithmetic. Quintilian, author of a manual on oratory, emphasizes that when a son is born, a father should set the highest expectations of him and assign a nurse with correct speech so that he will begin his education with every advantage.[26]

The question is whether girls of the upper strata received a comparable education, since in theory elite girls were married for the first time around age twelve to fourteen, at an age when elite boys would have begun their literary and oratorical training. If girls in the sub-elite married at a slightly later age, in their mid- to late teens, this later date may reflect not their continued education but the desire of the family to retain daughters as a source of labor in the home, farm, or shop. The later age may also reflect their delayed puberty or (as with boys) the desire of the family to postpone their daughters' social transition to adulthood until they were emotionally more mature. However, this later age at marriage is based on a statistical analysis of epitaphs (discussed further in chapter 4).[27]

Some women of the upper orders did receive a literary and philosophical education, closely associated with scholarly male relatives (fathers and husbands). Cornelia, the mother of the Gracchi, was not only the daughter of Scipio Africanus, but the niece of Aemilius Paullus, the conqueror of Macedon, who acquired the Macedonian royal library. Cornelia was probably the first Roman woman to be well educated in Greek literature. Hortensia, mentioned earlier in this section, learned rhetorical and oratorical skills from her father, the orator Quintus Hortensius. Another example is Laelia, daughter of the orator Gaius Laelius (mid-second century BCE). Elite women's education also enabled them to educate their sons, as with Cornelia, the mother of the Gracchi (mentioned earlier in this paragraph), who educated her sons, the tribunes Tiberius and Gaius Gracchus, "with such scrupulous care that although confessedly no other Romans were so well endowed by nature, they were thought to owe their virtues more to her education than to nature." A later Cornelia, the wife of Crassus and of Pompey, successively, was highly cultivated, as was her father. But families with old-fashioned views might give their daughters little education. In more cosmopolitan circles, women of the upper orders may have been educated to display cultivated Latin and Greek speech and to be conversant with Latin and Greek literature so that their conversation would reflect well on their husbands. They may have learned to write elegant letters, though the letters of Cicero's and Pliny's female correspondents (including Cicero's wife Terentia and Pliny's wife Calpurnia) are not included in the Cicero and

Pliny collections. Mothers were believed to transfer such cultivation to their children, beginning with speech.[28]

However, some elite men did not want female competitors in literature and rhetoric. Women who publicly displayed learning in a competitive manner were regarded as making a display of themselves contrary to female *pudor* (modesty), associated with *impudicitia* (unchastity). The highly educated Sempronia, a woman of the nobility who supported the conspiracy of Catiline in 63 BCE, is depicted in this manner:

> Now among those women was Sempronia, who had often perpetrated many deeds of masculine daring. In birth and appearance, in her husband too and children, she was quite favored by fortune; she was well versed in Greek and Latin literature, at playing the lyre, at dancing more skillfully than a virtuous woman needed to, and in many other accomplishments which are instruments of wantonness. But there was nothing which she held so cheap as modesty and chastity; you could not easily decide whether she was less sparing of her money or her reputation; her lust was so heated that she pursued men more often than she was pursued.

As Sallust's description of Sempronia suggests, a cultivated woman might be thought to pursue seduction, behaving like a Greek courtesan whose arts included playing music, singing, and reciting poetry. Julia, the daughter of Augustus, was another highly cultivated and witty matron who was branded with *impudicitia*; she was convicted for adultery and exiled. Even if a woman's display of cultivation was not intended to seduce, it might appear competitive with men. In the late first century CE, Juvenal's notorious Sixth Satire depicted educated women in unfavorable terms: "Don't let [a woman] know the whole of history. Let there be a few things in books that she doesn't even understand." In contrast, Pliny the Younger presents his wife Calpurnia's intellectual interests in a more flattering (to himself) light, since she was no threat to him. Calpurnia, probably in her mid-teens to Pliny's forty, was a fan of Pliny's own literary works and learned them by heart. Pliny depicts Calpurnia as "extremely intelligent" and as taking a passionate interest in his own literary production. She read his works and even attended one of his literary recitations—sitting behind a curtain for the sake of modesty. The devotion of Minicia Marcella to her studies (quoted at the beginning of this chapter) was also nonthreatening.[29]

Further down the social scale, most women in the sub-elite probably only had a primary education (reading, writing, and arithmetic). Skills such as letter-writing and accounting were of practical use, and it is hard to imagine women managing their property or working in family businesses without them. The wealthy had slave accountants and business representatives, but a prudent woman would want to read and approve their work. Women further down (sub-elite) may not have had such representatives. A literary and philosophical education is unlikely at this stratum. The (fictional) wealthy freedman Trimalchio boasted that he had "never listened to a philosopher." As both the Herculaneum tablets and Roman Egyptian papyri and other documents show, sub-elite women used documents, though they may have dictated to scribes and had letters and documents read to them, activities that were considered normal in a society in which many people were not fully literate. Even among the educated elite, it was considered normal to dictate to a scribe and to be read to, as the Romans had no eyeglasses or other aids to vision. The indefatigable encyclopedist Pliny the Elder (Pliny the Younger's uncle), aged fifty-five at the time of his death in the Vesuvian eruption, used readers and scribes.[30]

Below the middle class sub-elite, most people were illiterate, due to Rome's lack of a public education system and due to their toil from an early age as agricultural laborers, artisans, or slaves, not due to their lack of intelligence. Many women, employed from childhood in some form of domestic work as poor free or slave laborers, were also illiterate. Roman soldiers were perhaps the lowest (male) stratum that was expected to be literate, though not all were (subliterate people in the papyri, including soldiers signing hay receipts, are described as "slow writers").[31]

GIRLS IN PUBLIC LIFE

Children played a symbolic role in public life, representing the continuity of families and of the social order. The emperors' prospective heirs, starting with Gaius and Lucius Caesar, the grandsons of Augustus, were most prominent and may have given a higher profile to boys in Roman society. The daughters and sisters of emperors could not succeed to the purple and were symbolic mainly as future wives of possible adopted heirs or aristocratic allies, also representing dynastic continuity. At the level of decurions (city councilors), their sons might hold town magistracies while still boys, keeping their families in the public eye. The daughters and wives of decurions were also prominent in town public life as benefactors and priestesses, as will be described in chapters 9 and 10.

Girls also played a public role in religious practices, performing in choruses and dances at public festivals, even carrying ritual items at sacrifices. For these roles, the daughters of the elite were probably chosen (in towns, the daughters of decurions). Children whose fathers and mothers were still living and still married to each other were preferred, as more ritually pure, unpolluted by death. Under the high-mortality demographic conditions of antiquity, this status was relatively rare and regarded as especially fortunate. Termed generically *patrimi et matrimi*, the boys were termed *camilli* and the girls *camillae*. The Saecular Games of Augustus (17 BCE) featured a famous hymn by Horace, the *Carmen Saeculare*, sung by groups of twenty-seven boys and twenty-seven girls. Saecular Games were held again in 47 CE, 88, and 204, at which boys and girls may have performed. Boys and girls with both parents living were among the members of the ritual procession to dedicate the rebuilding of the Capitoline Temple of Jupiter, destroyed in the civil war of 69 CE. Prepubertal girls were distinguished in ritual from *virgines*, sexually mature but unmarried girls who were probably in their early teens. Twenty-seven *virgines* sang a hymn composed by the Latin poet Livius Andronicus in 207 BCE.[32]

Children and girls also belonged to associations that seem to be secular, termed *collegia iuvenum* (young people's associations) or, for girls, *iuvenae*. These are attested in inscriptions, as with the epitaph of eight-year-old Ursilia Ingenua who belonged to a young girls' association. What these groups did (besides provide opportunity for socialization) is not clear, but Roman society was oriented toward public spectacle and the girls may have sung, danced, or walked in procession on festival days. Older boys' youth associations performed displays of horsemanship, the so-called *ludus Troiae* or Troy Games.[33]

As will be seen in chapter 9, an important part of public life was elite benefaction: wealthy notables, including women, bestowed public buildings, feasts, and other gifts on their cities and towns. Among these benefactions were the *alimenta*, distributions of grain and money to boys and girls, mostly freeborn citizens and residents of the cities and towns. The *alimenta* were created by Trajan (emperor 98–117 CE) and imitated by many local aristocrats, including Pliny the Younger himself for the town of Comum in northern Italy. Some alimentary benefactions took place during the donor's lifetime and others were commemorative in nature, taking effect after the donor's death:

> Caelia Macrina, daughter of Gaius, left 300,000 (?) sesterces in her will for the construction of this building, and . . . sesterces for its decoration and upkeep. In honor of her son Macer, she also left 1 million sesterces to the citizens of Tarracina [a town in Southern Italy], so that from the income of this sum, by way of *alimenta*, (the following amounts) are to be paid to one hundred boys (and girls): to each citizen boy five denarii (= twenty sesterces) each month, to each citizen girl four denarii (= sixteen sesterces) each month, the boys up to sixteen years, the girls up to fourteen.[34]

The alimentary distributions were intended to help raise healthy male and female citizens of the towns and ensure the prosperity of the region; as seen earlier, they also could perpetuate the memory of the donor. Most alimentary distributions were bestowed on both boys and girls; typically, the girls received slightly less support and for a shorter time, perhaps because girls were thought to need less food and because they were assumed to marry earlier. An alimentary foundation from Sicca in Roman Africa provided for three hundred boys from ages three to fifteen, who received two and a half denarii a month, and for three hundred girls from ages three to thirteen, who received two denarii a month; if any children died, new ones were enrolled. The emperor Antoninus Pius (138–61 CE) created the *puellae Faustinianae*, a group of girls receiving alimentary distributions in honor of his deceased wife and empress Faustina the Elder. His adoptive heir and successor Marcus Aurelius (161–80 CE) endowed a different *puellae Faustinianae* in honor of his own deceased wife, Faustina the Younger. Both distributions were honored on imperial coin issues and a historical relief survives that depicted the empresses Faustina and Lucilla presiding over the distribution to the girls.[35]

SLAVE CHILDREN AND OTHER VULNERABLE CHILDREN

Families with no legitimate father, such as the de facto families of slaves, of citizen unions with noncitizens, and (in the first two centuries CE) the families of soldiers, were in a highly precarious situation. In Roman law, illegitimacy, though not a stigma in itself, so weakened the claims of children to inherit from their fathers or mothers that they were dependent on being named as heirs or legatees in wills. This situation did not favor the lower social strata, more likely to be intestate and illiterate.

Slaves could not be legally married, and their legal status as property rendered their families precarious. Slave men and slave women formed de facto marriages termed *contubernia*. The child of a slave woman was a slave, following its mother's status. Children of slaves were liable to be separated from their parents, for (as seen in section "Mothers and Other Caregivers") wet-nursing in the countryside or, at a later age, training in specialized occupations. Once trained, they might be sold away from their de facto families. Slave children might also be offered as surety in a loan, to be transferred to the creditor if the loan was not repaid. Owners acquired slave children by purchase, by encouraging female slaves to reproduce, or by collecting exposed infants. Because slave children were less expensive than adult slaves, and an owner acquired for free a slave child whom he fathered or picked up from the ground, owners regarded raising slave children as an investment. Slave children, furthermore, were liable to be put to work from an early age, approximately five to seven years old, performing domestic tasks and light agricultural work. Slightly older children performed more specialized tasks. Slave girls are attested as hairdressers (*ornatrices*), aged twelve, nine, and ten in three inscriptions; since elite Roman women's hairstyles were elaborate, this was a skilled occupation. Slave children also performed all-purpose labor which marked their skeletons, preserved at Herculaneum by the eruption of Vesuvius, with the wear resulting from physical toil.[36]

The children of serving soldiers during the Principate (from ca. 13 BCE to 197 CE) were illegitimate and, before the reign of Hadrian, lacked inheritance rights from their fathers. The emperor Hadrian (117–38 CE) allowed the children of soldiers to inherit from their fathers who died intestate; other legislation in 178 CE allowed children to inherit from their mothers who died intestate. The children of soldiers might also be noncitizens if their mothers were noncitizens. Military discharge diplomas, bronze tablets recording the discharge and grant of Roman citizenship to a veteran who had completed his decades-long service, also granted Roman citizenship to the veteran's children (for auxiliaries, only before 140 CE) and granted him the right of marriage with their mother. Civilians, in unions of citizen fathers with noncitizen mothers, did not fare so well; the children followed the mother's status and remained noncitizens. The union of a citizen mother with a noncitizen father was penalized by reducing the children to noncitizen status. In the town of Karanis in Roman Egypt, the mother Sempronia Gemella, who was a Roman citizen, preferred to declare her twin sons illegitimate and Roman citizens rather than risk their loss of citizenship if she declared their likely father, a noncitizen Egyptian.[37]

VULNERABILITY OF CHILDREN: FREEBORN VERSUS SLAVE

Freeborn and especially elite children quickly learned that they were different from and socially superior to slave children. A daughter of an aristocratic family would also learn to give orders to female slaves who might be of her own age or grown women. The daughters of elite families also learned early that they were less liable to corporal punishment, whereas slaves were "eminently beatable," in the translation of Richard Saller. It is unclear whether it was more acceptable for parents to use corporal punishment on daughters than on sons; despite anecdotes of early Roman husbands beating their wives for drinking wine, the main contemporary evidence for corporal punishment of wives (and presumably daughters) is from a different cultural context, Augustine's Christian North Africa. It was acceptable, however, for primary schoolmasters (*ludimagistri*) to hit their pupils, who seem to have spanned a wider social range.[38]

The sexual molestation or assault of freeborn boys and girls were regarded as typical of corrupt and evil governors, emperors, soldiers, and ancient tyrants, including Tarquinius Superbus's son, the rapist of Lucretia (510 BCE), and the *Decemvir* Appius Claudius, who planned to rape Verginia (450 BCE). In the middle and Late Republic, sexual assault or molestation of freeborn boys and girls may have been tried by the *comitia* (assembly) or handled by the families involved. In the Principate, seduction of freeborn boys and girls was criminalized as *stuprum* by the *Lex Julia de adulteriis* and violent sexual assault was criminalized by the *Lex Julia de vi*. That lower-status freeborn citizen children were protected by these laws is not clear; in Italy, many lower-status inhabitants were slaves. Lower-status peregrine provincials were not protected—they were peoples whose ancestors had been enslaved by the Roman conquerors, even if they themselves were not slaves.

Furthermore, the daughter of an elite family was sexually unavailable, required to be a virgin at first marriage. This status of *pudicitia* (sexual inviolability) contrasted markedly with that of slave girls, *ancillae*, who from an early age were regarded as sexually available. The eroticization of young slave boys and girls is repellent from our perspective, but Roman literary authors (all male and elite) represent it without particular shame. Slave child "darlings" (*deliciae*), as young as five in the case of Martial's Erotium (a little girl), were most likely to be sexually abused.[39]

Freeborn and more likely elite children may have been protected by their costume. The *toga praetexta*, bordered with a purple stripe, supposedly worn by both freeborn boys and girls, and the amulet or *bulla*, worn by boys were intended to mark freeborn and particularly elite children as sexually unavailable. Girls past puberty but before marriage may have worn only long tunic dresses, so the main

Funerary portrait from Hawara in Roman Egypt, imperial era. These realistic portraits, painted with wax pigments on wood, captured close likenesses of the deceased, buried with their mummies. The girl is older, and wears jewelry picked out in gold leaf (also used on her lips). This girl, like Minicia Marcella, may have died before she could be married. (John L. Severance Fund, The Cleveland Museum of Art)

marker of their elite status would be the quality of their clothing and the presence of attendants (as seen in chapter 5).

Elite boys were more protected against sexual advances, as their status as future fathers, magistrates, military officers, and senators required freedom from penetration. Such freedom was the male version of *pudicitia*. A man who had been sexually penetrated became effeminate and lost all respect in conventional Roman society, and unprovable rumors of such behavior circulated as vicious gossip. The primary schoolmaster Furius Philocalus was commemorated as exceptionally chaste toward his pupils, suggesting that not all schoolmasters exhibited such self-control.[40]

CONCLUSION

Roman children, at least at elite levels (the families of senators, equestrians, and decurions) and the moderately well-off sub-elite, appear to have had "childhood" in the sense of a separate life stage, distinct from adulthood, during which children were expected to play and attend school. The boundaries of this childhood were located below the well-off sub-elite, as the children of the poor and slave children had to work from an early age. Freeborn children of elite and respectable sub-elite status were protected from the physical punishment and sexual exploitation that were the lot of slave children in Roman society.

Girls may have had a shorter childhood and youth than boys, because they received less education and were expected to marry in their early to mid-teens. Pliny the Younger lamented that Minicius Fundanus had to spend his budget for his daughter Minicia Marcella's wedding clothing and jewelry upon "incense, perfumes, and spices" for her funeral. The motif of a young girl whose wedding procession torches were replaced by funerary ones reflects the emphasis on first marriage at a relatively early age for Roman women, particularly women of the upper orders. This age, and when women of the lower strata married for the first time, are discussed in chapter 4, which describes Roman marriage—how it was negotiated, dowries, customary wedding rituals, the sexual and emotional relationships of spouses, and the state's role in promoting marriage and repressing adultery.[41]

NOTES

1. Plin. *Ep.* 5.16.2–5, 7. On Minicia Marcella, see John Bodel, "Minicia Marcella: Taken before her time," *AJPh* 116.3 (1995), 453–60; Emily A.

Hemelrijk, *Matrona Docta: Educated Women in the Roman Elite from Cornelia to Julia Domna* (London, 1999), 60–61; Beryl Rawson, *Children and Childhood in Roman Italy* (Oxford, 2003), 85–86; Jo-Ann Shelton, *The Women of Pliny's* Letters (London, 2013), 275–81; Laura K. McClure, *Women in Classical Antiquity: From Birth to Death* (Hoboken, NJ, 2019), 175. *CIL* VI 16631 reads simply D(is) M(anibus) / MINICIAE / MARCELLAE / FUNDANI F(iliae) / V(ixit) A(nnis) XII M(ensibus) XI D(iebus) VII: "To the deified spirit of Minicia Marcella, daughter of Fundanus. She lived twelve years, eleven months, and seven days."

2. On boys, see *CIL* VI 28138, 33976; IX 2860. On such inscriptions, see Rawson, *Children*, 17–20; and Christian Laes, *Children in the Roman Empire: Outsiders Within* (Cambridge, 2011), 174–84, on boys holding office (at decurion level) at early ages.

3. On these approaches, see Laes, *Children*, 13–15, 48–49. Rawson, *Children*, and Richard P. Saller, *Patriarchy, Property, and Death in the Roman Family* (Cambridge, 1994), emphasize parental affection for children; both these authors tend to emphasize elite families' experiences.

4. On lack of evidence for girls, see Laes, *Children*, 2. On swaddling, Soranus *Gynaecology* 2.15.

5. See discussion of girls' costume in chapter 5.

6. On male life stages, see Rawson, *Children*, 139–40; Laes, *Children*, 83–98.

7. See discussion of infant burials in chapter 2.

8. On these roles for elite male children see Laes, *Children*, 165–84; Rawson, *Children*, 293–95, 299, 320–21 (imperial princes).

9. On *delicium*, see Rawson, *Children*, 261–63.

10. On evolutionary history, Saller, *Patriarchy*, 1–8.

11. Tac. *Dialogue on Oratory* 28.2, 4–6, 29.1; Gellius *Noctes Atticae* 12.1.5–23; Plut. *Cato the Elder* 20.2–3. On Cornelia, see Cic. *Brutus* 21; Quintilian *Institutio Oratoria* 1.1.6. On Agricola, see Tac. *Agricola* 4; Hemelrijk, *Matrona Docta*, 68–69; Shelton, *Women*, 179, 182, 184. On decadence discourse, see Suzanne Dixon, *Reading Roman Women: Sources, Genres, and Real Life* (London, 2001), 54–65.

12. On Ummidia Quadratilla, see Plin. *Ep.* 7.24; Shelton, *Women*, 240–55.

13. On Novatilla, see Seneca *Consolatio ad Helviam* 18.8; Shelton, *Women*, 184–85. On slave woman, see Cato *On Farming* 143.

14. Augustine *Confessions* 9.8.17. On this passage, see Laes, *Children*, 75–76.

15. Plin. *Ep.* 6.6. On *nutrices*, see Rawson, *Children*, 117–24; Laes, *Children*, 69–77; Shelton, *Women*, 177–82. On manumission, see Gaius *Institutes* 1.18–19; D. 33.2.34.1 (Scaevola); D. 40.2.11–13 (Ulpian).

16. D. 32.99.3; D. 50.16.210; letter, *P. Lond.* III 951 verso = Mary R. Lefkowitz and Maureen B. Fant, eds., *Women's Life in Greece and Rome: A Source Book in Translation*, 4th ed. (Baltimore, MD, 2016), no. 299. McClure, *Women*, 224 is skeptical about extensive wet nursing. On inscriptions, see, e.g., Emily A. Hemelrijk, *Women and Society in the Roman World: A Sourcebook of Inscriptions from the Roman West* (Cambridge, 2021), nos. 3.15–23.

17. On pedagogues, see Hemelrijk, *Matrona Docta*, 21–22; Rawson, *Children*, 163–67; Laes, *Children*, 113–18. On female *pedagogi*, see, e.g., Statilia

Tyrannis, pedagogue of Statilia Messalina, *CIL* VI 4459, 6331, 9754, 9758; Hemelrijk, *Women and Society*, nos. 3.24–27. On Pontius Aufidianus, see Valerius Maximus 6.1.3.

18. On family size, see Rawson, *Children*, 116–18, 245–47; on the demographic transition, see Paul Morland, *The Human Tide: How Population Shaped the Modern World* (New York, 2019), 103–04, 139–43.

19. Rawson, *Children*, 125.

20. On stepmothers, see Shelton, *Women*, 228–31. Wicked (jealous) stepmothers were a cliché; see, e.g., Seneca *Controversiae* 9.5–6; Ovid *Metamorphoses* 1.147. On grandmothers, see Shelton, *Women*, 237; Plin. *Ep.* 7.24; Quintilian *Institutio Oratoria* 6.pr.8. On Calpurnia Hispulla, the aunt of Pliny's wife Calpurnia, see Plin. *Ep.* 4.19.8; Shelton, *Women*, 102–3.

21. On foster children, see Hemelrijk, *Women and Society*, nos. 1.85–88.

22. On primary school, see Laes, *Children*, 122–31.

23. On excerpt, see *Corpus Glossariorum Latinorum* III, pp. 645–7 = Shelton, no. 131. On fees, 8 *asses* per pupil a month, see Horace *Satires* 1.6.75. On methods, see Quintilian *Institutio Oratoria* 1.1.25, 30. On punishment, see Martial 9.68.2. On Verginia, see Livy 3.44.6.

24. On *grammaticus*, see Laes, *Children*, 132–37. On rhetoricians supported by emperors, see, e.g., Suet. *Vespasian* 18; Dio 53.60. On girls tutored at home, see Rawson, *Children*, 199–200. On female grammarians, see *L'Année Epigraphique* 1994, 1903 = Hemelrijk, *Women and Society*, no. 3.28. Slave women are attested as *lectrices*, readers; see, e.g., Hemelrijk, *Women and Society*, nos. 3.30–32.

25. On Hortensia, see Appian *Civil Wars* 4.32–4; Valerius Maximus 8.3.3. On Carfania, *ibid.*, 8.3.2.

26. Quintilian *Institutio Oratoria* 1.1.1, 1.1.5. Education's association with status is emphasized in Michael Peachin, ed., *The Oxford Handbook of Social Relations in the Roman World* (Oxford, 2011).

27. On postponement of coming of age for boys, see Fanny Dolansky, "*Togam virilem sumere*: Coming of age in the Roman world," in *Roman Dress and the Fabrics of Roman Culture* (Toronto, 2008), ed. Jonathan Edmondson and Alison Keith, 47–70.

28. On Cornelia, see Plut. *Tiberius Gracchus* 1.5; Cic. *Brutus* 211; Quintilian *Institutio Oratoria* 1.1.6; Tac. *Dialogue on Oratory* 28. On Cornelia, wife of Pompey, see Plut. *Pompey* 55.1–2; Hemelrijk, *Matrona Docta*, 17, 28, 54–55. On education of women, see Rawson, *Children*, 197–209; Shelton, *Women*, 115–19; Hemelrijk, *Matrona Docta*, esp. 17–95; McClure, *Women*, 219. On old-fashioned views, see, e.g., Seneca *Consolatio ad Helviam* 17.3–4; Plin. *Ep.* 4.19. On women conveying culture, see Tac. *Dialogue on Oratory* 28–29 (quoted previously).

29. On Sempronia, see Sall. *Catilinarian War* 25.1–3. On Julia, see Macrobius *Saturnalia* 2.5.2; Hemelrijk, *Matrona Docta*, 17, 22. On history, Juvenal 6.448–51. On Calpurnia, see Plin. *Ep.* 4.19.2–4; Shelton, *Women*, 116–18. On Pliny and Calpurnia, see Shelton, *Women*, 115–19.

30. On Trimalchio, see Petronius *Satyrica* 71. On levels of literacy, William V. Harris, *Ancient Literacy* (Cambridge, MA, 1989); in Roman Egypt, see Raffaella Cribiore, *Writing, Teachers, and Students in Graeco-Roman Egypt* (Atlanta, 1996). The extensive writing painted and graffitied on the walls of Pompeii does not imply widespread literacy. For example, see Alison E. Cooley and M. G. L. Cooley, eds, *Pompeii and Herculaneum: A Sourcebook* (London, 2013), nos. D96–118 (graffiti); F2–84 (electoral notices). Elite women owned slave readers, Hemelrijk, *Women and Society*, nos. 3.30–32.

31. On women as slow writers, see Jane Rowlandson, *Women and Society in Greek and Roman Egypt: A Sourcebook* (Cambridge, 1998), pp. 301–2.

32. Horace *Odes* 4.6; *CIL* VI 877 = *ILS* 5050 = Hemelrijk, *Women and Society*, no. 5.63; Tac. *Histories* 4.53; Livy 27.37.5–15; Rawson, *Children*, 315–20.

33. Emily A. Hemelrijk, *Hidden Lives, Public Personae: Women and Civic Life in the Roman West* (Oxford, 2015), 192.

34. *CIL* X 6328 = *ILS* 6278 = Hemelrijk, *Women and Society*, no. 6.12; *Hidden Lives*, 148; on the *alimenta*, see *Hidden Lives*, 148–54.

35. Rawson, *Children*, 59–65; Pliny, *CIL* V 5262 (donation of 500,000 HS to fund alimentary distributions at Comum); Plin. *Ep.* 1.8.10–11, 7.18.2. On Trajan, see Plin. *Panegyricus* 26.5–28. Sicca, *CIL* VIII 1641 = Jo-Ann Shelton, *As the Romans Did: A Source Book in Roman Social History* (Oxford, 1988), no. 47. On Antoninus Pius, see SHA *Antoninus Pius* 8.1. On Marcus, see SHA *Marcus* 26.8.

36. On slavery in general, see K. R. Bradley, *Slavery and Society at Rome* (Cambridge, 1994); Sandra R. Joshel, *Slavery in the Roman World* (Cambridge, 2010). On child labor, also applying to free poor, see Laes, *Children*, 148–221. On training of slaves, see Rawson, *Children*, 192–94, e.g., D. 32.65.3; *ornatrices*, *CIL* VI 9726, 9731; *CIL* X 1941. On the slaves at Delos who apparently offered their own children as surety toward loans paying for their own manumission, see Laes, *Children*, 162–63. On slave breeding, see Plut. *Cato Maior* 20–21; Columella *On Farming* 1.8.19.

37. On soldiers, see Sara Elise Phang, *The Marriage of Roman Soldiers, 13 B.C.–A.D. 235: Law and Family in the Imperial Army* (Leiden, 2001); on Sempronia Gemella, Rowlandson, *Women and Society*, no. 71.

38. Saller, *Patriarchy*, 133–53; "beatable," 137.

39. Martial 5.34, 37; Rawson, *Children*, 261–62. On problems in studying this topic, see Laes, *Children*, 222–76.

40. On Philocalus, see *summa quom castitate in discipulos suos*, *CIL* X 3969.

41. On Minicia, Plin. *Ep.* 5.16.

4

MARRIAGE

INTRODUCTION

Roman legitimate marriage, *iustum matrimonium*, joining a husband and wife "for the purposes of procreating children," was essentially a social and familial institution rather than romantic and personal. In the words of the *Rules of Ulpian*, an epitome of Roman law attributed to the jurist Ulpian (ca. 170–220s CE),

> Matrimony is lawful when legal marriage takes place between those contracting it, if the male has arrived at puberty, and the female is nubile, and when both consent, if they are legally independent; or their parents give their consent, if they are under their control.

Marriage joined two families and was regarded as a monogamous partnership; husband and wife were ideally devoted to one another, but romantic love was not expected. The procreation of legitimate children was regarded as necessary to perpetuate society, transmit property within the family lineage, and maintain family lineages. However, other aspects of Roman marriage did not fit this patriarchal pattern; women's property remained separate within marriage, and they did not legally become members of their husbands' families.[1]

MARRIAGE WITH AND WITHOUT *MANUS*

An important aspect of Roman marriage in the period of our study was that women's property remained separate from that of their husbands. In archaic Rome, women entered the state of *manus* in marriage—coming under the "hand" of their husbands and becoming subordinate to them; their property merged with that of their husband (or that of the husband's paterfamilias if still alive), and they owned nothing of their own. This model of Roman marriage was emphasized by earlier classical scholarship, because it provided precedent for the legal status of women in later Western European societies. *Manus* marriage was obsolete by the mid-Republic and continued to exist mainly to qualify candidates for high priesthoods at Rome. The major *flamines* (priests) of Jupiter, Mars, and Quirinus had to be the sons of patrician parents married with *manus*, by the ancient rite of *confarreatio* (the bride and groom shared a cake of spelt, *far*, a variety of wheat, emmer, termed farro in modern Italy). As marriage with *manus* became rare, it became harder to find qualified candidates for these priesthoods, and the emperor Tiberius (14–37 CE) relaxed these rules. In the spirit of antiquarianism, Gaius, a jurist writing in the middle second century CE (ca. 110–after 179), describes the creation of *manus* marriage by three different legal procedures: *confarreatio*, *coemptio* (a mock ritual "sale" of the bride), and *usus*. None of these were used for regular marriage without *manus* (*sine manu*), the dominant form in the Late Republic and Empire.[2]

CONUBIUM

Marriage *sine manu* did not require a legal procedure or official ceremony to come into existence; it required only *conubium* (the right to marry), consent, and the consensus of being married (*affectio maritalis*). Not all people had *conubium*. Slaves lacked it altogether; though they often formed de facto marriages (*contubernium*), the children of a slave mother were both illegitimate and slaves. Roman citizens generally did not have *conubium* with non-Romans (Latins before 89 BCE and/or peregrines before 212 CE). In such cases, the children had the status of their mothers, unless the mother was a Roman citizen and the father a peregrine, in which case the *Lex Minicia* decreed that the child was peregrine. Noncitizen Italians were promoted to Roman citizen status as the result of the Social War of 92–89 BCE, and the emperor Caracalla gave the citizenship to all members of the empire in 212 CE. But the legal sources indicate that in a world without systematic birth certificates or identification papers, and in which many people were illiterate, individuals might be uncertain as to their status and form illicit marriages without knowing it.[3]

Other categories of persons were forbidden legitimate marriage. After the passing of the *Lex Julia de maritandis ordinibus* and the *Lex Julia de adulteriis* in 18 BCE (discussed in sections "The *Lex Julia de maritandis ordinibus*" and "The *Lex Julia de adulteriis*"), convicted adulterers and adulteresses could not marry anyone, and former slaves could not marry senatorials (senators, their wives, their children, and grandchildren). All free persons were forbidden to marry prostitutes, pimps, gladiators and beast fighters, and convicted criminals. In the views of many jurists, a freedwoman could not marry any man but her own patron (former owner). Serving soldiers, in a ban attributed to Augustus, were not permitted legitimate marriage till their discharge, when various troops received a document termed a military diploma that granted them *conubium* with their wives. Service in the army had been lengthened to many years (twenty to twenty-five years for legionaries, twenty-five years for auxiliary soldiers, twenty-eight for navy), and many soldiers formed de facto marriages with women, displaying the intention of marriage. But the Roman authorities reiterated that these were not legitimate marriages and that the children of such unions were illegitimate. The marriage ban for soldiers was probably repealed by Septimius Severus in 197 CE, as a favor to the army.[4]

Partners in incestuous relationships, including brothers with sisters and ascendants with descendants, were also forbidden to marry. The Romans termed these relationships *incestum* and regarded them as abhorrent, causing a conflict of the Roman authorities with provincial customs of close-kin marriage, especially the marriages of brothers and sisters in Egypt. It has been suggested that the Egyptian "sibling marriages" in fact involved the marriage of an adopted child (usually a girl) to her adopted brother, a strategy that was intended to keep property within families and that did not produce the genetic problems ensuing from biological sibling marriage. The Senate made an exception for the incestuous marriage of the emperor Claudius (41–54 CE) to his niece Agrippina the Younger, the mother of Nero (whose father was her previous husband, Lucius Domitius Ahenobarbus). The term *incestum* was also used for Vestal Virgins' illicit sexual relations with any men, for which they could be punished by death.[5]

AGE OF SPOUSES AT FIRST MARRIAGE

The bride and groom had to be of legal age to marry, twelve for Roman women and fourteen for Roman men. The Roman legal and literary sources suggest that women could be married from age twelve, but most of this evidence for the early marriage of women pertains to the senatorial order and the imperial family, which preferred to marry women off early to consolidate political alliances. In contrast, husbands at first marriage were grown men in their late twenties or older and might, in subsequent marriages, be much older than their wives. Studies of tombstone inscriptions that mention the age of the deceased enable us to estimate the age at first marriage for members of the sub-elite. These studies compared the age of young men commemorated by their parents with the age of men commemorated by their wives or children and did the same for the epitaphs of young women (twelve and up). The commemoration-shift method suggests that sub-elite women were married in their middle to late teens, and nearly all by age twenty. This estimate is also supported by the likelihood that women's full puberty (culminating in menstruation) did not occur at age twelve, but some years later at fourteen to sixteen or even later, as has been the case in premodern European populations subject to malnutrition and disease. The sub-elite, able to afford tombstones, were less likely to be malnourished but were subject to the same disease burden as the general population. Chronic illness can stunt physical growth and maturation. Men's puberty may have been delayed as well at sub-elite levels; the average age for the recruitment of Roman soldiers was eighteen to twenty, not fourteen. But it is also plausible that families wished to delay their daughters' entry into marriage slightly until they were more socially and emotionally mature, as marriage meant entry into adult life for women. In poor families, which did not have large staffs of slave servants and laborers, young women may have stayed with their birth families for a few more years to provide domestic labor.[6]

The Augustan marriage legislation (see *"Lex Julia de maritandis ordinibus"* and *"Lex Julia de adulteriis"*) may have affected the age at first marriage for men and women of the senatorial and equestrian orders, as its penalties applied to unmarried and childless men between twenty-five and sixty and women between twenty and fifty, inducing men to marry by age twenty-five. This was also the age at which men launched their political careers, and having a child qualified a man for preferment for political appointments. This slightly reduced the age of senatorial men at first marriage.

However, that the age at which women should be married was set at twenty, not fifteen, supports the evidence of the tombstone inscriptions.

Nonetheless, in the case of a man who married for the second, third, or subsequent time to a girl being married for the first time, a very large age gap could result between husband and wife. Pliny the Younger was about forty when he married Calpurnia, in her early or mid-teens; Cicero was even older when he married his third wife Publilia, also in her early or mid-teens. The age asymmetry was probably reduced when a woman married for the second or subsequent time.[7]

CHOICE OF SPOUSES

If partners had *conubium* and did not belong to any of the prohibited categories, their marriage plans would begin with betrothal negotiations. These negotiations were usually undertaken by the paterfamilias of the bride (in a first marriage when she was still in her teens) and of the groom, or the groom himself. All parties had to consent to the marriage—bride, groom, and their patres familiarum if still alive. In practice, the prospective bride in her first marriage probably had little say in the choice of husband and would have to be satisfied with recommendations such as Pliny's, describing the youngish man Minicius Acilianus to his friend Junius Mauricius, who was looking for a husband for his own paternal niece:

> His native place is Brixia, one of the towns in our part of Italy, which still retains intact much of its honest simplicity along with the rustic virtues of the past. His father is Minicius Macrinus, [a distinguished equestrian] . . . Acilianus himself has abundant energy and application, but no lack of modesty. He has held the offices of quaestor, tribune, and praetor with great distinction, sparing you the necessity of canvassing on his behalf. He has a frank expression, and his complexion is fresh and high-colored; his general good looks have a natural nobility and the dignified bearing of a senator. I personally think these points should be mentioned, as a sort of just return for a bride's virginity.

It is not known if Minicius Acilianus was related to Minicius Fundanus and his daughter Marcella (see chapter 3). Judging by his career, Acilianus was probably in his thirties, and Junius Mauricius' niece, a virgin, was being married for the first time. Pliny emphasizes the good moral character of Acilianus and his family but waffles upon the subject of Acilianus's wealth; either Acilianus's family was not wealthy and this was a drawback or, less plausibly, the family was wealthy and Pliny thought that Junius Mauricius (a Stoic) would disapprove. Doubtless in lower social strata similar negotiations went on, where family friends and relatives suggested possible matches.[8]

We lack comparable letters recommending young women but can reconstruct their probable content. In women, virginity (in their first marriage), modesty, and sexual fidelity were probably assumed to be basic, nonnegotiable requirements. Also, in women marrying for the second or later time, having borne children was an asset, not a drawback. Agrippina the Younger was presented as a suitable bride for the emperor Claudius (41–54 CE) by his adviser Pallas, who praised her "proven fecundity" and extremely distinguished family. Agrippina had been previously married to Lucius Domitius Ahenobarbus and already had a son, the future emperor Nero. As also seen in this passage, elite Romans wanted to marry into distinguished families; to avoid marrying down, Pallas advised consanguineous marriage (Claudius was Agrippina's uncle).[9]

Beyond that, the traditional characteristics of a good wife are repeated in many tombstone inscriptions. They included frugality, industry (at housekeeping), piety (toward family elders, the gods, and the family *sacra*), an agreeable temperament, and devotion to her husband and family. To this the Roman elite in practice added virtues that benefited women and their husbands in a sophisticated, socially competitive society, such as an elegant appearance and cultivated speech—the way a mother spoke Latin and Greek was thought to influence her children from an early age. As was stated in chapter 3, women of the upper *ordines* received an education that enabled them to appreciate their husbands' level of culture, though they were not encouraged to use their education to compete with men. It seems unlikely that an urbane aristocratic man actually wanted a wife of such *pudicitia* and modesty that she never wore festive clothing or jewels, never left the house, and chose spinning wool over learning Greek and Latin literature (a requirement of an educated person). Furthermore, as chapter 6 will show, women of the upper orders probably had to manage large and complex households and estates.[10]

DOWRY

The next phase in negotiating a marriage was the dowry settlement or contract. As dowry, the bride's family provided a substantial gift of money, real estate, and/or household goods (depending on their means) to the groom's family. Since no marriage contract was required in Roman law, the documentary evidence of the marriage was usually provided by the dowry tablets, which recorded the transfer of the bride's dowry (still her father's property, if he was alive) to the groom or his father. The dowry tablets might describe in detail how the dowry was to be managed during the marriage and returned after the marriage ended due to the death of a spouse or divorce. Within the marriage, the husband possessed the dowry but was expected to manage it carefully and not squander it. In the upper orders, dowry might consist of land or real estate, capital from which the profits were used to support the wife. At the end of marriage, the dowry was returned to the wife or her father. It would help her to remarry, the dowry property being transferred to her new husband. The wife or her father needed to sue for the dowry's return, the *actio rei uxoriae* (suit for return of wife's property), but granting these suits was usually automatic and no conflict was usually involved.

A dowry was not *legally* required for marriage, but a woman would be in difficult economic conditions without one if the marriage ended. The necessity of dowry is underlined in a letter of Pliny's where he states that he contributed 100,000 HS to the dowry of Calvina, the daughter of an acquaintance, because her father had left her only debts, and 50,000 HS to the daughter of Quintilianus (not the famous orator), "as she is to marry so distinguished a man as Nonius Celer, whose public duties oblige him to keep up a certain amount of style, she ought to be provided with clothing and attendants in keeping with her husband's rank." This concept that a woman's status should be displayed in her public appearance is explored further in chapter 5.[11]

The average sizes of Roman dowries at various social levels are not known, as only a few examples survive in literary and documentary sources. Dowry items at the level of senatorial and equestrian families would consist of land, houses, villas, slaves, and large sums of money, as we have already seen from Pliny's benefactions. In his legal oration *Apology*, Apuleius, writing in the mid-second century CE, thought that 300,000 sesterces (HS) would be regarded as a low sum for a dowry and 400,000 HS would be a high sum. The emperor Tiberius gave a disappointed candidate for Vestal Virgin a dowry of 1,000,000 HS. Satirists thought that 1,000,000 HS was a notoriously large dowry; it was also the property qualification for a Roman senator. Approximately, a year's income (the property qualification for each of the *ordines*) may have been considered normal for a dowry. Richard Saller has argued that Roman dowry did not comprise a massive proportion of the bride's family's estate or require the bride's family (if normally prudent) to go deep into debt. The returned dowry was often paid in three installments of cash. In his letters Cicero appears to have had trouble juggling returning his wife Terentia's dowry (worth 400,000 HS) upon their divorce and providing a dowry for his daughter Tullia's marriage to Marcus Cornelius Dolabella. Cicero then married a new wife, Publilia, with a huge dowry worth 1,000,000 HS.[12]

At sub-elite level, the possibility that a dowry was worth a year's income also seems to apply, given that a legionary soldier in the first century CE (till Domitian's reign) earned 900 HS a year, probably the lower boundary of sub-elite income. Sub-elite incomes between 900 and 5,000 HS appear credible. Though the full value of the dowries in marriage contracts from Roman Egypt is not given, items are frequently listed with their values and provide minimum estimates. Dowries at this level often contained valuable household items, jewelry, and women's clothing. Because clothing was disproportionately expensive in the ancient world, many of the clothing items in the marriage contracts cost 200–1,000 HS each, such as "a tunic and a little cloak and a cloak from Scyros worth 180 Augustan drachmas" in a contract dated from the mid-second century CE. A mid-third-century CE dowry contract listed a Dalmatian cape worth 260 drachmas, a white chiton worth 160 drachmas, a blue-green Dalmatian cape worth 100 drachmas, and a purple-bordered Dalmatian cape worth 100 drachmas. A drachma is roughly equivalent to a denarius, which equals 4 HS. Though valuable, these clothing items do not seem particularly luxurious or the prices inflated compared to those of other clothing from Roman Egypt. The dowry items may have been the bride's normal clothing, her family's contribution to the new household. A passage of Ulpian suggests that dotal items of clothing depreciated from the wife's wearing them. We will see in chapter 5 why ordinary clothing was so expensive, on a par with livestock in ancient Rome and furniture in today's economy.[13]

THE ROMAN WEDDING

No particular wedding ceremony was legally required, but Roman poetry and antiquarian tradition describe wedding rituals and a bride's elaborate costume. These descriptions are based on wedding poems (marriage epithalamia) and antiquarian authors, and it is not known whether all families (i.e., upper-class families) adhered to all elements of the traditional wedding any more than with modern weddings. That a senatorial bride spent the last months of her unmarried life spinning and weaving her *tunica recta* and her *flammeum* in the Late Republic and early Empire, when elite women probably did not do most of their own spinning and weaving, seems particularly unlikely.[14]

On the day before her wedding, the traditional Roman bride put her *toga praetexta* away and donned the *tunica recta*, a wide tunic of white wool that she supposedly had woven herself on an upright loom; on the night before her wedding, she slept in this tunic and in a yellow hairnet, also woven by her. However, there is much less evidence for these two items than for the *flammeum*, the wedding veil. On her wedding day, the bride donned the *flammeum*, a large veil of deep yellow-orange woolen cloth that covered her head and face; its color was associated with fertility and also provided ritual protection from harm as she left her father's house and proceeded to her husband's house. Under the *flammeum* she wore a wreath of *verbena*, leafy twigs which she had picked herself, or of flowers, also associated with fertility. Her hair was dressed in a much-debated style termed the *seni crines* or "six locks." Traditionally divided with the point of a spear that had been used to kill a gladiator, the six locks were twisted or braided and may have been piled into a bun and tied with *vittae*, woolen fillets. Unfortunately, the details of this hairstyle are not visible in depictions of brides in Roman art, where their hair is covered with the *flammeum*. On the wedding night, her husband would remove the veil and undo the belt of her tunic, tied with a "Hercules" knot that only he could undo.[15]

The description of the bride's costume is steeped in an antiquarian and religious context, linking the bridal costume with that of the Vestal Virgins (who wore their hair in a similar style) and the *flaminica Dialis*, the wife of the high priest of Jupiter at Rome. The *flaminica* also wore the *flammeum* and could not divorce her husband, rendering her a potent symbol of marital constancy. Though Pliny the Elder mentions that a Roman man used to give an iron finger ring to his prospective wife at betrothal, and that now gold rings are used, rings were much more important for denoting men's social status. The *flammeum* was the item most associated with a bride, and the visual symbol of a married woman was her *stola* or overdress, described in chapter 5.[16]

The core ritual of a Roman wedding was the *domum deductio*, the escorting of the bride from her father's house to her husband's house in a torch-lit procession with many guests (and witnesses). The procession attendants sang bawdy "Fescennine" songs that mocked the bride and groom; such mockery was believed to provide ritual protection from envy. They chanted "Io Hymen Hymenaeus"—the Greek god of marriage. Another ritual cry was "Talassio!" Children with both parents living (a sign of ritual purity and good fortune) carried items in the procession, including a distaff and spindle, symbols of the bride's domestic labor in her new household, and threw nuts (instead of the modern rice). At the street corner near the groom's house, she offered a coin at the neighborhood shrine. On arrival at the groom's house, the bride anointed the door posts with wolf's fat or lard and bound them with woolen ribbons. Her attendants or the groom lifted her over the threshold, and she proceeded into the house, where she offered a coin to her new husband's household gods. The groom offered her water and fire from his hearth, symbolizing her acceptance into his household. A ritual attendant (*pronuba*, often the bride's mother) may have joined the right hands of the couple, a gesture termed *dextrarum iunctio* and more prominent in sculpture than in literature. The bride recited the words "Where you are Gaius, there also I am Gaia." These rituals may have been followed by a banquet where the bride reclined at dinner with the groom (see chapter 8 on dining customs). At night, she entered the wedding bedchamber, which had also been adorned festively, where the marriage was consummated.[17]

A more tasteful marriage epithalamium (literally, a song sung "before the doors" of the bridal chamber) was written by the Late Republican poet Catullus (Poem 61). Written for the marriage of a Junia with a Manlius Torquatus, the poem repeats the traditional refrain "Io Hymen Hymenaeus" and depicts the bridal *flammeum* and yellow shoes, the wedding procession, and the groom's lifting the bride across the threshold. It suggests emotional and sexual anxiety. The bride is "full of desire for her bridegroom" but weeps (though the text is damaged at that point). The wedding attendants cry, "Come forth, O bride, if now you will, and hear our words." The poet urges, "You too, O bride, be sure you do not refuse what your husband claims, lest he go elsewhere to find it." The virgin bride is apparently frightened of the sexual act. Though Roman society as a whole was quite explicit about sexuality, young girls raised to display *pudicitia* were supposedly isolated from sexual matters. *Nupta verba*, "married women's words," were an euphemism for sexually explicit terms that were not supposed to be spoken around unmarried virgins. Catullus ends the epithalamium with the hope that Junia's son will resemble his father: "May he be like his father Manlius and easily be recognized by all." Such praise of children who resembled their fathers emphasized married women's *pudicitia*. It is likely that first-time brides were expected to demonstrate (possibly feigned) reluctance to leave their parental home and join the marriage procession, thus displaying proof of their virginity to the wedding guests.[18]

ASYMMETRY IN ROMAN MARRIAGE

Though female writers' perspectives on the experience of marriage are almost entirely lacking, Roman marriage was probably an asymmetrical experience in which women were expected to accede to their husbands' wishes, starting with possible sexual assault on the wedding night and continuing with women's emotional roles and the prevalence of a sexual double standard. An ethic of companionship, the frequency of death, the ease of divorce (see section "Divorce"), and partners who might be closer in age in subsequent marriages may have restored some balance.

Elements of rape symbolism appear in the *domum deductio* and wedding night. Catullus's epithalamium suggests the reluctance of a virgin bride. Some poetry was more explicit, such as the Fescennine verses or the fourth-century CE poet Ausonius's *Cento nuptialis*, a depiction of a wedding night constructed from lines of martial epics emphasizing penetration by swords or spears. The origin story of Roman marriage was the capture of the Sabine women, a legend of earliest Rome (eighth century BCE). Romulus, the first king of Rome, and his band of followers had no wives, and so they descended upon the neighboring Sabine people and carried off their women, making the captives into wives. The *domum deductio* was regarded as a reenactment of this capture. In his *Roman Questions*, a collection of explanations of Roman customs, Plutarch wonders why first-time brides are sad, while women marrying for a second or later time are happy. Whether Roman husbands routinely raped their virgin brides is uncertain. The "reluctance" of virgin brides was part of the ideal of female *pudicitia*, which emphasized modesty and chastity to ensure the control of paternity, thus preserving property transmission within families. First-time brides may have been encouraged to weep and resist when the *domum deductio* came to take them to their bridegrooms' houses, thus displaying their *pudicitia* to the public. In real life, the bride's family might know the groom, and the prospective bride was allowed to meet with her future husband (with a chaperone present) before the wedding, so that he was at least not a stranger. But the fact that grooms were often much older than their brides, especially women marrying for the first time, created a gender asymmetry that cannot be wished away.[19]

Other elements of gender asymmetry in Roman marriage include the emotional work that women were expected to do and the sexual double standard. Greco-Roman literature stereotyped women as quarrelsome. An ideal of Roman marriage was that the couple lived together in harmony (*concordia*), never quarreling, a feature that epitaphs praised, describing the deceased couple as living together without a single quarrel. It seems that women were expected to maintain this *concordia*, soothing and being agreeable to their husbands. In epitaphs and eulogies women are praised for displaying agreeableness and for sacrificing their own interests to those of their husbands. In practice, the relative ease of divorce (in comparison with later Christian European societies until quite recent history) gave women some leverage within marriages, as did their dowries and their own ownership of property (discussed in chapter 6). It is noteworthy that Pliny, depicting his own marriage as ideal, emphasizes the youth and docile personality of his wife Calpurnia.[20]

The ideal of female *pudicitia* was part of a general double standard for male and female sexual behavior. Women, maintaining their *pudicitia*, were expected to be faithful to their husbands within marriage and sexually unavailable to other men; their only option was divorce and remarriage. A stock praise for fathers in Roman society was that their children resembled them, because (it was understood) their wives had been faithful to them. Men were bound by no such requirement of fidelity. Though Catullus 61 suggests that the groom gives up his *concubinus* (boy slave sexual partner), there is much more evidence that husbands could have sexual relations with their own slave women, female mistresses or prostitutes, or slave boys or young male prostitutes. Only two sexual behaviors were inappropriate for Roman elite men: adultery with other men's wives, which was criminalized by the *Lex Julia de adulteriis* (discussed later in this chapter), and undergoing sexual penetration by other males, a role which was suitable only for male prostitutes or slaves. Oral sex was also regarded with disgust, as contaminating the mouth with which men spoke, spoiling their public identities.[21]

DIVORCE

If her marriage was incompatible, a Roman woman had more freedom to divorce than in medieval and early modern Christian Europe (until very recent times in some nations). To leave her husband, she needed the permission of her paterfamilias while he was alive, but after his death, she could initiate divorce if she had a "good reason" (though in ideological literature, men initiate most divorces). A first husband might also well predecease a young wife, due to the age gap between them. In subsequent marriages, which were required by the Augustan marriage legislation, a Roman woman might well have more choice of whom to marry and take part in the negotiations herself, especially if her father had also passed away; the age gap with her spouse might also be less extreme.[22]

Divorce required mutual consent (though it could be undertaken unilaterally by either spouse) and had no legally required form, though "Take your things with you" (*tuas res tibi habeto*) seems to have been a stock phrase. Augustus introduced the requirement of a written notification and witnesses, especially in the case of divorce for suspected adultery. Since the property of husband and wife was already separate, the main legal process of divorce was the return of dowry to the wife or to her paterfamilias if he was alive. If the woman had initiated the divorce, the husband could withhold a fraction of the dowry (up to one-half as *retentiones propter liberos*) for the support of their children, as fathers had legal custody of the children, whom they had *patria potestas* over. Women did not have legal custody of their children, though it seems to have been socially accepted that mothers might continue to live with their young children. If the woman's morals were in question, short of an adultery prosecution, the husband could exact *retentio propter mores* (withholding on account of morals) from the dowry. The return of dotal property was important, not just for the woman's birth family, for it enabled the woman to remarry. A woman of the upper social strata might have inherited substantial property, which always remained separate from the dowry and from her husband's property, but this was not always the case. Pliny the Younger says that he gave a young woman, Calvina (of his own class), a substantial sum of money to help her constitute her dowry, since she had inherited only debts from her deceased father.[23]

GIFTS BETWEEN HUSBAND AND WIFE

Roman women were unlikely to seek wealth through marrying a much richer husband. First of all, in marriage without *manus*, there was no community of property in marriage; the property of the husband remained separate from that of the wife. Second, Roman law forbade gifts between husband and wife. The jurists' discussions of this ban on gifts show that quite substantial gifts were envisioned "by which a woman is made richer." The general purpose of the ban was, in Ulpian's words, "to prevent [the husband and wife] from being plundered reciprocally because of

Detail from a sarcophagus in the Baths of Diocletian, Rome, Italy, late imperial era. This detail displays a popular motif on sarcophagi: the hand clasp of bride and groom, representing their bond as husband and wife. (Pabloborca/Dreamstime.com)

their mutual love"; Paulus put it more harshly that "marriages would become for sale." Ulpian explained the ban on gifts as "so that the richer partner should not fall into comparative poverty and the poorer partner become rich." Shared items of daily use, such as food, items of clothing, slaves, or even gifts of consumable luxuries such as wine or perfumes, were not included in the ban. Third, Roman wives were for quite a long period at a disadvantage in inheriting from their husbands or children (if their children predeceased them). (More detail is provided on these issues in chapters 6 and 11.) Marriage with *manus* had legally incorporated a wife into her husband's *familia*, giving her the same rights to inherit from her husband as their children. Marriage without *manus*, by far the most prevalent form in the Late Republic and Empire, did not incorporate the wife into her husband's *familia*; she remained in her birth family, if her *pater* was still alive, or was *sui iuris*, independent. She was not one of her husband's "automatic heirs" (*sui heredes*, inheriting automatically upon his intestacy). Her husband could make a will and leave her a bequest or trust (*fideicommissum*), but the Augustan marriage legislation restricted bequests between husband and wife to one-tenth of their estates unless they had children. As mentioned earlier, the Augustan legislation also outright banned freed persons and stigmatized persons from marrying presumably much wealthier senatorials.[24]

All these legal restrictions promoted what sociology and anthropology term "assortative mating" or "status endogamy"—the tendency of people to marry within the same social and economic stratum. Roman senatorial and equestrian families tended to marry within these orders; there was some overlap, though, between senatorials and wealthy equestrians, who might be promoted into the senate. We know from tomb inscriptions that the Roman military also practiced an occupational endogamy, the daughters of veterans often marrying soldiers. Freedpersons also tended to marry one another, once they obtained their liberty, except in the case of *patronus* and freedwoman (see section "Manumission and Freed Status"). People in stigmatized professions, such as actors and actresses, other stage performers, prostitutes and panderers (of both sexes), and gladiators and beast fighters, probably married one another because they were not permitted to marry others.[25]

An unequal marriage was more likely to reverse gender roles, in which a poorer husband married a wealthy wife. A man might seek a wife with a large dowry, since he would possess the dowry during their marriage (though he was legally obligated to return its value upon the end of the marriage). But that many such unequal marriages were made seems unlikely; we have seen that the jurists disapprove of unequal partners. A "richly dowered wife" (*uxor dotata*) seemed to have power over her husband, reversing accepted gender roles, and providing a satirical motif that may not have reflected reality. In Roman satire, gold-digging did not occur so much through marriage, but through inheritance; greedy individuals sought bequests and legacies by ingratiating themselves with unrelated wealthy old people, the trope being based on the elite custom of leaving significant bequests to unrelated friends and acquaintances.[26]

The exception to status endogamy was the marriage of a *patronus* (a slave's former owner) to his own freedwoman (*liberta*). Because female slaves (*ancillae*) were assumed to be sexually available and similar to prostitutes, the status of the *liberta* troubled the jurists, and they sought to tie her to the union with her *patronus*, whether it was a marriage or a concubinage (a durable and monogamous relationship of a man of higher status with a woman of inferior status). She could not leave her *patronus* without his consent. She also did not have full disposition of her property, as her *patronus* was also her *tutor legitimus* (statutory guardian, who authorized certain property transactions). She could only obtain release from guardianship by bearing four children, not three, which might be a hardship as the Augustan *Lex Aelia Sentia* required slaves to be at least thirty years old when formally manumitted. More is said of the *liberta* and her status in chapter 7.[27]

THE *LEX JULIA DE MARITANDIS ORDINIBUS*

Augustus's marriage legislation put unprecedented constraints on Roman marital behavior. The laws are usually spoken of together, but were separated by years, the *Lex Julia de maritandis ordinibus* ("Julian Law on the marriage of the orders") and *Lex Julia de adulteriis coercendis* ("Julian Law on punishing adultery") in 18 BCE and the *Lex Papia Poppaea* in 9 CE. They are often called the *Leges Juliae*, though there are many other laws with that name that were promulgated by Julius Caesar and Augustus. Augustus appears to have been concerned that the senatorial order was not reproducing itself and that men were not marrying. As we will see, even with these laws the senatorial order turned over very quickly, new families replacing old ones, but the power structure of the empire was itself to blame for this.[28]

The marriage laws also, by reinforcing traditional morality and punishing sexual immorality, promoted Augustus's legitimacy as emperor. As *Pater Patriae* (father of the fatherland), he wielded the authority to regulate the social and moral behavior of the citizen body, in keeping with the traditional role of the paterfamilias and the Roman Republican censor. The censor was a magistrate who took the census every five years and examined the moral behavior and economic qualifications of the senatorial and equestrian orders, demoting members for immorality. In 46 BCE Cicero had advised Caesar that "lust must be checked, and increasing the population must be promoted."[29]

The *Lex Julia de maritandis ordinibus* prescribed that all Roman citizens between certain age limits should be married and procreate children or face restrictions on their capacity for inheritance; citizens who had children gained inheritance and other privileges. Women between the ages of twenty and fifty, and men between twenty-five and sixty, should be married; the unmarried (*caelibes*) and childless married couples (*orbi*) were forbidden to receive bequests or legacies from persons related more distantly than the sixth degree. This still permitted the childless and unmarried to inherit from their immediate families, within the sixth degree of relationship. These restrictions were a significant penalty for the Roman upper orders, for whom leaving bequests to unrelated persons (clients, patrons, friends, and acquaintances) was an important social obligation. Married couples could also only inherit one-tenth of each other's estates if they had no children, and an additional tenth for each child, allowing for infant mortality: "A common son or daughter whom they lost after the name-day [the ninth day of life] adds one-tenth, but two lost after the name-day add two-tenths." Similarly, "a son aged 14 or a daughter aged 12 or two children aged 3 or three children [living] after their name day" allowed a husband and wife to inherit from one another in full. It should be remembered that as many as a third of all infants died in their first year, and half of all children died before age ten.[30]

The *Lex Julia de maritandis* granted to women of free birth who gave birth to three children the *ius trium liberorum*, the "right of three children," exempting them from *tutela*, guardianship (discussed in chapter 6). Freedwomen had to have four children to obtain the *ius liberorum*. It seems that the *ius liberorum* counted all children that a woman gave birth to, even if not all survived. To require three children to survive to legal adulthood would have put a brutal childbearing requirement on women. A woman of free birth would have to give birth to more than five to six children, and a freedwoman required to have four children for her *ius liberorum* would have had to give birth to ten to twelve children. If only three births were required, the *ius liberorum* was relatively easy to attain The *ius trium liberorum* is discussed in more detail in chapter 6.[31]

The *Lex Julia de maritandis ordinibus* also required citizens to remarry. If a marriage ended through death of one spouse or divorce, the partner was required to remarry; women between ages twenty and fifty were required to remarry within eighteen months of a divorce and within two years of widowhood; men between ages twenty-five and sixty were also required to remarry. The *Lex Papia Poppaea* gave widows an additional year and divorced women an additional six months, but also eliminated loopholes that the Roman elite had been using in an attempt to escape the marriage law.[32]

It is not certain how far down the social scale the *Lex Julia de maritandis ordinibus* and the *Lex Papia Poppaea* applied. These laws were clearly aimed at the senatorial and equestrian orders, whose numbers were small enough to arouse demographic anxiety and who had significant wealth to bestow external legacies and bequests. In the Western province of Spain, the "Flavian Municipal Law" from the town of Irni dictated the political and legal institutions of municipalities organized along Roman lines; similar inscriptions were found at Malaga and Salpensa (ca. 91 CE). As fragments of the *Lex Irnitana* cover post-Augustan *tutela* and manumission, it is likely that the *Lex Julia de maritandis ordinibus* also applied (though the inhabitants of Irni were of Latin status). In Roman Egypt, the *Gnomon of the Idios Logos* suggests that the *Lex Julia de maritandis ordinibus* applied to well-to-do citizens in the provinces. Women with property worth 20,000 HS or more were taxed if they were childless; men with 100,000 HS or more and women with 50,000 HS or more were unable to receive inheritances if they were childless. These people were well-to-do but below the equestrian census of 400,000 HS and might represent decurions (city councilors) and medium landowners. A Latin marriage contract from Roman Egypt states that the marriage is being made in accordance with the *Lex Julia de maritandis ordinibus*. But less wealthy families, who left inheritances only to close relatives, might be less motivated by the penalties. In the census declarations from Roman Egypt, widows tended not to remarry and often moved back in with birth relatives. The jurists write, however, as if the Augustan marriage laws applied to all citizens of "respectable" moral status—status that the *Lex Julia de adulteriis* and its interpretation defined.[33]

THE *LEX JULIA DE ADULTERIIS*

The *Lex Julia de adulteriis coercendis* was also passed in 18 BCE. It made adultery a capital crime for the first time in Roman history; previously, adultery and other forms of illicit sexuality had been punished within the family, by the paterfamilias of an adulterous woman and a "council" of family elders. Now Augustus established a standing court (*quaestio perpetua*) to try cases of adultery. The *Lex Julia de adulteriis* required the husband of the adulterous woman to divorce her and report the case within sixty days of discovering the adultery. If the husband did not divorce his wife, he himself could be prosecuted for *lenocinium* (pimping), having a financial motive for keeping his adulterous wife, whether it was retaining her dowry or receiving a hush-up payment from her lover. After the sixty-day limit, outsiders could report the adultery for up to four to six months. The case then went to trial; the emperor presided over prominent cases in Italy. If the adulterous woman and her lover were convicted, half of the woman's dowry and one-third of her property were confiscated; her lover lost half of his property. The confiscated property went to the imperial treasury.[34]

The most sensational feature of the adultery law was the so-called *ius occidendi* (right to kill) clause permitting a father to kill his married daughter and her lover if he caught them in the act of adultery. The adulterous woman's husband was not permitted to kill his wife and could kill her lover only if the lover was a person of low or stigmatized status (slave, freedman, actor, male prostitute, pimp, gladiator, beast fighter). The father had to catch the adulterous pair in his house. The *ius occidendi* was probably based on the father's *vitae necisque potestas* (power of life and death) over his children, which husbands did not have over their wives. It also echoed elite Roman beliefs that their ancestors had punished adultery in this way. This *ius occidendi* was used very rarely in practice. Several rescripts provide evidence of actual cases and show that the father or husband risked being charged and sentenced for murder, with the alleged adultery considered as an extenuating circumstance. In demographic terms, due to the age gap in Roman marriage, married women's fathers were unlikely to still be alive, much less have the vigor for double homicide.[35]

The father's right to kill may have been included mainly as a deterrent to adultery, frightening potential lovers. It echoed similar legends from the early Republic in which a father kills his daughter for unchastity, even when she did not consent to the illicit sexual relationship, as with Verginia, killed by her father to save her from the lust of Appius Claudius. One Pontius Aufidianus killed his daughter and her male pedagogue when he caught them having an affair. The larger comparison might be with extralegal "honor killings" in various traditional societies, particularly the Middle East and South Asia, in which male family members slay women for premarital or extramarital sexual relations or as rape victims.[36]

Other than the *ius occidendi*, though the *Lex Julia* made adultery a capital crime, conviction did not result in death for the elite. Senatorial and equestrian adulterous partners were punished with exile; the adulterous woman was exiled to an island and her lover to a different island. It is not known if the exile was permanent; some Mediterranean islands, such as Capri or Rhodes, were more pleasant places to live than others. The adulterous partners were also formally stigmatized in law, becoming infamous (*infames*), a status shared with prostitutes, pimps, stage performers, gladiators, and criminals convicted of other capital crimes. It is not known whether the *Lex Julia de adulteriis* was enforced for lower social strata (subelite and poor), but it is likely that if they were convicted, their punishment was corporal (sentenced to hard labor). In the lower strata, we only know of the punishment of soldiers; a centurion who committed adultery with his commander's wife was exiled.[37]

The *Lex Julia de adulteriis* also defined other forms of illicit sexuality and may have legislated "respectable" forms of behavior, though the evidence is increasingly indirect. *Stuprum* was any form of illicit sexual relations outside marriage, defined mainly for women, who thus were forbidden premarital as well as extramarital sexual relationships. Jurists' interpretation of the *Lex Julia de adulteriis* seems to have defined persons to whom the law did not apply. Among these were the women "with whom *stuprum* is not committed," probably including prostitutes and women with "disreputable" occupations (among the *infames*). Exactly how far down the social scale a woman was still thought to be "respectable" is uncertain. Ulpian claimed that

> we ought to regard as a *mater familias* a woman who has not lived dishonorably; for her behavior separates and distinguishes a *mater familias* from other women. It will make no difference whether she is still married or a widow, free born or freed; for neither the state of matrimony nor birth make a *mater familias*, but good morals.

But the attitudes toward freedwomen suggest that many Romans did not agree with this definition. Late legal writings state that "adultery cannot be committed with any woman who keeps a business or shop," and Constantine I (emperor 306–37) extended the ban on senatorial marriages with infamous persons to senatorial marriages with *tabernariae* (barmaids) and *popinariae* (cookshop girls).[38]

Tacitus claims that the *Lex Julia de adulteriis* was resented by the elite; "an excess of immorality was followed by an excess of laws."

Members of the aristocracy seem to have pushed back against the law almost immediately; Augustus's own daughter Julia the Elder and her daughter Julilla were banished for adultery (though Augustus did not try them in the public court). According to Tacitus, outsiders were motivated to report adultery to the criminal court because as *delatores* (public informers) they received rewards for doing so from the public treasury (augmented by the confiscated property of adulterers); wealthy households thus became targets. In practice, because of the sexual double standard in Roman culture, elite men greatly resented the state's attempt to control their marital and sexual lives; in contrast, the laws reinforced general attitudes about women's sexual roles and behavior.[39]

The *Lex Julia de adulteriis* reinforced already existent social attitudes about married women's sexuality in which their modesty and chastity (*pudicitia*) were a source of honor. Infidelity, in contrast, was profoundly dishonoring. Under Augustus's adultery law, the adulterous woman and her lover were punished, stigmatized, and isolated from society; her husband risked contamination with dishonor (prosecution for *lenocinium*) if he did not divorce and prosecute her; an archaic, violent form of punishment (killing in the act) was also endorsed in theory. Emphasizing women's sexual fidelity in marriage, these attitudes and provisions were intended to ensure paternity, protect property transmission within families, and maintain the honorable reputation of both families. The number of people deviating from such norms was probably much fewer than Roman moralists liked to claim. In particular, it is likely that the *Lex Julia de adulteriis* reinforced attitudes about women's behavior in public spaces, where they might encounter strange men. Roman women were not confined to their houses, as was the Greek ideal. But women were likely to have attendants as chaperones when they went out in public, and their reputation was at risk if they were accosted or publicly followed by men who were not their husbands. The implications for women's dress in public are discussed in chapter 5.[40]

IMPACT OF THE *LEGES JULIAE*

Roman marriage was still an enduring institution, but it is not clear whether the Augustan marriage legislation "worked" in the demographic sense. Its main functions may have been ideological. The Roman senatorial order failed to sustain itself in demographic terms. In a classic series of articles published in his *Death and Renewal*, Keith Hopkins showed that senatorial families failed to perpetuate the same level of political success for more than a generation or two. Many such families disappeared altogether in a generation or two and were replaced by the promotion of equestrians into the senate. Finer-grained studies have supported these conclusions. From the first century CE to the third, the ethnic origins of senators shifted from Italy to Southern Gaul and Spain, to Greece and Asia Minor, North Africa, and finally the Balkans.[41]

There were doubtless multiple reasons for senatorial families' ephemeral nature, but instead of biological causes—infertility from hot baths, lead poisoning, and so on—that are difficult to prove, or blaming elite women for not wanting to bear children (as did the ancient male authors), the causes were probably structural. Partitive inheritance, the distribution of parental estates among all surviving children rather than en bloc to the eldest male child as in later European primogeniture, tended to reduce the wealth of descendants. It may have caused senatorial families to fall below the property qualification for the senatorial order. The heads of families could make wills that reduced this tendency, but the Romans felt a strong incentive to treat all *sui heredes* fairly, creating strong incentives to reduce family size. As was discussed in chapter 2, the high rate of infant and child mortality makes it impossible to tell how much contraception, abortion, or postnatal exposure were used to limit family size. However, the high rate of infant and child mortality made partitive inheritance a workable strategy in the short term because the surviving number of heirs tended to be small; fathers were survived by one, two, or three children, not nine or ten. The Augustan marriage legislation supposedly incentivized childbearing but may have promoted the production of three ever-born children to qualify for the *ius liberorum*, not all of whom were likely to survive infancy and childhood; three children were below the replacement fertility rate.[42]

Elite males also had many socially obligatory expenses that reduced the transmission of estates to their children. For the sake of prestige and honor, they made extensive benefactions to towns and cities and to individuals (as Pliny did to provide women with dowries) and testamentary bequests and legacies to nonfamily members. Even "extravagance" was obligatory when it expressed social status, as will be seen in chapter 5. The general consensus of current economic historians of the classical world is that the Roman empire was more capitalist than has traditionally been supposed, but it was still harder to make money quickly than in modern capitalist economies; legal experts and moralists advised the careful husbandry of estates.

Finally, perhaps most of all, the emperors had a strong interest in hindering the development of powerful, enduring senatorial families, which might become rivals to the imperial power; they preferred to promote so-called new men into the *ordines*. Women were an essential part of this political economy, creating marriage alliances and keeping property in circulation in the form of dowry. A woman's marriage brought an infusion of property into the groom's family, even if this dowry had to be returned when the marriage ended.

CONCLUSION

Marriage was a central element of the Roman family and of women's lives in Roman society. Except for the women who were not legally permitted marriage, marriage was probably expected of all women, except those who became Vestal Virgins. The *matrona* or materfamilias, a married woman of the upper *ordines*, was an icon of Roman womanhood, at least in public culture. Other women, especially freedwomen and those who were legally unable to marry, were not permitted to share in her status (though they aspired to it).

In this highly stratified and status-conscious society, there was even a prescribed costume for *matronae*, the *stola* (overdress worn over a long tunic), not worn by other women, such as unmarried women, prostitutes, or slave women. In general the Romans believed that one should be able to tell people's status at once from how they were dressed and adorned; women of the upper orders could be distinguished from their slave attendants and from women of lower status. The social context of Roman costume is the subject of the next chapter.

NOTES

1. *Rules of Ulpian* 5.2.

2. On *manus* marriage, see Tac. *Annals* 4.16; Gaius *Institutes* 1.108–114; Jane F. Gardner, *Women in Roman Law and Society* (London, 1986), 11–14; Susan Treggiari, *Roman Marriage: Iusti Coniuges from the Time of Cicero to the Time of Ulpian* (Oxford, 1991), 16–32; Judith Evans-Grubbs, *Women and the Law in the Roman Empire: A Sourcebook on Marriage, Divorce, and Widowhood* (London, 2002), 21–22. Earlier scholarship affected general works, e.g., Sarah B. Pomeroy, *Goddesses, Whores, Wives, and Slaves: Women in*

Classical Antiquity (New York, 1975), 152–54. On marriage without *manus*, see Gardner, *Women*, 13–14; Treggiari, *Roman Marriage*, 30.

3. Treggiari, *Roman Marriage*, 43, 52–53; Gaius *Institutes* 1.55–6; *Rules of Ulpian* 5.5, 5.8; Paulus *Sententiae* 2.19.6.

4. On *Lex Julia*, see Evans-Grubbs, *Women*, 149–50; D. 23.2.4.6 (Paulus); *Rules of Ulpian* 16.2. On soldiers, see Sara Elise Phang, *The Marriage of Roman Soldiers, 13 B.C.–A.D. 235: Law and Family in the Imperial Army* (Leiden, 2001); Evans-Grubbs, *Women*, 158–60. On evidence for women working and living in military camps, see Penelope M. Allison, *People and Spaces in Roman Military Bases* (Cambridge, 2013).

5. Treggiari, *Roman Marriage*, 37–39; Evans-Grubbs, *Women*, 136–40. On adopted sibling marriage, see Sabine R. Huebner, *The Family in Roman Egypt: A Comparative Approach to Intergenerational Solidarity and Conflict* (Cambridge, 2015), 159–61. On Claudius and Agrippina, see Tac. *Annals* 12.6–7; Gaius *Inst.* 1.62. However, cousin marriage was tolerated; see Treggiari, *Roman Marriage*, 113–19.

6. On early marriage, see John Crook, *Law and Life of Rome, 90 B.C.–A.D. 212* (Ithaca, NY, 1967), 100; Gardner, *Women*, 38–40; Treggiari, *Roman Marriage*, 39–40. On epitaphs, see Richard P. Saller, *Patriarchy, Property, and Death in the Roman Family* (Cambridge, 1994), 25–42. Puberty was "13 plus" according to Treggiari, *Roman Marriage*, 40; 14 to 16 in sub-elite, Saskia Hin, *The Demography of Roman Italy: Population Dynamics in an Ancient Conquest Society 201 BCE–14 CE* (New York, 2013), 150–52.

7. On Pliny, see Jo-Ann Shelton, *The Women of Pliny's Letters* (London, 2013), 101. On Cicero and Publilia, Plut. *Cicero* 41.3–4; Treggiari, *Marriage*, 96, 102.

8. Plin. *Ep.* 1.14.4–9; Shelton, *Women*, no. 48. On betrothal, see D. 23.1; Evans-Grubbs, *Women*, 88–91; Gardner, *Women*, 42–43; Treggiari, *Roman Marriage*, 39–40, 120–21. For Acilianus, see Shelton, *Women*, 84. For other recommendations, see Plin. *Ep.* 1.10, 6.26, 6.32.

9. Tac. *Annals* 12.2.

10. On this competitive society, see Emily A. Hemelrijk, *Matrona Docta: Educated Women in the Roman Elite from Cornelia to Julia Domna* (London, 1999), 7–9.

11. Gifts: Plin. *Ep.* 2.4; 6.32; Shelton, *Women*, 281–85. On dowry, Evans-Grubbs, *Women*, 91–98; Treggiari, *Roman Marriage*, 323–64. On the necessity of dowry, D. 23.3.2 (Paulus); 24.3.1 (Pomponius). On its return, *Rules of Ulpian* 6.4–6.

12. Apuleius *Apology* 92. On Tiberius, see Tac. *Annals* 2.86. On Cicero, see Plut. *Cicero* 41.3–4. On dowry size, Saller, *Patriarchy*, 211–15; Gardner, *Women*, 71–81, 97–116. On instances of dowries, see Treggiari, *Roman Marriage*, 345. On Cicero and Tullia, see Treggiari, *Roman Marriage*, 47.

13. Examples of contracts, see *P. Mich.* VII 434 + *P. Ryl.* IV 612; *Oxyrhynchus Papyri* X 1273 (texts, Evans-Grubbs, *Women*, 126–28). On sub-elite, see Evans-Grubbs, *Women*, 122–28, 132–35. On depreciation of dotal clothing, see D. 23.3.10.pr.

14. On antiquarian, see Treggiari, *Roman Marriage*, 160. On spinning and weaving done by a woman's slave women, see D. 24.1.31.pr; Gordon Williams, "Some aspects of Roman marriage ceremonies and ideals," *JRS* 48 (1958), 16–29; Karen K. Hersch, *The Roman Wedding: Ritual and Meaning in Antiquity* (Cambridge, 2010), 108–9.

15. Judith Lynn Sebesta, "Symbolism in the costume of the Roman woman," in *The World of Roman Costume* (Madison, WI, 1994), ed. Judith L. Sebesta and Larissa Bonfante, 46–53, 48; Laetitia La Follette, "The costume of the Roman bride," in Sebesta and Bonfante, *The World of Roman Costume*, 54–64; Alexandra Croom, *Roman Clothing and Fashion* (Stroud, 2010), 112; Kelly Olson, *Dress and the Roman Woman: Self-Presentation and Society* (London, 2008), 21–25; Hersch, *Roman Wedding*, 69–114. On the *flammeum*, the main element of bridal costume, see Olson, *Dress*, 22; Hersch, *Roman Wedding*, 94–106; Lucretius 2.361–2; Petronius *Satyrica* 26.1; Martial 12.42.3; Plin. *Natural History* 10.148; Festus 82L. On the *tunica recta* and hairnet, see Plin. *Natural History* 8.124; Festus 364L. On *seni crines*, see Festus 454L. On the spear, see Plut. *Roman Questions* 87; Plut. *Romulus* 15.5; Festus 55L. On the *verbena* wreath, see Festus 56L. On the knot, see Festus 55L.

16. On the *Flaminica Dialis*, see chapter 10. On rings, see Richard Hawley, "Lords of the rings: Ring-wearing, status, and identity in the age of Pliny the Elder," in *Vita Vigilia Est: Essays in Honour of Barbara Levick* (London, 2007), ed. Edward Bispham and Greg Rowe, 103–11; iron ring, Plin. *Natural History* 33.4.12.

17. Treggiari, *Roman Marriage*, 167–68; Williams, "Aspects"; Hersch, *Roman Wedding*, 140–226. On water and fire, see Plut. *Roman Questions* 1.

18. On *nupta verba*, see Festus 175L.

19. Treggiari, *Roman Marriage*, 3–4, 103; Shelton, *Women*, 82–83. On Sabines, see Livy 1.9. On "sad," see Plut. *Roman Questions* 105. On weeping, see Hersch, *Roman Wedding*, 145–46.

20. Plin. *Ep.* 4.15; Shelton, *Women*, 101, 105–7, 109–10. On the companionate ideal with separate spheres (men outside, women inside the home), see Columella *On Farming* 12.pr.6–8; Tac. *Annals* 3.34; Plut. *Moralia* 139d–140a, 141b; cf. Dio 56.3.3, versus ideal that wife should obey husband, Plin. *Panegyricus* 83; Dion. Hal. *Roman Antiquities* 2.25.4; Valerius Maximus 9.1.3. On women prone to excess, see Livy 34.3.1–4; Tac. *Annals* 3.33. For the "without a quarrel" theme in epitaphs, see, e.g., Emily A. Hemelrijk, *Women and Society in the Roman World: A Sourcebook of Inscriptions from the Roman West* (Cambridge, 2021), nos. 1.16, 17, 19, 20.

21. On children resembling their fathers, see Plin. *Ep.* 6.26; Catullus 61; Lucretius *De rerum natura* 3.894–901; Horace *Odes* 4.5.21–4; Beryl Rawson, *Children and Childhood in Roman Italy* (Oxford, 2003), 85; Shelton, *Women*, 170. On men's sexuality, see Craig Williams, *Roman Homosexuality*, 2nd ed. (Oxford, 2010), also Holt N. Parker, "The teratogenic grid," in *Roman Sexualities* (Princeton, NJ, 1997), ed. Judith P. Hallett and Marilyn B. Skinner, 47–65.

22. Treggiari, *Roman Marriage*, 90 (e.g., Suet. *Galba* 3.4); Hemelrijk, *Matrona Docta*, 9.

23. Suet. *Augustus* 34; D. 24.2.9; 38.11.1.1. On divorce, see Gardner, *Women*, 72, 81–95; Evans-Grubbs, *Women*, 187–202; Treggiari, *Roman Marriage*, 435–82; the formula was also *tuas res tibi agito*, "look to your own affairs" (D. 24.2.2.1).

24. On gifts between husband and wife, see Ulpian: D. 24.1.1, 24.1.3.pr; Paulus, D. 24.1.2; Gardner, *Women*, 68–73; Evans-Grubbs, *Women*, 98–100; Treggiari, *Roman Marriage*, 366–74. On permissible goods that might be shared, see D. 24.1.18 (Papinian), 24.1.21.pr (Ulpian). On small luxuries, see D. 24.1.31.8.

25. On status endogamy in army, see Ramsay MacMullen, *Soldier and Civilian in the Later Roman Empire* (Cambridge, MA, 1963), 100–3. On gladiators, see Valerie M. Hope, "Fighting for identity: The funerary commemoration of Italian gladiators," in *The Epigraphic Landscape of Roman Italy* (London, 2000), ed. Alison E. Cooley, 93–113.

26. On dowry, Treggiari, *Roman Marriage*, 329–31; on inheritance, Edward Champlin, *Final Judgments: Duty and Emotion in Roman Wills, 200 B.C.–A.D. 250* (Berkeley, CA, 1991), and on *captatio* (legacy-hunting), see 87–102.

27. On freedwomen, see Matthew J. Perry, *Gender, Manumission, and the Roman Freedwoman* (Cambridge, 2014). On rape of captives and Roman slave- and freedwomen, see Sara Elise Phang, "Intimate conquests: Roman soldiers' slave women and freedwomen," *Ancient World* 35.2 (2004), 207–37.

28. Dio 54.16.1, 55.2.5–6, 56.1–56.9, 56.10.1–2; Suet. *Augustus* 34.1–3; Cic. *Pro Marcello* 7.23. Shelton, *Women*, nos. 33–35; Mary R. Lefkowitz and Maureen B. Fant, eds., *Women's Life in Greece and Rome* (Baltimore, MD, 2016), nos. 141–42.

29. Treggiari, *Roman Marriage*, 58–60; Thomas A. J. McGinn, *Prostitution, Sexuality, and the Law in Ancient Rome* (Oxford, 1998), 78–81; Beth Severy, *Augustus and the Family at the Birth of the Roman Empire* (London, 2003), 51–56, 60–61; Shelton, *Women*, 18–19. Cicero *Pro Marcello* 7.23.

30. *Rules of Ulpian* 15.2–3, 16.1; Gardner, *Women*, 77–78; Treggiari, *Roman Marriage*, 60–80; McGinn, *Prostitution*, 70–78; Evans-Grubbs, *Women*, 83–87.

31. Treggiari, *Roman Marriage*, 70–71, 382; McGinn, *Prostitution*, 73, 76–77; Evans-Grubbs, *Women*, 37–38.

32. On remarriage, Treggiari, *Roman Marriage*, 61–66; Evans-Grubbs, *Women*, 220–21.

33. In *Lex Irnitana*, see Evans-Grubbs, *Women*, 30–31; Egypt, *Gnomon of the Idios Logos* §29, 30, 32; social impact, Treggiari, *Roman Marriage*, 77–78; McGinn, *Prostitution*, 75, 81; *P. Mich.* VII 434 + *P. Ryl.* IV 612; Evans-Grubbs, *Women*, 126–27. On widows, see Roger S. Bagnall and Bruce W. Frier, *The Demography of Roman Egypt* (Cambridge, 1994), 126–27; Huebner, *Family*, 95–105.

34. On elders, see Dion. Hal. *Roman Antiquities* 2.25.6; Livy *Periochae* 48; Valerius Maximus 6.3.8. On emperor, see Plin. *Ep.* 6.31.4–6. On adultery law, Gardner, *Women*, 127–32; Treggiari, *Roman Marriage*, 277–90; McGinn, *Prostitution*, 140–47 (main features); Evans-Grubbs, *Women*; Shelton, *Women*, 167–72.

35. On *ius occidendi*, see Treggiari, *Roman Marriage*, 279–82; McGinn, *Prostitution*, 202–7. Treggiari (*Roman Marriage*, 285) thinks it was mainly intended as a deterrent and McGinn (*Prostitution*, 206) that it was "meant to be used." On the statute, see D. 48.5.25 (24).pr.-4; *Collatio* 4.2.3 (Paulus); Paulus *Sententiae* 2.26.1; *Women's Life*, nos. 143–45, 148–49. On real instances, see D. 48.5.39 (38).8 (husband who kills wife receives exile instead of death); *Codex Iustinianus* 9.9.4; *Women's Life*, no. 147.

36. On archaic anecdotes, see Valerius Maximus 6.1.3, 6.1.6; Livy 3.44–8; Diodorus Siculus 12.24.2–4. Honor killings are discussed briefly in McGinn, *Prostitution*, 11–12 (post-classical influence from Islam confuses the issue).

37. Plin. *Ep.* 6.31.4–5; McGinn, *Prostitution*, 142–43; on military, Sara E. Phang, "Elite marriage and adultery in the camp: Plin. *Ep.* 6.31.4–6 and Tac. *Hist.* 1.48," in *Present but Not Accounted For: Women & The Roman Army* (forthcoming), ed. L. L. Brice and E. M. Greene.

38. Ulpian: D. 50.16.46.1; Gardner, *Women*, 33, 121–25; Evans-Grubbs, *Women*, 58–60. On the social scale, see Treggiari, *Roman Marriage*, 34, 297 (lower classes were "not worth the attention" of the law); Evans-Grubbs, *Women*, 19, 72; McGinn, *Prostitution*, 72–76. In the *Gnomon of the Idios Logos* §29, 30, 32, the *Leges Juliae* apply to people with property worth 20,000 HS and more. On *tabernariae*, see Paulus *Sententiae* 2.26.11; *CTh* 4.6.3.

39. Tac. *Annals* 3.27; cf. Tac. *Histories* 1.2. On Julia, see Macrobius *Saturnalia* 2.5.

40. Treggiari, *Roman Marriage*, 105, 311–19; McGinn, *Prostitution*, 10–14, 213.

41. Keith Hopkins, *Death and Renewal* (Cambridge, 1983).

42. On family size and possible limitation, see Treggiari, *Roman Marriage*, 404–5.

5

DRESS AND STATUS

INTRODUCTION

Clothing and fashion are among the most obvious elements of daily life. In the modern United States, outside of certain professions and subcultures (e.g., lawyers, Wall Street, Congress, the military, police, Hasidim, Mennonites), clothing and fashion are regarded mainly as forms of self-expression; because clothing is cheap, clothing selection is relatively unconstrained by social and economic status. It is often not possible to tell a person's wealth and social status from how they are dressed. Fashion is still constrained by gender roles; though sartorial choices have greatly broadened for women, they have not done so for men.

In the classical world, social status and gender and the production and cost of clothing constrained what men and women could wear; you were what you wore, as one scholar has said. The study of the social context of costume in antiquity is a rapidly growing field precisely because of its challenges. Items of clothing or even remains of fabric are very rarely preserved from antiquity. Painted details on stone statues and reliefs (customarily painted in bright colors) have not survived the weathering of time. Ancient writers often did not bother to explain customs that they took for granted. In many instances our main source is a dictionary, *On the Meaning of Words*, by Verrius Flaccus, an antiquarian author of the Augustan

era, which was abridged by the second-century CE writer Sextus
Pompeius Festus. Festus in his turn was abridged by Paul the Dea-
con, a Christian writer at the turn of the eighth century CE. Verrius
Flaccus, Festus, and Paul (not to be confused with the jurist Julius
Paulus from the early third century CE) were particularly interested
in ritual and religion. They are major sources for women's and
priestesses' garments. Other antiquarian authors, most from Late
Antiquity, commented on the meaning of words in Virgil's *Aeneid*
and in Horace.

Male authors again provide most of our information—much of it
disapproving—on women's dress and ornament. These passages,
such as Livy on the third-century BCE *Lex Oppia*, are difficult to
interpret. They reflect the ambiguity of women's status: on the one
hand, elaborate or expensive dress and adornment made women
conspicuous, giving them a public identity and presence, implying
elite women's possession of wealth. On the other hand, such clothing and adornment were linked with women's gender and sexuality, risking transgression of the matronal ideals of *pudor* (modesty)
and *pudicitia* (sexual unavailability). Male authors often project sexual ambivalence onto women by depicting their dress and adornment as intended to seduce and deceive.

It should be understood that much of men's writing about women
was intended for other men; men wrote about women's appearance and behavior as a way of fashioning their own masculinity.
Men were assumed to dress simply, in plain tunics and togas, and
were mocked by other men when they indulged in "feminine"
adornment, such as silk clothes, jewelry, and perfume. The mas-
culine/feminine dichotomy even extended to language. Praise of
a "masculine" unadorned elegant prose style might be contrasted
with "feminine" prose style (also used by men), with florid use of
metaphor and exotic words, termed prose "cosmetics."

DRESS AND SOCIAL STATUS

What women wore strongly reflected their social and economic
status, as is assumed in this passage by the Roman legal writer
Ulpian (late second century CE):

> If someone accosts respectable young girls (*virgines*), even though
> they are in slave women's clothing (*ancillari veste*), he is understood
> to commit a lesser offense: a much lesser offense if the women were
> dressed as prostitutes and not as respectable women. Therefore, if
> a woman has not been wearing the clothing of a matron (*matronali*

habitu) and someone has accosted her or abducted her companion, he is not liable to the action on *iniuria*.

Iniuria, "outrage" or "insult," was penalized not as a crime but as a civil delict (tort), in which the wronged party sued the perpetrator for damages. It could range from hitting someone or damaging their property to, as here, sexually harassing women by accosting them on the street, pursuing them, or abducting their attendants. The women's fathers or husbands would bring suit for *iniuria*; a respectable woman might be able to bring suit for *iniuria* herself if she was accosted but would require a male representative to speak for her in court. As *infames*, prostitutes or pimps could not bring suit at all.[1]

Clearly the action for *iniuria* applied only if the woman was of higher social status, and that status was shown by her dress. Ulpian assumes that *virgines* (unmarried girls, probably under twelve), married women, slave women (*ancillae*), and prostitutes were all dressed differently. He does not explain *how* they were dressed, because he assumes that his readers would know. This chapter will first examine evidence for the distinct costumes of unmarried girls, married women (*matronae*), and prostitutes. Other distinct costumes had ritual contexts, such as the costume of traditional Roman brides and of Vestal Virgins. Slave women do not appear to have had distinctive costume. However, the evidence for these costumes is prescriptive (it represents traditions and ideals of how people should behave), and other evidence, both literary and artistic, suggests that every detail of these costumes was not worn and that the boundaries of acceptable dress were often more vague. It is notable that Ulpian does not use specific terms for clothing, such as the *stola* and *palla*, garments associated with high-status married women, but only the generic *vestis* (clothing). Second, this chapter will explore other ways of signaling social status with clothing, through the type, quality, and color of the fabric in an economy where clothing was disproportionately expensive because it was made by hand from the thread and cloth upward. Hand production of clothing limited its availability and made it a form of wealth and a status symbol. Even dyes, such as the famous Tyrian purple, could be expensive and a marker of economic status.

GARMENTS ASSOCIATED WITH SOCIAL ROLES: INTRODUCTION

In Roman society, certain garments were associated with social roles. The most well-known garment, of course, is the toga, worn by male citizens (and by children). Married women of high social status wore the *stola*, a long, sleeveless overdress worn over a long tunic dress. Other women wore only long tunic dresses. Over the *stola*, women of high social status were expected to wear the *palla*, a mantle that hid their body, when outside in public. Women of lower status may not have worn the *palla*; these extra layers of clothing were expensive, as will be seen later. There is a tradition that prostitutes and women convicted of adultery were required to wear the toga, but it seems unreliable. Noncitizen men and women in native costume will have been conspicuous in "Romanized" settings such as urban centers. This section will examine first aspects of clothing construction that limited their shapes, and then examine more closely garments associated with social roles.

GARMENT CONSTRUCTION

Modern garments are usually shaped by cutting pieces to fit the body and sewing them together, which results in many pieces of wasted material. In the ancient world, the high value of woven fabric made ancient clothing makers reluctant to cut into fabric. The rectangular front and back of a short-sleeved tunic were stitched together along their edges to produce the shoulder and arm seams and side seams; the neck opening was produced by leaving the body unstitched between the shoulder/arm seams, not by cutting into the fabric. Additional rectangular pieces might be stitched onto the body of the tunic to produce long sleeves, or sleeves might be woven in one piece with the body on the loom, a full-fashioning process that is normally seen today only in sweaters. It is not known whether cutting into fabric was a ritual prohibition (suggested by the myth of the three Fates, who spun, measured, and cut the thread of life) or whether tailors were merely reluctant to waste fabric and risk unraveling.[2]

Garments were held on the body and shaped with draping, knots, brooches, and belts. The toga, worn by Roman citizen adult males and children, was held on and shaped by draping alone. According to artistic evidence, the tunic worn by Roman matrons in the Late Republic and early Empire left the shoulder/arm seams unstitched; the cloth along these seams was fastened together at intervals with knots of fabric. Garments might be fastened and shaped with brooches, large pins with notable regional styles. Men's tunics were shaped by belts worn at the waist, with some of the fabric pulled over the belt; women's tunics were belted under the breasts. These relatively loose and unfitted clothing styles accommodated a wide range of body types and were convenient in warm weather; as we have seen, the average temperature in the early Roman Empire was higher than the modern Mediterranean's (in the nineteenth and twentieth centuries). In cold weather, men and women added more layers of clothing.[3]

Styles changed in the third century CE onward, when mosaics show that men wore tunics that were more closely fitted, with long, tight sleeves and narrower bodies, and long trousers or leggings that were fitted to the leg and may have included feet, as with medieval hose or modern tights. Women also appear in tunics with long, more fitted sleeves. Makers of clothing seem still to have been reluctant to cut into cloth; sleeves could be woven to fit upon the loom, and this was possible also with men's trousers, though how they were made is still unclear. The styles of Late Antiquity have been attributed to the influence of northern and western provincial cultures (Gaul, Germany, and the Danube) but are as likely to be due to the colder and more unreliable weather patterns of the third century CE onward. Bold ornament, taking the form of separately woven and tapestried appliques and bands, became popular, especially on men's clothing, and was used to denote rank. A general increase in ostentation corresponds to the increased socioeconomic inequality of the later Empire.[4]

GARMENTS ASSOCIATED WITH STATUS, AGE, AND GENDER

Roman men's dress was a marker of masculinity as well as citizen status. Tunics were worn above the knee, and sleeves were (before the later Roman Empire) short, as long sleeves were regarded as effeminate and unsuitable for men. The toga in particular was a marker of the political class, symbolizing adult male citizenship: in the words of Virgil in the *Aeneid*, the Romans were the toga-wearing people who dominated all other peoples. Augustus enforced men's wearing of the toga in public places, particularly in the Forum and Roman Senate.[5]

The toga became increasingly ostentatious and ceremonial, worn only for formal occasions or not worn at all. A relatively simple version of the toga was worn by Roman men in the Republic. Augustus promoted the wearing of a more voluminous toga, which expanded to 5 meters in length and 2.5 meters in width and thus became less affordable for the poorer citizens. The enlarged toga required an assistant to put it on properly and discouraged any physical labor which risked dislodging the drapery and folds.[6]

In social terms, the toga was strongly associated with male elite status and public roles. Elite men were expected to wear the toga at formal public appearances, such as religious ceremonies, giving speeches, holding political office, or appearing in court or before the emperor. Augustus even required all male Roman citizens to wear the toga when they entered the Forum. His *Lex Julia theatralis* (discussed in section "Theaters and Spectacles") required at least senators and equestrians to wear togas at the theater. Lower-status men, especially outside Rome, had less cause to wear the toga. Juvenal says that in many parts of Italy "no man wears the toga until he is dead," the ancient version of a man's wearing a business suit only in his funeral casket. However, the clients or political and social dependents (free men, not slaves) of important Romans needed to wear the toga when they formally greeted and attended on their patrons.[7]

Status indicators appeared on the toga and on the tunic worn under it: underage boys and girls and Roman magistrates wore the *toga praetexta*, bordered with a purple stripe. Equestrians wore two narrow vertical stripes (*clavi*) on the front of their tunics, and senators and their sons wore broader vertical stripes. However, such vertical stripes on the body of tunics were a widespread fashion that muddled these status indicators. The toga was worn during the daytime; Roman men's evening dress, worn to banquets, was more casual, featuring a tunic and matching mantle termed *cenatoria* (dinner-party clothing).[8]

The toga was also a marker of masculinity as well as status, because of its associations with men's citizenship and public roles. It was the garment that the Roman orator rehearsed and performed in, though his more impassioned gestures might disarrange it. Except for the aforementioned stripes, the toga and the man's tunic underneath were relatively simple and unadorned; the toga itself was white (or the off-white of unbleached wool), in keeping with an elite philosophical preference for simplicity and lack of adornment as appropriate to masculine men and "masculine" oratory. Such austere manly style was contrasted with a "feminine" love of elaborate adornment, cosmetics, and jewelry, regarded by the moralistic male authors as extravagant, deceptive, and un-Roman, and equated with a flamboyant "Asiatic" oratorical style. Female adornment to display wealth and social status thus might backfire; as we will see, the ideal costume for *matronae* emphasized their modesty.[9]

Underage boys and girls of free birth (and probably of higher status) wore the *toga praetexta*, which was bordered with a purple stripe, a symbolic color that provided ritual protection from harm. Under the *toga praetexta*, a boy wore a short tunic and a girl a long tunic that reached her feet. There is more evidence for boys wearing the *toga praetexta*, which they exchanged for the *toga virilis* or plain white toga of an adult male when they reached puberty (at age fourteen to sixteen, though there was no fixed age). The sculptural evidence for young girls wearing the *toga praetexta* is limited; instances are seen on the friezes of the *Ara Pacis*, depicting the Augustan imperial family. Physically active children could not be expected to keep the *toga praetexta* on, so children may not have worn the *toga praetexta* for daily wear, but only for public appearances and ritual occasions. Due to its elite associations, poor and country children of free birth may not have worn the *toga praetexta*; slave children of course did not wear it. As seen in chapters 3 and 7, the *toga praetexta* separated freeborn children from sexually vulnerable slave children. The daily dress for a young girl, then, was the long female tunic, falling to her feet as was appropriate for female tunics.[10]

Both sexes ceased to wear the *toga praetexta* after puberty. Boys exchanged the *toga praetexta* for the all-white *toga virilis* after they reached puberty, on average around age fourteen to sixteen, when they dedicated their *toga praetexta* and protective amulet (*bulla*) to their family's household gods. The age of donning the *toga virilis* could vary, as parents chose to have their sons enter adult life sooner or later depending on circumstances and personal maturity. According to the Christian author Arnobius, young girls dedicated their *togae praetextae* to Fortuna Virginalis when they reached twelve years of age, the traditional age of marriage. But girls did not immediately don the *stola*, the garment of married women that was analogous to the toga. Unmarried *virgines* past puberty may have worn only a long tunic dress, which rendered their status ambiguous.[11]

The costume of the traditional Roman bride has already been described in chapter 4: the *tunica recta*, which she supposedly spun by hand and wove herself; the *flammeum* or orange-yellow veil that covered her head and face; under it, she wore a wreath of twigs symbolizing fertility, and her hair was dressed in the obscure "six locks" style. The bride's costume, as we have seen, emphasized the traditional role of a Roman wife and mother; it had religious associations, the hairstyle resembling that of the Vestal Virgins and the *flammeum* also being worn by the *flaminica Dialis*, the wife of the high priest of Jupiter at Rome. The *flaminica Dialis* was not permitted to divorce her husband; her relationship symbolized the perfect, harmonious marriage.[12]

After her wedding day, a married woman of the upper orders donned the clothing of a *matrona*, the *stola* and *palla*. In the Republic and first century CE, *matronae* wore the *stola*, a sleeveless long tunic that was worn over a regular long tunic dress and that was decorated with an embroidered or banded hem, the *instita*. The term *instita* refers to a sewn-on element and may also refer to the straps that fastened the *stola* at the shoulders. Festus calls *matronae* "those women who had the right to wear the *stola*," and Valerius Maximus relates that a man summoning a *matrona* to court was not permitted to touch her body, "so that the *stola* should be left inviolate from the touch of an alien hand." Both tunic dress and *stola* extended to the feet, displaying a large extent of expensive fabric and making physical labor difficult. Over the *stola*, when outside in public, the *matrona* wore a *palla*, an enveloping mantle; she wore the mantle over her head, covering her hair. (Indoors, she did not have to cover her hair.) This traditional costume of the *matrona*, hiding her body in several layers of clothing, emphasized her *pudicitia* and modesty. In his *Ars Amatoria* or "Art of Love," a satirical handbook for young men on how to seduce women, the poet Ovid announces that his book is not intended for *matronae*: "Stay away, slender fillets (*vittae*), symbol of modesty, and you, long hem (*instita*), who cover half the feet." The *vittae* or woolen hairbands are not depicted in surviving portrait statues of Roman empresses and high-status women, who often have elaborate hairstyles that are used to date women's statues.[13]

It is uncertain, however, if all married women or even all *matronae* wore the *stola*. As discussed in chapter 1, *matrona* was a term that indicated women of relatively high status, namely, senatorial, equestrian, and decurial women; the far more numerous married women of lower status were probably not regarded as *matronae* and did not wear the *stola*. This might explain why the *stola* appears in surviving portrait sculpture for only a short time, in the first century CE. Augustus may well have emphasized the wearing of the *stola* by matrons, as he did the wearing of the toga by male citizens.[14]

After the first century CE, the *stola* seems to have disappeared from use, and respectable women were distinguished by the *palla* alone. The passage of Ulpian discussed earlier does not describe married women as wearing the *stola*. By that time, no single dress style may have distinguished a *matrona*, other than the *palla*, long skirts, and the absence of provincial non-Roman styles.

The *palla* itself dictated matrons' modest behavior in public. It covered the head; according to Valerius Maximus, Gaius Sulpicius Gallus (mid-second century BCE) divorced his wife for going with her head uncovered in public. The *palla* was draped rather than pinned at the neck or shoulder, and keeping it on (as with the toga) required a dignified posture, holding the arms close to the body and making no sudden, expansive movements. This restrained posture is seen in the more numerous surviving public statues of women wearing the *palla*. Women furthermore needed to carefully adjust the drapery to achieve the elegant effect seen in statues and to walk slowly to avoid disarranging it. Slave women probably wore shorter skirts that did not impede movement, while still longer than men's tunics, which were belted to the knee.[15]

Some Latin sources claim that prostitutes and convicted adulteresses wore the toga, specifically a dark-colored toga, to distinguish them from matrons in *stola*s and citizen men in white togas. Having abandoned *pudicitia*, prostitutes and adulteresses no longer merited the costume of a faithful wife and mother. The evidence is conflicting; some of it is humorous or satirical, as the Romans found the concept of a woman in men's clothing incongruous. There is much other literary evidence for prostitutes dressing in other kinds of clothing, including extravagant dresses. Furthermore, Roman men in mourning or appearing as defendants in court cases also wore dark-colored togas, the *toga pulla*, and would have not welcomed confusion with prostitutes. Kelly Olson suggests that the literary association of matrons with the *stola* and prostitutes with the toga perpetuated itself rhetorically without regard to actual social practice.[16]

Since the women in D. 47.10.15.15 are clearly outside in public, a *matrona* would be distinguished by her enveloping *palla*; at this date, *matronae* may no longer have worn the *stola*. Their daughters (the respectable unmarried girls) may have worn the *toga praetexta*. Slave women would not have been thus cloaked, though they may have worn shorter shawls or capes. That prostitutes did not cover their heads and bodies in public is the most plausible inference; we cannot assume that prostitutes were distinguished by their wearing the toga. In short, it was probably the extent to which a woman's body was covered that indicated her reputable status (and protection from harassment on the street). This spectrum of modesty conflicted with the use of dress and adornment to display status, discussed in section "Clothing as Signs of Economic Status."

CLOTHING AS SIGNS OF ECONOMIC STATUS

Today, thread, cloth, and clothing are produced in industrial factories and may contain artificial fibers unknown before the late nineteenth and twentieth centuries—polyester, rayon, nylon, and acrylic. Clothing is likely to have been produced on another continent, shipped across the world. This mass-produced clothing is relatively cheap and affordable, and fashions—not just colors but styles, silhouettes, and details—change with great speed, giving rise to the phenomenon of "fast fashion": clothing that may be worn once or twice and discarded. The international clothing industry accordingly generates serious ecological burdens, whether the use of toxic chemicals in the processing and production of natural and artificial fibers, the use of fossil fuels for long-distance shipping, or the problem of disposal of discarded clothing. Textile and garment workers, located mainly in East, Southeast, and South Asia, are among the lowest-paid and most exploited workers in the world. The great majority of these workers are women.[17]

Only one of these features was present in the Roman world: the great majority of textile workers were poorly paid or enslaved women (outside Egypt, which had a tradition of male weavers). Textiles were limited to natural fibers: wool, linen, and silk. The Romans imported cotton from India on a limited scale, and Pliny the Elder, the natural history encyclopedist, thought that cotton grew on trees. Silk was imported from China, the land of the *Seres* (silk people), through trade with the Persian Empire and India. The Greeks and Romans did not know that silk was spun by insects, silkworms, or the larvae of the silk moth *Bombyx mori*, and recounted legends about its source. In any case, silk was extremely expensive, a luxury fabric (as will be seen). The main fibers used in the Roman world were wool, from sheep and to a lesser extent, goats, and linen, which is produced from the long, tough stem fibers of the flax plant. Wool was the dominant textile industry in Roman Italy; the dominant flax producer was Roman Egypt.[18]

All textiles were made by hand labor, including thread, cloth, and finished garments. Roman spinners of thread used the drop spindle, a rod attached to a circular weight (spindle whorl), twisting thread by hand from a mass of unspun fibers and winding the thread on the rod. The weight of the spindle whorl helped maintain a constant tension on the thread, keeping it twisted and producing an even thread. The unspun fibers were held on a stick termed a distaff. Spinning wheels were an invention of the medieval Islamic period and spread to Western Europe.[19]

In classical antiquity, weaving was also performed on handlooms, usually a warp-weighted loom or two-beam loom. In weaving, the warps are the vertical threads; the weft consists of the horizontal threads which are threaded over and under the warp threads by a shuttle. In a warp-weighted loom, the warp threads are suspended and held under tension by weights tied to their bottom ends; in a two-beam loom, the warp is stretched vertically between top and bottom horizontal beams of a frame. Larger looms were used in artisan workshops. Hand spinning and weaving were very laborious, time-consuming processes, which shaped the consumption of fabric and the nature of fashion in the Greek and Roman periods.[20]

Accordingly, woven fabric and clothing were disproportionately expensive in the ancient commercial economy, compared with today when mass-produced garments are disproportionately cheap. It was possible to buy many kinds of clothing and personal adornment in Rome in the early second century BCE, the time of Plautus's *Pot of Gold*, but this passage was also meant to seem comically extravagant in "Madison Avenue" fashion, depicting women as in debt to many shopkeepers.

> There stands the launderer, the embroiderer, the goldsmith, and the wool-worker; the dealers in flounces and tunics; those who dye garments in flaming red, violet, and brown; or those who make garments with sleeves, or those who sell exotic perfumes; retailers in linen and shoemakers; squatting cobblers and producers of slippers; sandal-makers are standing there, and producers of mallow garments are standing there; the launderers are demanding pay, and the menders of clothes are demanding pay; sellers of women's breast-bands are standing there, and sellers of girdles are also standing there.

Most women who were not wealthy probably had relatively fewer clothes: a daily outfit, a higher quality outfit for festivals and ceremonies, and cold-weather gear such as a mantle or hooded cape. The mantles of the poorest did double duty as bed coverings. Wealthy people owned more clothing, but to change your dinner outfit many times during a banquet (as does Martial's Zoilus) was mocked as gauche ostentation, and to wear jewelry only once or twice and to tear up expensive clothing, as did the emperor Heliogabalus, was grossly extravagant. A wealthy, fashionable woman might display her wealth and status through owning many pieces of clothing, but their styles were unlikely to change much because of the constraints on design, discussed previously. She might have her clothes redyed to change their color. She would supplement her status display through hairstyles, which were more subject to changes in fashion, cosmetics, and elaborate jewelry.[21]

The high prices of spun thread, finished cloth, and clothing are attested in the emperor Diocletian's (284–305 CE) *Edict on Maximum Prices* (301 CE), an attempt to curb inflation by setting maximum prices for a comprehensive list of goods and services. Finished cloth and clothing items appear to be ten to one hundred times more expensive than raw, unspun wool or linen. The cost of dyeing also increased the value of fiber, even unspun. The *Edict*'s wages set for textile workers (spinners, weavers, tailors, and fullers or clothes cleaners), in contrast, are by the piece or day and much lower than the value of the fabric they produced. Prices for clothing from earlier periods of the Empire are lower, but still extremely high relative to other goods and services. In a comparison of "real" prices with the price of grain, only meat, livestock, and slaves (discussed in chapter 7) were as or more expensive.[22]

Cloth and clothing were regarded as substantial financial investments and sources of wealth in themselves, due to the labor required to produce textiles. Items of clothing appear in dowry contracts from Roman Egypt (where Greek legal influence persisted) alongside gold jewelry, showing that the brides and their families were not poor and that they considered garments to be a significant form of wealth. The Roman jurists write of clothing as significant property alongside slaves and houses, featuring in important legal transactions such as dowry (paid by the wife or her father to the husband, and returned when the marriage ended), gifts between husband and wife, and legacies. The depreciation of clothing through wearing might be accounted for in estimating its value. Launderers, *fullones*, who pounded woolen clothes in cold-water solutions of fermented urine (which contains ammonia, a cleanser) and then rinsed them in cold water, were responsible for any damage to the garments they cleaned.[23]

The high value of clothing even influenced crime. Thieves might specialize in stealing clothing as the most expensive item, other than jewelry, that people carried on their bodies. Some thieves mugged people for clothing, leaving their victims naked. Others stole clothing from the public baths of Rome and lesser cities and towns, where people undressed before exercise and bathing.

Well-to-do bathers brought slaves to guard their clothing; others paid public bath attendants to guard them. Unscrupulous fullers, who were paid to clean clothing, made double the amount by also renting out the clothing; the jurists regarded this practice as theft. The value of clothing is also seen in the legend that the soldiers guarding Jesus's crucifixion gambled for his clothing. Even in the upper strata, expensive clothing might lead to chicanery; Pliny the Younger depicts his arch-enemy Marcus Aquilius Regulus, an unscrupulous legal expert, attempting to persuade a wealthy woman to revise her will and bequeath him the very expensive clothing she is wearing.[24]

To return to our opening passage, it is likely that Ulpian's "respectable" women, from well-to-do families, would have displayed their status through the quality of the fabric they wore, the use of silk, and the use of colors produced by expensive dyes, such as purple, scarlet, and saffron. Silk was imported at great expense from the Near East, originating in China, but sometimes silk cloth was unraveled and rewoven for the Greek and Roman markets. Purple dye was produced by fermenting the ink glands of several species of marine murex snails. This process required thousands of snails to produce a small amount of purple dye, and accordingly purple dye was a luxury good, though it was not restricted to the emperors even in Late Antiquity. Only certain grades of purple were reserved for the "imperial purple," a particularly dark shade that required repeated dyeing. Less costly purple-dyed thread was used widely as decoration, for the toga praetexta's stripe and for *clavi* and, from the third century onward, decorative patches on men's clothing. Scarlet was also an expensive dye, made from the tiny insect cochineal (*coccus*), a pest on desert plants and imported from the Near East. Saffron was made from the dried stamens of crocus flowers, used as a flavoring and as a dye; large numbers of stamens had to be collected to produce a substantial amount of dye. Other natural dyes are less associated with luxury, but still added to the value of a garment. The deeper the dye, the more valuable the fabric was, so that even black-dyed clothing was ostentatious. Still more extravagant garments, out of reach of nearly all, were ornamented with spun gold and with jewels, such as the cloth of gold cloak worn by the empress Agrippina or the jeweled garments of the emperor Caligula.[25]

Much of our artistic evidence for clothing colors in the Roman world is lost. One could easily think that ancient Greeks and Romans wore white clothing, because surviving sculptures and reliefs in marble and limestone have been scoured white by weather. In classical times, these sculptures and reliefs were painted in bright colors, the microscopic traces of which have been identified by recent archeologists. A range of colors of clothing is thus attested, supported by the literary tradition and by surviving fresco paintings from Pompeii and mummy portraits from Roman Egypt. White itself was a high-status color because it required bleaching of wool or linen and avoidance of physical labor that might soil it. A Roman political candidate was termed *candidatus* because his toga was further whitened with chalk.[26]

Low-status women (such as Ulpian's slave women) would probably wear undyed, unbleached garments in the natural colors of linen and wool (including tan and gray shades from brown and black sheep). They would own few pieces of clothing, some of which did double duty as bed covers. The quality of their fabrics would be lower, especially if produced within the household. Subsistence households probably still did their own spinning and weaving, whether in rural Italy or in the provinces. By the first century BCE, well-to-do households in Rome and the provinces may not have required the women of the family to spin and weave. They would have worn fabrics spun and woven by specialist slaves or artisan workshops. It is likely, however, that their slaves wore homespun fabric produced within the household. Very wealthy households with few slave women probably dressed the slaves in livery bought on the market, though Trimalchio's household slaves dressed in silk are an extreme extravagance intended as satire. Low-status women, furthermore, probably wore clothing that had been mended or patched; once a garment wore out or was damaged, the taboo on cutting fabric no longer applied, and usable cloth was pieced together into *centones* or patchwork. Wearing homespun fabric became an attribute of rusticity, showing that you were poor and lived far from commercial centers—except when the emperor Augustus (27 BCE–14 CE) made a point of wearing it to suggest archaic virtue, discussed in section "Dress as Social Competition versus State Ideology."[27]

DRESS AS SOCIAL COMPETITION VERSUS STATE IDEOLOGY

The sources for women's dress and fashion show a tension between the "official" ethic of modesty and women's desire to display wealth and status (social competition). Augustus may have promoted matrons' wearing the *stola* and *palla* as part of his marriage legislation, though no law requiring the wearing of the *stola* or *palla* has survived. In his rhetorical work *De pallio*, the Christian author Tertullian (writing in the late second and early third centuries CE, thus long after this period) claims that early in the reign of Tiberius (14–37 CE) the augur Lentulus promoted a law that penalized matrons who did not wear the *stola* with the punishment for *stuprum*, a nonspecific sexual offense. Ovid's focus on *matronae* as wearing the *stola* suggests opposition to Augustus's policy. It is difficult to interpret references to the *stola* as always attesting its use, as the *stola* became a metaphor for the *matrona* and her traditional role. However, the Vestal Virgins may have continued to wear the *stola* as part of their ritual costume (in the reign of Domitian).[28]

Though much literary evidence for female display is probably exaggerated, surviving artistic evidence suggests that elite women in the first and second centuries of the Empire competed for display in clothing and especially in elaborate hairstyles. Portrait statues of the empresses, which were distributed to Italian and provincial cities alongside the portraits of the emperors, display elaborate hairstyles that were imitated by local elite women. There were few other sources of visual images in the Roman world: wall paintings (such as those surviving from Pompeii) did not travel, and other than the obscure *acta Senatus* (minutes of the Roman Senate) and *tabula alba* (white boards) that recorded laws and decrees, there were no newspapers or broadsheets, let alone photographs. Women in remoter parts of Italy and the provinces looked to the empresses' portraits as evidence for the imperial court's high fashion. Many of these hairstyles are very elaborate, requiring the assistance of a hairdresser, and were probably not worn by non-elite women. Slave women are depicted wearing their hair in a simple bun or otherwise tied up; slaves only had their hair cut short or shaved on the day of their manumission. Across all classes and ages, Roman women wore their hair up; even young girls were depicted with their hair in braids or buns that were pinned up on the head. Wearing one's hair loose was a symbol of emotional distress, used in Roman art to represent women in trouble (being pursued by rapists or grieving over their capture in war). Loose hair was also worn by female mourners, discussed in chapter 11.[29]

Jewelry was another form of display for women, and also a form of movable wealth, listed in the dowry documents discussed in chapter 4. As female adornment, women's jewelry attracted male

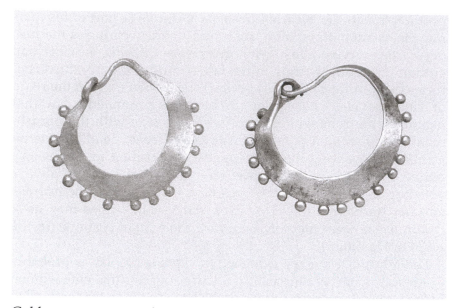

Gold crescent earrings decorated with gold balls, Roman, first century CE. These small earrings (3/4 inch) and other jewelry might be part of a woman's movable wealth. Even women who could not afford gold jewelry and precious stones wore jewelry made from other metals and glass or pottery beads. (The Metropolitan Museum of Art)

moralizing. Roman men did not wear jewelry other than signet rings and the bracelets (*armillae*) awarded as military decorations. Men represented women's jewelry as a singularly feminine form of ornament, extravagant and potentially decadent. The famous matron Cornelia, the mother of the Gracchi (mid-second century BCE), is reported to have owned little jewelry and to have said, "My children are my jewels." Seneca the Younger, praising his mother Helvia, says that "jewels and pearls did not move you," implying that adornment led to adultery. Such attitudes were mocked in an anecdote about Augustus's daughter Julia, later banished for adultery, who one day donned a revealing dress and was scolded by her father; the next day she appeared in modest clothing, and was praised by Augustus. She replied, "Today I dressed to be looked at by my father, yesterday by my husband." This focus on jewelry as a form of *luxuria* (luxury, extravagant expenditure on pleasures) also obscured its role as movable wealth in a society where gold coinage (*aurei*) had intrinsic value as precious metal, not fiduciary currency. Elite women's wealth, as seen in chapter 6, was significant, but men belittled it by referring to it as female ornament.[30]

In general, women may have used expensive cloth (such as silk), dyes, and elaborate hairstyles and jewelry to display their wealth and social status, conveying their membership in elite socioeconomic strata and their share in their husbands' status. The convention of matronly modesty competed with this display. The tension is reflected in men's satire and invective depicting elaborately adorned women as meretricious—similar to prostitutes in their avarice, deception (hiding physical imperfections), immodesty, and promiscuity. If prostitutes always wore dark-colored togas, or if matrons always wore *stolas*, this discourse would not have been so widespread.[31]

Marble portrait bust of Empress Claudia Octavia, Rome, Italy, ca. 50–70 CE. Claudia Octavia, daughter of the emperor Claudius (r. 41–54) and first wife of the emperor Nero (r. 54–68), was divorced, banished, and executed by Nero. The portrait shows an elaborate hairstyle with front locks, curled sides, and long ringlets. Imperial portraits were sent to the provinces and, in the absence of printed or other media, popularized the hairstyles of the imperial capital. (Purchase from the J. H. Wade Fund, The Cleveland Museum of Art)

But outside the genres of moralism, satire, and invective, men of the upper social strata probably expected their wives and daughters to dress in a way that reflected their wealth and social status. Pliny the Younger, writing at the turn of the second century CE, gave money to an acquaintance to help him pay for his daughter's dowry, so that she would be maintained in a lifestyle appropriate to her status. The shock of the late fourth- and fifth-century CE Roman elite when some elite Roman women began to practice extreme Christian asceticism, espousing virginity and renouncing all display of wealth and personal adornment, illustrates the previous standard.[32]

CONCLUSION

The diversity of clothing suggests that Roman women's economic roles were complex and stratified, the subject of chapter 6. They participated in the complex and commercial Roman economy that current scholarship emphasizes. It is even likely that, contrary to the image of *matronae* spinning wool, slave women were the main producers of clothing.

NOTES

1. D. 47.10.15.15. Thomas A. J. McGinn, *Prostitution, Sexuality, and the Law in Ancient Rome* (Oxford, 1998), 332; translation is McGinn's. On *iniuria*, see Bruce W. Frier, *A Casebook on the Roman Law of Delict* (Atlanta, GA, 1989). "You were what you wore": McGinn, 162.

2. On the avoidance of cutting, see Kassia St. Clair, *The Golden Thread: How Fabric Changed History* (New York, 2019), 161; Elizabeth W. Heckett, "Clothing patterns as construction of the human mind: Establishment and continuity," in *Ancient Textiles: Production, Craft, and Society* (Oxford, 2007), ed. Carole Gillis and Marie-Louise B. Nosch, 208–14, on the full-fashioning of the Roman toga; Alexandra Croom, *Roman Clothing and Fashion* (Stroud, 2010), 18–19; Mary Harlow, ed., *A Cultural History of Dress and Fashion in Antiquity* (New York, 2017), 3–5.

3. Glenys Davies and Lloyd Llewellyn-Jones, "The body," in Harlow, *Cultural History*, 49–69, 53.

4. Croom, *Roman Clothing*, 35–39.

5. Jonathan Edmondson, "Public dress and social control in late Republican and early imperial Rome," in *Roman Dress and the Fabrics of Roman Culture* (Toronto, 2008), ed. Jonathan Edmondson and Alison Keith, 21–46. On Romans, see Virgil *Aeneid* 1.286. On Augustus, Suet. *Augustus* 40.5; 44.2.

6. On the dimensions of a toga, see Croom, *Roman Clothing*, 44–45. On assistance, see Tertullian *De pallio* 5.1–2.

7. Juvenal 3.171–2. On the toga, see Shelley Stone, "The toga: From national to ceremonial costume," in *The World of Roman Costume* (Madison, WI, 1994), ed. Judith Lynn Sebesta and Larissa Bonfante, 13–45; Michele George, "The 'dark side' of the toga," in Edmondson and Keith, *Roman Dress*, 94–112.

8. On *clavi*, see Croom, *Roman Clothing*, 33; they even appear on women's tunics in the Egyptian mummy portraits. On men's dinner party clothing, Edmondson, "Public dress," 23; wearing it in public was inappropriate, e.g., Suet. *Nero* 51.

9. On these themes, see Kelly Olson, *Dress and the Roman Woman: Self-Presentation and Society* (London, 2008), 80–95; Amy Richlin, "Gender and rhetoric: Producing manhood in the schools," in *Roman Eloquence: Rhetoric in Society and Literature* (London, 1997), ed. William J. Dominik, 90–110.

10. Stone, "Toga," 13; Judith Lynn Sebesta, "Symbolism in the costume of the Roman woman," in Sebesta and Bonfante, *The World of Roman Costume*, 46–53, at 47–48; Croom, *Roman Clothing*, 144–45; Olson, *Dress*, 15–20; "The appearance of the young Roman girl," in Edmondson and Keith, *Roman Dress*, 139–57; Macrobius *Saturnalia* 1.6.7; Cic. *Verrines* 2.1.113; Propertius 4.11.33–34; Festus 282 4L.

11. Arnob. *Adversus Nationes* 2.67. On boys, see Fanny Dolansky, "*Togam virilem sumere*: Coming of age in the Roman world," in Edmondson and Keith, *Roman Dress*, 47–70. On girls, see Olson, "Appearance." Girls may have been unmarried till their mid-teens; see Richard P. Saller, *Patriarchy, Property, and Death in the Roman Family* (Cambridge, 1994), 36–42.

12. Sebesta, "Symbolism," 48; Laetitia La Follette, "The costume of the Roman bride," in Sebesta and Bonfante, *The World of Roman Costume*, 54–64; Croom, *Roman Clothing*, 112; Olson, *Dress*, 21–25. On the *flammeum*, the main element of bridal costume, see Olson, *Dress*, 22; Lucretius 2.361–62; Petronius *Satyrica* 26.1; Martial 12.42.3; Plin. *Natural History* 10.148; Festus 82L. On the *tunica recta* and hairnet, see Plin. *Natural History* 8.124; Festus 364L. On *seni crines*, see Festus 454L. On the spear, see Plut. *Roman Questions* 87; Plut. *Romulus* 15.5; Festus 55L. On the *verbena* wreath, see Festus 56L.

13. On *matronae*, see Sebesta, "Symbolism," 48–49; McGinn, *Prostitution*, 149, 153–54, 157, 332–34; Olson, *Dress*, 25–41; Croom, *Roman Clothing*, 89–90; Andrew B. Gallia, "The Vestal habit," *Classical Philology* 109.3 (2014), 222–40; Emily A. Hemelrijk, *Hidden Lives, Public Personae: Women and Civic Life in the Roman West* (Oxford, 2015), 297–98; Meghan J. DiLuzio, *A Place at the Altar: Priestesses in Republican Rome* (Princeton, NJ, 2016), 37, 154–55; Festus 112L; Valerius Maximus 2.1.5a; 6.1.pr.; Cic. *Verrines* 2.1.113; Ovid *Art of Love* 1.31–32. On Ovid, see Ioannis Ziogas, "Stripping the Roman ladies: Ovid's rites and readers," *Classical Quarterly* 64.2 (2014), 735–44.

14. On *stola*, see Emily A. Hemelrijk, *Matrona Docta: Educated Women in the Roman Elite from Cornelia to Julia Domna* (London, 1999), 14–15; *matrona stolata* in documentary sources refers exclusively to senatorial or equestrian women. On Augustus, Dio 54.10.3–5; McGinn, *Prostitution*, 154–55.

15. Croom, *Roman Clothing*, 89–90, 104–5; Davies and Llewellyn-Jones, "The body," 57–58; "Gender and sexuality," in Harlow, *Cultural History*, 87–104, at 88–89; cf. Hemelrijk, *Hidden Lives*, 297–98; on walking, Mary Harlow, "Dressed women on the streets of the ancient city: What to wear?" in *Women and the Roman City in the Latin West* (Leiden, 2013), ed. Emily A. Hemelrijk and Greg Woolf, 225–41, 231–32.

16. Sebesta, "Symbolism," 50; McGinn, *Prostitution*, 168–69; Croom, *Roman Clothing*, 108; Olson, *Dress*, 40–41.

17. On the modern textile economy, see St. Clair, *Golden Thread*, 2–3, 16; Adam Minter, *Secondhand: Travels in the New Global Garage Sale* (Bloomsbury, 2019).

18. Croom, *Roman Clothing*, 16–18; Eva Andersson Strand and Ulla Mannering, "Textiles," in Harlow, *Cultural History*, 13–35.

19. Croom, *Roman Clothing*, 16–18; Strand and Mannering, "Textiles," 20–25.

20. By comparison, a meter of medieval Norse sail cloth took twenty hours to weave; in medieval England, thirty yards of "good broadcloth" took about twelve days to weave: St. Clair, *Golden Thread*, 109–11, 123. These were probably denser fabrics.

21. Plautus *Aulularia* 508–22. On expensive clothing, see Croom, *Roman Clothing*, 18–19, 28–29; in dowry documents, *P. Oxy.* X 1273, XVI 1901. On Zoilus, see Martial 5.79. On Elagabalus, see SHA *Heliogabalus* 32.1. On display, Eve D'Ambra, *Roman Women* (Cambridge, 2007) 112–28.

22. On the chapters (XIX–XXIX) on textiles in the Price Edict, A. H. M. Jones, "The cloth industry under the Roman empire," *Economic History Review* 13 (1960), 183–192. On real prices, Walter Scheidel, "Real wages in Roman Egypt: A contribution to recent work on pre-modern living standards," Princeton-Stanford Working Papers in Classics (Princeton, 2008), https://www.princeton.edu/~pswpc/pdfs/scheidel/020802.pdf

23. On fullers, see D. 47.2.12.pr. On dowry, gifts, etc., Chapter 4, see sections "Dowry" and "Gifts between Husband and Wife" in this book.

24. On thieves, see Croom, *Roman Clothing*, 28–29; Garrett G. Fagan, *Bathing in Public in the Roman World* (Ann Arbor, MI, 1999), 36–38, e.g., Plautus *Rudens* 382–85; D. 47.17.1; Seneca *Letters* 56.2; Petronius *Satyrica* 30.7–11; curse tablets, 37. On fullery, see D. 47.2.19.4, 47.2.48.4. On gambling, see Lk. 10:30; Matt. 27:35. Pliny and Regulus, Plin. *Ep.* 2.20.9.

25. On silk, see Olson, *Dress*, 14. On dyes, see Judith Lynn Sebesta, "*Tunica ralla, tunica spissa*: The colors and textiles of Roman costume," in Sebesta and Bonfante, *The World of Roman Costume*, 65–76; Croom, *Roman Clothing*, 24–27; Agrippina, Plin. *Natural History* 33.19.63; Caligula, Suet. *Gaius* 62.

26. On painted, Harlow, "Dressed women," 237. On *candidatus*, Edmondson, "Public dress," 27.

27. On production of fabric for the market, see Sebesta, "*Tunica ralla*," 70; Kersten Dross-Krüpe, "Production and distribution," in Harlow, *Cultural History*, 37–48.

28. Plin. *Ep.* 4.11.9; Gallia, "Vestal," 238. DiLuzio, *Place*, 172–74, argues that Vestals did not wear the *stola* (not being married) and that Cornelia Cossa was dressed as a lay woman for her execution. On Tertullian *De pallio* 4.9.

29. Amy Richlin, "Emotional work: Lamenting the Roman dead," in *Essays in Honor of Gordon Williams: Twenty-Five Years at Yale* (New Haven, CT, 2001), ed. Elizabeth Tylawsky and Charles Weiss, 229–48; Amy

Richlin, *Arguments with Silence: Writing the History of Roman Women* (Ann Arbor, MI, 2014), 267–88, at 276–78.

30. On Cornelia, see Valerius Maximus 4.4.pr.; Helvia, Seneca *Consolatio ad Helviam* 16.1; Julia, Macrobius *Saturnalia* 2.5.5.

31. Olson, *Dress*, 5, 7, 96–112.

32. On dowry, Plin. *Ep.* 6.32.

6

ECONOMIC LIFE

INTRODUCTION

Women's participation in the economic life of the Roman Empire was substantial, but their economic roles were shrouded by the social expectations of female domesticity: women's work was inside the home, while men's work was out of doors, whether as farmers, soldiers, or public officials. Accordingly, there is ample information about the economic status of women of the upper social strata whose wealth was in land and real estate, which they could manage at a remove from within their homes. This wealth was mainly inherited. These elite women had a high degree of control over property (relative to women in other patriarchal societies, such as medieval and early modern Europe). Their main difficulties with managing and inheriting property stemmed from the institutions of *patria potestas*, *tutela mulierum* (guardianship of women), and Roman inheritance laws that favored children and other relatives over wives. Because of demographic realities, the first two institutions, *patria potestas* and *tutela*, had relatively minimal impact. Women in these strata had household staffs of slaves and freedpersons and managed domestic work rather than performing it.

In the sub-elite strata, women sought to conform to the domestic ideal, even if economic necessity required them to work. Accordingly, female occupations as represented in Latin inscriptions were limited to "feminine" occupations that were regarded as appropriate for women and that served other women's needs, from secretary to hairdresser. Women do not seem to have worked in "men's" occupations. Many of these women in "feminine" occupations were slaves or freedwomen but appear to be relatively privileged; slavery itself was highly stratified in the Roman world.

In the lower strata of Roman society, we know very little about female agricultural laborers and female textile workers. Spinning and to a lesser extent weaving were traditionally female activities, practiced in the home, as seen in legends of early Rome and the traditional costume of Roman brides. By the later Republic and Empire, textile production was a commercial enterprise, probably carried out by slave women. At the bottom of society, "dirty" tasks such as cleaning were carried out by slaves. Almost completely invisible is the subsistence household, too poor to own slaves, where women would have carried out nearly all tasks essential to the household's survival.

THE ECONOMIC STATUS OF ELITE WOMEN

A substantial proportion of Roman property owners, estimated as 20 percent to as much as a third, were female. Their possession and management of property are attested in extensive legal sources and were restricted by two institutions, *patria potestas* and *tutela mulierum*. However, these restrictions had less impact because of demographic realities and the Augustan *ius trium liberorum* (right of three children), which freed women from *tutela* if they gave birth to three children. Separate property was usual in Roman marriage; except in *manus* marriage, husbands did not control women's inherited property. Elite women whose fathers were deceased and who had had three children were thus able to manage their property in their own right. Not legal but social factors may have constrained their economic activities; to maintain propriety, they carried out economic transactions through subordinate managers and representatives. Nonetheless, many elite women in the Roman Empire became very wealthy; some gave their wealth back to the community as benefactions, which will be discussed in chapter 9.[1]

Patria Potestas

The first restriction on Roman women's property ownership was *patria potestas*, affecting mainly younger unmarried women (until their mid-teens) and younger women who were married without *manus*, the most prevalent form of marriage in the middle and later Republic and Empire, as long as their fathers were alive. The Romans regarded *patria potestas* as a uniquely Roman institution: in the *Institutes*, a textbook of Roman law, the jurist Gaius writes that "there are virtually no other peoples who have such power over their children as we have over ours." The father or paterfamilias had *potestas* over both his sons and daughters and over his direct descendants in the male line—that is, over his sons' children, but not his daughters' children, who were in the *potestas* of their own fathers.[2]

The paterfamilias owned all the property in the family; as long as he was alive, neither his sons nor daughters or any of his direct descendants in the male line could legally own property. In theory, a great-great-grandfather of ninety could still be alive and hold *potestas* over four generations of descendants in the male line, each of whom had to ask the paterfamilias for enough money "to buy a bar of chocolate," as David Daube, a scholar of Roman law, put it colorfully (and anachronistically, chocolate being unknown in Europe before colonization of the New World). According to Daube, a great-great-granddaughter would also need to ask.[3]

In practice, since the adult men of wealthy families needed to manage their own financial affairs, adult children *in potestate* (subject to *patria potestas*) were allotted personal funds, a *peculium*, which they were allowed to manage though they did not legally possess these funds. An adult daughter *in potestate* might also have a *peculium*. The legal institutions of *patria potestas* and the *peculium* applied further down the social scale: Gaius discusses the *peculium* of a daughter, plying "some common trade like sewing or weaving."[4]

Furthermore, due to the late marriage of Roman men and the general high mortality rate, three or more generations of family members were unlikely to be alive simultaneously. According to demographic simulations, a Roman man was lucky if his father was still alive when he was thirty, around the time he would expect to marry. Grandfathers who were still living when their grandchildren were growing up or adults were relatively rare, remarked on by Pliny the Younger describing the healthful location of a mountain Italian town, Tifernum Tiberinum: "Here there are many elderly people: you can see the grandfathers and great-grandfathers of young men."[5]

In contrast, many low-lying coastal areas of Italy and crowded cities—most of all Rome itself, with approximately a million inhabitants by the first century CE—were unhealthy, as seen in chapter 2. The coastal areas were infested with malaria, and the cities were also infested with infectious diseases that spread in crowded conditions. In these areas, sons and daughters in power (*in potestate*) could expect to be legally independent and inherit their fathers' property while still relatively young. Women may have often become *sui iuris* (legally independent) by age thirty.[6]

When a paterfamilias died, his estate was divided between both sons and daughters, a strategy known as partitive inheritance, rather than being left entirely to the first-born son (primogeniture, the form of inheritance in medieval and early modern English aristocracy). In the wealthiest Roman families, a daughter's inheritance may have been limited by the *Lex Voconia* (169 BCE), which forbade the institution of daughters as heirs to the estates of men in the first (wealthiest) census class; the law permitted daughters to receive legacies of up to one-half the paternal estate. The application of the *Lex Voconia* depended on the continuation of the Republican census, which lapsed during the chaos of the Late Republic. In any case, the *Lex Voconia* did not affect Roman women from less wealthy families. Dowries, as discussed in chapter 4, represented only a part of a daughter's patrimony, in contrast with societies in early modern Europe (e.g., Renaissance Italy) where a daughter might receive her entire share of the family estate as a large dowry. There are instances in which Roman daughters received smaller inheritances than sons, but the evidence is inconclusive. In short, Roman women expected to receive part of their share of their fathers' wealth as dowry and part as inheritance. Women whose brothers happened to predecease them (in infancy and childhood or later life) would receive larger inheritances. Demographic simulations suggest that approximately a third of fathers died without sons, leaving daughters as heirs.[7]

Tutela Mulierum

After the death of her paterfamilias, a woman became *sui iuris* and able to own property but was still subject to guardianship of women (*tutela mulierum*). *Tutela mulierum* was distinct from *tutela impuberum*, guardianship of underage children, in which the *tutor* (guardian) actually administered the child's property and carried out all transactions involving it. A woman's guardian was needed to authorize a limited number of legal and financial transactions, including making a will and alienating so-called *res mancipi*: real estate in Italy, slaves, cattle, horses, mules, and donkeys, but not other animals. A *tutor* was also needed to draw up a dowry which contained any *res mancipi*. For all other property transactions, an independent woman did not need a *tutor*'s authorization, and literary authors speak casually of elite women's financial transactions as if no guardians were involved.[8]

A woman's *tutor* was designated in one of three ways. A *tutor testamentarius* was nominated in her father's will; a *tutor legitimus* was assigned from her nearest living male agnate relative, usually her brother or her father's brother; and a *tutor* could be appointed by an official, such as the city praetor at Rome, a provincial governor, or a city magistrate. For example, at Herculaneum in ca. 40–50 CE, the town magistrate Nassius Cerialis appointed Quintus Vibius Ampliatus as guardian to Cornelia Thallusa, "so that no guardianship may diverge from a lawful guardianship in accordance with the *Lex Iulia Titia*." The *tutor* of a freedwoman was automatically her *patronus*, her former owner. Freeborn women were eventually allowed to select their own *tutores*, rather than being subject to their brothers' or paternal uncles' guardianship, a practice that originally was intended to keep control of property within the agnatic lineage.[9]

However, the *tutor*'s powers appear to have been quite limited. A *tutor* did not own or legally possess a woman's property, he was not required to actively manage it, and the transactions that he had to authorize were limited in number. By far the greatest number of daily economic transactions were small scale and did not require a *tutor*'s authorization: buying or selling food and drink, medicines, cosmetics, papyrus, writing tablets, pots and dishes, or paying fees for minor services. Even larger transactions, such as buying clothing or furniture, repairing or renting property, or *buying* slaves, livestock, and real estate, did not require a *tutor*. In general, nonlegal sources speak of adult women as buying, selling, and making loans and wills as independent actors without mentioning their guardianship at all. In contrast with the guardianship of children, a burden which men tried to evade, the guardianship of women attracted relatively little attention from Roman legal experts.[10]

IUS LIBERORUM

Furthermore, the Augustan marriage legislation freed women from guardianship if they bore three children (four children in the case of freedwomen). This was termed the *ius liberorum*, the "right of [three/four] children," and it brought with it other privileges as well, such as the right of husband and wife to inherit more than one-tenth from each other. Freeborn women who had given birth to three children thus were liberated from *tutela* and were able to make wills, constitute dowries, and alienate *res mancipi*, including real estate in Italy, slaves, and livestock. In 263 CE the Egyptian woman (a Roman citizen at this date) Aurelia Thaisous also called Lolliane applied to the prefect of Egypt "for permission to conduct her affairs without a guardian," emphasizing that she was literate, though literacy was not required for the *ius liberorum*.[11]

It was even possible for the emperor to grant the *ius liberorum* as a favor to people who had no children, such as the Vestal Virgins (high priestesses at Rome). Though childless, Pliny the Younger was granted the *ius liberorum* by the emperor Trajan (98–117 CE), and he petitioned Trajan to grant the *ius* to his acquaintance Suetonius (author of the *Twelve Caesars*), who also had no children. The poet Martial bragged that the emperor (Domitian, 81–96 CE) had granted him the *ius liberorum*: "Farewell, wife!"[12]

We come to the problem whether the *ius liberorum* counted three live births even if the children died soon afterward, or whether the children were required to survive to a certain age (e.g., one year, six years, or puberty). In a society where each woman needed to give birth to five or six children just to keep the population stable, giving birth to three children was relatively easy to achieve, but the high rate of infant and child mortality made their survival much more difficult to achieve. Several passages suggest that the *ius liberorum* took account of infant and child mortality, counting all children that lived past eight or nine days, the day of the name-day ceremony. As seen in chapter 4, the *Lex Julia de maritandis ordinibus* allowed husband and wife to inherit more than one-tenth of their estates from each other only if they had children. According to the *Rules of Ulpian*, a summary of Roman legal concepts, they were permitted to inherit an additional one-tenth if they had one child, and another one-tenth for each child that survived past its name-day. If the husband and wife had three children or the equivalent, they were permitted to inherit in full from each other: one child who survived past puberty, or two children who lived more than three years, or three children who survived past their name-day. The jurist Paulus stated only that the children needed to be born alive and full term. These provisions were reasonable, as we have seen that a third of all infants died in the first year of life, and approximately half of all children died before age ten. The city charter of Malaga in Spain, a standardized document modeled on Roman legal institutions, enabled a prospective magistrate's preferment ahead of his runner-up if he had children: one child who survived to puberty or marriageable age (for a girl), or two children who survived past their name-day. Awareness of infant mortality also appears in Ulpian, concerning the identification of a baby born to a widow after her husband's death (this is discussed further in chapter 11). The baby was inspected at birth, twice a month until it was three months old, once a month until it was six months old, every two months from six months to a year old, and every six months from a year old till it became able to speak. It was inspected at these diminishing intervals because the jurists believed that it might die and another man's child be substituted.[13]

Written registration of births existed, but few such registrations survive. In a tablet from Herculaneum, "Lucius Venidius Ennychus has solemnly declared that a daughter has been born to him by his wife Livia Acte," followed by a list of witnesses. Whether such registrations were kept systematically, on the scale of parish registers in early modern England, is unknown. As we have seen in chapter 3, many inhabitants of the Empire were illiterate. In the absence of written documentation, the authorities could call on a family's members and social circle as witnesses to a birth, once a child was named on its eighth or ninth day of life, due to name-day announcements and celebrations.[14]

The jurists disagreed whether stillborn or deformed infants counted toward the *ius liberorum*. Ulpian and Terentius Clemens argued that they did:

> Someone will ask, if a woman has given birth to someone unnatural, monstrous, weak or something . . . not of human appearance . . . whether she should benefit, since she gave birth. And it is better that even a case like this should benefit the parents; for there are no grounds for penalizing them because they observed such statutes as they could, nor should loss be forced on the mother because things turned out ill.

Paulus argued that they did not, saying that "those who are stillborn, seem neither born nor begotten, since they could never be called children." The jurists were uncertain whether a child removed by cesarean section after the mother's death was said to be born and counted toward the *ius*. Thus it is less certain whether stillbirths or infants that died in the first hours or days of life counted toward the *ius liberorum*; they were of ambiguous status, not yet members of society, as was seen in chapter 2.[15]

"WOMANLY WEAKNESS"

The Roman jurists (who were all male) justified *tutela* of women in terms of women's "weakness of mind" or "womanly weakness," *infirmitas sexus* or *imbecillitas sexus*. Gaius states that "it was the wish of the ancients that women, even those of full age, should be in guardianship as being scatterbrained (*propter animi levitatem*)." The idea that women are silly creatures may have derived from Greek philosophical ideas and might have originated in the substantial age gap between Roman elite husbands and wives, first-time brides being in their mid-teens. But adult women were significant economic actors, as Roman legal sources and surviving documents show, and the notion of *infirmitas sexus* was not credible to Gaius, who says:

> There seems . . . to have been no very worthwhile reason why women who have reached the age of maturity should be in guardianship; for the argument which is commonly believed, that because they are scatterbrained they are frequently subject to deception and that it was proper for them to be under guardians' authority, seems to be specious rather than true. For women of full age deal with their own affairs for themselves.

Other jurists continued to reiterate the concept of *infirmitas sexus*, but they appear to be rhetorically defending it.[16]

In fact, Roman legal writing *assumes* that a legal subject is male but that male gender is generic; unless the legal institution excludes it, the generic male also includes females, as jurists admitted. Thus, an explanation of the legal aspects of buying and selling (as long as the goods were not *res mancipi*), describing parties with male genders, could as easily apply to women who were *sui iuris*. However, women appear explicitly in family law; a man could not be said to give birth or to have a dowry.[17]

In Roman law, women did still have certain disabilities as economic actors. They could not provide surety for other people's loans and thus were restricted from the role of banker. This may have excluded women from the largest-scale forms of commerce. Furthermore, women were unable to represent others' interests in court, as will be seen in chapter 9. However, the main restriction on women's economic actions was not legal but social. Respectable women were expected to display modesty (*pudor*, related to *pudici-tia*, chastity) in public (discussed in chapters 1 and 5). Buying, sell-ing, and negotiating in public with strange men might be regarded as immodest activities, and a common attitude in male-authored sources (both legal and literary) was that lower-status women who sold food and drink in taverns and cookshops were prostitutes. Wealthy women with extensive business interests (inherited land and property, even industry and commerce) probably used male representatives (*institores*, usually translated as "business man-agers") to manage their economic interests. But Roman women fur-ther down the social scale might not have had the privilege of using representatives.[18]

The biases of the male jurists are also seen in contrast with the petition and response system of the imperial era. Individuals could submit petitions (letters) to the emperors, or to their legal secre-taries, asking for resolution or clarification of legal problems. The emperors' replies were termed *rescripta*, rescripts (from Latin "to write back"). A large proportion of imperial rescripts are addressed to women and address them in person rather than through male relatives or *tutores*, suggesting that the women were regarded as acting independently even if they formally had guardians. Ulpian says that "there is no doubt that women can conduct and conclude business transactions."[19]

WIDOWS AND INHERITANCE

Roman women's economic and legal disabilities made widow-hood a probable time of hardship for all but the wealthiest. In gen-eral, the importance of elite women as property owners should be understood demographically: high mortality and chance death were likely to leave many women *sui iuris* and heirs of property when relatively young. As we have seen in chapter 4, women's property remained separate in marriage, not merged with their husbands'. High mortality and chance death were likely to leave many wives widowed. The Augustan marriage legislation required women of the upper orders to remarry within eighteen months of divorce and two years of widowhood, or face restrictions on inher-itance from outsiders. The *ius liberorum* may have freed widows from this requirement. But it is not certain whether the legislation applied to everyone below the senatorial and equestrian *ordines* or whether the authorities bothered to enforce it below the elite. Receiving bequests from outsiders was a particularly Roman elite custom and may not have motivated sub-elites and provincials to comply with the Augustan marriage laws. We know from Roman Egypt's census declarations, which attest sub-elite to poor families, that many widows in Roman Egypt did not remarry.

Demographic realities also determined whether women would achieve the *ius liberorum* and liberation from *tutela*. If a woman's children had to survive for a year or more, the *ius liberorum* would have been harder to achieve and would explain why the *ius liberorum* became a status marker of sorts, emphasized by women in papyrus documents. As we have seen, legal texts suggest that all births were counted toward the *ius liberorum* and may have made it relatively easy to achieve.[20]

A major concern of Roman widows was how to care for their children, who might still be young. Women were forbidden to exert *tutela impuberum*, guardianship over their underage children. It was a woman's husband's responsibility to appoint a *tutor* in his will for their minor children. Alternatively, the nearest male agnate relative would be selected, or the magistrate would appoint a *tutor* (as with *tutela* of women). In all these cases, the *tutor* of a minor child was expected to exert more active control over the property. *Tutela* of children conflicted with a widow's obvious interest in managing her children's economic affairs and ensuring that they were provided for. In practice, many widows exerted de facto guardianship over their children, especially in the Eastern Empire and in Roman Egypt, perhaps due to non-Roman cultural influence. This practice clashed with the Roman authorities, who repeatedly pronounced that women should not exercise guardianship over their children and that they could not guarantee legal protection to all parties if women did so. In the later Roman Empire, widows were finally granted the right of legal guardianship over their children by Theodosius I (in 390 CE), on the condition that they not remarry.[21]

Women were also at a disadvantage in inheritance law, as will also be discussed in more detail in chapter 11. Wives in archaic marriages with *manus* had been counted among the *sui heredes* or "automatic heirs" to a husband's estate, on a par with his children. In marriages without *manus*, the order of succession to an estate upon the husband's death without a valid will was his children, then his agnate (birth) relatives, then other blood relatives, and finally his wife. The Romans "disliked being intestate" and adult men would probably have wills, in which they could explicitly make their wives heirs or legatees or place them in charge of a trust to transmit to their children. However, sudden death made intestacy a risk. A woman also had limited inheritance rights with respect to her own children, who were in the *potestas* of their father and thus belonged to his family, not her own. The *SC Tertullianum* and the *SC Orphitianum* (178 CE), two legal provisions of the second century CE, allowed women with the *ius liberorum* to inherit from their own children and allowed children intestate inheritance rights from their mothers, respectively.[22]

ELITE WOMEN'S ECONOMIC ACTIVITIES

In their day-to-day economic activities, women of the upper *ordines* (senatorial, equestrian, and decurial) did not perform domestic tasks such as cooking, cleaning, and childcare but managed a staff of household servants (slaves and freedpersons). A wealthy household would have a slave or freedman *dispensator* (steward), a manager of the household who kept accounts. A prudent and diligent materfamilias would consult with him frequently and probably inspect his accounts herself. If she had inherited property and was *sui iuris* but did not have the *ius liberorum*, she would also communicate with her *tutor* to authorize sale of real estate, slaves, and livestock. If she had the *ius liberorum*, she did not need a *tutor* to authorize these actions. She might, as seen earlier, still use a male representative to conclude financial transactions. She would communicate with the managers of her own properties and authorize the purchase of equipment and sale of produce. A woman of the upper *ordines* would also employ a legal advocate if she wished to sue or was sued (her freedom to act in court will be discussed in chapter 9). She also would keep up an extensive correspondence with family members, friends, and social connections and maintain a social schedule, attending banquets, entertainments, and religious rites. Such a social letter survives from a distant Roman military camp, Vindolanda on Hadrian's Wall (near the Scottish border). Extensive social correspondence also survives from Roman Egypt, suggesting that the habit of social letter-writing had filtered down to the sub-elite.[23]

To what extent the materfamilias directed the daily tasks of the household servants probably depended on her temperament and the size of the household. The Christian theologian Jerome gives a glimpse of an upper-class woman's daily life managing the household:

> The virgin, who is not married, thinks about God's matters . . . But the woman who is married thinks about worldly matters, how to please her husband . . . Over there, babies are chattering, the household is

in uproar, children hang on her mouth for kisses, expenses are being counted up, the outgoings prepared. Here, a team of cooks is rounded up to pound the meat, a crowd of weaving women is buzzing.

The prudent and diligent paterfamilias (the *bonus* paterfamilias or "good householder" of Roman legal texts) would inspect his slaves' work, and the materfamilias would probably do so too, especially concerning the female servants. Issuing reprimands and arranging for the punishment of slaves was part of this work, discussed in chapter 7.[24]

Estate and property management is mentioned in elite men's letters such as Cicero's letter about his new house or Pliny's sale of wine from his estates. In practice, husband and wife might be partners in managing each other's estates even though the properties were legally separate; Cicero speaks of inspecting a forest that belonged to his wife Terentia. In another letter, Cicero, in exile (58 BCE), expresses distress that Terentia is planning to sell a block or row (*vicus*) of houses, probably to send money to him in Greece. He urges her not to liquidate her property on his behalf.

> Dearest, you tell me that you are going to sell a row of houses. This is dreadful. What in the name of heaven, what is to happen? . . . Just this I will say: if my friends are loyal, money will not be lacking; if not, you cannot achieve results with your money. For pity's sake, pitiable that we are, don't let our unfortunate boy be utterly ruined!

Instances of elite women's financial and political efforts on behalf of their husbands are described in chapter 9.[25]

Estate management by women is attested in the Herculaneum tablets and the papyri (in both regions, the families are of decurial or lower status, town or village elites). A tablet records the sale of harvest from a female landowner's estate near Herculaneum: "Nico, slave of Herennia Tertia, has exacted a promise that 1,800 HS are duly paid in good coin on next March 1 on account of the sale of the Cadianus farm's produce. Lucius Annius Agathemerus has given a pledge." Inscriptions on amphorae (large storage jars, usually for wine or oil) show that female owners of estates exported their produce. The Roman Egyptian Arsinoe writes to her sister Sarapias that she will visit a tenant farmer herself about collecting rents that apparently belonged to Sarapias: "if indeed he will give them to me, for you should have sent me a letter addressed to him." Female estate owners also owned brick and tile production yards, using clay from their own lands; brick and tile stamps survive with female owners' names.[26]

Women of the upper social strata also bought land and real estate. At the level of the elite, huge sums are quoted. Sulla's daughter Cornelia Fausta bought one of Marius's estates on the Bay of Naples for 75,000 drachmas (denarii), which she later sold to Lucullus for 2,500,000 drachmas. Pliny the Younger tells us in detail about his sale of some of his own land near Comum to one Corellia, a sister of his mentor Corellius Rufus, who bought this land for the sum of 700,000 sesterces (HS), using as intermediary Pliny's freedman Hermes. The sale was, however, below the market price of 900,000 HS. Pliny makes it sound as if she negotiated a bargain with Hermes without involving him, though Pliny himself had discussed a sale with Corellia earlier. Shortly afterward, she offered to pay the remaining 200,000 HS, possibly because she wanted to maintain their friendship and avoid gossip in their mutual circles.[27]

The Roman world lacked the elaborate, impersonal banking systems of the modern world. Individuals who made loans on a more professional basis are termed bankers, but in a society based on patronage, many loans were based on personal ties between friends, relatives, patrons and clients, or political allies. Women participated in both systems. Thus women contracted loans—sometimes quite large sums—and received payments from bankers through these representatives and through letters. The literary sources attest that personal loans might be risky. Clodia Metelli, sister of the tribune Clodius (Cicero's enemy), loaned gold to Caelius; when she sought its return in court, Cicero, defending Caelius, attacked her sexual and personal reputation. Cicero himself received a loan from a woman named Caerellia that was later represented as an improper transaction by his enemies, supporters of Mark Antony.[28]

In the Herculaneum documents, on July 19, 69 CE, "I, Venustus, slave of Ulpia Plotina, daughter of Marcus, have written that I have received 1,000 denarii from Lucius Cominius Primus to pay off what is owed from 15,000 denarii." Lucius Cominius Primus was a businessman who made loans, some large, and who seems to have been in debt for this huge sum (60,000 HS) to Ulpia Plotina, a very wealthy woman who may have been a relative of the future emperor Trajan's wife Plotina. In another document of 59 CE, Lucius Cominius Primus made a cash loan of 1,000 HS "to Pompeia Anthis, on the authority of her guardian Gaius Vibius Erytus." It is not clear that either Ulpia Plotina or Pompeia Anthis were present at these transactions. Pliny the Younger speaks casually of borrowing money from his mother-in-law for the purchase of an estate worth 3 million HS.[29]

Other women at Pompeii received payments from the banker Lucius Caecilius Jucundus for auctioned property. In these documents, these women are represented by men, but whether the men were relatives, *institores*, or guardians is not stated. It is plausible that even if a woman had the *ius liberorum* and did not need a guardian, she still chose to employ a man as a representative. If she accompanied him to Jucundus's offices (which is not clear), he would be both witness and chaperone for propriety. A large transaction read: "I, Decimus Volcius Thallus, wrote at the request of Umbricia Ianuaria that she had received from Lucius Caecilius Iucundus 11,039 HS, less commission from her auction [of unspecified property]."[30]

Other women made loans more directly. In Roman Egypt, Didyme, daughter of Heron, made a loan of 372 drachmas (equivalent to 1,488 HS) to two women, Taorsenouphis and Tephorsais (Tebtunis, 140 CE). Other women provided smaller loans with the debtor's clothing items as collateral; at Pompeii, the lender Faustilla gave small loans as a pawnbroker, making notes on the walls of her lodging such as "Vettia, 20 denarii, interest 12 asses." Such loans are also attested in Roman Egypt; a female letter-writer instructs the recipient to recover her property, worth two minas (800 HS) from the lender Serapion, including "a dalmatic cape the color of frankincense, a dalmatic cape the color of onyx, a tunic, a white cape with a real purple border, a striped face-cloth . . ., a purple linen garment," and other household items.[31]

In general, the full history of women's roles in the Roman economy —which recent scholarship has shown to be more complex, commercial, and interconnected than was previously believed—is still unwritten, and this is even truer of women in the lower social strata, below the level of the upper *ordines* and the sub-elite middle stratum.

LOWER-STATUS WOMEN'S OCCUPATIONS: URBAN

At the sub-elite level, below the "notables" of small cities and towns but above the poorest strata, women in Roman Italy and the Latin west are best attested through Latin epitaphs, which were most popular in Rome and Italy but are found throughout the Latin-speaking western and northern provinces, in urbanized areas and in the vicinity of military camps. Most of these epitaphs attest women in family relationships as wives (*uxores, coniuges*), mothers, daughters, or slaves or freedpersons of patrons. The emphasis on women's domestic roles also appears in funerary reliefs and statues. Many of the sub-elite apparently wanted to represent women in their domestic roles, aspiring to Roman tradition and the behavior of the social elite. However, other women of the middle and lower social strata proudly represented their occupations as artisans and shopkeepers.

Some epitaphs recording women's occupations display a distinct bias toward "feminine" or what we might term "pink-collar" occupations. Of these, midwife (*obstetrix*), healer or doctor (*medica*), hairdresser or lady's maid (*ornatrix*), wet nurse or childcarer (*nutrix*), woman's attendant (*pedisequa*) are most common. Women's occupations also included fine crafts such as embroidering with gold thread and jewelry-making. The feminine of male occupational terms ending in *-arius*, such as *purpuraria*, suggests sellers of items, here seller of purple-dyed (wool or clothing). However, other women attested in epitaphs and in grave reliefs depicted themselves in less stereotypically gendered occupations: shopkeepers, sellers of market produce, a maker of shoes, or an owner of three shops related to the wool industry.[32]

Women tend not to appear in occupations that required heavy labor (such as building or blacksmithing) or extensive training or apprenticeship (other than the *medica*). It is most likely that *medica* meant "healer" as well as "doctor" as there were no formal medical schools and many medical practices were based on folk beliefs. Cato the Elder's *On Farming* and Pliny the Elder's *Natural History* record a wide range of traditional remedies using food items such as cabbage, herbs, animal products, and magic charms and amulets. However, some *medicae* were trained in Greek medicine. Other occupations in which a woman might be literate included the possible teacher Statilia Tyrannis, "pedagogue of Statilia," and the female secretary Grapte, "secretary of Egnatia Maximilla." Fields of "higher learning" such as oratory, philosophy, astronomy, mathematics, and literature were taught by men to elite boys and young men. However, female teachers would have been most socially appropriate for elite girls. Little is known about elementary teaching for girls because in elite families, educated slaves instructed the owners' children.[33]

Freedwomen seem to have engaged most vigorously in commercial activities. One employment opportunity was grain shipping. To increase grain shipments to Rome, Claudius (emperor 41–54 CE) awarded certain privileges, including the *ius liberorum*, to freedmen and freedwomen who built ships. The passage explicitly states that he awarded women the *ius quattuor liberorum*, indicating that these women were freedwomen. These women must have been wealthy and literate. Due to crop failures, storms at sea, and shipwrecks, the occupation of grain shipper was a financially risky one, though a passage of Ulpian indicates that shipowners were not also the captains of their ships. However, the successful grain shipper could make a large fortune, as did the fictional freedman Trimalchio. Other freedwomen may also have made fortunes through commerce, glimpsed in the advertisement of real estate at Pompeii: "For lease, in the estate of Julia Felix daughter of Spurius: elegant baths for respectable people, shops with upper rooms, and apartments." Julia Felix, who was illegitimate by birth, had come to own an entire apartment block in the city, recently remodeled with luxurious baths, apartments, and shops on its lower floors.[34]

When women appear as benefactors in honorific inscriptions such as that of Eumachia at Pompeii, the source of their munificence is rarely stated, but it is possible that it was commercial. It is also possible that the female "mothers" of occupational guilds (*collegia*) were something more than financial patrons, having some connection with the professions. Both these phenomena are discussed in chapter 9.[35]

If it was not purely epigraphic, several reasons are possible for the tendency of lower-status women's occupations to emphasize "feminine" categories. One is economic supply: the ideology of *pudicitia* may have motivated women of higher status to avoid professions and trades where they would encounter strange men or face the public. Women of low status, probably slaves or freedwomen in Roman Italy and poor freeborn women elsewhere, filled these occupations, facing elite disdain (see section "Lower-Status Women's Occupations: Urban"), so that "feminine" occupations provided a more respectable image. Another is economic demand for tasks that women could perform with greater propriety, tending to other women's bodies, as midwives, healers, nurses, hairdressers, maids, and attendants in public (in Latin, a *pedisequa* is a woman attendant or errand-runner). It would not be reputable for men to carry out these tasks, as Roman elite men were fearful that male slaves or freedmen would seduce/be seduced by their wives and daughters. Many of these female providers of bodily services were slave women, as will be discussed in chapter 7.

Though these occupations were practiced by slave women of wealthy households, it is not always possible to determine the legal status of people in Latin epitaphs, and freedwomen or freeborn women of lower status may also have practiced these occupations for hire for clients who couldn't afford to buy and keep slaves. Numerous contracts for wet nurses survive from Roman Egypt, showing that women charged fees for this service.[36]

STIGMATIZED OCCUPATIONS: URBAN

The Romans closely associated occupations with social status, stigmatizing certain occupations as "infamous" and disgraceful: prostitutes of either gender, managers of brothels, stage performers, gladiators, and beast fighters. Low-status commercial occupations, such as street sellers or auctioneers, were also shaming in elite eyes, and Cicero sweepingly rejected all such commercial occupations as unbefitting free (elite) men. The stigma was attached to people's public roles; the elite had no objection to carrying out commercial activities through intermediaries. So it is not surprising to find female occupations closely tied to gender roles and to honor/disgrace.[37]

The so-called *infames* (or infamous persons) included female actors and stage performers, prostitutes, and procuresses. Little is known about how actors and performers recruited new members; from comparable societies, it is likely that there were families of professional performers, and the more because Augustus's marriage legislation forbade the *infames* to marry any other citizens. The families of gladiators and beast fighters might marry, though the fighters were also recruited from those condemned to the arena. In the case of prostitution, the procurers or procuresses appear to have bought slave girls, often quite young ones, and raised them to be prostitutes.

Not among the *infames* but regarded similarly were the *tabernariae*, *hospitae*, and *popinariae*—barmaids, inn women, and cookshop women, who served hot food at the equivalent of fast-casual restaurants or street stalls. Elite men regarded the *tabernariae* and *popinariae* as borderline prostitutes, and graffiti suggest that some barmaids worked as prostitutes on the premises. The emperor Constantine (306–37 CE) added *tabernariae* and shop women to the list of persons whom persons of the senatorial order were forbidden to marry.[38]

Female sellers of market produce and other food that required cooking may also have been looked down upon by the Roman elite. These were all occupations that made women "open" to the public, degrading their sexual/gender reputation in men's eyes. For their part, the fruit and vegetable sellers and even the entertainers left behind epitaphs that present them as conventional mothers of families.[39]

Another occupation not related to prostitution but that was stigmatized was the *libitinarii*, or undertakers and corpse-handlers, who prepared the dead for funerals, carried out cremations and later burials, and disposed of unclaimed dead bodies. These activities were ritually polluting and the *libitinarii* were made to live apart (and possibly marry only each other). The *libitinarii* may have included female *praeficae* (hired mourners), who performed ritual grieving in funeral processions, wailing while wearing torn and dirty clothing and unbound hair. Women's grief was thought to be more intense than men's, but elite women might not want to show it in so theatrical a manner.[40]

Both epitaphs and tombstone reliefs tend to present a conventional view of gender roles, depicting women in the mold of the traditional *matrona* even when their marriages were not legitimate, as was the case with the wives of Roman soldiers in the first two centuries CE. The tombstone reliefs present a more tranquil and idealized portrayal of family life than is plausible at this social level. Below the elite, families might have only a few slaves (one or two on a farm, one to do heavy labor around the house) and the wife and children of the family might carry out more household tasks. Slave women or freedwomen in service occupations such as secretary, hairdresser, or attendant were at their owners' or employers' beck and call. It is also plausible that the wives of artisans and merchants, though they are depicted as domestic wives in epitaphs, assisted with the family business or took on management roles due to the household cycle.[41]

Even less is known about women in the lowest social strata, such as agricultural laborers and unskilled artisans. The traditional view of women's roles, going back to Homer, assigned them to domestic tasks within the house; the out-of-doors, whether farming or warfare, was the men's realm. This schematic view of gender roles cannot have applied in daily life to free subsistence farming families, where women probably worked in the fields when their fathers, husbands, or sons were absent on military service, as has been suggested by Nathan Rosenstein for Italy in the middle Republic. Even without warfare, the so-called household cycle—family members enter through marriage or birth, pass through childhood, adulthood, and old age, and die at unpredictable times—removed men from the family via death or illness. Poor women in agricultural households are likely to have performed the whole range of household tasks—fetching firewood and water, cleaning the house, cleaning and mending clothes, spinning and weaving, cooking, preserving food, disposing of waste, and tending the sick.[42]

Lower-status women who lived in cities, such as the tenement districts of imperial Rome and Ostia, had slightly easier lives because of urban amenities. Large cities and towns were likely to have aqueducts that brought water to public fountains, though women might still have to fetch water from these fountains to their homes; only the wealthy had water piped from the aqueducts to their urban residences, used for garden fountains and baths as well as cooking and washing. Sellers of charcoal provided fuel for iron braziers, used for both cooking and heating in urban dwellings. Bread was sold in cities, and the grain might be free (provided to citizen heads of household). Women and their families could use the public baths. They could have their clothes cleaned at fulleries (commercial laundries). In cities, residents could also purchase prepared food at the so-called *popinae* or cookshops. The children of both rural and urban lower-status households probably helped with the work from an early age.[43]

But to pay for such urban services, women needed to earn money. As aforesaid, there were a limited number of reputable occupations for women. Spinning thread may have been an option, performed as piecework for weavers, since spinning took more time and required more laborers than weaving. Wet-nursing was also an option that may have allowed a woman to preserve her sexual reputation, since wet nurses were supposed to abstain from sex (lest they become pregnant, which would cause their milk to dry up). Other impoverished women turned to the disreputable occupations discussed earlier.

LOWER-STATUS WOMEN'S OCCUPATIONS: RURAL

A depiction of a woman's household tasks on a farm is provided by Cato's *On Farming*:

> See to it that the *vilica* performs all her duties . . . She must visit the neighboring and other women very seldom, and not have them either in the house or in her part of it. She must not go out to meals, or be a gadabout . . . She must be neat herself, and keep the household neat and clean. She must clean and tidy the hearth every night before she goes to bed . . . She must keep a supply of cooked food on hand for

you and the servants. She must keep many hens and have plenty of eggs. She must have a large store of dried pears, sorbs, figs, sorbs in wine lees, preserved pears and grapes and quinces . . . All these she must store away diligently every year. She must also know how to make good flour and to grind spelt fine.

He depicts the *vilica*, a slave or freedwoman who was the wife of the *vilicus* or bailiff of a country farm that was owned by an elite owner, though independent female *vilicae* are possible. Certainly his advice to "let her fear you" is directed at controlling a slave woman, but the other aspects of managing the household were probably universal to farm households across the Mediterranean.[44]

At this level, women are likely to have engaged in spinning and weaving, the traditional domestic work of women. By the middle and Late Republic, commercial production of textiles by slave workshops was probably routine (see later in this section), but spun thread and cloth remained disproportionately expensive, as has been seen in the discussion of dowry items in chapter 4. Cato the Elder (234–149 BCE) is recorded as having paid one hundred denarii for a tunic, toga, and shoes, but Cato was notoriously frugal; a graffito from Pompeii advertises a tunic for one denarius seven asses, which is implausibly low. A woman might do some of her spinning and contract out the rest, as seen in a letter from Roman Egypt: "I sent out three minas to be spun, at an obol per stater weight in all 17 drachmas 5 obols, and I myself spun the other four minas and put into them a colored black thread." Spinning could be performed while doing other tasks such as minding children, tending the sick, or cooking, but weaving was a skilled task often performed by male artisans; in Egypt, most weavers' apprentices were boys, and only slave girls were apprenticed to weavers. The female servants of a wealthy woman are likely to have done spinning and weaving for her, as Columella fulminates and as related in a passage of the Digest on a husband's gift of wool to his wife to be spun and made into clothing by her slaves.[45]

The lowest-status women were agricultural slaves, "the most silent women of Greece and Rome," in the words of Walter Scheidel. These women are glimpsed in literary passages that depict them as pathetic (gleaners collapsing in the summer sun; the gleaners in Ruth 2:8–11, 21) or alien and barbaric, the women of foreign peoples who are so tough that they give birth in the fields and immediately resume their toil. It is not even certain how many women were agricultural slaves. Modern scholars have assumed that most slave field laborers were men, toiling on large "plantation" farms (*latifundia*) that specialized in wheat, wine, or olive production. To study the presence of women in agricultural labor, modern scholars have suggested the use of comparative evidence from more recent agrarian societies. In these, plough agriculture (where the worker directs a plough that is pulled by oxen) is typically performed by men, as is other heavy labor that requires greater strength; hoe agriculture is more often performed by women, as are other tasks that require stooping. Women might provide more of the labor in specialized agriculture such as vegetable farming, which requires hoeing, weeding, and picking, or tending and herding smaller animals. The herding of large livestock (sheep and oxen) was regarded as men's work in antiquity, especially when the herders took their flocks into the mountains to graze, a practice termed transhumance. Varro suggests providing the herders with women to help domesticate the herders (regarded as unruly and rough).[46]

It is also possible that villa agriculture in Roman Italy employed slave women as spinners and weavers, producing garments at least for the slave household and probably for the commercial market. "Industrial" textile workshops were also located in cities. The population of the city of Rome needed an immense quantity of clothing, even if most lower-status people did not buy new clothes frequently but wore them until they wore out. The wealthy were more likely to buy new clothing more often, as it was regarded as auspicious to wear new clothing for major holidays and events. The Roman army was a major market for clothing. Ulrike Roth has conjectured that the city of Rome needed 1.5 million tunics (for both men and women) a year. This rate of production demanded far more spinners of thread than weavers of cloth, approximately 10 hours of spinning for every hour of weaving; assuming that a spinner produces 100 meters an hour, a tunic required 150 hours to spin and weave. The large numbers of spinners were probably women, because spinning was regarded as exclusively a female occupation in the Greco-Roman world; the agricultural writers mention spinning and weaving as practices on villa farms. The women producing textiles on villa farms (and in urban workshops) were probably slaves, contributing to a more substantial population of female slaves than has hitherto been assumed and suggesting that the slave population was self-reproducing.[47]

In general, an entirely male adult labor force was probably insufficient to produce the necessities of life for the urban populations of Roman Italy, above all Rome itself. The cities were major commercial centers, but not producers of food or of the raw materials for textile production and other crafts. Rome imported grain, oil, and wine on a large scale from other parts of the Mediterranean as well as Italy. These products were relatively imperishable, but in the absence of refrigerated transport, fresh food (including meat, fruit, and vegetables) had to be produced and transported locally, and the women and children of smallholders and slave farms probably grew vegetables, picked fruit, and tended animals such as pigs and poultry.

LANIFICIUM: ELITE IDEOLOGY AND SERVILE REALITY

This brings us to the "performative" working of wool (*lanificium*) by elite Roman women. As we have said, by the first-century BCE, spinning wool was unlikely to be an economic necessity for elite Roman women. Woolworking nonetheless is invoked as a symbolic behavior representing women's domestic industry and virtue, appearing in tombstone epitaphs. Spinning and weaving were regarded as women's work, so defining of female gender that women were depicted with spindles or wool baskets on their tombstones or described as *lanifica*, "spinner of wool" (a domestic rather than professional description). Roman male authors believed that in the past, Roman matrons had spun and woven the garments of the household; in Livy, the legendary Lucretia stays up late at night spinning wool, a demonstration of her devotion to the household and her feminine virtue (equated with marital fidelity). The traditional Roman bride was supposed to spin and weave her bridal tunic, the *tunica recta*, and yellow veil, the *flammeum*; it is not known how many Roman brides did this. But it is unlikely that wealthy Roman women of the Late Republic and Empire still spun and wove clothing on a large scale; it also is not known if these women actually spun fine wool as a small-scale leisure activity with the same social function as embroidery in later Western (and Chinese) societies. The wide range of garments' quality and price—the diversification of clothing as a commodity—reflects the commercial production and sale of clothing. If women of the family did the spinning and weaving of clothing themselves, this would result in a much narrower range of products. The domestic ideal of *lanificium* represented a simple, self-sufficient economy in which the family produced everything they needed, including spinning and weaving, and women as guardians of the household economy were praised for thrift and for spending little outside it. This economic model was archaic by the Late Republic and imperial era. It is probable that elite women took the credit for their slave women's spinning and weaving; this type of claim is seen also in the performance of religious rites. Even women of lower status displayed allusions to woolworking on their tombstones, but it is likely that they contracted out some of the work (as seen in the discussed papyrus). Slave women were probably the main producers of spun thread and woven cloth, whether on villa farms or in urban workshops.[48]

However, Augustus invoked the symbolism of *lanificium* when he required the women of his family—his wife Livia, his sister Octavia,

Thermopolium (street restaurant) in Pompeii, Italy, first century CE (before CE 79). The openings in the counter probably held jars of food. Lower-status women may have worked in such establishments, which provided food to other lower-status people who did not have cooking facilities in their tenement homes. (Allan T. Kohl/Art Images for College Teaching)

his daughter Julia, and his granddaughter Julia the younger—to spin and weave wool. Augustus made a point of wearing their homespun fabric himself at a time when no wealthy Romans needed to do so. He thus laid claim to the notional simplicity and austerity of the earlier Republic, and asserted the virtue of his women (the Julias were later tried for adultery). Augustus promoted the ideology of the traditional *matrona* and traditional marriage, seen in his legislation against adultery and suggested by the dates of the antiquarian evidence for the traditional costumes of Roman brides and matrons. Augustus may have tried to legislate

Glass spindle whorl, Roman, ca. 1st–2nd century CE. The whorl originally held a wooden stick. The weight of the spindle whorl assisted with twisting the thread, which was wound around the stick. (The Metropolitan Museum of Art)

the wearing of the *stola*, as with the toga. This campaign may have failed to persuade elite women of the metropolis; the depictions of women wearing the *stola* are short-lived, and some women's portrait sculpture displayed their elaborate hairstyles uncovered by the *palla*. Public sculpture of women, however (discussed in chapter 9), tended to emphasize their modesty.[49]

Matrona ideology was perhaps aspirational, more often invoked by women from social groups that might be anxious about their status as Roman citizens and as reputable legally married women. Freedwomen in Roman Italy might display the tokens of *lanificium* on their tombstones. One of the most frequently cited ideological matron's epitaphs, describing her as *lanifica pia pudica frui casta domiseda*, "wool-working, pious, modest, frugal, chaste and stay-at-home," names her as Amymone "wife of Marcus," a Greek woman's name that suggests a freedwoman. On the edge of the Roman Empire, well-to-do Palmyrene women were depicted with spindles (as well as jewelry and local forms of dress) on their tombstones. Roman cavalrymen from the northwest frontier often have elaborate tombstones which show the deceased reclining (at his notional funeral banquet) and accompanied by his wife, dressed in a *palla* and long skirts, sitting in a chair with a wool basket at her side. Some of these date from the period when Roman soldiers were not permitted legal marriage;

the soldiers formed de facto marriages that aspired to the status of *iustum matrimonium*.[50]

CONCLUSION

In conclusion, this survey of women's economic roles shows that elite women's ownership of property was significant and that they were accorded many property rights not granted to women in later medieval and early modern European societies. They were probably a substantial part of all property owners. Marriage tended to consolidate property, not through the production of joint property regimes, but through inheritance to the couple's children. Despite being wealthy in their own right, elite women were not accorded political power or military or judicial authority; they participated in public life as priestesses and benefactors, discussed in chapters 9 and 10.

For sub-elite women, economic opportunities appear much more restricted given the constraint on women's roles due to the need to maintain women's *pudicitia*. Occupations that did not face the public are plausible, though poorly attested. Occupations that provided personal services to other women, thus maintaining both their own propriety and that of their clients, are better attested, from female healer and midwife (*medica, obstetrix*) to hairdresser or lady's maid (*ornatrix*) to female slaves (*lectrices*) who read aloud for their owners to a grammar teacher of girls. There is a major overlap of these occupations with slave status, discussed in chapter 7.

Women also are found in stigmatized occupations that were regarded as sexually dishonorable, such as prostitutes and entertainers. These labor markets may have been influenced by the codification of female roles in the *Lex Julia de maritandis ordinibus* and *Lex Julia de adulteriis*, separating sexually "respectable" women from sexually disreputable ones. Since the full texts of these laws do not survive, it is more likely that prevailing gender roles shaped both women's labor markets and the *Leges Juliae*.

In the lowest social strata, the least well-attested women of all toiled as poor freehold farmers and as agricultural slaves or "sweatshop" textile producers. Though invisible, their labor (and that of their children) helped to feed and clothe the urban populations of Rome and Italy, which depended on the importation of grain, oil, and wine and the regional production of fresh food and textiles. Much of what is indicated for the economic life of lower-status women of uncertain status pertains also to slave women, who are discussed in chapter 7.

NOTES

1. On a substantial proportion of Roman property owners, 20 percent to a third, being female, see Richard P. Saller, "Household and gender," in *The Cambridge Economic History of the Greco-Roman World* (Cambridge, 2007), ed. Walter Scheidel, Ian Morris, and Richard Saller, 87–112, 97; "The Roman family as productive unit," in *Companion to Families in the Greek and Roman Worlds* (Malden, MA, 2011), ed. Beryl Rawson, 116–28, 120; cf. Emily A. Hemelrijk, *Hidden Lives, Public Personae: Women and Civic Life in the Roman West* (Oxford, 2015), 23–24. On separate property, see Jo-Ann Shelton, *The Women of Pliny's* Letters (London, 2013), 58–59.

2. Gaius *Institutes* 1.48.

3. *On patria potestas*, see Jane F. Gardner, *Women in Roman Law and Society* (London, 1986), 5, 71–72; Judith Evans-Grubbs, *Women and the Law in the Roman Empire: A Sourcebook on Marriage, Divorce, and Widowhood* (London, 2002), 20–21; Richard P. Saller, *Patriarchy, Property, and Death in the Roman Family* (Cambridge, 1994), 102–32. Daube quoted in Saller, *Patriarchy*, 119.

4. D. 15.1.27 (Gaius); Gardner, *Women*, 9–10.

5. Plin. *Ep.* 5.6.6.

6. On Tifernum Tiberinum and regional variations, see Robert Sallares, *Malaria and Rome: A History of Malaria in Ancient Italy* (Oxford, 2002), 269–71. On simulated populations and when children lost fathers, see Saller, *Patriarchy*, 12–69; Hemelrijk, *Hidden Lives*, 23–24. By age fifteen, one-third of women may have lost their fathers; by age twenty-five, 49–61 percent of women had done so.

7. On *Lex Voconia*, see Gardner, *Women*, 76–77, 170–75; Susan Treggiari, *Roman Marriage: Iusti Coniuges from the Time of Cicero to the Time of Ulpian* (Oxford, 1991), 383. On reduction of woman's inheritance by dowry, see Gardner, *Women*, 163–64, 179–81. On smaller inheritances, see Treggiari, *Marriage*, 385–87; Edward Champlin, *Final Judgments: Duty and Emotion in Roman Wills, 200 B.C.–A.D. 250* (Berkeley, CA, 1991), 117; Shelton, *Women*, 245, e.g., Plin. *Ep.* 7.24. On not reduced, see Saller, *Patriarchy*, 204–24; Saller, "Household," 97. On one-third, see Saller, "Household," 97 n. 53.

8. On *tutela mulierum*, see Mary R. Lefkowitz and Maureen B. Fant, *Women's Life in Greece and Rome: A Source Book in Translation*, 4th ed. (Baltimore, MD, 2016), nos. 135–57; Gardner, *Women*, 14–22; Evans-Grubbs, *Women*, 23–47; Saller, "Household," 97. Contrast with *tutela* of underage children, Saller, *Patriarchy*, 181–203. Lin Foxhall, *Studying Gender in Classical Antiquity* (Cambridge, 2013), 93, is incorrect in saying that "women could not make wills."

9. E.g., see *L'Année Epigraphique* 2006, 303 = *Tabulae Herculanenses* 13 = Alison E. Cooley and M. G. L. Cooley, *Pompeii and Herculaneum: A Sourcebook* (London, 2014), no. G12; cf. *P. Oxy.* IV 720 = Jane Rowlandson, *Women and Society in Greek and Roman Egypt: A Sourcebook* (Cambridge, 1998), no. 140 (247 CE) in which Aurelia Ammonarion requests the prefect of Egypt to appoint as her guardian Aurelius Ploutammon.

10. On *tutela impuberum* (guardianship of minors), Saller, *Patriarchy*, 181–203.

11. Gaius *Institutes* 1.145, 1.194; Paulus *Sententiae* 4.9; Dio 55.2; Gardner, *Women*, 21; Evans-Grubbs, *Women*, 37–42; Treggiari, *Marriage*, 66–71; Shelton, *Women*, 20–23. On Aurelia Thaisous, see *P. Oxy.* XII 1467 = Rowlandson no. 142 = Evans-Grubbs, 39 = *Women's Life*, no. 174.

12. On Vestals, see Dio 56.10.2; on Pliny and Suetonius, Plin. *Ep.* 10.2, 10.94–5, cf. 2.13; on wife, Martial 2.92.

13. *Rules of Ulpian* 15.2, 16.1a; Paulus *Sententiae* 4.9; D. 25.4.1.10 Ulpian; Treggiari, *Marriage*, 69–71; Thomas A. J. McGinn, *Prostitution, Sexuality, and the Law in Ancient Rome* (Oxford, 1998), 73, 82. On Malaga, see Treggiari, *Marriage*, 67. Tim G. Parkin, *Demography and Roman Society* (Baltimore, MD, 1992), 116–18, is not reliable on *tutela* (passages cited are on *tutela* of children). On widows, see Evans-Grubbs, *Women*, 261–62.

14. On declarations, see *L'Année Epigraphique* 2006, 306 = *Tabulae Herculanenses* 5 + 99 = *Pompeii and Herculaneum*, no. G1. Cf. *C. Pap. Lat.* 156 = Rowlandson, no. 70 (Alexandria, 148 CE); *P. Mich.* III 169 = Rowlandson, no. 71 (Karanis, 145 CE), birth of twin sons with unknown father to Roman citizen mother; *P. Petaus* 2 = Rowlandson, no. 72. On the problem of documentation, see Jane F. Gardner, "Proofs of status in the Roman world," *Bulletin of the Institute of Classical Studies* 33 (1986), 1–14.

15. D. 50.16.135 Ulpian; cf. D. 50.16.153; D.50.16.129 Paulus; D. 50.16.132 vs. 50.16.141.

16. Gaius *Institutes* 1.144, 1.190; Gardner, *Women*, 16–17; Evans-Grubbs, *Women*, 46–48, 51–52; Suzanne Dixon, *Reading Roman Women: Sources, Genres, and Real Life* (London, 2001), 73–88. On women's lack of legal knowledge, see D. 1.16.9.5; 2.8.8.2; 2.13.1.5; 22.6.9.pr; 50.17.110.4. On women in court, see D. 3.1.1.5.

17. Generic terms (male includes female, but not female male), e.g., D. 31.45.pr. The generic term for "man" in Latin is *homo* (pl. *homines*); the pronoun *quis* (someone) is also used. The term *mulier* (woman) and related terms such as *uxor* (wife) or *ancilla* (slave woman) are rare outside the family law chapters.

18. On surety, see the *SC Velleianum*, D. 16.1; Gardner, *Women*, 75–76, 152; Evans-Grubbs, *Women*, 152; Treggiari, *Marriage*, 378–79. On *institores*, see Saller, "Household," 98. Elite women's names appear in property markers denoting the owner, such as brick stamps or inscriptions on lead pipes; some record empresses, such as Plotina, Matidia, and Sabina, *CIL* XV 7305–6, 7313a, 7377, 7398a, 7433, 7435 = *Women's Life*, no. 350. Elite women in public roles are discussed in chapter 9.

19. Ramsay MacMullen, "Women in public in the Roman Empire," in *Changes in the Roman Empire: Essays in the Ordinary* (Princeton, NJ, 1990), ed. Ramsay MacMullen, 162–68 at 163–64; Ulpian, D. 3.5.3.1.

20. Few women could afford to be *univirae*; Shelton, *Women*, 40, 51.

21. On *tutela impuberum*, see Gardner, *Women*, 146–49, 151; Saller, *Patriarchy*, 181–203; Beryl Rawson, *Children and Childhood in Roman Italy* (Oxford, 2003), 250–51; *tutela impuberum* is "a man's duty," Gaius D. 26.1.16; cf. *Codex Iustinianus* 2.12.18 (Alexander Severus). On conflict, see Evans-Grubbs, *Women*, 236–47; and on regional custom, see Evans-Grubbs, *Women*, 248–60. On guardianship, also see Judith Evans-Grubbs, "Promoting *pietas* through Roman law," in Rawson, *Companion to Families*, 377–92.

22. On "disliked being intestate," see Treggiari, *Marriage*, 381. On inheritance between spouses, see Gardner, *Women*, 192–97; Treggiari, *Marriage*, 326–27, 379–96. On intestate inheritance, see Jane F. Gardner, "Roman 'horror' of intestacy?" in Rawson, *Companion to Families*, 361–76.

23. On social life, chapter 8, see sections "Introduction" and "Stereotypes of Domestic Seclusion and *Otium*."

24. Jerome *Against Helvidius* 20; discussed, Treggiari, *Roman Marriage*, 425–26.

25. Cic. *Fam.* 5.6.2; Plin. *Ep.* 8.2; Cic. *Att.* 2.4.5; *Fam.* 14.1.5; Shelton, *Women*, 58–62.

26. On Nico, see *L'Année Epigraphique* 1999, 449 = *Tabulae Herculanenses* 12 = *Pompeii and Herculaneum*, no. H18 = Hemelrijk, *Women and Society*, no. 3.127. On amphorae, see Hemelrijk, *Women and Society*, no. 3.73–76. On Arsinoe, see *P. Oxy.* XXXIII 2680 = Rowlandson, no. 172. On bricks and tiles, Laura K. McClure, *Women in Classical Antiquity: From Birth to Death* (Hoboken, NJ, 2019), 252.

27. Cornelia, Plut. *Marius* 34.2; Corellia, Plin. *Ep.* 7.11, 14; Shelton, *Women*, 201–3.

28. Cic. *Pro Caelio* 13.30–1; *Att.* 12.51.3; Dio 46.18.4. On banking and business, see Jean Andreau, *Banking and Business in the Roman World* (Cambridge, 1999). On the risk to women in loans, see Dixon, *Reading*, 70–71, 93–98, and on Clodia 133–57.

29. *L'Année Epigraphique* 1993, 461 = *Tab. Herc.* 52 + 90,5 = *Pompeii and Herculaneum*, no. H65 = Hemelrijk, *Women and Society*, no. 3.133; *L'Année Epigraphique* 1993, 462a = *Tab. Herc.* 70 + 71 = *Pompeii and Herculaneum*, no. H66; Plin. *Ep.* 3.19.8–9.

30. On Umbricia Ianuaria, see *CIL* IV 3340.25 = *Pompeii and Herculaneum*, no. H110 = Hemelrijk, *Women and Society*, no. 3.132. Cf. *CIL* IV 3340.22 = *Pompeii and Herculaneum*, no. H107 (to Histria Ichimas, 6456 1/2 HS); *CIL* IV 3340.23 = *Pompeii and Herculaneum*, no. 108 (to Umbricia Antiochis, 645 HS minus fees); *CIL* IV 3340.24 = *Pompeii and Herculaneum*, no. H109 (to Umbricia Antiochis, 6,252 HS for sale of a slave); *CIL* IV 3340.40 = *Pompeii and Herculaneum*, no. H111 (to Tullia Lampyris, 8560 HS).

31. On Didyme, see *P. Kron.* 17 = Rowlandson, no. 103. Faustilla, *CIL* IV 4528 = *Pompeii and Herculaneum*, no. H61 = Hemelrijk, *Women and Society*, no. 3.134. Letter: *P. Oxy.* 1 114 = Rowlandson, no. 191.

32. On occupations, see Sandra R. Joshel, *Work, Identity, and Legal Status at Rome: A Study of the Occupational Inscriptions* (Norman, OK, 1992), 173–82 (list of occupational titles); Gardner, *Women*, 233–53; Treggiari, *Marriage*, 374–79; "Jobs in the household of Livia," *Papers of the British School at Rome* 43 (1975), 48–77; Eve D'Ambra, *Roman Women* (Cambridge, 2007), 94–105. On bias in occupational titles, see Foxhall, *Studying Gender*, 97; Saller, "Household," 106; "Productive unit," 122–23. A sample of occupations appears in *Women's Life*, nos. 350–51, 400–402, 407; Hemelrijk, *Women and Society*, nos. 3.1–70. Less gendered commercial and artisan occupations: Miriam J. Groen-Vallinga, "'Desperate' housewives? The adaptive family economy and female participation in the Roman urban labour market," in *Women and the Roman City in the Latin West* (Leiden, 2013), ed. Emily A. Hemelrijk and Greg Woolf, 295–312; Claire Holleran, "Women and retail in Roman Italy," in Hemelrijk and Woolf, *Women*, 313–30.

33. On *medicae*, see *Women's Life*, nos. 464–67, 467; Hemelrijk, *Women and Society*, nos. 3.1–8; Holt Parker, "Women and medicine," in *A Companion to Women in the Ancient World* (Malden, MA, 2012), ed. Sharon L. James and Sheila Dillon, 107–24; Rebecca Flemming, "Gendering medical provision in the cities of the Roman west," in Hemelrijk and Woolf, *Women*, 271–93. On educators, Statilia Tyrannis, *CIL* VI 6331; Grapte, *CIL* VI 9523 = *ILS* 7397; both = *Women's Life*, no. 419. On apprenticeship, see Saller, "Household," 106.

34. On shipping, see Suet. *Claudius* 18–19.1. On Julia Felix, see *CIL* IV 1136 = *ILS* 5723 = *Pompeii and Herculaneum*, no. H73 = Hemelrijk, *Women and Society*, no. 3.125. On Julia Felix's property, see Eve D'Ambra, "Women on the Bay of Naples," in *Companion to Women*, 400–13, 405–9.

35. On the grain trade, see Peter Temin, *The Roman Market Economy* (Princeton, NJ, 2013), 32–35. On ship owner versus captain, see D. 14.1.1.1; 14.1.1.16 (Ulpian). *Women's Life*, no. 347, lists the epitaph *CIL* X 1030 = *ILS* 6373 as a female shipper, but this seems only based on the iconography; *CIL* XV 8166 and *IG* XIV 2412.1 = *Women's Life*, no. 351, a bronze tag from an oil amphora, labeled "Of Coelia Mascellina," attests a woman exporting olive oil from Baetica (Spain).

36. E.g., Rowlandson, no. 213 (13 BCE). However, this and other such contracts are for nursing slave foundlings, as it was cheaper to raise a child slave than to buy an adult.

37. Cic. *On Duties* 1.150–1. On the *infames*, Catherine Edwards, "Unspeakable professions: Public performers and prostitution in ancient Rome," in *Roman Sexualities* (Princeton, NJ, 1997), ed. Judith P. Hallett and Marilyn B. Skinner, 66–95; McGinn, *Prostitution*, 44–69 (legal disabilities of); *The Economy of Prostitution in the Roman World: A Study of Social History & the Brothel* (Ann Arbor, MI, 2004).

38. On *tabernariae* and related occupations equated with prostitutes, McGinn, *Economy*, 16–19, 31, 80; on Constantine, *Theodosian Code* 4.6.3. On *tabernariae* in general, Holleran, "Women and retail," 319–20.

39. Epitaphs: e.g., Hemelrijk, *Women and Society*, nos. 3.96–99 (inn keepers).

40. On *libitinarii*, see *L'Année Epigraphique* 1971, 88 = *Roman Social History*, no. 5.13 (Puteoli).

41. Alexandra Croom, *Running the Roman Home* (Stroud, 2011), 56–58.

42. On the household cycle, see Tim G. Parkin, "The Roman life course and the family," in Rawson, *Companion to Families*, 276–90. On domestic stereotype, see Treggiari, *Roman Marriage*, 375. On the problem of female agricultural labor, see Walter Scheidel, "The most silent women of Greece and Rome: Rural labour and women's life in the ancient world (I)," *Greece & Rome* 42 (1995), 202–17; "The most silent women of Greece and Rome: Rural labour and women's life in the ancient world (II)," *Greece & Rome* 43.1 (1996), 1–10; Ulrike Roth, *Thinking Tools: Agricultural Slavery between Evidence and Models*, BICS Supplement no. 92 (London, 2007); Saller, "Household," 103; "Productive unit," 121; Foxhall, *Studying Gender*, 99.

43. Croom, *Roman Home*, 17–18, 21, 35, 42–43, 52–57, 61–72, 101–8. On child labor, see Saller, "Household," 107–10; cf. Varro *On Farming* 1.17.2.

44. Cato *On Farming* 143. On the *vilica*, see Ulrike Roth, "Inscribed meaning: The *vilica* and the villa economy," *Papers of the British School at Rome* 72 (2004), 101–24; Saller, "Productive unit," 121–22.

45. Plut. *Cato Maior* 4.3. "For a tunic, 1 denarius 7 asses," *CIL* IV 10664 = *Pompeii and Herculaneum*, no. H28 too low for a new purchase, may represent cleaning or mending. On apprenticed girls, see *Stud. Pal.* XXII 40 = Rowlandson, no. 204 (140 CE). Letter: *P. Oxy.* XXXI 2593 = Rowlandson, no. 205. On spinning by slave women, see D. 24.1.31.pr.–1 (Pomponius). On spinning in general, see Croom, *Roman Home*, 56–60; Columella *On Farming* 12.3.6–7.

46. Scheidel, "Silent women" (1995), 204; on shepherds, see Scheidel "Silent women" (1996), 5; Roth, *Thinking Tools*, 19–20. Varro *On Farming* 2.1.26, 2.10.1, 61.

47. Roth, *Thinking Tools*, 21 and n. 79; on 100 meters, see ibid., 81; and on 150 hours to produce, see ibid., 81–82; Columella *On Farming* 1.8.19.

48. On the ideology, see Daniela Cottica, "Spinning in the Roman world: From everyday craft to metaphor of destiny," in *Ancient Textiles: Production, Craft, and Society* (Oxford, 2007), ed. Carole Gillis and Marie-Louise Nosch, 220–28; Lena Larsson Lovén, "Wool work as a gender symbol in ancient Rome, Roman textiles and ancient sources," in Gillis and Nosch, *Ancient Textiles*, 229–36. On Lucretia, see Livy 1.57.4–6. On contemporary women not spinning, see Columella, *On Farming* 12.pr.9.

49. On spinning, see Suet. *Augustus* 74; on toga, see *ibid.* 44.2. On Augustus, see Lovén, "Wool work," 233; Judith Lynn Sebesta, "Women's costume

and feminine civic morality in Augustan Rome," in *Gender and the Body in the Ancient Mediterranean* (Oxford, 1998), ed. Maria Wyke, 105–17; Beth Severy, *Augustus and the Family at the Birth of the Roman Empire* (London, 2003), 137; McGinn, *Prostitution*, 154, 157; and Andrew B. Gallia, "The Vestal habit," *Classical Philology* 109.3 (2014), 222–40, 230–31 on Tertullian *De pallio* 4.9 (Caecina Severus urged the Senate to force matrons to return to wearing the *stola*; the augur Lentulus moved a law that women not wearing the *stola* were to be punished for *stuprum*).

50. On Amymone, see *CIL* VI 11602 = *ILS* 8402 = Hemelrijk, *Women and Society*, no. 1.4. On Palmyra, see Cottica, "Spinning," 223–24.

7

SLAVERY AND MANUMISSION

INTRODUCTION

A substantial number of women in the Roman world—the exact proportion may never be known—were slaves (*servae* or *ancillae*). Their symbolic status is illustrated in the ancient Roman festival of the *Matralia*, held at Rome on June 11, in which freeborn *matronae* (married women) invited an *ancilla* into the temple of Mater Matuta, a goddess of fertility. The *matronae* then drove the *ancilla* out of the temple with harsh words and blows. The meaning of this ritual (as with many archaic Roman festivals) is disputed, but it illustrates a stark and real division between freeborn Roman women and slave women. In the Roman social hierarchy and even among slaves themselves, slave women occupied the lowest level. They are almost invisible as rural workers, though they must have contributed to agricultural labor, the textile economy, and the slave supply. Wealthy urban households preferred male slaves in most occupations; female slaves performed occupations that provided personal services to the women of the owner's family. In low-income households, a female slave may have been regarded as a lower-cost, all-purpose servant. In contrast with *matronae*, slave women were not permitted bodily integrity, whether immunity to corporal punishment or the sexual inviolability termed *pudicitia*. The history of slave women is not entirely dismal. Some slave women obtained their freedom and appear in Latin inscriptions and reliefs as members of free families and as an integral part of the city of Rome's working-class community. In this chapter, the term "owner" has been used in preference to "master" and "mistress" except in direct or paraphrased quotations from ancient sources.[1]

SLAVERY IN THE ROMAN WORLD

As introduction, this section gives an overview of general practices of slavery in classical antiquity. Ancient Greece and Rome were two of world history's true slave societies, in which economic production depended on slave labor and the social hierarchy was shaped by slavery. Other slave societies existed in the New World from ca. 1500 CE, including the American South from colonial times to after the American Civil War (1861–65), the Caribbean, and Latin America. New World slavery was highly racialized. Most New World slaves were Black people brought from sub-Saharan Africa. Though substantial racial mixing took place with white settlers and Native Americans, the doctrine of racialized slavery, especially in the United States, was that any Black ancestry made the descendant also Black. This color bar impeded escape for runaway African slaves and prevented the assimilation of freed slaves. The rate of manumission was also very low. White American colonists' attitudes and beliefs about race further exaggerated the perceived differences between owners and slaves and discouraged assimilation, leaving a legacy of racism that still exists today.

The racialized slavery of the New World did not exist to any comparable degree in the ancient Mediterranean world. Roman slaves were prisoners of war, taken captive from defeated peoples, starting with the early Romans' own Italian neighbors and in the later Republic and early Empire, including Carthaginians, Spanish, Greeks, Syrians, Gauls, Germans, Britons, Jews, and Dacians. The ethnic origins of slaves were declared when they were sold. People from North Africa, Egypt, and rarely sub-Saharan Africans (encountered as traders) were not preferentially enslaved. Other slaves in the Roman world were enslaved by bandits, pirates, and slave traders or were the result of natural reproduction.

However, Greek and Roman slavery, in particular its legal institutions and philosophical arguments in favor of slavery, strongly influenced New World slavery. Many of the forms of New World slavery based on race existed in the Roman world without an emphasis on race, including the "social death" of slaves, the treatment of slaves as property, the absolute vulnerability of slaves' bodies, and the sexual exploitation of female slaves.[2]

SLAVERY WITHOUT RACE?

The physical differences between Roman slave owners and slaves appear to have been regarded as trivial. This made flight easier for Roman slaves, who could merge into the free population unless their owners had marked them in some way with branding, tattoos, or slave collars (discussed in section "The Reality of Roman Slavery"). Elite freeborn individuals were able to escape from crises wearing slaves' clothing, a trope that to be plausible depended on a lack of physical difference. During the triumviral proscriptions, loyal slaves exchanged clothing with their owners so the owners could escape into exile. In the civil war and Gallic revolt of 69–70 CE, army officers escaped from mutinies and routs by donning slaves' clothing. As we have seen in chapter 5, the clothing of slaves resembled those of poor free Romans; only the male citizen's toga and the matron's *stola* (long overdress) were garments forbidden to slaves. On the other hand, the disguises might not withstand close inspection, as many slaves bore the physical marks of toil, corporal punishment, and identifying tattoos and brands (see section "The Reality of Roman Slavery"), as well as "servile" mannerisms that differentiated them from owners.[3]

Trivial physical differences also gave rise to legal conflicts over status when a free person was claimed by another to be a slave or vice versa. Free people might be kidnapped by bandits and enslaved, described in section "The Reality of Roman Slavery." In short, a male or female slave in the Roman world might be physically indistinguishable from his or her owners, and the owners relied on other features of slavery (such as legal status and cruel punishments) to emphasize the divide between owners and slaves. Manumission of Roman slaves was relatively common, and a large population of freedpersons—former slaves—developed, especially in Roman Italy. Freedpersons still had a legally distinct and subordinate status, but were Roman citizens. In a generation or two, the children of freedpersons disappeared into the free population.

THE REALITY OF ROMAN SLAVERY

This is not to deny the brutality of Roman slavery. Slave prisoners of war were taken by force from their homelands, chained, and sold to slave traders, who might transport them across long distances and separate family members from each other. Celebrating recent conquests, Roman triumphal art depicted abject captives in chains as proof of Roman victory over "barbarian" peoples. Roman militarism did not accept defeat, and peoples who had been defeated by the Romans were regarded as deserving their fate.[4]

Other slaves were enslaved by bandits or pirates, who kidnapped free travelers and sold them to slave traders. Being enslaved by bandits or pirates was both a suspenseful plot twist in Greco-Roman fiction and a very real danger for travelers in remote areas and even in Italy: both Cicero and Pliny the Younger knew of acquaintances who had disappeared in this way. The young Julius Caesar, traveling to take up a junior office in Asia, was captured by pirates, negotiated his freedom, and took his revenge on them.[5]

A citizen who was enslaved underwent what scholar Orlando Patterson has termed "social death." In Roman law, he or she underwent a legal death, *capitis deminutio maxima*, losing citizenship, associated rights, and other legal bonds and relationships, including marriage, property ownership, and (for a man) *patria potestas* over his children. Noncitizens (who were most often enslaved as captives of war) did not have these rights to begin with. Citizens who were enslaved by the enemy and won back to the Roman Empire were able to restore their rights, property ownership, and obligations in a process termed *postliminium*. Citizens wrongly enslaved within the empire also could use a procedure, *vindicatio in libertatem*, to claim their free status.[6]

Slaves were treated as objects and as property according to Roman law. The linguist and agricultural writer Varro calls slaves *instrumentum vocale*, "speaking equipment" grouped with animals and with the *instrumentum* or physical equipment of Roman farms. Slaves were legally *res mancipi*, a form of property (along with houses, land in Italy, and livestock) sold by mancipation, a legal procedure with ancient roots. The prices of slaves ranged widely, depending on skills, age, and gender (discussed in this section "The Reality of Roman Slavery"), but were probably on the same order as livestock. Slaves were included in women's dowries alongside land, clothing, and household implements. They were treated as collateral for the purpose of securing a loan, where, if the debtor defaulted on repayment, their slaves, put up as surety on the loan, became the creditor's property. Slaves might even be leased, the renter paying the owner for a short period of service. In Roman wills, slaves might find themselves manumitted—or legated as estate property, even divided between heirs or legatees (in practice, the slave would work for one or the other legatee or they would share his labor). In law, slaves had no family and could not own property.[7]

When slaves were sold, the seller was required to declare any physical defects, with the addition that defects might also be mental, such as insanity, obstinacy, or a tendency to run away. The process of slave sale at auction was highly demeaning. Slaves were exhibited unclothed so that any physical defects could be seen and were inspected closely. Slave dealers, furthermore, had a bad reputation (as with today's used-car salesmen) for hiding defects in the merchandise, dyeing slaves' hair, feeding them more to disguise malnutrition, and applying plasters to hide scars and brands. Some of the Roman elite's contempt for slaves arose from the slaves' having been exhibited under such degrading conditions.[8]

However, Roman slavery itself displayed a de facto hierarchy, in which some slaves were relatively privileged, educated, given positions of authority, and became wealthy. Educated slaves who spoke Greek (the common language of the Eastern Mediterranean by the third century BCE, spoken by educated Romans as well as Latin) might serve as wealthy Romans' accountants and secretaries, their children's caretakers and instructors, and their wives' hairdressers and maids. Such high-status household slaves had close contact with their owners and a greater likelihood of manumission. Male slaves of the emperor, belonging to the imperial household or *familia Caesaris*, might have important responsibilities in the imperial administration, particularly in the treasury. These privileged slaves were skilled professionals as well as property. They did not themselves own property, but were permitted a *peculium*, a fund that they could manage (the sons and daughters of a paterfamilias also were allowed *peculium*). Wealthy slaves even had sub-slaves of their own, so-called *vicarii*.[9]

In contrast, slaves from societies that were less developed than Greek and Roman or Near Eastern civilizations, and who knew neither Greek nor Latin, were likely to become low-status servants, factory workers, or field hands, employed in menial labor and with little chance of freedom. Cicero spoke contemptuously of enslaved Britons (captured in Julius Caesar's brief foray into Britain) as unlikely to be literate or educated in Latin or Greek. Britain did not become part of the Roman Empire until 43 CE.[10]

The prices of unspecialized slaves were very substantial for lower-income Romans. In a survey of data from Roman Egypt and other areas of the Empire, the mean price of slaves aged six to fifteen was 880 drachmas (equivalent to denarii, or 3,520 sesterces [HS]). The mean price of slaves aged sixteen to twenty-five was 1,000–1,220 drachmas or 4,000–4,880 HS; the median price (to rule out skewing by individual high prices) was 980–1,100 drachmas or 3,920–4,400 HS. The cost of a slave was prohibitive for lower-status men, representing several years' wages. A first-century CE legionary soldier (from Augustus to Domitian) earned 900 HS a year; the soldiers owning a slave may have saved for several years or drawn upon family money. Child slaves were substantially cheaper, as low as 300 denarii or 1,200 HS.[11]

For all slaves, however, the owners' bigotry against them persisted. This prejudice was not racially based, but it could be ethnocentric: despite admiring classical Greek literature and philosophy, many Romans looked down on the present-day Greeks, whom they had conquered, as a "servile" people. Many Romans also despised slaves because they were slaves, degraded by their inferior position in life. This contempt arose from the fact that owners had power of life and death over slaves and could humiliate them and inflict corporal punishment, violating their physical integrity in ways that free citizens were in most cases exempt from. In the Republic, the right of *provocatio* protected free citizens' bodies from assault by magistrates, and, except for treason or parricide, freeborn citizens' most severe capital punishment was exile rather than death. In the Principate, treason against the emperor was exceptional and might be punished with death, but members of the senatorial and equestrian orders were still usually punished with exile.[12]

In contrast, slaves received both brutal corporal punishment and exacerbated death penalties. Roman fathers probably did not beat their children, reserving violent corporal punishment (explicitly *verbera*, beatings) for their slaves. Extreme forms of capital punishment, such as crucifixion, were usually reserved for slaves, though after the first century CE, low-status freeborn criminals increasingly also received severe punishments such as condemnation to the mines and being thrown to wild beasts in the arena. Slaves were answerable for any misdeed with their bodies, the reason why many elite slaves and freedmen were employed in financial administration in the Roman Empire.[13]

The Roman satirist Juvenal depicted women as particularly cruel to slaves, taking out their resentment of their husbands on them.

If her husband slept with his back turned last night, the wool-girl (or secretary: *libraria*) has had it, and the hairdressers must remove their tunics, and the Liburnian slave [litter-bearer] is told he is late and has to pay for someone else's sleep. One breaks the canes, another reddens under the whip, another under the strap.

The wife "keeps torturers on retainer." Juvenal is interested more in the viciousness of the wife to her husband rather than to her slaves; the passage is based on the elite male belief that women were more anger-prone and irrational than men. Nonetheless, there was a real association of torturers and corpse-handlers at Puteoli in Italy that removed slaves for corporal punishment and execution. Female heads of household, in managing their slave staff, also were responsible for punishing them, just as with male owners.[14]

Coercion manifested in brutal ways of discouraging flight. Shackles were often used, particularly when transporting slaves. Iron collars survive from Roman sites with the inscription *tene me quia fugio*, "restrain me, I am a runaway." This inscription was even abbreviated to TMQF, and the collar might have a plaque that said, "Return me to so-and-so." It is not likely that all slaves (particularly elite slaves) wore these collars, but more collars probably existed than have been found, because metal tended to be reused. Other slaves were tattooed or branded to deter flight. The tattooing is parodied in Petronius's *Satyrica*, where the two main characters disguise themselves by painting the runaway-slave inscription over their entire faces. The risk was high that if unmarked slaves escaped, they would merge into the free population and be untraceable because they were not racially different from the free population. Roman owners believed that slaves could be distinguished by the whip scars on their backs, but not all could.[15]

The ownership of slaves was also highly stratified and reflected the steep social pyramid of Roman society. Imperial households and wealthy senators might have hundreds of slaves, many in highly specialized occupations, a display of their owners' wealth and status. These owners provided *columbaria* (funerary sites housing multiple urns) for these slaves which recorded their names and occupations. Well-to-do households might have several dozen slaves. Sub-elite families may have had a few slaves for essential domestic work, farm work (if the owners resided in a town), and child minding. A Roman soldier might have a slave or two.[16]

The scale of ownership is also shown by the *Lex Fufia Caninia* of 2 BCE, which restricted manumission in wills. An owner with two to ten slaves might free up to half his slaves; an owner with ten to thirty slaves might free up to one-third; an owner with thirty to one hundred slaves might free up to one-fourth; and an owner with one hundred to five hundred slaves might free up to one-fifth. Owners with more than five hundred slaves might not free more than one hundred at a time.[17]

WOMEN AS SLAVES

So far, we have spoken of slaves in the mass and as generically male, and most of these features apply to female slaves as well. The Romans celebrated a holiday called *Compitalia*, the crossroads festival, during which they hung woolen decorations on crossroads shrines: a woolen doll for each free member of the household, and a woolen ball for each slave, not differentiating male and female slaves, suggesting the non-gendered and fungible nature of slaves as undifferentiated, easily replaced bodies.[18]

But female slavery in the Roman world was in some ways starkly differentiated from male slavery. There may have been fewer female slaves altogether in the total slave population, though statistics are lacking. Female slaves' occupations and opportunities for promotion and wealth accumulation were much more limited than those of male slaves. Female slaves' chances of manumission were more dependent upon their owners. Female slaves were sexualized: used against their will as sexual partners, they lacked the *pudicitia* or "sexual honor" of freeborn Roman women, a contrast seen in the vignette of the *Matralia* that opened this chapter. Female slaves were probably used in slave-breeding, producing more slaves for their owners. After manumission, freedwomen were still inferior to freeborn women in Roman law.

THE POPULATION OF FEMALE SLAVES

Estimating the population of female slaves in the Roman world is tied to a scholarly debate over the sources of Roman slaves. It has been estimated that slaves comprised about 10 percent of the total population of the Roman Empire, but as much as 1–1.5 million out of 6 million in Roman Italy. Actual statistics on the proportion of female slaves are lacking, but the female slave population was probably below that needed to replace the slave population entirely through natural reproduction. The debate on this topic has focused on the sources of slaves. As remarked earlier, slaves were obtained from conquest (and kidnapping by bandits and pirates) and from slave reproduction (children born from slave mothers). Scholarship previously emphasized that the slave supply was obtained from conquest during the Roman Republic, shifting to slave reproduction during the Principate, as sources from conquest dwindled. However, this is a false dichotomy, as the historian Keith R. Bradley has emphasized. Some slave reproduction must have occurred during the Republic, when the enslavement of female captives was also routine. Cato and Varro, writing about slave management on rural farms during the last two centuries of the Republic, indicate that slave-worked farms had some women. Furthermore, in the Principate captives continued to be acquired on a large scale from major campaigns such as the conquest of Britain in 43 CE, the Jewish War of 66–70, and the emperor Trajan's conquest of Dacia (modern Romania). It is likely that the army acquired captives on a lesser scale in minor border conflicts.[19]

There must have been a substantial number of female slaves to perform "domestic" tasks and replenish the slave population. Spinning, discussed later in this section, was regarded as "women's work" in the Roman world, and it is unlikely that male slaves spun. Female slaves were also needed for the production of more slaves. Columella states that he rewarded his slave women for producing children, giving time off to women who gave birth to three children and freedom to those who gave birth to more than three. He does not say that he selected their partners, as actual "breeding" would require, but all three agricultural writers thought that male slaves worked harder if they had access to female slaves. Cato the Elder even charged his male slaves money for access to female slaves. Slaves, particularly more privileged slaves, may have been allowed to form de facto marriages and have children. The children of slave mothers were born as slaves, their status following from their mother, and the property of their owners, as the Roman jurists agreed. Owners might sell slave children once they were old enough to work (at six or seven years) and if their labor was not needed on the owner's own estates. The threat of breaking up slave families was used to discipline slaves. However, keeping "home-bred" slaves in the household also benefited the owners as a cheaper source of slaves than buying them on the market. "Home-bred" slaves were also preferred by their owners as they had only known slavery and were not traumatized by the experience of capture.[20]

Another source of slaves was the practice of infant exposure. Though exposure resists quantification, some infants whom parents did not want or could not afford to raise were exposed (abandoned) in public places or on hillsides where other households or slave traders might pick them up to raise as slaves, using wet nurses to feed the infants. The practice was an economic gamble, as half of all infants and children might die from common illnesses before they reached ten.

Whether they were home-bred, bought on the market, or picked up as exposed infants, many domestic slaves appear to be little more than children. Slaves in positions of authority in the slave household, such as *dispensator* (steward, accountant) in an urban household or *vilicus* (bailiff) on a farm, were adults, as were slaves that performed heavy agricultural labor. The youth of many slaves was partly a reflection of the age structure of ancient society, which despite infant and child mortality had a large proportion of young people, in contrast with modern societies that have completed the demographic transition and have many old people. The youth of slaves also enabled adult owners and overseers to dominate them. A slave child was considered able to do useful work after reaching five years of age. However, no matter how old he was, a male slave was likely to be called "boy" (Latin *puer*) by his owner. Female slaves might be children as well; in epitaphs from the city of Rome, four *ornatrices* (hairdressers, an occupation that required training) are all in their preteens.[21]

The argument that there were fewer female slaves than males is based on the small number of occupations for slave women that are attested in agricultural writers and inscriptions. The elite treatises on agriculture, Cato's *On Farming*, Varro's *On Farming*, and Columella's *On Farming*, date from the second century BCE to the first century CE and describe slave-worked villas (farms) with almost entirely male labor forces, as does Digest 33.7 (a list of workers needed on a farm). Of thirty-four rural occupations in D. 33.7, only seven are female: *vilica* (bailiff's wife), *ancilla*, *focaria* (a woman who tends the hearth), *lanificae* (woolworkers), a female custodian of the farmhouse, and women who bake bread and prepare other foods. Columella lists thirty-seven rural occupations, of which only one is female, the *vilica*.[22]

OCCUPATIONS OF FEMALE SLAVES

Cato's description of the *vilica* is one of the most detailed descriptions of a slave woman's tasks, and the portrayal of domestic labor also can apply to a free smallholder's wife.

See that the *vilica* performs all her duties. If the master has given her to you as wife, keep yourself only to her. Make her regard you with fear. Restrain her from extravagance. She must visit the neighboring and other women very seldom, and not have them either in the house or in her part of it. She must not go out to meals, or be a gadabout . . . She must be neat herself, and keep the farmstead neat and clean. She must clean and tidy the hearth every night before she goes to bed.

This description presents the *vilica*'s duties as domestic, restricted to the villa farmhouse, and not sharing outdoor labor with the male slaves. Her behavior is subject to discipline; she must not waste time visiting other women or practice unauthorized religious cults, but she is authorized to worship the household gods on behalf of her owners. The picture is idealized. Women probably provided supplemental outdoor labor on farms as needed because of the agricultural cycle and the household cycle (in which family members are born and progress through childhood, adulthood and old age, subject to random mortality). If no able-bodied men were available at harvest time, women would pitch in. Depending on the fluctuating needs of the local labor force, slave women probably also assisted with tilling vegetables and herbs, tending flocks, picking olives and fruits, and gleaning grain; as the "most silent women of Greece and Rome," they also are poorly attested in textual sources.[23]

The slave women also apparently produced textiles for the slave household and for the market, but Cato, Varro, and Columella do not focus on this. Ulrike Roth has argued that women's production of textiles on rural estates was economically significant, though there were also textile workshops in cities and towns, probably also staffed with slave women. Spinning thread was highly labor intensive, requiring approximately ten spinners to every one weaver and many more hours of spinning than weaving. Spinning was also a low-intensity task that could be carried out simultaneously with other tasks such as tending flocks, watching cooking pots, or nursing or minding children. Spinning was "women's work" that men probably ignored, except in anecdotes about virtuous Roman women in past times. But the scale of textile production to clothe the population of Rome and Roman Italy required much labor. Even though lower-income inhabitants probably did not buy clothing very often, wearing their few items until they wore out, approximately 1.5 million tunics were needed yearly, each taking about 150 hours to spin and weave. Other items of clothing, such as togas, cloaks, and mantles, were also needed. Some of this production may have been domestic, carried out by free women (adults and young girls) and household slaves, but some of it was commercial, intended for sale, and probably employed thousands of slave women in the countryside and in urban workshops.[24]

In contrast, the proportion of slave women employed in urban households was limited, skewed by upper-income households' preference for male servants. In such households, female slaves appear in "feminine" occupations, such as *obstetrix* (midwife), *nutrix* (nurse), *ornatrix* (hairdresser or lady's maid), *pedisequa* (foot-woman or attendant), *sarcinatrix* (tailor), and *unctrix* (masseur, who helped her female owner clean her body with oil in the baths). These occupations all provided personal services involving close physical contact, which would be inappropriate for male slaves. The servile hierarchy is shown in the household of Livia Augusta (the first empress, wife of Augustus) where an *a veste* (slave in charge of clothing) and *ad unguenta* (slave in charge of perfumed oils) were probably male supervisors of an *ornatrix* and an *unctrix* (more than one of each occupation is attested). Some female slaves who provided personal services were literate: secretaries, scribes who took down dictation, slaves who read books aloud, even a *libraria* (librarian?). But the great number of slaves in such elite households were male. Of fifty occupations in the household of Livia, seven were explicitly female, twenty-seven definitely male, and fifteen unspecified but probably male; a *delicium* (a child page or "pet") could be either male or female. Of thirty-nine occupations cited in inscriptions from Rome, five are female: *cantrix* (singer), *quasillaria* (spinning woman), *textrix* (weaver), *tonstrix* (barber), and *vestifica* (tailor). Many of these occupations were highly specialized, such as a mirror holder or a caretaker of pearls, who took care of her owner's jewels. These servants existed mainly to display their owner's wealth and status, and when they were not performing their specialized functions, they would be in attendance on their owners, providing retinues.[25]

Male slaves had positions of greater authority in the household, such as the *dispensator* (accountant, steward) or *actor* (general manager), akin to the butler in an English great house, or the secretaries who assisted Cicero and Pliny the Elder with their research. Such slaves had greater chances of promotion, both before and after manumission. Freedmen of the imperial household might be promoted in the financial administration. The *nutrix* (nurse) of a wealthy Roman was also likely to be manumitted, but only out of affection, and it is likely that such domestic-service slave women, unless they married, stayed on as servants after manumission.[26]

Further down the social scale, slave women seem to be regarded as "all-purpose" slaves, multifunctional domestic workers owned by poorer or stingy owners. In documents, when an owner owns just one or two slaves, they are as likely to be female as male. In Apuleius's *Metamorphoses*, the narrator Lucius (still in human form) meets the "sharp as a needle" slave girl Photis, who does everything for her owner the stingy moneylender Milo and his wife, including making the beds, cooking, and serving dinner, tasks that in a wealthy household would be handled by different servants. Many documents and inscriptions also attest sub-elite men buying or selling slave women. These men, though not poor (they owned a slave), do not seem distinguished by particular wealth or status; many were ordinary Roman soldiers. The owner of a single slave woman probably expected sexual services (discussed in section "Sexual Identity of Female Slaves") as well as domestic labor; if the slave woman was young, he could expect her to give birth to new slaves, though he would have to pay the expense of raising the infants to an age where they could work for him or be sold. A particularly money-grubbing owner might also prostitute his slave woman, though the Roman emperors and jurists tried to discourage such practices, both through the legal stigma attached to pimping and through clauses against the prostitution of females in slave sale contracts.[27]

A large number of slave women were probably prostitutes. It was common for brothel owners to buy slave girls, often at quite young ages, and raise them within the brothel to teach them the trade. Slave boys were also prostituted. In Roman society, homosexuality was defined differently from today, as it was regarded as acceptable for a freeborn male to penetrate a male of inferior status (slaves or prostitutes), an act that still displayed his masculinity, while it was inappropriate for a freeborn male to be penetrated (anally or orally), a role which assimilated him to a woman, slave, or prostitute. Slave women working in taverns, bars, and hostels also had the reputation of being prostitutes. In some respects, however, all female slaves were likened to prostitutes, because they were assumed to be sexually accessible to their owners.[28]

SEXUAL IDENTITY OF FEMALE SLAVES

Slave women were regarded as sexually accessible and as providing sexual services. They were among the women "with whom *stuprum* [illicit sexual activity] is not committed," as seen in chapter

4. Slave women lacked *pudicitia*, the sexual inviolability of freeborn Roman unmarried girls and of matrons, who ideally had sex only with their husbands. Though he casts it in the male gender, the rhetorician Seneca the Elder remarked that "*impudicitia* is a crime in a freeborn person, a necessity for a slave, and a duty for a freed person." *Impudicitia*, the opposite of *pudicitia*, meant sexual availability and a lack of sexual reputation.[29]

According to the imperial biographer Suetonius, Cestius Gallus, a notorious senator in the Julio-Claudian era, reportedly was served dinner by his nude slave women, a practice that would be humiliating for freeborn women. Even if they were not forced to go naked as servants, *ancillae*'s bodies had been exposed in the slave market upon the auction block, open to the public gaze as the reverse of the matron hidden from prying eyes in her *stola* (long tunic dress) and *palla* (mantle). Apuleius depicts Milo's slave girl Photis as sexually attractive, a stock character attribute of young *ancillae* in Latin literature. Artemidorus, the author of a well-known book of dream interpretation in antiquity, writes that to dream of "covers and sacks for the deposit of bed linens" signifies concubines and freedwomen.[30]

The owner of a slave woman, whether he was the paterfamilias of the household or a son (having the slave in his *peculium*), had a right to her sexual services, but men outside the household did not. Men outside the household were not permitted to sexually assault or seduce its slave women—but only because in doing so, they were interfering with another man's property and offering insult to his household as a whole. Harassing or seducing a slave woman was considered an attempt on the *pudicitia* of the paterfamilias' wife and daughters.[31]

Many slave women formed de facto marriages, termed *contubernia*, with fellow slave men. These unions had no legal existence; their children were illegitimate and, if the woman was still a slave when she gave birth, also slaves. But slave marriages appear to have been long-lasting and affectionate, commemorated in epitaphs. Slave families aspired to win their liberty; often if one member attained freedom, he or she would strive to purchase the freedom of the other members. Freedperson families also greatly cherished children who were born in liberty. The mixture of statuses in freedperson families is well attested in epitaphs from the city of Rome.

MANUMISSION AND FREED STATUS

Manumission had various forms and was restricted by the emperor Augustus. An owner could manumit slaves in his or her will; he could also liberate his slaves before an appropriate magistrate; the form was often quite casual. As part of his conservative social legislation, Augustus sought to limit and formalize manumission. As seen earlier, the *Lex Fufia Caninia* (2 BCE) limited how many slaves could be manumitted in a will. The *Lex Aelia Sentia* (4 CE) restricted formal manumission to slave men and women over thirty years of age, unless the slaves were freed for overriding personal reasons, such as a family relationship (natural children or marriage). Such a restriction was motivated by a fear that indiscriminate manumission was freeing too many undeserving slaves (in the view of the historian Dionysius of Halicarnassus) and ensured that owners would reap the fruit of slave women's more fertile years, from their mid-teens to their mid-twenties. In general, the manumission of slave women depended on their owners to a greater extent than with elite male slaves, who had more opportunity to save money to purchase their freedom.[32]

Manumission over age thirty also made it harder for freed women over age thirty to have children to meet the stricter definition of the *ius liberorum* (right of children) for freedwomen. A freedwoman's guardian was her *patronus*, her former owner (if male). Where free women had to bear only three children to attain the *ius liberorum* and get rid of a *tutor*, freedwomen had to bear four children after their manumission to attain the *ius*. The *Lex Junia* acknowledged that many slaves were manumitted informally under age thirty but allowed them to become only "Junian Latins," inferior to full Roman citizens. Junian Latins could attain Roman citizenship if they married and produced a child who lived to the age of one year, presenting the child to the appropriate magistrate (a procedure termed *anniculi probatio*). Such a document is preserved in the Herculaneum tablets, where the freedman Venidius Ennychus reports the birth of a daughter and then presents her for the *probatio* before a magistrate.[33]

Freedwomen's status in Roman law was still subordinate to that of their former owners, their current patrons, to whom they owed obligatory respect and services. It appears that the Roman jurists thought that a freedwoman ought not to marry anyone but her male patron, whom she could also live with respectably in concubinage (an unmarried but long-term, monogamous relationship). One jurist declared that if a freedwoman lives with anyone but her patron, "I declare to you that she does not have the honorable name of *mater familias*." In this view, it was immoral for the freedwoman to marry or live with other men than her patron. These strictures reflect the Roman elite's view that former slave women retained the sexually dishonorable and promiscuous status of slave women, though not all agreed. Ulpian admitted a freedwoman to the category of materfamilias if she had "good morals."[34]

The jurists envision a hierarchical relationship of the freeborn male *patronus* and his freedwoman. Patrons in general were permitted to speak more harshly to their own freedmen than to freeborn men, and could even strike them. The *patronus* could berate his freedwoman or administer "light chastisement," though he could not beat her like a slave. The freedwoman was obliged to have her *patronus* as *tutor* (guardian), requiring his authorization for various legal transactions, including making a will (see chapter 6), and was obliged to leave part of her inheritance to him or his children.[35]

But Roman slave ownership, especially in urban regions with a high slave and freed population, took many forms and the strict hierarchy envisioned by the jurists may not always have existed. Some patrons were themselves former slaves of the same owner, creating a relationship with a greater possibility of shared experience. Some patrons were female and could not impose the strict hierarchical relationship envisioned by the jurists (since they themselves could not be guardians). Female patrons were restricted from marrying freedmen, but the framing of this policy (in the reign of Claudius, 41–54 CE) suggests that it was aimed at the upper classes.[36]

As aforesaid, the most likely slaves to be manumitted were relatively high-status house servants, who had constant contact with their owners' families and personal relationships with them. A much larger proportion of these higher-status slaves were freed than in slavery in the American South. It is not known what proportion of *all* Roman slaves were manumitted. Probably most menial and agricultural workers were never freed.

For slaves without hope of manumission, or who lived in terror of their owners, running away was an option—if they succeeded. There were professional slave-catchers, though their work was more difficult because Roman slavery was not racialized. If a slave or slave woman succeeded in running away, beginning a new life in another area, his or her owner was still able to claim him or her in Roman law. The Roman jurists also discuss the reverse phenomenon, a free person who was enslaved by accident and purchased in good faith. Such enslavements might befall travelers in the countryside, especially in remote locations, who were captured by bandits who were themselves slave traders or sold captives to slave traders.

The difficulty of determining slave or free status is displayed in the case of Petronia Justa from the Herculaneum tablets. This complex legal case occupied numerous tablets. Petronia Justa claimed that she was freeborn, but her possible stepmother Calatoria Themis claimed that she was the freedwoman of her possible father Petronius. A freedwoman owed deference and days of service (*operae*) to a former owner and could be reduced to slavery under certain circumstances, for example, as a punishment for a crime.[37]

Nevertheless, freedpersons, including freedwomen, formed Roman Italy's most vigorous commercial class. Freedmen could not run for public office but were permitted to become *severi Augustales*, local priests of the imperial cult. The most prominent freedman in Latin literary sources is fictional, the exaggeratedly wealthy Trimalchio, living on the Bay of Naples, who made his fortune through shipping. But his parallels (perhaps not quite so wealthy) are attested in inscriptions. The emperor Claudius (41–54 CE) invited Junian Latins and freedwomen to build ships for the grain trade, offering "to Latins the rights of Roman citizens, and to women the right of four children" if they provided ships. These freedwomen who built ships were probably wealthy and literate and needed experience in various kinds of industry and commerce. It is typical of the Roman sources' focus on women of the upper orders that we know so little about them, except for possible epitaphs.[38]

The number of "working-class" freedwomen—not wealthy, and working as artisans or shopkeepers—was much larger. Some of them adopted the role of mothers of families; these family epitaphs record both freed members and children born in freedom. The role of *matrona* was aspirational at this social level, imitated in clothing, posture, and objects such as woolwork baskets on their tombstone reliefs. Other freedwomen are recorded for posterity in carved reliefs that emphasized their role as shopkeepers, showing us what ancient Roman storefronts looked like. The relief from Ostia termed "Two Monkeys and a Snail" by modern scholars depicts a female shopkeeper standing behind a counter laden with plates of round objects—possibly fruit or baked items—and handing one to the buyer on the left. Under the counter are cages with live animals, including rabbits; two monkeys sit to the right of a basket that probably holds live snails, as a snail is carved over the shopkeeper's right shoulder. Sadly, this was probably not a pet shop; the animals were meant to be eaten, though the monkeys seem beyond the range of all but extremely wealthy epicures and may have been pets. The impression of the storefront reliefs is that Roman shopkeepers, who

Limestone funerary tablet, from Roman Cyprus, first century CE. The bilingual inscription commemorates the freedwoman (former slave) Julia Donata, freedwoman of Olympos, in both Latin and Greek. (The Metropolitan Museum of Art)

were probably freed-people, including freed-women, were proud of their work.[39]

CONCLUSION

Slave women in the Roman world faced a double degree of oppression—as slaves and as women. As slaves, they underwent a "social death" and became property; they were liable to cruel punishments; if they were captives in war, their children might be taken from them. The Column of Marcus Aurelius (erected by his son Commodus after 180 CE) shows the capture of German women by Roman soldiers, emphasizing the brutality of capture; a soldier drags away a boy from his mother's arms and another soldier pulls a captive woman by her unbound hair. Female slaves also experienced the sexual vulnerability of lower-status Roman women in an absolute degree. *Ancillae* were sexually exploited by their owners and as prostitutes. It was concern for the owner's propriety than the slave woman's rights that led to the institution of a covenant in slave sales against prostituting slave women. Being a *leno* or *lena* (brothel manager, pimp) was a disgraceful profession for freeborn Roman citizens, penalized by the *Lex Julia de adulteriis*.

Finally, slave women who were manumitted still faced additional hardships. They were required to bear four children rather than three to gain the privileges of the *ius liberorum*, including freedom from guardianship. A freedwoman's male former owner or *patronus* still possessed many owner-like rights over her; he was her guardian, and she could not make a will without his consent; she had to leave part of her estate to him in her will; he had the right to marry her, and the Roman jurists regarded it as inappropriate for the freedwoman to marry other men than her *patronus*. Not all freedwomen had male former owners, however, and the freedwomen of women may have been less constrained by social expectations.

NOTES

1. Ovid *Fasti* 6.551–8; Plut. *Camillus* 5.2; *Roman Questions* 16–17; on the related *ancillarum feriae*, Plut. *Camillus* 33; *Romulus* 29; Macrobius *Saturnalia* 1.11.36; Keith Bradley, *Slavery and Society at Rome* (Cambridge, 1994), 18. A good introduction to Roman slavery is Sandra R. Joshel, *Slavery in the Roman World* (Cambridge, 2010).

2. On the influence of classical slavery, David Brion Davis, *Inhuman Bondage: The Rise and Fall of Slavery in the New World* (Oxford, 2006), 40–47. On ancient precursors of racial slavery, see Frank M. Snowden, Jr., *Before Color Prejudice: The Ancient View of Blacks* (Cambridge, MA, 1983); Benjamin Isaac, *The Invention of Racism in Classical Antiquity* (Princeton, NJ, 2004); the topic is developing faster and cannot be explored here. Racist English and German classical scholarship in the nineteenth century fostered the interpretation of classical civilization as "white."

3. Appian *Civil Wars* 4.44, 4.46; Tac. *Histories* 2.29, 4.36, 4.50. On Appian, see Holt N. Parker, "Loyal slaves and loyal wives: The crisis of the outsider-within and Roman *exemplum* literature," in *Women and Slaves in Greco-Roman Culture* (London, 1998), ed. Sandra R. Joshel and Sheila Murnaghan, 152–73. On clothing, see Joshel, *Slavery*, 132–33. On inspection, see *Collected Ancient Greek Novels* (Berkeley, CA, 2008), ed. B. P. Reardon, 39.

4. Bradley, *Slavery*, 25; on triumphal art (with illustrations), see Joshel, *Slavery*, 68–69, 84–85.

5. Cic. *Pro Cluentio* 21; Plin. *Ep.* 6.25, 10.65; Julius Caesar, Suet. *Julius* 4; Bradley, *Slavery*, 37–38.

6. On social death, Orlando Patterson, *Slavery and Social Death: A Comparative Study* (Cambridge, 1982).

7. Varro *On Farming* 1.17.1: *instrumenti genus vocale et semivocale et mutum, vocale, in quo sunt servi, semivocale, in quo sunt boves, mutum, in quo sunt plaustra.* On loans, see, e.g., *L'Année Epigraphique* 1993, 462b = *Tabulae Herculanenses* 74 = *Pompeii and Herculaneum: A Sourcebook* (London, 2014), ed. Alison E. and M. G. L. Cooley, no. H67. On lease of slave, e.g., see *P. Wisc.* 16.5 = Jo-Ann Shelton, *As the Romans Did: A Source Book in Roman Social History* (Oxford, 1988), no. 182.

8. Bradley, *Slavery*, 53–54.

9. Ibid., 15; Joshel, *Slavery*, 31, 47.

10. Cic. *Att.* 4.17.6.

11. Walter Scheidel, "Real slave prices and the relative cost of slave labor in the Greco-Roman world," *Ancient Society* 35 (2005), 1–17, at 5.

12. Republic: Jill Harries, *Law and Crime in the Roman World* (Cambridge, 2007), 14–15; imperial, 35-6.

13. On punishment of elite children versus slaves, see Richard P. Saller, *Patriarchy, Property, and Death in the Roman Family* (Cambridge, 1994), 133–54; on the two-tier punishment system, see Peter Garnsey, *Social Status and Legal Privilege in the Roman Empire* (Oxford, 1970); Harries, *Law and Crime*,

36–37. On bodies, Sandra R. Joshel, *Work, Identity, and Legal Status at Rome: A Study of the Occupational Inscriptions* (Norman, OK, 1992), 30.

14. Juvenal 6.474–9.

15. On collars, see Joshel, *Slavery*, 119–20, e.g., *ILS* 8731, 9454. On tattooing, see C. P. Jones, "*Stigma*: Tattooing and branding in Graeco-Roman antiquity," *JRS* 77 (1987), 139–55, at 147–48, 150. On painting, see Petronius *Satyrica* 103.

16. On the households, see Susan Treggiari, "Jobs in the household of Livia," *Papers of the British School at Rome* 43 (1975), 48–77; Joshel, *Work, Identity*, 71-5.

17. Gaius *Institutes* 1.43; Bradley, *Slavery*, 9–11; Joshel, *Slavery*, 46.

18. Richard P. Saller, "Symbols of gender and status hierarchies in the Roman household," in Joshel and Murnaghan, *Women and Slaves*, 85–91, at 87. On the fungible nature of slaves, Joshel, *Slavery*, 92.

19. On numbers, see Joshel, *Slavery*, 8. On the slave supply controversy, see Bradley, *Slavery*, 31–56; Joshel, *Slavery*, 67; Matthew J. Perry, *Gender, Manumission, and the Roman Freedwoman* (Cambridge, 2014), 44.

20. Columella *On Farming* 1.8.19; Plut. *Cato Maior* 21.2; Varro *On Farming* 1.17.5, 2.10.6; Columella *On Farming* 1.8.5, 11.1.14. On slave reproduction, see Joshel, *Slavery*, 124–25, 131–32; on slave families, see Henrik Mouritsen, "The families of Roman slaves and freedmen," in *Companion to Families in the Greek and Roman Worlds* (Malden, MA, 2011), ed. Beryl Rawson, 129–44.

21. On child slaves, see Christian Laes, *Children in the Roman Empire: Outsiders Within* (Cambridge, 2011), 167–71, 189; on useful work, see D. 7.7.6.1 Ulpian; cf. D. 21.1.37; on *ornatrices* and their training, see D. 32.65.3 (Marcian); on epitaphs, see *CIL* VI 9726, 9728, 9731, *CIL* X 1941.

22. On slave labor in general, see Bradley, *Slavery*, 57–80. On occupations on rural estates, see ibid., 59–60; Perry, *Gender*, 45.

23. On *vilica*, see Cato *On Farming* 143. On this pattern in free smallholders during the Republic, see Nathan S. Rosenstein, *Rome at War: Farms, Families and Death in the Middle Republic* (Chapel Hill, NC, 2004). On women on slave-worked farms, see Walter Scheidel, "The most silent women of Greece and Rome: Rural labour and women's life in the ancient world (I)," *Greece & Rome* 42 (1995), 202–17; "The most silent women of Greece and Rome: Rural labour and women's life in the ancient world (II)," *Greece & Rome* 43.1 (1996), 1–10; Ulrike Roth, *Thinking Tools: Agricultural Slavery between Evidence and Models*, *BICS* Supplement no. 92 (London, 2007). On household gods worshiped by slaves, cf. the *lararium* in the kitchen of the House of Sutoria Primigenia at Pompeii; Joshel, *Slavery*, 144–45.

24. Roth, *Thinking Tools*, 21 and n. 79; on spinning, see ibid., 81; on 150 hours to produce, see ibid., 81–82.

25. On occupations, see Joshel, *Work, Identity*, 173–82 (list of occupational titles); Joshel, *Slavery*, 149–50, 182; Bradley, *Slavery*, 59–60; Perry, *Gender*, 43–68, esp. 43, 46–47; Treggiari, "Jobs in the household of Livia." On bias

in occupational titles, see Joshel, *Work, Identity*; Lin Foxhall, *Studying Gender in Classical Antiquity* (Cambridge, 2013), 97; Saller, "Household," 106. On mirror holder and tender of pearls, see *CIL* VI 7297, 7884.

26. Bradley, *Slavery*, 78–80; Joshel, *Slavery*, 41; Perry, *Gender*, 64–65.

27. On Photis, see Apuleius *Metamorphoses* 2.7, 11, 3.13; Bradley, *Slavery*, 57. On a contract of sale, see *P. Oxy.* 95 = Shelton, no. 181. On soldiers, see Sara Elise Phang, *The Marriage of Roman Soldiers, 13 B.C.–A.D. 235: Law and Family in the Imperial Army* (Leiden, 2001), 231–40 (many appearing in epitaphs as freedwomen). On prostitution, see Thomas A. J. McGinn, *Prostitution, Sexuality, and the Law in Ancient Rome* (Oxford, 1998), 288–319; Vespasian decreed that if a slave woman had been sold under the agreement that she would not be prostituted, and she was prostituted, she should be free (D. 37.14.7.pr).

28. McGinn, *Prostitution*, 306–11; Thomas A. J. McGinn, *The Economy of Prostitution in the Roman World:A Study of Social History & the Brothel* (Ann Arbor, MI, 2004), 55–61. On women working in taverns, bars, and hostels, see Joshel, *Slavery*, 196. On assumption that slave women are prostitutes, see Perry, *Gender*, 37.

29. Seneca *Controversiae* 4.pr.10.

30. Suet. *Tiberius* 42.2; Artemidorus *On Dreams* 1.74. On *pudicitia*, see Rebecca Langlands, *Sexual Morality in Ancient Rome* (Cambridge, 2006), 14–29, stressing that *pudicitia* was differentiated by status; cf. McGinn, *Prostitution*, 155–56, 331–35. On sexual use of slave women, see Bradley, *Slavery*, 28, 49–50, 113; Joshel, *Slavery*, 99; Perry, *Gender*, 8–22. On the general disgrace of sale, see Joshel, *Slavery*, 101–7. On literary trope, see Perry, *Gender*, 13–15. On Artemidorus, see Bradley, *Slavery*, 141.

31. D. 47.11.1.2; McGinn, *Prostitution*, 332–33; Langlands, *Sexual Morality*, 99, 136–37, 205–206; Perry, *Gender*, 20–25; on insult, D. 47.10.9; 47.10.10; 47.10.15; also D. 48.5.6.pr (action for corrupting a slave) applied to seduction.

32. On *Lex Aelia Sentia*, Perry, *Gender*, 64–65. On unrestricted manumission, Dion. Hal. *Roman Antiquities* 4.24.4–8.

33. *L'Année Epigraphique* 2006, 305 = *Tabulae Herculanenses* 89 = *Pompeii and Herculaneum*, no. G3. On the *ius liberorum* for freedwomen, see Perry, *Gender*, 88–92, 136–37.

34. D. 24.2.11.pr; D. 23.2.41.1; Ulpian, D. 50.16.46.1. On this respect, see Joshel, *Slavery*, 41–44. On patron and freedwoman, see Perry, *Gender*, 94, 131–32.

35. On striking, see D. 47.10.7.2; on chastisement, see D. 47.10.11.1; 47.10.7.2; Perry, *Gender*, 73–78.

36. Perry, *Gender*, 96–128, examines various freedperson epitaphs.

37. On Petronia Justa, see *Pompeii and Herculaneum*, nos. G5–11 (pp. 215–18); cf. Emily A. Hemelrijk, *Women and Society in the Roman World: A Sourcebook of Inscriptions from the Roman West* (Cambridge, 2021), nos. 2.58–60.

38. On *ius liberorum*, see Suet. *Claudius* 19.1; this book, section *"Ius Liberorum."*

39. Joshel, *Slavery*, 209. On the shopkeepers, see Claire Holleran, *Shopping in Ancient Rome* (Oxford, 2012); and on this relief, *ibid.*, 213; other instances, Hemelrijk, W*omen and Society*, nos. 3.77-93 (performers), 3.94–95 (gladiators), 3.96–99 (inn and bar workers); see also Eve D'Ambra, Roman Women (Cambridge, 2007), 25–27, 138–40; Claire Holleran, "Women and retail in Roman Italy," in *Women and the Roman City in the Latin West* (Leiden, 2013), ed. Emily A. Hemelrijk and Greg Woolf, 313–30.

8

SOCIAL LIFE

INTRODUCTION

Around 100 CE, Claudia Severa, the wife of a Roman military officer, sent a birthday invitation to Sulpicia Lepidina, the wife of the equestrian commander Flavius Cerialis, at the fort of Vindolanda in north Britain.

> Claudia Severa to her Lepidina greetings. On 11 September, sister, for the day of the celebration of my birthday, I give you a warm invitation to make sure that you come to us, to make the day more enjoyable for me by your arrival, if you are present. Give my greetings to your Cerialis. My Aelius and my little son send him their greetings. I shall expect you, sister. Farewell, sister, my dearest soul, as I hope to prosper, and hail.

The letter was written with ink on wood and, as with many other records of the Roman army and associated civilians found at Vindolanda, was buried in oxygen-free boggy conditions that preserved it to this day. The letter imitates the polite forms of Roman letters in literary collections—but as a woman's letter, it is paralleled by papyri from Roman Egypt, because the collections of elite men's letters were edited to remove the letters of their female interlocutors. It may be a draft, related to the draft of a more personal letter to Lepidina. Though Claudia Severa's letter reflects the Roman frontier setting, which will not be discussed in detail here, it also shows common social events and phenomena in Roman women's lives: birthday parties and women's socializing with each other.[1]

Roman social life was maintained through the writing of letters. In the absence of modern forms of rapid communication, letters were an essential social obligation. Such letters survive not just in Cicero's and Pliny the Younger's collections but in large numbers of papyri and tablets, written by the sub-elite. A letter typically ended with numerous greetings to people who were not the main addressee, but related to them as family members or friends. Often we do not know how all these people were related, but greeting them by name made the reading of a letter (almost always out loud) a vicarious social gathering. Below the elite, the subliterate could pay a scribe or reader to write or read a letter aloud. Outside Roman Egypt, very few women's letters survive. The letter of Cornelia the mother of the Gracchi to Gaius Gracchus, begging him to not follow his brother Tiberius's path, is probably a forgery. The imperial biographer Suetonius quotes correspondence of Augustus with Livia, but not Livia's own letters, and notes that Livia herself wrote "short harsh letters" reprimanding young Claudius.[2]

What was social life like for Roman women? Again, social status and identity greatly influenced social life and leisure. Social expectations, such as the system of *pudicitia*, may have most affected women in the elite strata, but the evidence is ambiguous. The easiest way to guard women's *pudicitia* would have been the seclusion of women within the home, not being permitted to travel freely, dine with men, use public baths, or attend the theater or the games. None of these were the case. Roman women were to be found in all parts of the city, according to our (admittedly, manipulative) male informants. Women could dine with men and use public baths, even those where men and women bathed together. They could attend the theater and the games, though from the reign of Augustus (27 BCE–14 CE) onward, women's seating was segregated. To protect their *pudicitia*, elite women depended on an entourage of attendants. Sub-elite women might be attended in public by friends, relatives, or one or two slaves. Vulnerable women of the lowest classes, believed to lack *pudicitia*, had no attendants at all.

The nature of social life and leisure also depended on women's cultural and personal identity, on their agency as individuals. Here generalizations may be impossible. Images of women in Roman literature are also heavily weighted by elite authors' praise and blame. It was possible for some elite women to socialize freely and even to be highly reputed as literary patrons (patronage is discussed in chapter 9), if their *pudicitia* was assured. These instances (Cornelia the Mother of the Gracchi, Livia the first empress, and Julia Domna the Severan empress) are older women; the first two were widowed. Other women, the mistresses of love poetry, *may* have chosen a "countercultural" identity, as did the Late Republican poet Catullus, "away with the grumblings of grim old men." However, this imaginative literature is extremely difficult to interpret and will not be discussed in detail in this book.[3]

In practice, social life with other women, or in the company of one's husband, was probably safest for women of the upper orders, as was appearing in public surrounded by an entourage of servants. Social life with other women or with family members was also safest for lower-status women. In many Islamic countries and India, women display such self-segregating behavior. Finally, slave women by definition did not have leisure (free choice of how to use their time); their social lives were in theory restricted to their owners' household, though in practice Roman slaves appropriated free time and social contacts whenever and wherever they could, resisting their owners' dictates.[4]

STEREOTYPES OF DOMESTIC SECLUSION AND *OTIUM*

Male-authored sources present an ideal of domestic female behavior. As seen in chapter 1, Livy praises the legendary Lucretia for staying at home and spinning wool, while other women of her age were attending parties. Latin epitaphs of women praised them for *lanificium*, woolworking, implying that they remained within the home. *Domiseda*, "stay-at-home," might even be used in epitaphs (though rarely). In his notorious satire against women and marriage, the late first-century CE poet Juvenal contrasted present-day women with the women of the past, made virtuous by poverty and toil: "hard work, short sleep, hands chafed and hardened from handling Tuscan fleeces," though earlier in the satire he describes the deity *Pudicitia* herself as an unattractive peasant woman. Juvenal implies that wealthy women no longer performed such domestic labor, but lower-status women still performed such domestic toil in subsistence households.[5]

Even if women appeared outside the home, the ideal of *pudicitia* prescribed modest behavior in public. In 195 BCE Cato the Elder upbraided Roman matrons for leaving their homes, entering the Forum, and demonstrating in public against the *Lex Oppia*, met with in chapter 5 and discussed in chapter 9. The early first-century CE orator Seneca the Elder is best known for the *Controversiae*, a series of elaborate rhetorical exercises used to train young men as orators. Each exercise sets a premise, and the orators in training declaimed for or against it. The premise in question requires establishing that a woman is chaste, as shown by her behavior:

> Let her have companions old enough . . . to make the shameless respect their years. Let her go about with her eyes on the ground. In the face of an over-attentive greeting, let her be impolite rather than immodest. Even where she has to return a greeting, let her show confusion and blush deeply.

The context, as in the passage of the *Digest* cited in section "Dress and Social Status," is probably response to strange men rather than to acquaintances.[6]

As will be seen in chapters 9 and 10, women of the upper orders engaged in public life as patrons and benefactors and held prominent religious roles as priestesses and lay officiants. It is doubtful that they carried out such roles while blushing, stammering, and looking at the ground and by "being rude rather than immodest." Praise of female modesty and chastity was culturally obligatory. Praising the *pudicitia* of matrons was thus praise of their husbands and sons, upholding family status. Nonetheless, male authors' hostility to women's extramarital sexual activities created an atmosphere of anxiety around women's sexual behavior that may have constrained women's other behaviors.[7]

The other stereotype found in Roman moralists is that of present-day women's leisure, *otium*, contrasted with the domestic toil of women in the distant past. *Otium* was an ambivalent concept in Roman culture. Signaling freedom from business (*negotium*), *otium* might be productively used by men of the upper orders for intellectual activities, such as studying or creating literature or philosophy. In contrast, the lower social strata were prone to misusing *otium* on luxury and idle activities. Women misusing *otium* was contrasted with women of the past who displayed *industria* (hard work) at domestic tasks such as woolwork. Pliny the Younger depicts the elderly senatorial widow Ummidia Quadratilla, recently deceased at nearly eighty, as having spent her "women's *otium*" on watching a troupe of pantomime actors whom she personally owned. According to Pliny, Ummidia also played dice games, another time-wasting activity. In fact, as will be seen in chapter 9, she had built an amphitheater and a temple and restored a theater where the actors probably performed.[8]

It appears that Roman women of the upper strata (and those below, though their social obligations are not as well documented) spent much "idle time" on emotional labor—social obligations that maintained family relationships and friendships. In the upper orders, such emotional labor might have political influence. In the letter quoted in the opening of this chapter, the middle-ranking officer's wife Claudia Severa, by extending a deferential invitation to the wife of a superior officer, is clearly performing such emotional labor by asking about the health of her husband and addressing her warmly. Her related drafts suggest anxiety over her relationships with her husband Brocchus and with Lepidina. In a society based on patronage and personal power, maintaining a good social relationship with other officers might help her husband retain his rank or obtain promotion. Because of the way elite men's collections of letters were edited, women's letters directly exerting such influence are rarely preserved.[9]

That the letter reflects a genuinely warm friendship is another possibility. If Claudia Severa and Sulpicia Lepidina were both of equestrian (or at least decurion) status, there were few women of similar background to socialize with on the frontier of northern Britain. Close female friendships are attested in a number of Latin epitaphs; the friends commemorated each other or shared a tomb, and the formula *amica optima* was used.[10]

An instance of an elite woman's refusing to perform emotional labor is shown by Cicero's sister-in-law Pomponia, the wife of Cicero's brother Quintus and sister of Cicero's friend Caecilius Atticus. Pomponia's marriage to Quintus was deteriorating. In 51 BCE the three couples had been traveling in Italy all day. Quintus proposed that the three families host a dinner, suggesting that the women invite the women and the men the men. Pomponia was apparently tired, and refused, saying sarcastically that "I'm just a guest here." It may have been the women's work to organize the dinner. When the dinner was served, she refused to join the guests and rejected the offer of food from the dinner, also refusing to share her bed with Quintus. The account is filtered through Cicero, who sees Pomponia as behaving unreasonably.[11]

Elite women may have socialized outside the home mainly with relatives or with other women; they were accompanied by their husbands when they attended dinner parties (discussed in section "Dining") and public events. As suggested in chapter 5, women's costume, demeanor, and attendants would be subject to scrutiny. Women of the upper orders frequently traveled in carriages or litters (couches carried on poles, screened by curtains), in part to avoid walking through the muddy streets in long skirts, but in part to avoid being seen in public. The litter-bearers provided a retinue, though traveling matrons were probably also accompanied by their personal servants or friends. Men also used litters. Satirists depicted the use of litters as privileges of the wealthy, akin to limousines in modern society. But elite women's use of carriages and litters suggests that the system of *pudicitia* was not merely rhetorical. Even when they traveled on foot, elite women were likely to be accompanied by an entourage of servants and dependent clients.[12]

In the lowest social strata, women could not live in domestic seclusion because they needed to work to support themselves and their families. They traveled on foot (or rode animals such as donkeys) and were unlikely to have attendants. Slave women were exposed to the public eye from the point of their sale, exhibited in the slave market, subject to buyers' physical inspection. Poor free women, whether freeborn or freedwomen, might be exposed to the public as sellers of food and wine in taverns and bars, and female sellers of other goods were also exposed to the public, as were women who performed agricultural labor.

The literature of *pudicitia* makes it appear as if certain public spaces in the Roman city (or military camp) excluded women. Women appear to have been excluded from the Senate House (*Curia*), reserved for mature male citizens elected to it (the term "senator" derives from *senex* or old man). According to Tacitus, the empress Agrippina the Younger went to great lengths to overhear proceedings of the Senate, moving its meetings to the imperial palace, where she listened from behind a curtain so that she was not visible. Tacitus depicts a case of adultery in a military camp in which a commander's wife entered the barracks to watch soldiers at drill and committed adultery in the headquarters itself with Titus Vinius, a junior officer of senatorial rank. In such highly rhetorical passages, Tacitus paints images of female transgression, suggesting archaic prohibitions and supporting his themes of the unlicensed influence of women and uncontrolled power of the emperors. In contrast, in his *Art of Love*, a manual for would-be seducers, Ovid depicts women (sexually available, though not prostitutes) as found throughout the city of Rome: in the Gardens of Pompey, the Portico of Livia, a temple of Isis, the theater, the games, women's groups, and the seaside resort of Baiae. Even the Forum itself did not exclude women; Ovid depicts it as a place where the god of Love might strike a woman listening to an orator. Ovid allows for women's presence in public spaces but sexualizes that presence. Both authors ignore the reality of women in public life.[13]

At the level of smaller cities and towns, as chapter 9 shows, elite women were funding and perhaps organizing (though exactly how is unknown) the construction of public buildings: temples and shrines, baths, theaters and amphitheaters. Their portrait statues appeared in city forums, and indeed at Rome itself, starting with (to omit legendary women) Cornelia the Mother of the Gracchi, though in imperial Rome itself images of the emperors and empresses soon dominated. Smaller cities and towns afforded more locations for statues of local aristocrats, including women. Special cases of gendered space are discussed in the next sections: theaters and amphitheaters, public baths, and dinner parties.[14]

THEATERS AND SPECTACLES

One area of gendered space was the theater or amphitheater (circus). These were major institutions in Roman society, not only providing mass entertainment (the so-called bread and circuses) but also associated with religion and public benefactions. The *ludi* were also religious festivals and occurred at intervals through the year, featuring chariot races (*ludi circenses*) and theatrical performances (*ludi scaenici*), both publicly funded. Religious features included offerings to the gods and performances of hymns, as at Augustus's *Ludi Saeculares* in 17 BCE. Gladiatorial games began as privately funded munificences (*munera*) presented at Republican aristocratic funerals but merged with the public spectacles. Rome's large amphitheater (the Colosseum, built by the Flavian emperors) and Circus Maximus were famous throughout the Empire.

Spectacles were also held by smaller cities, offered by local aristocrats as benefactions. Providing spectacles enabled local aristocrats to display their generosity. As with football games in modern nations, the Roman games often displayed intense local patriotism, smaller cities striving to outdo each other in the expense and quality of their spectacles. Long-range trade was probably encouraged by the pursuit of exotic animals for the beast shows, though these shows also decimated the exotic large animals of the Roman world.

Women were permitted to watch theatrical shows. The content spanned a range from traditional Greek tragedy to the low and often raunchy comedy of pantomime shows. Women were in the theater audience for the emperor Nero's own performances, which ran so long that at least one woman gave birth there (the audience could not leave while the emperor performed). Pliny the Younger remarks disapprovingly on Ummidia Quadratilla's preference for watching her own troupe of pantomime actors, whom she did not permit her young adult grandson to watch. Pantomime comedy was often sexually explicit and the performers, as with all stage performers, were *infames* (legally stigmatized persons of ill repute). Ummidia would have been young in the days of Caligula (emperor 37–41 CE) and Nero (54–68), a more uninhibited period than Pliny's own day (around 100–110). But women were never excluded entirely from watching at the theater.[15]

Despite the cruelty of the gladiatorial and beast-fighting shows, featuring both professional fighters and criminals who were sentenced to die in the arena, women were permitted to watch these shows. Women were excluded from watching only Greek-style athletic games where male contestants competed in the nude. Satire and graffiti depicted women as attracted to gladiators—the imaginary matron Eppia runs off to Egypt with an unattractive gladiator named Sergius, and gladiators at Pompeii were hailed in graffiti as *suspirium puellarum*, "who makes all the girls sigh." But men do not seem to have had a general objection to women watching the games; in real life, a social and legal gulf separated senatorial and equestrian women from gladiators and condemned criminals, both being *infames*, legally stigmatized persons with restricted rights.[16]

The Principate introduced segregated seating in the theater for women. During the Late Republic, elite women had been able to sit next to men and socialize with them. Augustus passed a law, the *Lex Julia theatralis*, which decreed precisely where each rank of society was to sit in the theater. Senators sat in the front row, and equestrian men in the first fourteen rows, displaying their rank by wearing white togas and tunics with broad (senatorial) or narrow (equestrian) stripes. The mass of lower-status men, termed *pullati* or "clad in dark clothing," sat behind the first fourteen rows. Women were relegated to the back/top of the theater, behind the *pullati*. The law had been anticipated in previous decades by a law requiring senators to sit in front and by the *Lex Roscia* of 67 BCE which required equestrians to sit in the first fourteen rows. The *Lex Julia theatralis*'s seating women at the back meant that they could not see the events as well. Only women of the imperial family and the Vestal Virgins were allowed to sit in the front with senatorial men. In the women's section, women of the upper orders received privileged seating, and those of the lower strata sat behind *them*. The poets craned their necks to catch a glimpse of their mistresses in the women's rows.[17]

The entire Roman social order was thus visible at a glance at the rows of the theater. However, it is not certain that the *Lex Julia theatralis* was in force throughout Roman Italy or the provinces, and Ovid's evidence shows that at that time it was not applied to the *ludi circenses* or the amphitheater (where the larger seating area may have reduced the problem of different social strata coming into close contact). However, the subsequent emperors continued to enforce the seating rules, so the women's area probably was also extended to the amphitheater.[18]

PUBLIC BATHS

Roman public baths were another area that women were not excluded from, though gender-segregated options existed. Public baths had elaborate suites of bathing rooms heated by furnaces that both heated the water and conducted hot air through hypocausts, channels under the floors, that warmed the rooms above. Using the public baths was not only about getting clean but an all-purpose social activity. Romans cleaned their bodies with oil, applying the oil to the skin and scraping it off with a metal instrument called a strigil, taking dirt with it. The bathers progressed through the baths in a prescribed order, changing out of their clothes in an *apodyterium* or changing room, bathing first in a *tepidarium* or medium-hot pool, where they would clean themselves with oil, then soaking or steaming in a *caldarium* (hot pool) or *laconicum* (an even hotter, sauna-like room), returning to the *tepidarium* and finally cooling off in a *frigidarium* or cold pool. The progress was leisurely; the baths were a major place for men to socialize (we are best informed about men). They also offered other amenities, including wine and other drinks, snacks, exercise grounds for ball players or weight lifters, and even libraries. Large public baths, or *thermae*, covered large areas and were all-purpose recreation centers. Smaller baths, *balneae*, may not have had all of these amenities.[19]

There is surprisingly little information about how Roman women used the baths. At first glance, using the public baths (where everyone was naked at least in the bathing rooms) would seem problematic in a culture that idealized women's modesty in public, and where matrons did not go outside without their *palla* (mantle). The late first-century CE poet Martial says that his poems are "full of naked men at the baths" and not for matrons. Roman antiquarian authors believed that in the mid-Republic, when public baths were supposedly first introduced, there were separate men's and women's baths and that men and women started bathing together in the Late Republic and early Empire. Hadrian and subsequent emperors are supposed to have repressed mixed-gender bathing, though the source, the *Scriptores Historiae Augustae*, is late and unreliable.[20]

Archeology shows that some public baths might have two sets of bathing rooms, one for men and one for women, or have only one suite of rooms and furnaces but with separate hours for women and for men, attested in an inscription from Vipasca, a town in Roman Spain. At Vipasca women were given the morning hours to use the baths, from dawn to the seventh hour (counted from midnight), and men bathed from the eighth hour to nightfall. The Roman business day started very early in the morning, and the charter of Vipasca assumed that women did not work. These segregated hours were probably employed elsewhere. In Roman Italy, some municipal benefactors (local aristocrats) funded separate men's and women's baths. At Corfinium, the municipal magistrate Quintus Avelius Priscus Severius Severus Annavus Rufus (the many names are typical of the late second-century CE date) built "Avelian" women's baths. At Lanuvium, one Marcus Valerius restored "at his own expense" the men's and the women's baths. Alfia Quarta, a female benefactor, gave the women of Marruvium a women's baths with multicolored stone decoration, and Caesia Sabina of Veii funded free bathing and a supply of oil for the women of Veii. Benefactions by women are discussed in more detail in chapter 9.[21]

Other public baths, constructed in the first century CE, appear to have been mixed-gender baths where men and women bathed together. Satirists depicted promiscuous women as attending these baths, as did Christian authors. A range of options thus existed for women: separate men's and women's establishments, partitioned baths, or mixed-gender baths. Some mixed-gender baths, such as the Suburban baths at Pompeii, blatantly advertised sexual activity with explicit frescoes on the walls. It is still not clear how women, especially women of higher status, used the mixed-gender baths without risking sexual harassment or aspersion cast upon their *pudicitia*. Some scholars have suggested that the Romans had a casual attitude toward nudity in the public baths, not sexualizing nudity any more than we sexualize partial nudity at a public pool or beach in modern society (though it depends on the particular pool or beach and on the time of year). In contrast, Garrett Fagan suggests that the Romans did not lay aside their status hierarchy with their (status-signifying) clothes when they went to the public baths. At minimum, a bather was accompanied by a slave to help him clean his body with oil. The emperor Hadrian (117–38 CE) is said to have spotted an elderly veteran rubbing his back against the wall of the public baths, because he had no slave attendant to scrub his back, and gave the man a slave of his own; the next day, when Hadrian went to the baths, he saw many old men rubbing their backs against the wall, and reproved them. The wealthy and well born found other means than clothing to display their status in the baths, such as arriving with an entourage of attendants, being waited on by these slave as they proceeded through the bathing rooms, using expensive implements and unguents, and being presented with an elaborate choice of clothes as they dressed (all these are from satirical sources). A *matrona* attending a mixed-gender public bath would probably be accompanied by a retinue of female slaves and a male bodyguard, who acted as chaperones and screened her from the public eye. Very wealthy households had their own private bath houses, where women who wished to maintain a reputation for *pudicitia* could bathe alone, or bathe with men away from the public eye. However, the paradox of *pudicitia* was that it was displayed in public behavior; maintaining it in public was more prestigious. Women further down the social scale may have attended the mixed-gender baths with their husbands and family members. In an epitaph, a husband praises his deceased wife for never going to the baths without him, and in another epitaph, a husband addresses the passers-by: "You who read this, go bathe in the baths of Apollo, as I used to do with my wife. I wish I still could."[22]

Women's presence in men's baths could still be depicted as abnormal behavior. This behavior might be sexualized, as in Ovid's description of the obscure ritual of Fortuna Virilis on April 1, when women of lower (slave or freed) status bathed in the men's baths, allegedly to beg the deity Fortuna Virilis to make them more attractive to men. Women's use of men's baths might display their general arrogance, as with the consular matron who demanded that the small Italian town of Teanum Sidicinum clear out its men's baths for her personal use, punishing the town magistrates for not making the bath ready quickly enough, or the woman in Juvenal's Sixth Satire who uses the men's baths at night, works out with weights, and worships the god Silvanus, a deity worshipped only by men. All these baths in these unreliable instances seem to be normally reserved for men.[23]

At all times, more moralizing about excessive bathing was directed at men, for the relaxation that the baths and associated indulgences represented was thought to make them effeminate, literally softening and soaking their drier and harder constitutions. Women's moister constitutions presumably were not altered by using the baths.[24]

DINING

Women also dined with men in the Roman world. Cornelius Nepos explains the Roman custom to his Greek readers, as Greek women did not normally dine or drink with men unless the women were courtesans (*hetairai*). When inviting friends and relatives to dine with them, it was considered correct etiquette for an elite Roman man to send invitations to the male guests and his wife to send invitations to the female guests. Augustus's widow Livia invited both senatorial and equestrian men and their wives to a banquet at the dedication of a statue of the Deified Augustus; Tiberius took offence and invited the men himself. Quoted at the beginning of this chapter, a wooden tablet survives from the Roman fort of Vindolanda on Hadrian's Wall, ca. 100 CE, where an officer's wife, Claudia Severa, invited the equestrian commander's wife, Sulpicia Lepidina, to her birthday party. It may have been a women-only party, or Claudia's husband would invite the prefect Flavius Cerialis, Lepidina's husband, and other officers. Officers' wives regularly accompanied their husbands to the frontiers from the first century CE onward and, at least in peacetime, social occasions were part of military life for senatorial and equestrian officers.[25]

The upper-class Roman home had at least one *triclinium* (dining room), which was outfitted with three couches around a table; diners reclined on the couches rather than sitting in chairs. Each couch was large enough to hold several people. In the older Republic, matrons had been seated in chairs at dinner; by the Late Republic and imperial era, they also reclined at dinner, normally with their husbands or with female relatives and friends. Macrobius depicts a lavish banquet attended by the high priests and priestesses of Rome in the mid-first century BCE: four Vestal Virgins and the *flaminica Martialis* and her mother reclined in one *triclinium*. As will be seen in chapter 10, the Vestals' chastity was closely guarded; they could not recline with men, but neither were they seated in chairs in the archaic manner. It was considered normal for married women to recline with their husbands on the same couch. At more uninhibited banquets, women reclined with men who were not their

Roman public baths at Bath, Roman Britain, 1st–4th c. CE. Roman women may have attended public baths at separate hours from men or in the company of male relatives or slave attendants. Wealthy families might have private bath complexes. (Wellcome Collection)

husbands, to the condemnation of moralists. Middle-status homes, of well-to-do sub-elite families, also had *triclinia* that allowed reclining for dinner. Lower-status homes, especially in cities, were small tenement apartments without room for *triclinia*; many people dined out at cookshops, where they sat on stools or stood.[26]

A related theme in moralistic literature was that women in early Rome were forbidden to drink wine. Valerius Maximus and Plutarch relate that women's relatives used to kiss them in order to sniff whether they had been drinking, and Dionysius of Halicarnassus says that the ancient Roman king Romulus put women to death for adultery and for drinking wine, a custom attributed to the early Roman paterfamilias by Cato the Elder. One Egnatius Metellus (or Mecenius) was said to have beaten his wife to death for drinking wine. These legends were all attributed to the early or at latest middle Republic, but the behavior of Monica's nurse (related in chapter 3) to her charges suggests that these legends were imitated by some families. The rationale was that drunkenness made women promiscuous as well as careless household managers. Drunken women were already mocked in ancient Greek comedy and satire. However, other traditions allowed Roman women to drink wine.

Festus relates that *matronae* drank a wine called *murrina* or *muri-ola*, Gellius states that they were allowed to drink raisin wine and spiced wine, and Varro states that old women drank *passum*, raisin wine. Women were permitted to drink at dinner, though they did not join the men's *commissatio*, a party solely for the purpose of getting drunk. In his *Art of Love*, Ovid depicts women as reclining at dinner with men and drinking wine, which he paints as an aid to seduction, though he condemns excessive drunkenness in women: "a woman who is dead drunk deserves any sexual union whatsoever." Clement of Alexandria, advising Christian women on how to attend banquets, urged them to dress modestly (avoiding purple, perfumes, cosmetics, and jewelry) and to drink in moderation, not allowing themselves to become drunk.[27]

Below the elite, Roman women of the lower strata also drank wine. *Sportulae*, handouts of food and wine as well as coins, were common at public banquets and other sponsored events. Water was not always safe to drink, and wine contributed a part of the daily calories for the poor or slaves living on a subsistence diet. The alternative to wine was *posca*, a drink made from vinegar.[28]

Though Ovid's *Art of Love* is not a straightforward handbook of etiquette, he advises women who would be courted by men to display attractive table manners, somewhat resembling the Renaissance author Erasmus of Rotterdam's *On Civility in Children* or the eighteenth-century *Rules of Civility*. Because the Romans ate with their fingers, Ovid advises women to use their fingers daintily and not put their entire hand into a dish. One hand appears to have been reserved for eating, as in Islamic societies today. Ovid advises women not to eat too much, but to stop before they are full, a dictum that philosophical authors also upheld for men. He suggests that some women ate their meal before being invited out, presumably so they would display less appetite.[29]

Despite the moralists, it was socially significant that elite Roman women regularly attended dinner parties and banquets, because of the semipublic nature of these events in the political class (senatorial order). Roman politicians built support and alliances during social gatherings, including banquets; this motivated the sumptuary legislation of the second century BCE, restricting expenditure at banquets, both on food and drink and on displays such as silver plate. These laws fell into disuse by the first century BCE, but the custom of political banquets continued. Under the Empire, imperial favor or disfavor was often shown by invitation to and seating at banquets, a pattern that was imitated lower on the social scale by wealthy patrons toward poor clients. Roman women were thus able to observe the political and social operations of their male peers and even to contribute to them (though the satirist Juvenal ridiculed women who monopolized dinner-party conversation with discussion of literature or philosophy).

Literary evidence for food at Roman meals varies widely, from depictions of extravagant luxury at the superrich (fictional) Trimalchio's house or imperial banquets, to the baseline staples enumerated for slaves' rations in Cato the Elder's *On Farming*. These staples were wheat, olive oil, and wine; legumes such as beans or lentils provided protein, as did cheese and fermented fish products. When middle- and lower-strata people ate meat, it was probably pork, as pigs are more economical to raise than cattle or sheep. Slave women and poor freeborn women are most likely to have received insufficient protein in their diets to support the repeated pregnancies of the ancient world's high-fertility demography. On the other hand, economic historians have suggested that the general quality of life in the Roman Empire was relatively high by the standards of other premodern societies that experienced frequent famines.

At the high end, the range of foods eaten seems limited only by the extravagance of epicures and the imagination of literary authors. The cookbook attributed to Apicius, a notorious epicure who committed suicide when his income could no longer supply his accustomed level of luxury, describes many dishes that might have been served by the first-century CE wealthy, with extensive use of expensive spices (especially pepper) imported from India and Asia. However many other dishes used simpler ingredients. Reconstructing these dishes is difficult (as with most premodern cookbooks) because the amounts or proportions of ingredients are not specified; a Roman cook, usually a male slave rather than a woman, would have been accustomed to making dishes from experience. Cooking was not a major feature of women's idealized domestic labor; spinning and weaving, rather than baking bread or cookies, were ideal feminine accomplishments.[30]

COUNTERCULTURAL SOCIAL LIFE

A part of modern social life is free choice of whom to associate with, let alone have sex with or marry. Women in the Roman world often had little choice about who they would marry. Most of the sources for this book have depicted features of daily life that were considered normative or obligatory (or, in the case of mortality, inescapable). Even actions that were undertaken by choice, such as the benefactions described in chapter 9, followed a more or less prescribed form, as did epitaphs and many personal letters.

In contrast, love (elegaic) poetry emphasizes subjective perception and emotional responses, almost always from the male lover's point of view. In his *Ars Amatoria* (*Art of Love*), the Augustan-era poet Ovid presents a plausible and detailed picture of young women, perhaps sub-elite in status, who were sexually available— not prostitutes, but free to seek love affairs with young men. The women in the *Art of Love* and in elegy have been suggested to be freedwomen, and the identification of Catullus's "Lesbia" with the aristocratic Clodia, sister of the tribune Clodius Pulcher, has been questioned. The overall reality of countercultural love elegy has also been questioned; young Roman men and women could well have read such poetry for vicarious reasons, seeking an imaginative escape from the constraints of a society that expected young women to marry men chosen by their fathers and that imposed severe punishments for adultery.

The Late Republic–era poet Sulpicia presents the point of view of a woman. Some modern critics have doubted her very existence, arguing that she was a persona adopted by the closely associated poet Tibullus.

CONCLUSION: OTHER SOCIAL EVENTS

Many of the private events described in previous chapters were also opportunities for women to socialize, involving family members or wider circles of acquaintances. The name-day of infants, on the eighth or ninth day of life, was an opportunity for celebration, as were birthday parties (more typically celebrated by adults than by children). Betrothals and weddings were other social events, as were, more sadly, funerals (described in chapter 11). Many of these also featured feasts, sometimes prescribed by the ritual.

Social events that were peculiar to the Romans, but private and secular rather than public or religious, included the witnessing and reading of wills. For all but soldiers, a legitimate Roman will (*testamentum*) required seven witnesses, typically men, but also women. The witnessing was taken seriously but seems also to have been an opportunity for a social gathering. Women were able to make wills (see discussion in chapter 11). Pliny the Younger relates that a woman named Aurelia (he provides little other information about her, her family, or her age) invited him and six others to witness the drawing up of her will. Pliny's most despised acquaintance, the jurist and orator Marcus Aquilius Regulus, turned up and attempted to negotiate Aurelia into adding a codicil legating him the very expensive clothing that she was wearing. The reading of a will, after the testator's death, was also a solemn but eagerly anticipated social event, as people used their wills to leave legacies to and praise people they approved of and to pass over and disparage their enemies.[31]

Dramatic public events brought out women spectators as well as men. Women came to witness the battle of Cremona in 69 CE, bringing food to the combatants, as Tacitus's *Histories* relates. Women should be assumed present as onlookers at major events—the urban conflicts of the Late Republic; the fall of the city of Rome to the Flavians in December 69; the triumphs of Republican generals and Roman emperors. Pliny depicts Roman women as among the witnesses of Trajan's arrival (*adventus*) as emperor.

Women also were participants in religious festivals, discussed in chapter 10. But triumphs and spectacles also had a religious aspect; the dividing line is blurry. At the Saecular Games, boys and young women sang a hymn (Horace's *Carmen Saeculare*). Chapters 9 and 10 focus on women's roles in two kinds of public events: as civic benefactors and as priestesses and lay participants in religious rituals.

NOTES

1. *Vindolanda Tablets* II 291 = Mary R. Lefkowitz and Maureen B. Fant, *Women's Life in Greece and Rome: A Source Book in Translation*, 4th ed. (Baltimore, MD, 2016), no. 324 = Emily A. Hemelrijk, *Women and Society in the Roman World: A Sourcebook of Inscriptions from the Roman West* (Cambridge, 2021), no. 4.2. On related letters, see *Vindolanda Tablets* II 292 + 294 = *Women's Life*, no. 272, addressing Lepidina less formally. On frontier society, see Lindsay Allason-Jones, *Women in Roman Britain* (London, 1989); Alan K. Bowman, *Life and Letters on the Roman Frontier: Vindolanda and Its People* (New York, 1994); Elizabeth Greene, "Female networks in military communities in the Roman West: A view from the Vindolanda Tablets," in *Women and the Roman City in the Latin West* (Leiden, 2013), ed. Emily A. Hemelrijk and Greg Woolf, 369–90; Lee L. Brice and Elizabeth M. Greene, ed., *Present but Not Accounted For: Women and the Roman Army* (Cambridge, forthcoming).

2. On Cornelia, see Cornelius Nepos fr. 2 = *Women's Life*, no. 309. On Livia, see Suet. *Claudius* 4.1–6, 3.2.

3. Catullus 5.2–3.

4. On elite women's social lives, see Susan Treggiari, *Roman Marriage: Iusti Coniuges from the Time of Cicero to the Time of Ulpian* (Oxford, 1991),

414–27; Emily A. Hemelrijk, *Matrona Docta: Educated Women in the Roman Elite from Cornelia to Julia Domna* (London, 1999).

5. On Lucretia, Livy 1.57; an epitaph, *CIL* VI 11602; on hard work, Juvenal 6.9–10, 286–90.

6. Livy 34.2; Seneca *Controversiae* 2.7.3.

7. On these complexities, see Rebecca Langlands, *Sexual Morality in Ancient Rome* (Cambridge, 2006).

8. On Ummidia, see Plin. *Ep.* 7.24. For negative depictions of women's leisure, see J. P. Toner, *Leisure and Ancient Rome* (Oxford, 1995), 29–30, with caution.

9. For a definition of emotional labor, see Amy Richlin, "Emotional work: Lamenting the Roman dead," in *Essays in Honor of Gordon Williams: Twenty-Five Years at Yale* (New Haven, CT, 2001), ed. Elizabeth Tylawsky and Charles Weiss, 229–48 = Amy Richlin, *Arguments with Silence: Writing the History of Roman Women* (Ann Arbor, MI, 2014), 267–88.

10. On *amica optima*, see Hemelrijk, *Women and Society*, nos. 4.3–10.

11. Cic. *Att.* 5.1.3–4 = Jo-Ann Shelton, *As the Romans Did: A Source Book in Roman Social History* (Oxford, 1988), no. 60; Matthew Roller, "Horizontal women: Posture and sex in the Roman *convivium*," *AJPh* 124.3 (2003), 377–422, 398.

12. On travel, Treggiari, *Roman Marriage*, 421–22; in the city, Mary Harlow, "Dressed women on the streets of the ancient city: What to wear?" in *Women and the Roman City in the Latin West* (Leiden, 2013), ed. Emily A. Hemelrijk and Greg Woolf, 225–41.

13. On Agrippina, see Tac. *Annals* 13.5. On adultery, see Tac. *Histories* 1.48. On places, see Ovid *Art of Love* 1.66 (gardens), 72–3 (*Porticus Liviae*), 77–8 (temple of Isis), 79–88 (Forum), 90–134 (theater), 135–69 (games), 253–4 (women's festivals), 255 (Baiae). On Tacitus, see Sara Elise Phang, "Elite marriage and adultery in the camp: Plin. *Ep.* 6.31.4–6 and Tac. *Hist.* 1.48," in Brice and Greene, *Present but Not Accounted For* (Cambridge, forthcoming).

14. On Cornelia's statue, Plin. *Natural History* 34.31; *CIL* VI 10043 = Hemelrijk, *Women and Society*, no. 7.1. On public statues of women, see section "Women in Municipal Public Life."

15. Suet. *Nero* 23.2; Plin. *Ep.* 7.24; Jo-Ann Shelton, *The Women of Pliny's Letters* (London, 2013), 246–49. On *infames*, see Catherine Edwards, "Unspeakable professions: Public performance and prostitution in ancient Rome," in *Roman Sexualities* (Princeton, NJ, 1997), ed. Judith P. Hallett and Marilyn B. Skinner, 66–95; Jane F. Gardner, *Being a Roman Citizen* (London, 1993), 110–54; Thomas A. J. McGinn, *Prostitution, Sexuality, and the Law in Ancient Rome* (Oxford, 1998), 21–69.

16. On Eppia, see Juvenal 6.102–13; Keith Hopkins, *Death and Renewal* (Cambridge, 1983), 23–24. On *suspirium puellarum*, see *CIL* IV 4342 = Hemelrijk, *Women and Society*, no. 4.26.

17. Elizabeth Rawson, "*Discrimina ordinum*: The *Lex Julia theatralis*," *Papers of the British School at Rome* 55 (1987), 83–114; Emily A. Hemelrijk, *Hidden Lives, Public Personae: Women and Civic Life in the Roman West* (Oxford, 2015), 212, 217–18. On looking up, Rawson, "*Discrimina ordinum*," 89, 91.

18. On Ovid, see n. 12; cf. *Amores* 3.2.1–84 = Shelton, no. 347.

19. Garrett Fagan, *Bathing in Public in the Roman World* (Ann Arbor, MI, 1999), 10.

20. Martial 3.68.1–4; antiquarian, Varro *On the Latin Language* 9.68; Vitruvius *On Architecture* 1.10.4. On Hadrian and other emperors, *SHA Hadrian* 18.10; *Marcus* 23.8; *Alexander* 24.2.

21. On Vipasca, see *ILS* 6891 = E. M. Smallwood, ed., *Documents Illustrating the Principates of Nerva, Trajan, and Hadrian* (Cambridge, 1966), no. 440 = Hemelrijk, *Women and Society*, no. 4.47. On Corfinium, see *L'Année Epigraphique* 1961, 109 = Fagan, *Bathing*, no. 88; Lanuvium, *CIL* XIV 2121 = *ILS* 5683 = Fagan, *Bathing*. no, 46; Marruvium, *CIL* IX 6377 = *ILS* 5684 = Fagan, *Bathing*, no. 151; Veii, *CIL* IX 3811 = *ILS* 6583 = Fagan, *Bathing*, no. 213.

22. On mixed-gender bathing, see Fagan, *Bathing*, 24–29, 34–36, 47; Roy Bowen Ward, "Women in Roman baths," *Harvard Theological Review* 85.2 (1992), 125–47; J. P. Toner, *Leisure and Ancient Rome* (Cambridge, 1995), 53–64; both Ward and Toner are uncritical of sources. Suburban baths: Laura K. McClure, *Women in Classical Antiquity: From Birth to Death* (Hoboken, NJ, 2019), 244–45. Mixed-gender disapproved by Plin. *Natural History* 33.153; Quintilian *Institutio Oratoria* 5.9.14. On mixed bathing encouraged by Elagabalus, see *SHA Heliogabalus* 31.7; repressed by emperors, n. 20 above. On an egalitarian outlook, see Fagan, *Bathing*, 189. On veterans, see *SHA Hadrian* 17.5–7. On ostentation, see Fagan, *Bathing*, 215–18, e.g., Lucian *Nigrinus* 34. Epitaphs: *L'Année Epigraphique* 1987, 179 = Hemelrijk, *Women and Society*, no. 1.7 (Ostia, 2nd/3rd c. CE); *CIL* XIII 1983 = *ILS* 8158 = Shelton, no. 56.

23. On Fortuna Virilis, see Ovid *Fasti* 4.145–52. On Teanum, see Gellius *Noctes Atticae* 10.3.1–3; on woman, Juvenal 6.418–447.

24. Seneca *Letters* 86.12; Columella *On Farming* 1.16.19–21. On Hannibal's soldiers at Capua, see Livy 23.18.11–17.

25. On Greek versus Roman, see Nepos pr. 6. On invitations, see Treggiari, *Roman Marriage*, 414; Dio 57.12.5; *Vindolanda Tablets* II 291.

26. Treggiari, *Roman Marriage*, 423–25; Roller, "Horizontal women." On archaic manners, see Varro in Isidorus *Etymology* 20.11.9; Valerius Maximus 2.1.2. On Vestals, Macrobius *Saturnalia* 3.13.11. On this scene, see Meghan J. DiLuzio, *A Place at the Altar: Priestesses in Republican Rome* (Princeton, NJ, 2016), 57. Children still sat, as shown in Nonius 372L; Suet. *Claudius* 33; Tac. *Annals* 13.16.

27. On legends, see Plut. *Roman Questions* 6; Dionysius of Halicarnassus *Roman Antiquities* 2.25.6; Valerius Maximus 2.1.5, 6.3.9; Gellius *Noctes*

Atticae 10.23.1–4. On *matronae* drinking sweet wine, see Festus 131L; Gellius *Noctes Atticae* 10.23.2; Varro in Nonius 551M. On table manners, Ovid *Art of Love* 1.229–52, 3.760–64; quoted, 765–66; cf. Juvenal 6.300–305. On Clement of Alexandria, see Treggiari, *Roman Marriage*, 423.

28. Hemelrijk, *Hidden Lives*, 145–46.

29. Ovid *Art of Love* 3.754–6.

30. For examples of recipes in Apicius, see Shelton, nos. 93–95.

31. Plin. *Ep.* 2.20.

9

PUBLIC LIFE

INTRODUCTION

The ideal *matrona*'s role was supposedly wholly domestic, in the stylized words of Seneca the Younger describing his mother's conduct:

> Throughout the sixteen years during which her husband was governor of Egypt, she was never seen in public, never admitted a provincial to her house, sought no favor from her husband, nor suffered any to be sought from herself.

Pliny the Younger praises Plotina, wife of the emperor Trajan (98–117 CE), in similar terms:

> Many distinguished men have been dishonored by the ill-considered choice of a wife or weakness in not getting rid of her; thus their fame abroad was damaged by their loss of reputation at home, and their relative failure as husbands denied them complete success as citizens. But your own wife contributes to your honor and glory, as a supreme model of the ancient virtues . . . How modest she is in her attire, how moderate the number of her attendants, how unassuming she is when she walks abroad! This is the work of her husband, who has fashioned and formed her habits; there is glory enough for a wife in obedience.

These passages represent an ideal of modesty and *pudicitia* for high-status Roman women (the wife of a provincial governor and the wife of an emperor). In some respects these passages are accurate, for women were excluded from many areas of public life in the Roman world. However, elite women's de facto influence, though depicted negatively in these two passages, was undeniable. Elite women also acted to protect their husbands' interests in emergencies. In other respects these passages are highly misleading, for women of the upper orders took part in other aspects of public life, especially in smaller cities and towns in Roman Italy and the Mediterranean, using their wealth to become civic benefactors and priestesses (more context on women's religious activities is provided in chapter 10). These roles, as will be seen in this chapter, were extremely public.[1]

Roman empresses, termed *Augustae*, did not govern in their own right. They were the wives, mothers, and other female relatives of emperors (the title Augusta was not limited to the emperor's consort). The Roman state, from the founding of the Republic onward, did not permit women to hold political offices or military commands, to serve in the military, or to vote. In practice, empresses and women of the senatorial and equestrian orders wielded very considerable unofficial influence, though assessing its strength and impact is difficult because of the male-authored sources' hostility to women's influence, seen above in the quotations on Helvia and Plotina. A man's representation of a woman's modesty in public was probably conventional, intended to persuade his audience of his own bona fides as well as of her good repute.

Women were also excluded from representing others in court, a major public role for Roman elite men, and in general, public speaking was regarded as inappropriate for women, a violation of their ideal of modesty. This restriction did not exclude Roman women from access to the law. Women could employ male advocates and frequently petitioned the emperor in their own written voices and were responded to directly; imperial rescripts to women are addressed to them, not to their guardians or advocates.

Though Roman women were excluded from public life in terms of officeholding, the empresses played an important public role as symbolic representatives of the imperial power and as actual representatives of dynastic continuity. They bestowed majestic public buildings on Rome and other cities. As with the emperors themselves, empresses were the focus of reverence in the imperial cult (discussed in chapter 10).[2]

Roman women were not excluded at the municipal level, where they could be public priestesses and even hold some municipal magistracies (most often in the Greek cities of the east). As we have seen, elite women possessed considerable wealth, usually attained through inheritance, but in some cases through trade and commerce. Women were permitted to employ this wealth for public benefit as benefactors, usually at the municipal level. These were important roles, as the cities and towns of the Roman Empire depended on local funding for building and repairing public buildings, providing amenities such as public baths and spectacles, and feeding poor children.

In a society that emphasized hierarchical relationships, including patron-client relationships, women of the upper social strata were also able to be patrons. The model of female patronesses took its inspiration from the empresses. It was imitated by sub-elite Romans; women appear in honorary inscriptions as the *matres* (mothers) of *collegia*, voluntary associations of artisans and members of religious cults. Across the Empire, the role of "mother" was an acceptable model for female social power, from the empresses to the female members of *collegia*. A major part of public life for women in the Roman world was participation in religious activities, discussed in chapter 10; this chapter concerns secular aspects of public life.

EXCLUSION FROM PUBLIC LIFE: THE REPUBLIC

The Republic's exclusion of women from political power was ancient, embedded in the downfall of the monarchy (753–510 BCE). In the Republic, women could not hold political office (senator, quaestor, aedile, tribune of the plebs, praetor, consul, or censor), military commands, or governorships (propraetor, proconsul, and in the imperial period legate). Nor could they vote. The reasons for these exclusions were probably rooted in the military organization of the Republic. In the early and middle Republic, the most powerful magistrates, praetor and consul, were war leaders. Young men were required to serve ten military campaigns before they could run for office. In the middle and Late Republic, as the Roman *imperium* grew, many of these offices became less military; the urban praetor stayed at Rome and his main responsibility was administering law. Proconsuls and propraetors became governors, less and less expected to command. For young aristocrats, the custom of serving ten campaigns lapsed, replaced by oratorical careers. Augustus's reorganization of the Principate demilitarized some provinces altogether, and ensured that many senators' distinguished careers saw very little military service, chiefly a year or two as military tribune (distinct from tribune of the plebs). Nonetheless, women were still excluded from these offices. In the late second or early third century CE, Ulpian writes, "Women are removed from all civil and public functions and therefore are neither able to be judges (*iudices*) nor to undertake a magistracy nor to bring a prosecution nor to intervene [legally] on behalf of another nor to be procurators [financial officials]." In fact, women were permitted to bring lawsuits on their own behalf, as will be seen.[3]

Elite women in the Republic did wield influence and social power, as representatives of noble families and the mothers and wives of powerful men. As the practice of *manus* marriage declined, women whose fathers were deceased could possess wealth in their own right, giving them social power. They were permitted to display their wealth, as personal adornment (the focus of the *Lex Oppia* debate, mentioned in chapter 5). They could also display wealth through expenditure on religious dedications and ceremonies such as expiatory *lectisternia* (discussed in chapter 10).

The second century BCE was a period of rapid social change for the Roman Republic. The nobility was becoming extremely wealthy from the conquests of the Eastern Mediterranean, and the proper use of wealth was a moral concern, giving rise to sumptuary laws (laws which restrict conspicuous consumption). The *Lex Oppia* had been passed in 215 BCE as part of the response to Hannibal's invasion of Italy. It decreed "that no woman was to own more than a half-ounce of gold, wear [brightly] colored clothes, or ride in a carriage in the city or a town . . . except to attend public religious rites." In 195 repealing the law was proposed. The women, "displaying . . . no female modesty," assembled to support the repeal. Then censor and in charge of public morals, Cato the Elder defended the law, claiming that without the law, women would run out of control. He upbraided them for making their demands in public:

> What sort of conduct is this, all this running out into public places, blocking streets and accosting other women's husbands? Couldn't you all have asked your own husbands the very same thing at home? . . . And yet not even at home should the proposing or repealing of laws . . . have been any concern of yours, not if modesty kept married women within their proper limits.

The plebeian tribune Lucius Valerius defended the repeal of the *Lex Oppia*, saying that men were permitted to wear purple as magistrates and priests; women, who were not permitted to hold public office, should be allowed adornment to allow them to show distinction.

> Magistracies, priesthoods, triumphs, insignia, prizes or spoils of war are not accessible to them. Elegance, grooming, a fine appearance—these are women's insignia. These are their pride and joy. This is what your ancestors called woman's embellishment.

The women demonstrators succeeded in inducing the repeal of the *Lex Oppia*. Livy's depiction of women's wealth represents it as adornment, trivializing elite women's considerable economic power.[4]

Women's assertiveness over the *Lex Oppia* was part of a tradition of spontaneous collective action, attributed to archaic Rome in the anecdote that the Sabine women, taken captive and made into wives, stopped a war of the Romans versus the Sabine men, literally coming between the two battle lines. Women also took collective action to introduce the worship of new gods, described in chapter 10. Another instance of women's collective action appears in the Late Republic, when the triumvirs (Octavian, Antony, and Lepidus, 43–42 BCE) sought to tax the wealthiest 1,400 Roman matrons. Led by Hortensia, who was skilled in oratory, the matrons appeared in the Forum, where Hortensia defended their right not to be taxed: "Why should we be taxed when we have no part in public office?" The wealth of women of the upper orders was their major source of social power. The triumvirs backed down, reducing the number of women taxed, and levying a tax on men who owned more than 100,000 sesterces (HS). Again, wealthy women's economic power was considerable, and they resisted attempts to reduce it. As this chapter will show, though they were excluded from public office, their ownership of property enabled them to hold public roles as patrons and benefactors.[5]

WOMEN AS PATRONS

The Roman world was a highly hierarchical society, emphasizing vertical social relationships, especially those of patrons (persons of higher status) and their clients (persons of lower status). A male *patronus* might be a wealthy senator who was able to do favors for his friends (*amici*) and clients (*clientes*), represent them in court, and exert political influence on their behalf; clients sought his advice and assistance. Clients lined up every morning to ritually greet their patron in the formal courtyard of his great house. Furthermore, an ex-owner was the legal *patronus* of the freed person whom he had manumitted.[6]

Elite women were not forbidden to be patrons (Latin *patronae*). In the legal sense, when they owned and manumitted slaves, these women became their *patronae*. Individual educated aristocratic women were also literary patrons from the Late Republic onward. At her home in Misenum, Cornelia the mother of the Gracchi hosted dinners for Greek men of learning. The empress Plotina herself was a patron of the Epicurean philosophical school at Athens. We have also seen in chapter 6 that elite women could make large loans to their social connections. But women were not able to represent clients in law (discussed in section "Women in the Law Courts"), an important role of male patrons.[7]

Furthermore, male authors often depict elite women's influence and de facto power in highly negative terms. An early such historical (as opposed to legendary) representation is Cicero's *Pro Caelio*, a defense of Caelius against Clodia, an aristocratic woman whom Caelius had borrowed a large sum of money from and who was suing for its return. Cicero proceeded to demolish Clodia's personal and sexual reputation, depicting her as immoral and promiscuous, probably with little basis in fact. Another powerful woman of the Late Republic who received this treatment was Fulvia, Mark Antony's wife, who became embroiled in the civil wars that broke out after the assassination of Julius Caesar in 44 BCE. Fulvia and Mark Antony's brother Lucius led the defense of the siege of Perusia, a city in central Italy, against its besieger Octavian (the future emperor Augustus). Fulvia was mocked with sexual insults by both Octavian's soldiers, who inscribed crude insults on lead sling stones, and by Octavian himself, who penned verses in more erudite but similar terms. Fulvia appears to have been loyal to Mark Antony's interests, a pattern that repeats itself in accounts of elite women's behavior.[8]

Elite women were permitted to exert influence and take unprecedented action on behalf of family members, particularly husbands. In such instances, their loyalty appeared praiseworthy as long as they did not step beyond the bounds of appropriate female behavior. When Cicero was exiled in 58 BCE at the instigation of the tribune Publius Clodius (the brother of Clodia), Cicero's wife Terentia exerted herself to raise money and send it to him (his distress at her selling her property is quoted in section "Elite Women's Economic Activities") and kept him up to date on events at Rome. The woman who is the subject of the "Laudatio Turiae," a funeral eulogy inscribed on stone, also helped her husband when he was exiled during the triumviral proscriptions in 43–42 BCE. She not only sent him money and news but went to the triumvir Lepidus and petitioned him for mercy toward her husband. According to the "Laudatio Turiae," she was beaten and dragged out by Lepidus's henchmen. Other loyal wives risked their lives to save their husbands during this period of brutal political purges.[9]

In the early Empire, the first empress, Livia Augusta, the wife and later widow of Augustus (27 BCE–14 CE) and mother of Tiberius (14–37 CE), wielded great influence and de facto power, though she held no formal offices other than chief priestess of the Deified Augustus after his death. Livia was honored as a goddess in the Greek East and as *mater patriae* (mother of the fatherland); she sponsored building projects, such as the *porticus Liviae* at Rome. This level of female influence was unprecedented in Rome, and male authors (writing long after the fact) depicted it negatively. Imperial women were wealthy in their own right and could help secure prestigious and lucrative appointments or blight a man's public career. But even Agrippina the Younger, the mother of Nero, who governed behind the throne during his minority, had to listen to proceedings of the Senate from behind a curtain.[10]

These allegations of female influence were extended to the wives of provincial governors in a famous passage of Tacitus's *Annals*, a debate in the Senate over whether provincial governors should be permitted to bring their wives to their provincial posts. Aulus Caecina Severus, a senator with a severe reputation, opposed this policy:

> There was point in the old regulation which prohibited the dragging of women to the provinces or foreign countries . . . [Women] paraded among the soldiers; they had the centurions at beck and call . . . It was to the wife that the basest of the provincials at once attached themselves; it was the wife who took in hand and transacted business. There were two potentates to salute in the streets; two bodies of government; and the more headstrong and autocratic orders came from the women, who, once held in curb by the Oppian law and other laws, had now cast their chains and ruled supreme in the home, the courts, and by now the army itself.

This exceedingly hyperbolic passage generalized from scattered incidents and invoked the emperor Tiberius's jealous suspicions about his nephew Germanicus, a military commander who had recently suppressed a mutiny on the Rhine and led a punitive expedition into Germany. Germanicus's wife, Agrippina the Elder, a granddaughter of Augustus, accompanied Germanicus on his campaign and notably stemmed a panicked rout of the Roman army by exhorting them at the Rhine bridge. Such a military role was highly unusual, even though Agrippina's behavior followed the pattern of a wife defending her husband's interests. Tiberius was also at odds with his mother Livia, who wielded great influence at Rome. In Tacitus's words, to owe promotion to a woman (especially on the traditionally all-male frontiers) undermined men's masculinity and impugned the woman's *pudicitia*. In fact the wife of a governor or commander had no official power over his bureaucrats, officers, and soldiers. Tacitus insinuates her unprovable boundless influence, *muliebris impotentia* ("uncontrolled power" rather than impotence).[11]

Could an elite Roman man acknowledge a female patron in his own words, in contrast with allegations of women's influence long after the fact? Such texts, whether inscriptions or literature, are valuable contemporary firsthand evidence. They seem to be relatively rare. As we will see, women could not perform one of a patron's most important roles, representing their clients in the law courts. Seeking out imperial women as patrons seems to have required a cautious and indirect approach; perhaps both parties were afraid of the type of insinuations Tacitus makes. In his treatise *On Architecture*, Vitruvius thanks Octavia, Augustus's sister, for helping him get a promotion. Pliny the Younger promises to recommend an acquaintance to Plotina. In fact, Plotina as Trajan's widow became a patron of the Epicurean school of philosophy at Athens, helping to settle a dispute over the appointment of its successor. The pattern suggests itself that an older woman who was a widow (such as Cornelia the mother of the Gracchi, Livia after the death of Augustus, or Plotina) was better placed to be a patron, to wield influence, and to receive honors.[12]

In the mid-third century CE, a man named Quintus Veturius Callistratus thanked the Vestal Campia Severina for securing his promotion to a financial post:

To Campia Severina, most revered Vestal Virgin, whose genuine chastity confirmed by repeated public praise the senate crowned;

> Quintus Veturius Callistratus, most eminent man [i.e., equestrian], by her support was appointed procurator of the private revenues of the libraries of our Augustus, and his procurator.

Notably, Veturius stresses the Vestal's chastity, which was theoretically assured. In another such dedication, Aemilius Pardalas thanks the Vestal for his promotion to an equestrian officership. The Vestal Virgins, as seen in chapter 10, were aristocratic high priestesses of the Roman state religion, often wealthy and highly influential.[13]

In other inscriptions (discussed in section "Women as Patrons and *Matres* of *Collegia*"), elite women who became the patrons of cities and towns or *collegia* were praised in similar terms. Advertising the modesty and chastity of the empress or of senatorial women asserted their virtue, increasing the prestige of the men associated with them (emperors, senatorial husbands, or clients). Praising a female patron for modesty and chastity (or as metaphorical "mother" as shown in section "Women as Patrons and *Matres* of *Collegia*") was a statement that her influence was acceptable and did not exceed the bounds of propriety; it assured that her de facto power was not *muliebris inpotentia*.

WOMEN IN THE LAW COURTS

Roman law and social customs restricted women's participation in court proceedings. Women were permitted to sue on their own behalf, speaking as their own advocates, but this behavior was considered immodest. Valerius Maximus relates the story of Carfania (Gaia Afrania in some versions), a noblewoman of the second-century BCE Republic who prosecuted her own lawsuits and made herself obnoxious in men's eyes. He hints that Carfania was accused of or tried for *calumnia*, "vexatious litigation." Conviction for *calumnia* brought with it the legal stigma known as *infamia*. Persons with *infamia* (*infames*) were not permitted to litigate on their own behalf at all and included such socially disapproved persons as prostitutes, pimps, stage performers, and gladiators, as well as those convicted of capital crimes. It was acceptable for women to speak in their own defense or to appear in court as witnesses. Valerius Maximus praises Maesia of Sentinum for speaking "bravely" in her own defense, though the details of her case are not preserved.[14]

Women were not permitted to litigate on behalf of others. They therefore could not be lawyers or advocates for clients, a very important role for men of the political class, who represented clients in court and gained prestige and fame through winning their cases (and took no pay, as they were usually wealthy in their own right). Cicero is only the most famous of such legal orators; his speeches have been preserved because they were regarded as brilliant examples of Latin prose. As an exception, women might litigate on behalf of their children or other dependents; avenging harm done to family members was an acceptable motive for women to enter the courts. Women were also permitted to make accusations of treason when the state itself was in danger. But they were not permitted to be *delatores* (informers), who accused others of capital crimes and were rewarded with pay from the public treasury. The *delatores* were regarded as a dishonorable occupation and a necessary evil; the Roman jurists thought that women should be protected from such dishonorable behavior.

Passages from the jurists suggest that the opprobrium against women's litigation was because their public appearance and speech in court violated the code of matronly modesty. Ulpian stated that the restrictions were "so that women not get themselves mixed up in other people's lawsuits contrary to the modesty suitable to their sex, (and) so that women not discharge men's duties." The emperor Constantine I (306–37 CE) put it more luridly in 315 CE: "so that women not rush irreverently into scorn of their matronly modesty (*matronalis pudor*)." In section "Womanly Weakness", we have seen the legal doctrine of *infirmitas sexus*, "womanly weakness" or frivolity. The jurists also regarded women as more likely to be ignorant of legal affairs, though other groups, such as peasants and soldiers, were also ignorant of the law.[15]

Yet, as seen in chapter 6, wealthy Roman women engaged in numerous property transactions and needed to protect their financial interests. They did so indirectly, appointing representatives to speak for them in court. They might be represented by *tutores* (guardians) if they still had them, or they might delegate an independent advocate or a male family member, as did Demetria daughter of Chaeremon, an Alexandrian woman, who in 55 CE applied to the governor of Egypt to appoint her grandson Chaeremon as her advocate in court proceedings, since she was "unable to be in attendance in court on account of womanly weakness," though her old age was also probably the cause.[16]

The petition and response system acknowledged women's access to legal assistance in their own right. When women sent petitions to the emperors asking for their judgment in legal cases, they did so in their own voices, not through male representatives or guardians (though some extant petitions do mention guardians). The emperors' rescripts spoke to the women directly, not to their male representatives or guardians. At least a fifth of all extant imperial rescripts are addressed to women.[17]

Women who were not citizens had more difficulty in obtaining access to the law. The provincial governors adjudicated cases involving *peregrini* (noncitizens) and judged as they saw fit, a procedure termed *cognitio extra ordinem*. *Cognitio* was not necessarily unfavorable. Whether the women seemed to be from local non-Roman elites and whether they spoke Greek or Latin probably mattered, as did their overall appearance and conduct.[18]

WOMEN IN MUNICIPAL PUBLIC LIFE

In the Roman world, women engaged in public life at the municipal level as public priestesses and benefactors of smaller cities and towns, throughout Italy and in both the Eastern (Greek-speaking) and Western empires. These municipalities, especially in the Latin-speaking West, might have formal charters that laid out the organization of the city or town along Roman legal lines as a *municipium* or *colonia*. Such cities usually had two governing magistrates, the *duumviri* (Board of Two Men), elected annually, and a town council (*curia*) staffed with fellow decurions, the local elite of the area. The property qualification for decurions is not known; 20,000–400,000 HS seems plausible up to the equestrian census or beyond, if not socially qualified for equestrian status. Families at the wealthiest end of this spectrum ran for office. In running for office, the candidates would typically make promises to the citizens to provide the city or town with repairs to public buildings, new public buildings, baths, temples, amphitheaters, feasts, distributions of money, or games, at their own expense. They thus funded the amenities of their cities or towns, which the imperial government for the most part did not supply. This practice of politically motivated benefaction is termed euergetism; it enabled the urbanized areas of the Roman world to enjoy a relatively high standard of living.[19]

Women did not hold magistracies in the cities and towns of the Latin West. The exclusion of women from male public offices characteristic of Rome itself was upheld for the provincial municipalities. An exception was the post of public priestess, *sacerdos publica* or *flaminica* (priestess of the imperial cult), usually held by women of decurion status. It is plausible that the role of priestess made a woman's public role more acceptable, as with the Vestals, though virginity was not expected of public priestesses, many of whom were married and had children (see Junia Rustica later in this section). The religious (cultic) activities of public priestesses will be discussed in chapter 10. As part of their secular activities, public priestesses might make substantial benefactions to their cities in their own right. Women also played the roles of civic benefactors without holding any particular office.[20]

At Pompeii, in the early first century CE, the public priestess Eumachia donated a large and impressive building adjoining the town's forum. The purpose of the building is unknown; it may have been a market or multipurpose gathering place, attractively decorated. One of its dedicatory inscriptions read:

> Eumachia, daughter of Lucius, public priestess, in her own name and that of her son, Marcus Numistrius Fronto, built at her own expense the *chalcidicum*, crypt and portico in honor of Augustan Concord and Piety and also dedicated them.

The fullers (commercial launderers and dyers) of Pompeii erected a dedication and statue to Eumachia, but that does not mean that the building was a fullery (commercial laundry), as fulleries were usually located on city and town outskirts because they smelled bad, using fermented urine to clean wool clothing. Eumachia's family may have become wealthy from other commercial activities, such as producing bricks and tiles; in any case, they were probably of decurion rank. Eumachia is represented in an elegant statue, depicting her as an idealized matron, wearing a *stola* and *palla* that modestly covers her head. The statues that adorned the Eumachia building included a shrine to Augustan Concord and Piety and statues of Aeneas and Romulus, imitating the decoration of the Portico of Livia (7 BC) and the Forum of Augustus.[21]

Other notable benefactors of Pompeii were the freedwoman Vibidia Saturnina and Aulus Furius Saturninus, who "rebuilt and decorated the Temple of Venus which had been damaged with old age" and gave 54,000 HS to the town "on account of their priesthood." The temple of Venus also bore an inscription stating that Vibidia Saturnina and Aulus Furius Saturninus "gave to the town councilors and Augustales 20 HS each and to the townsfolk [8?] HS and to the *Venerii* 4 HS." The *Venerii* were perhaps temple slaves.[22]

Another notable benefactor was Junia Rustica of Cartima, a town in Roman Spain.

> Junia Rustica, daughter of Decimus, first and perpetual priestess in the town of Cartima, restored the public porticoes, that had collapsed due to old age, gave land for a bathhouse, reimbursed the public revenues, set up a bronze statue of Mars in the forum, gave at her own expense porticoes next to the bathhouse on her own land with a pool and a statue of Cupid, after giving a feast and public shows.

In addition to this astonishing list of buildings and services, Junia Rustica also erected, at her own expense, statues of herself, her husband Gaius Fabius Fabianus, and her son Gaius Fabianus Junianus. These benefactions cost in all an estimated 60,000 HS. Junia's family and that of her husband were probably of decurion rank and could have made their fortunes through silver mining or growing olives and exporting olive oil (major industries of Roman Spain). The building of public baths was a major expense, as they required water supply, fuel, and furnaces to heat the water.[23]

In a study of female benefactions in the Roman West, temples and shrines were the most popular type of building funded by women benefactors (125 such inscriptions, with 143 female benefactors). Public infrastructures, such as roads, city walls, aqueducts, or bridges, were less popular (29 inscriptions recording 21 female benefactors), largely because they were extremely expensive. Theaters, amphitheaters, and circuses were also less popular (20 instances with 14 benefactors). Other public buildings, such as porticoes and baths, were popular (51 inscriptions with 46 benefactors). Public statues were frequently erected by female benefactors. Another popular type of benefaction was sponsorship of an event, such as a festival, theatrical shows, or a public banquet with distributions of food and money to the populace. Over half of all public buildings built by women are in Roman Italy, 30 percent in North Africa, and 10.5 percent in Roman Spain. Women avoided Rome itself, where the imperial family monopolized benefactions. The female benefactors of municipalities in the Latin-speaking West provided for their cities in much the same way as men, though they could not hold public offices other than priestess. It is likely that their wealth was inherited, but it can also have been made through commerce, especially when the benefactor appears to be a freedwoman.[24]

Senatorial and equestrian women also made benefactions at the municipal level. The wealthy senatorial widow Ummidia Quadratilla, whom Pliny the Younger describes as an elderly but vigorous matron who enjoyed a game of checkers and the performances of her own pantomime troupe, is probably also the Ummidia Quadratilla of Casinum in Italy who bestowed benefactions on the town, building an amphitheater with the dedication "Ummidia Quadratilla, daughter of Gaius, built the amphitheater and the temple for the citizens of Casinum at her own expense," and repairing a theater commemorated with a now fragmentary inscription, reconstructed as reading

> Ummidia Quadratilla, daughter of Gaius, restored the theater that had been adorned at the expenses of her father and had collapsed from old age, for the citizens of Casinum at her own expense. To celebrate the dedication she gave a banquet to the decurions, the people, and the women.

Pliny snipes at Ummidia Quadratilla for indulging "womanly idleness" (*otium*) with board games and the pantomimes, which were sexually explicit and associated with prostitution. He may have felt competitive; he also bestowed benefactions on his native town of Comum.[25]

Elite women's benefactions, especially when they involved building or organizing citywide events, required considerable planning and people-wrangling skills, even if elite women probably employed male managers to draw up architectural plans and oversee the male workers. Very little is known about *how* these women carried out their benefactions, whether, as is plausible, the *collegia* or guilds of workmen lobbied them with projects. It has been suggested that Ummidia watched her pantomime troupe perform in order to keep them in training for spectacles and increase their value.[26]

The practice of elite women's benefactions suggests a conflict between public spectacle and the ideology of matronly modesty. The announcement of a benefaction was probably a local public event with elaborate spectacle: the woman making the benefaction was formally received by the city councilors (municipal senate) and was profusely thanked. In the inscription of Junia Rustica, the town of Cartima proceeded to vote her and her husband public statues and, in what appears to be competitive gift-giving, she offered to pay for them. The dedication of a public building might be a citywide event, with speeches, entertainments, a public banquet (mainly for the city's upper classes), and handouts of food and money to the masses. The dedication of a temple demanded even more ritual, seen in Tacitus's account of the dedication of the new Capitoline Temple at Rome (the old temple had burned in the civil warfare in 69 CE). In all such events, the wealthy female benefactor probably played a central role and appeared in suitably splendid attire that displayed her rank. Yet when her public statue was erected, it was typically that of a matron in modest pose and dress, her arms held close to her body, her body hidden by a long tunic, *stola*, and enveloping *palla* that covered her hair. On closer inspection, the conflict is only apparent: as shown by other inscriptions dedicated to elite women as *patronae* of cities and associations, the emphasis on the benefactor's matronly modesty and *pudicitia* conferred legitimacy on her actions, as did her modestly cloaked statue.[27]

OTHER WOMEN IN PUBLIC ROLES

If Pompeii is a typical example, women in the cities of the Latin West also expressed public support for male candidates. Pompeii's walls were painted and graffitied with political statements of support, periodically whitewashed over to make room for new advertisements. Cnaeus Helvius Sabinus (probably no relation to Seneca's mother Helvia) ran for town aedile in 79 CE before the eruption of Vesuvius; his numerous supporters included women named Caprasia, Biria, Parthope (with Rufinus), Iunia, and Aegle. A typical statement was "I beg you to elect Cn. Helvius Sabinus aedile, worthy of public office. Maria asks this." The name Maria might be the feminine of the Roman name Marius and not a Jewish/Christian name. All these women were probably of relatively low status. The preservation of these texts suggests that women's public activity might have been recorded on ephemeral media such as painted walls and boards that are now lost.[28]

In the Greek-speaking East, women from wealthy and prominent families also held locally significant public roles, including priestesses of local cults as well as the imperial cult and magistracies usually held by men, such as *grammateus* (secretary of the town council), *gymnasiarch* (in charge of the city's gymnasia and exercise and cultural clubs), *gerousiarch* (in charge of groups for older men), magistrate in charge of theatrical shows, and more. These offices were highly honorary and the women's actual roles are unclear. It was more plausible that a Greek woman of notable family would fund a gymnasium and the attendant spectacles, such as youth parades and literary competitions, than concern herself with its daily activities. Many of these women, furthermore, came from families whose male members had held these honors. Nonetheless, the women held prominent public roles, even as representatives of their families and continuators of family tradition.[29]

In all these instances of female benefactors and officeholders, the importance of public display, even in "honorary" roles, should not be underestimated. Imperial Greco-Roman society was conducted very much in public, emphasizing public ceremony and spectacle. Women's dedications of honorific statues and of major public buildings are likely to have been accompanied by festivity and public speeches, though it is uncertain whether the women themselves would have given the speeches; women were not trained in oratory. Below the senatorial, equestrian, and decurion orders, women of sub-elite and ordinary status observed this public display and may have sought to imitate it as the so-called *matres* (mothers) of *collegia* (voluntary associations).[30]

WOMEN AS PATRONS AND *MATRES* OF *COLLEGIA*

A feature of public life below the municipal level was voluntary associations, *collegia* (sg. *collegium*, the source of the English word "college") or *sodalitates*, to which ordinary people belonged, organized by trade, religious cult, ethnicity, or other criteria. *Collegia* were extremely popular throughout Roman Italy. They served as funerary associations, collecting dues to fund members' funerals and remembrance feasts, not because the members were too poor to afford their own funerals (most members of *collegia* belonged to the middle strata) but to provide social cohesion. *Collegia* were also social associations, holding regular communal meals that were funded from the dues. They provided ambitious men of the sub-elite some opportunity for advancement through becoming magistrates of the *collegia*, with titles and honorific inscriptions that echoed those of city and town magistrates. The closest comparison is with the numerous fraternal orders and mutual aid societies that sprang up in eighteenth- to twentieth-century England and the United States.[31]

Prominent examples of Roman trade *collegia* were the *fabri* or builders and the *centonarii* or textile workers. Other *collegia* were adherents of a particular deity, such as Bacchus, or Aesculapius and Hygeia (the god of healing and his daughter). The *dendrophori*, or "bough-carriers," were votaries of the Great Mother (Cybele). Of some 2,500 *collegia* inscriptions, most in Roman Italy, about 200 record women associated with them.[32]

Building of Eumachia, Forum of Pompeii, Pompeii, Italy, early first century CE. A public priestess of Venus, Eumachia funded the construction of this imposing public edifice. The impressive building's purpose is unknown; it may have been a multifunctional gathering place rather than a wool market. (Jean-Jacques Serol/Dreamstime.com)

For the most part, the members of *collegia* were men. This was not exclusively the case, however, and *collegium* inscriptions that list the members attest that women might be members (depending on the trade and the gods). Women played a leading role in *collegia* in two ways: as patrons, who usually were of much higher social status than the *collegium* members, or as *matres collegiorum*, "mothers of the *collegia*."

The female patrons of *collegia* were of senatorial or equestrian rank and are honored by the *collegia* in rather exalted terms that praise their moral virtues, emphasizing their modesty and virtue as wives and mothers. In 224 CE, a *collegium fabrorum* erected an honorary inscription to Ancharia Luperca, the wife of chief centurion Laberius Gallo, *vir eminentissimus* (i.e., equestrian), co-opting her as patroness "because of the chastity of her morals and the purity of her traditional habits" and hailing her as "a honorable *matrona* of pure character and habits endowed with feelings of religious veneration." Such was the acceptable model to represent a woman of high status in public life, particularly one you wished to flatter. For the *collegium* members either thank their female patrons for a donation

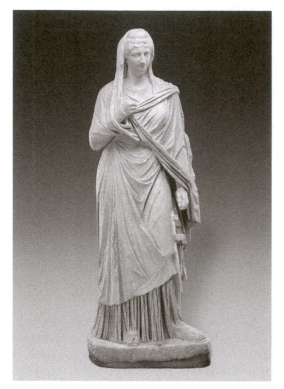

This portrait of the empress Faustina the Elder, wife of Antoninus Pius (138–61 CE), displays the modest bearing of a high-status Roman woman in long skirts and an enveloping mantle (*palla*) which covers her body and head. This costume belied the active role many elite women played in public life. Municipal benefactresses may have inspired Pius to create a grain distribution or alimenta for girls, the *puellae Faustinianae*, in honor of Faustina, who died in 140 CE. (The J. Paul Getty Museum)

or they seem to expect future favors from their female patrons— honoring them in advance. Many of these inscriptions are from the late second and third centuries CE, when the smaller cities and towns were suffering financially; the mode of funding by euergetism was beginning to fail as members of the decurion class became poorer. The epidemic known as the "Antonine Plague," which lasted approximately from 165 to 180 CE, the political instability of the late second and third centuries CE, and a colder climate that reduced crop yields all brought hardship to the Empire. In this period, the voluntary benefactions that sustained civic amenities became an obligatory tax (*munus*, pl. *munera*) upon the decurions.[33]

Women might hold public positions in *collegia* as *matres collegiorum*, mothers of associations. These women appear to be from the same social background as male members of the *collegia* and are not honored in exalted terms; they appear to have carried out some organizational functions that are not stated, presumably organizing feasts and funerals and keeping the rolls of members. They might contribute financially, but not on the scale of the decurion class and above. The role of "mother" is notable, as it provided women in public with an acceptably honorable role that did not risk sexual dishonor and that imitated the role of the empress as *mater patriae*, "mother of the fatherland."[34]

CONCLUSION: WOMEN AS PATRONS

Though women were excluded from public office (with the exception of public priestesses), elite women also played the role of patrons, exerting influence on behalf of and providing material assistance to clients. Unlike male patrons, women were unable to provide legal assistance to clients, being barred from representing others in court. Women could make extensive loans, as seen in chapter 6. They could also have exerted influence on behalf of men's promotions. Such influence and assistance was acceptable as long as it remained unobtrusive and in keeping with matronly modesty and *pudicitia*. Women's influence at the highest levels, as with the empresses, other imperial women, and governors' wives, was scrutinized with greater suspicion. Below the level of imperial politics, wealthy women may have been more free to play a public role in smaller cities and towns, making extensive benefactions to their municipalities. They pursued their own legal interests by using men as their legal advocates and mouthpieces in court.

Women also played a more symbolic role in public life as representatives of family and dynastic continuity, for which their honorable sexual reputation was essential. The empresses modeled this role as symbolic "mothers" of the state, which was imitated at successively lower levels of society. Women in chaste and maternal roles thus were guarantees of political stability; adultery threatened not just individual families, but the social order. The most acceptable public roles for women were, however, in religious life—as priestesses such as the Vestal Virgins and local public priestesses, and as participants in traditional rites and festivals in honor of the gods. These activities are the subject of chapter 10.

NOTES

1. Seneca *Consolatio ad Helviam* 19.6; Plin. *Panegyricus* 83.4–7.

2. On the empresses and other women of the imperial family, Eve D'Ambra, *Roman Women* (Cambridge, 2007), 148–66; Mary T. Boatwright, *Imperial Women of Rome: Power, Gender, Context* (Oxford, 2021).

3. D. 50.17.2. The exclusions are rooted in archaic Roman law and society; see Jane F. Gardner, *Being a Roman Citizen* (London, 1993), 85–108.

On the changes in the Principate, see Brian Campbell, *The Emperor and the Roman Army, 31 B.C.–A.D. 235* (Oxford, 1984).

4. On *Lex Oppia*, see Livy 34.1–7; Mary R. Lefkowitz and Maureen B. Fant, *Women's Life in Greece and Rome: A Source Book in Translation*, 4th ed. (Baltimore, MD, 2016), no. 196.

5. On Sabine women, see Livy 1.13. On Hortensia, see Appian *Civil Wars* 4.32–4; *Women's Life*, no. 199; Valerius Maximus 8.3.3.

6. On patronage in general, see Richard P. Saller, *Personal Patronage under the Early Empire* (Cambridge, 1982).

7. On Cornelia, see Plut. *Gaius Gracchus* 49; on her statue, see Plin. *Natural History* 34.31; discussed, Emily A. Hemelrijk, *Matrona Docta: Educated Women in the Roman Elite from Cornelia to Julia Domna* (London, 1999), 97–98, 101–2.

8. On Clodia, see Suzanne Dixon, *Reading Roman Women: Sources, Genres, and Real Life* (London, 2001), 133–56. On Fulvia, see Judith P. Hallett, "'Perusine glandes' and the changing image of Augustus," *American Journal of Ancient History* 2.2 (1977), 151–71.

9. On "Turia," see Emily A. Hemelrijk, "Masculinity and femininity in the 'Laudatio Turiae,'" *Classical Quarterly* 54 (2004), 185–97; more in chapter 11.

10. On influence, see Ramsay MacMullen, "Women in public in the Roman empire," in Ramsay MacMullen, *Changes in the Roman Empire: Essays in the Ordinary* (Princeton, NJ, 1990), 162–68. Livia, Dio 55.2.4, 55.8.2, 57.12.5; Suet. *Tiberius* 50.2; Messalina, Dio 60.16.2, 60.17.5, 60.18.2; Agrippina the Younger, Tac. *Annals* 12.59; Dio 60(61).32.3; Vespasian's concubine Caenis, Dio 65(66).14.3; Hadrian's wife Sabina, SHA *Hadrian* 4.1, 9; Julia Domna, Dio 75.15.6–7; Herodian 5.7.1; Dio 77(78).18.2, 78(79).4.2. On behind a curtain, see Tac. *Annals* 13.5. On governors' wives, see Tac. *Annals* 3.33–4; Plancina, Tac. *Annals* 2.43, 3.15–17.

11. On Caecina Severus, see Tac. *Annals* 3.33. On Agrippina, see Tac. *Annals* 1.69, cf. 2.55.

12. On Octavia, see Vitruvius *On Architecture* 1.pr.2. On Plotina, see Plin. *Ep.* 9.28; Saller, *Personal Patronage*, 65. On women as literary patrons, see Hemelrijk, *Matrona Docta*, 103–28; Beryl Rawson, *Children and Childhood in Roman Italy* (Oxford, 2003), 204–5, e.g., Statius, *Silvae* 2.7; Martial 7.21, 7.23, 10.64. On Plotina and Athens, see Plotina's letter of patronage to the Epicurean philosophical school at Athens, inscribed on stone, *ILS* 7784 = *Women's Life* no. 261; discussed, Hemelrijk, *Matrona Docta*, 116–17.

13. Saller, *Personal Patronage*, 64; Veturius, *CIL* VI 2132 = *ILS* 4928 = Emily A. Hemelrijk, *Women and Society in the Roman World: A Sourcebook of Inscriptions from the Roman West* (Cambridge, 2021), no. 4.31b; Pardalas, *CIL* VI 2131 = *ILS* 4929 = Hemelrijk, *Women and Society*, no. 5.17. On other dedications to Vestals, see Saller n. 142 (*CIL* VI 2130, 2133–34, 32414–18 = *ILS* 4930-33); Hemelrijk, *Women and Society*, no. 4.31. Hemelrijk, *Matrona Docta*, 254.

14. On Carfania, see Valerius Maximus 8.3.2; Maesia, 8.1; Jane F. Gardner, *Women in Roman Law and Society* (London, 1986), 284. On women in court, Judith Evans-Grubbs, *Women and the Law in the Roman Empire: A Sourcebook on Marriage, Divorce, and Widowhood* (London, 2002), 60–71.

15. Ulpian, D.3.1.1.5; Constantine, *Codex Iustinianus* 2.12.21; jurists, D. 1.16.9.5; 2.13.1.3.

16. *P. Oxy.* II 261 = Jane Rowlandson, *Women and Society in Greek and Roman Egypt: A Sourcebook* (Cambridge, 1998), no. 133 = Evans-Grubbs, *Women*, 53.

17. MacMullen, "Women in public," 163–64.

18. On *cognitio*, Jill Harries, *Law and Crime in the Roman World* (Cambridge, 2007), 28–42.

19. Emily A. Hemelrijk, "Public roles for women in the cities of the Latin West," in *A Companion to Women in the Ancient World* (Malden, MA, 2012), ed. Sharon L. James and Sheila Dillon, 478–90; Laura K. McClure, *Women in Classical Antiquity: From Birth to Death* (Hoboken, NJ, 2019), 249–54. On the cities, see Peter Garnsey and Richard Saller, *The Roman Empire: Economy, Society, and Culture* (Berkeley, CA, 1987), 33–40; scholarship in recent years stresses the dynamism of the Roman economy that created the local elite wealth that enabled such munificence; see Walter Scheidel, Ian Morris, and Richard Saller, eds., *The Cambridge Economic History of the Greco-Roman World* (Cambridge, 2007); Peter Temin, *The Roman Market Economy* (Princeton, NJ, 2013). On decurion census, see Emily A. Hemelrijk, *Hidden Lives, Public Personae: Women and Civic Life in the Roman West* (Oxford, 2015), 15.

20. Evans-Grubbs, *Women*, 71–80; Hemelrijk, *Hidden Lives*, 37–107.

21. On Eumachia, see Eve D'Ambra, "Women on the Bay of Naples," in *Companion to Women*, 400–413, 401–4; Alison E. Cooley and M. G. L. Cooley, *Pompeii and Herculaneum: A Sourcebook* (London, 2014), 156–60, nos. E55–E60. On dedication, see *CIL* X 810 = *ILS* 3785 = *Pompeii and Herculaneum*, no. E56. On statue programme, see *Pompeii and Herculaneum*, p. 158; cf. Hemelrijk, *Women and Society*, nos. 5.2; 6.2. A *chalcidice* or *chalcidicum* is a porch with columns; a crypt, a covered gallery, not a tomb. As usual, Eumachia's family tomb was located outside the city: *Pompeii and Herculaneum*, nos. E62–66.

22. *L'Année Epigraphique* 2008, 358 = *Pompeii and Herculaneum*, no. E31; *L'Année Epigraphique* 2008, 357 = *Pompeii and Herculaneum*, no. E30.

23. *CIL* II 1956 = *ILS* 5512 = Hemelrijk, *Women and Society*, no. 6.6; John F. Donahue, "Iunia Rustica of Cartima: Female munificence in the Roman west," *Latomus* 63.4 (2004), 873–91; on cost, see ibid., 877–88; on text, also Evans-Grubbs, *Women*, 77–78.

24. Hemelrijk, *Hidden Lives*, 117–19, 121–23, 123–25, 138–47.

25. Plin. *Ep.* 7.24. Amphitheater, *CIL* X 5183 = *ILS* 5628; theater, *L'Année Epigraphique* 1946, 174 = *ibid.* 1992, 244. Hemelrijk, *Women and Society*, no. 6.7. On Ummidia, Jo-Ann Shelton, *The Women of Pliny's* Letters (London, 2013), 240–55; Emily A. Hemelrijk, "Female munificence in the cities of the

Latin west," in *Women and the Roman City in the Latin* West (Leiden, 2013), ed. Emily A. Hemelrijk and Greg Woolf, 65–84, at 65–66; *Hidden Lives*, 109–11; David H. Sick, "Ummidia Quadratilla: Cagey businesswoman or lazy pantomime watcher?" *Classical Antiquity* 18.2 (1999), 330–48.

26. *ILS* 2927 = Tim G. Parkin and Arthur J. Pomeroy, *Roman Social History: A Sourcebook* (London, 2007), no. 7.22. On value, Sick, "Ummidia," 340–42.

27. On temple, see Tac. *Histories* 4.53. On competition, see Hemelrijk, *Hidden Lives*, 159–60; on legitimacy, see ibid., 174; on statues, see ibid., 297–99, also Glenys Davies, "Honorific vs. funerary statues of women: Essentially the same or fundamentally different?" in Hemelrijk and Woolf, *Women*, 174–99.

28. *CIL* IV 923, 9885, 3403, 1168, 7886 = *Pompeii and Herculaneum*, nos. F51–53, 56–57; Maria, *CIL* IV 7866 = *Pompeii and Herculaneum*, no. F58; Hemelrijk, *Women and Society*, nos. 6.49–54.

29. MacMullen, "Women in public," 167; Evans-Grubbs, *Women*, 76–77.

30. On oratory, see Amy Richlin, "Gender and rhetoric: Producing manhood in the schools," in *Roman Eloquence: Rhetoric in Society and Literature* (London, 1997), ed. William J. Dominik, 90–110.

31. On *collegia*, Jörg Rüpke, *Religion of the Romans* (Cambridge, 2007), trans. and ed. Richard Gordon, 206–14.

32. Hemelrijk, *Hidden Lives*, 181–225; Emily A. Hemelrijk, "Patronesses and 'mothers' of Roman *collegia*," *Classical Antiquity* 27.1 (2008), 115–62. Women's associations existed, but they were not widespread, e.g., *collegium mulierum*, *CIL* VI 10423; *curia mulierum*, *CIL* XIV 2120, MacMullen, "Women in public," 331–32.

33. On Ancharia, see *CIL* XI 2702 = *ILS* 7217 = Hemelrijk, *Women and Society*, no. 6.26. Hemelrijk, "Patronesses and 'mothers,'" 135. On the changes of the late second and third centuries CE, Kyle Harper, *The Fate of Rome: Climate, Disease, and the End of an Empire* (Princeton, NJ, 2017), 98–115 (epidemics), 131–36 (colder climate), 119–29 (instability).

34. Hemelrijk, "Patronesses and 'mothers,'" 141; *Hidden Lives*, 228–69. For examples of "mothers" at municipal level, see Hemelrijk, *Women and Society*, nos. 6.28–9 ("mothers" of cities), 30–33 ("mothers" of associations).

10

RELIGIOUS LIFE

INTRODUCTION

Women's roles in Roman religious practice were wide ranging; indeed, religion was the main aspect of public life that women were permitted to participate in. Participation during the Republic ranged from the highly prestigious and lifelong state priestesses, the Vestal Virgins and the *flaminicae*, to the roles of elite matrons in supplicating before the gods when public crises occurred and while introducing new gods. Women took part in many traditional festivals. Roman women both elite and of lower status participated in household rites, worshipping the *Lares*, *Penates*, and ancestral spirits of individual families. The transition to the Principate (and generally the expansion of the Empire) disrupted state religion and introduced the imperial cult or worship of deified emperors (or deified aspects of living ones). The imperial cult gave scope for women as public priestesses at municipal level. "Mystery" cults were also popular, including the worship of Bacchus, Magna Mater (Cybele), Isis, and Osiris, and increasingly Christianity. In discussing ancient religion, the term "cult" refers to the worship of an individual deity and does not indicate that that worship was unusual, deviant, or fanatical as in the popular English usage of "cult."

THE NATURE OF ROMAN RELIGION

Roman religion may seem highly alien to the more recent Judeo-Christian tradition, though perhaps less so to modern people familiar with Hinduism, Buddhism, or Shinto. Roman religion emphasized sacred places (temples or shrines), divination, and ritual practices such as festivals, processions, sacrifices, and votive offerings. Ordinary people may not have been encouraged to practice divination, which was monopolized by state priests. Otherwise religious sites and rituals were pervasive, part of daily geography and the yearly calendar. Again, much of our information, in particular for priestesses, derives from the antiquarian sources discussed in chapter 5. Religious practices were an area of public life that were open to Roman women (usually of higher status) as priestesses and lay participants, as seen from instances of women's religious activity from the early Republic onward.[1]

To ask "did the ancient Greeks and Romans believe in their gods?" (the way adherents of Judeo-Christianity or Islam do) is an anachronistic approach to polytheism, especially traditional Roman religion and the imperial cult (the worship of deified emperors). Pre-Christian Roman religion consisted not so much of beliefs as of practices: acts that are performed in accordance with tradition and that linked Romans to the gods in a contractual manner: if humans perform the rituals correctly, the goodwill or "peace" of the gods toward humans will be maintained. This goodwill, the *pax deorum*, was believed to be necessary for the state and society to remain stable and for agriculture to flourish. Angering the gods by neglecting the rituals led to conflict, pestilence, famine, and disaster. Typical ritual acts that pleased the gods were dedications, prayers, sacrifices, and ex-votos. Dedications were made in honor of a deity (they usually survive as inscriptions). Prayers or supplications might be traditional and prescribed (performed by public priests) or spontaneous and private. Sacrifices ranged from the ritual killing of a bull, ram, pig, or other large animal or smaller animal, to the offering of wine and incense, the harvest's first fruits, sacrificial cakes, wheat, or garlands. Animal sacrifice was not always necessary or within the means of poorer people. A subset of sacrifice was the expiatory offering: a special sacrifice made to appease the perceived wrath of the gods. Ex-votos are dedications or offerings made in the fulfillment of a vow to a deity, thanking the god(s) for their assistance. People also sought to ascertain the will of the gods through divination: scrutinizing the external world for signs of divine favor or displeasure. The Roman state maintained control over public divination, performed by groups of priests termed augurs, who inspected the sky for signs such as thunder and lightning or the flight of birds, and haruspices, who inspected the entrails of sacrificed animals. Priests and priestesses at famous sites, such as the Pythia of Delphi in Greece or the Sibyl of Cumae in Italy, gave prophecies. People also resorted to forms of private divination such as astrology.[2]

The other distinction from modern Judeo-Christian views of religion is the role of priest or priestess. Though an intermediary with the divine, a polytheist Greek or Roman priest or priestess performed sacred rites rather than explaining sacred beliefs (theology) or providing theological and moral guidance to laypeople. Roman nominally secular education, with its strong emphasis on moral examples from the past, provided moral guidance. As repositories of sacred lore about rites and the recognition and expiation of omens, the state priests of Rome told citizens what to do, not what to feel or believe. Religious rites had to be performed by a careful and respectful person who was free of ritual pollution; any mistake invalidated the ritual, requiring it to be performed again from the beginning.

Furthermore, the Judeo-Christian concept of priesthood as a vocation or calling often does not apply to polytheist priests. Except for the Vestal Virgins, who served thirty years or longer, and who risked being sacrificed if unchaste, and the other major state priests at Rome, especially the *flamen Dialis* (high priest of Jupiter) and his wife, being a polytheist priest or priestess was not a vocation or a lifelong commitment. Many of the municipal priestesses discussed in this chapter served only a year or two, unless described as perpetual. Their positions required the talents of an event organizer rather than an inner calling. For major festivals and sacrifices, many people and things (and animals and other items used for sacrifices) had to be brought together in one place at a given time—at the risk of displeasing the gods.[3]

STATE PRIESTESSES AT ROME

To assure the *pax deorum*, the Roman state maintained elite groups of public priests and priestesses whose work was to carry out traditional rites and perform divination on behalf of the Senate and People of Rome. These colleges were headed by the *pontifex maximus* or high priest and included the *pontifices, flamines, rex sacrorum*, augurs, haruspices, *decemviri sacris faciundis*, or "board of ten men in charge of sacred affairs," later increased to fifteen (*quindecemviri*), and *septemviri epulones* or "board of seven in charge of sacred feasts." The *rex sacrorum* or "king of sacred things" filled the ritual role of Rome's archaic kings, carrying out the king's religious rites but having no political power in Republican Rome. The most important *flamines* were the high priest of Jupiter, the *flamen Dialis*; the high priest of Mars, the *flamen Martialis*; and the high priest of Quirinus, the *flamen Quirinalis*. A college of lesser priests of Mars, the *Salii* or "Leapers," performed traditional dances in armor in honor of the war god. The augurs were responsible for performing auguries, forms of divination that ascertained the will of the gods from the flight of birds or the outbreak of thunder and lightning, or interpreting prodigies, unnatural happenings (such as a rain of blood or stones or the birth of deformed animals or infants) that required expiation to restore divine goodwill. Other augurs kept sacred chickens, whose feeding behavior was a portent of divine goodwill or disaster before battle. Haruspices were a subset of augurs who performed divination by sacrificing animals and inspecting their inner organs: normal organs portended goodwill, deformed or diseased organs were a portent of disaster.[4]

These colleges of priests were highly aristocratic. They were originally recruited exclusively from patricians. By the mid-Republic, as the patrician clans dwindled and plebeian clans became wealthy and prominent, the two groups gradually merged and, after plebeian campaigns for change, wealthy and prominent plebeians were admitted to the priesthoods. The high priests (at least, the *pontifex maximus*, the three major *flamines*, and the *rex sacrorum*) were required to be married by *confarreatio*, the ritual sharing of a cake of *far* (spelt) that created a marriage with *manus* in which the wife was subject to her husband's "hand" and unable to own property. As marriage without *manus* became more popular, the requirement of *manus* marriage for high priests tended to make them semi-hereditary.[5]

The state priesthoods were exclusively male, with the exception of four types of priestesses: the Vestal Virgins, the *flaminicae*, the *regina sacrorum*, and the little-known *Saliae*. The Vestal Virgins are best known: six in number, they tended the sacred fire in the temple of Vesta. As long as this fire remained alight, the Roman state would be secure. The Vestals were recruited from noble families and from girls whose fathers and mothers were both living, which

in antiquity's demographic conditions was rare and a sign of divine favor and purity. Boys and girls with two living parents (*patrimi et matrimi*) often played minor roles in religious worship. Of thirty-eight Vestals of known status, eight were definitely senatorial and fifteen probably senatorial; though fourteen Vestals' families cannot be identified, the priesteshood was dominated by the social elite. When a vacancy in the Vestal college opened, as many as twenty prospective Vestals, between the age of six and ten, were selected by the *pontifex maximus*; a new Vestal was then selected by lot, indicating divine favor. A Vestal was required to serve for thirty years, after which time she could retire. Many Vestals, however, remained Vestals all their lives.[6]

A Vestal was formally and legally separated from her birth family and enjoyed legal privileges. She was legally independent, no longer under her father's *patria potestas*, and free from *tutela mulierum* (guardianship of women). If she died intestate, her property reverted to the state rather than to her birth family. Vestals received a *stipendium* from the state and were also allowed to receive bequests in wills. Many Vestals became wealthy, and as seen in chapter 9, could act as patronesses because of their aristocratic status and great prestige and influence. The Temple of Vesta even acted as a proto-bank, as was the case with major temples in antiquity; aristocrats deposited money, valuables, and important documents (such as the wills of Mark Antony and Augustus) with the Vestals, who may have made loans; ordinary women were not permitted to be bankers.[7]

The Vestals were accorded privileges that prefigured those of the empresses. They were sacrosanct (inviolable). They were permitted to ride in a *carpentum* (covered carriage) and were preceded by lictors, though these lictors were not the same as those that preceded Roman magistrates, but special lictors for priests (*lictores curiatii*). The Vestals had special seating in the theater and amphitheater, a box on the lower level among men, whereas Augustus's *Lex Julia theatralis* (Julian Law regulating shows) required other women to sit in the upper levels. Because Vestals could not marry or have children and would be otherwise penalized by the *Lex Julia de maritandis ordinibus* (18 BCE), they were given the *ius liberorum*, the "right of children" normally allowed to women who gave birth to three children. The Vestals may have been the first mortal women to appear on Roman coins, depicted by moneyers (minor magistrates) who claimed descent (not directly, of course) from past Vestals.[8]

The Vestals, in contrast with other priestesses in the Roman world, were vowed to eternal virginity (up until they left the order). This eternal chastity, like the eternal fire of Vesta's hearth, was inviolable and assured the security of the Roman state. A Vestal's body was sacrosanct; she could not be touched. A Vestal who engaged in sexual activity committed *incestum* ("incest," used here for any sexual activity) and was put to death by being buried alive. The execution of Vestals for unchastity might occur even if she had not engaged in any sexual activity, because some disaster had come upon the Roman state and she was held responsible according to sacred law. Thirteen such executions are known from the whole span of Roman history; most occurred in the early Republic and are quasi-legendary, but several occurred in historical times (e.g., in 114 BCE; in 91 CE). A condemned Vestal was stripped of her ritual costume and apparently dressed as an ordinary matron; she was carried through the streets of Rome on a bier as in a funeral, to a location outside the Colline Gate, called the *Campus Sceleratus* or "Field of Wickedness," where an underground chamber was located. She was buried alive in this chamber with an oil lamp and small amounts of food and drink, apparently ritual provisions to avoid laying hands on her since she was sacrosanct and/or defiled. The Romans treated a man who had murdered his father in a similar manner, sewing him into a leather sack and throwing him into the sea.[9]

In contrast with the Vestals, the other high priestesses of Republican Rome, the *flaminica Dialis* and the *regina sacrorum*, wives of the *flamen Dialis* and the *rex sacrorum*, were married and served in partnership with their husbands. The *flaminica Dialis* was present at important festivals (see section "Women in the Festival Calendar"), and probably accompanied her husband at his ritual duties. In contrast with the traditional view that women in Roman religion were not permitted to sacrifice animals, the *flaminica Dialis* sacrificed a ram on market days (*nundinae*). She did not actually kill the animal but ritually confirmed its fitness for sacrifice by sprinkling offerings of wine and flour on its head and drawing a small sacrificial knife along its back. Professional slayers of sacrificial animals, the *victimarii*, then stunned the ram and killed it. It is uncertain whether priestesses other than the *flaminica Dialis* and *regina sacrorum* sacrificed animals; public municipal priestesses may have done so. Ordinary women were still allowed to make sacrificial offerings of wine, incense, perfume, cakes, grain, and flowers. Sacrificing large animals was beyond the means of poor people in any case.[10]

The *flaminica Dialis* was also in charge of marriage at Rome. According to Ovid, she advised women on the most auspicious days for weddings. Her costume featured the matron's *stola* and the *flammeum*, the deep yellow veil worn by Roman brides. The *flaminica Dialis* was not even permitted to divorce her husband, whereas divorce was relatively easy for all other citizens. She thus became a role model for marital fidelity. She was also subject to the host of strange ritual prohibitions that her husband the *flamen Dialis* endured: he could not leave the city of Rome or see an army mustered for battle, and he was not permitted to touch or even see beans (associated with death), ivy, dogs, goats, prisoners in chains, and corpses.[11]

The wives of the two other major *flamines*, the *flaminica Martialis* and the *flaminica Quirinalis*, may have shared their husbands' religious duties, but little is known about them. This is also true of the *regina sacrorum*, the wife of the *rex sacrorum*, who sacrificed a cow to Jupiter on the Kalends of each month. The wives of the lesser *flamines* (thirteen in number) are even more shadowy figures, as are the *Saliae*, virgin female dancers who may have accompanied the armored *Salii* or priests of Mars in their ritual war dance through the streets of Rome to open the campaign season in March. The *Saliae* are attested only in an antiquarian source and seem to have disappeared by historical times, as Roman men did not normally approve of women dressed as soldiers or gladiators.[12]

Despite the prestige of the major priesthoods, by the late Republic it became harder and harder to recruit them as confarreate marriage became an archaism. The emperors Augustus and Tiberius continued to have difficulty filling the post of the *flamen Dialis*. To make the office more attractive, Tiberius decreed that the *flaminica Dialis* was only subject to her husband's *manus* for the purpose of carrying out rituals. In all other aspects of her life, she was permitted the rights over property that a wife in marriage without *manus*, who was legally independent, had.[13]

The state priestesses officiated at some of Rome's major festivals, discussed in section "Women in the Festival Calendar." In general the state priesthoods were unique to the city of Rome, and when public priestesses (discussed in section "Imperial, Public, and Other Priestesses") appear in cities and towns outside Rome, they are priestesses of the imperial cult or of popular goddesses such as Venus or Ceres. However, the emphasis on the Vestals' chastity and on the *flaminica Dialis'* marriage is echoed elsewhere, in Roman festivals' emphasis on roles for *matronae* and *univirae* (women who had been married only once, remaining faithful to their husbands) and in the expectation that *matronae* play leadership roles in cult.[14]

WOMEN IN THE FESTIVAL CALENDAR

Rome had an extensive program of traditional festivals, reconstructed by first-century BCE antiquarians and recorded in a famous inscription, the *Fasti Praenestini*, and depicted in the poet Ovid's *Fasti* (of Augustan date). Women, both state priestesses and ordinary citizens, played a role in many of these. Many of the "public" festivals were probably celebrated mainly by the state priests and priestesses, who carried out rituals the meaning of which was obscure even to the antiquarian scholars of the first century BCE who recorded or reconstructed them. However, Roman women had roles in many of these festivals, often differentiated by social and sexual status; only *matronae* could attend some festivals, and even more exclusive festivals were only for *univirae*, women who had been married only once and not remarried after the death of their husband. This list is not to suggest that women attended only these festivals. Many of the public religious festivals involved the whole city of Rome.[15]

Carmentalia (January 11 or 15). For the two Carmentae, goddesses of childbirth.

Juno Sospita (February 1). Ritual for girls at Lanuvium, carried out by *virgines*.

Lupercalia (February 15). Young men ran naked through the city of Rome, flogging the bystanders, especially women, with thongs of goatskin from a freshly sacrificed goat.

Feralia (February 21). Old women and girls made sacrifice to the Silent Goddess, mother of the *Lares*. Feast for *Di Manes*.

Matronalia (March 1). Festival of Juno Lucina, a goddess of childbirth. Husbands prayed for their wives' health and gave them gifts; wives served their slave women ritual meals.

Liberalia (March 17). Old women sold sweet cakes and sacrificed on small altars. Freeborn boys donned the *toga virilis*.

Veneralia (April 1). Women propitiated Fortuna Virilis. Lower-class women bathe in men's baths. Matrons celebrate festival of Venus Verticordia.

Vinalia (April 23). Wine festival. Prostitutes propitiate Venus Erycina.

Floralia (April 27). Games and theatrical shows with nude actresses.

Bona Dea I (May 1). Festival for women only; matrons sacrifice a sow in private and drink wine.

Vestalia (June 9–15). *Matronae* make offerings at Temple of Vesta.

Matralia (June 11). In Temple of Mater Matuta, *univirae* adorn her statue; *matronae* bake ritual cakes; *matronae* invite slave woman into temple, drive her out again with blows.

Fortuna Muliebris (July 6). *Univirae* tend temple and statue of Fortuna Muliebris.

Nonae Caprotinae (July 7). Slave women hold a feast and a mock battle outside the city; in ancient times slave women saved *matronae* from an enemy army.

Diana on the Aventine (August 13). Rites at Diana's shrine at Aricia.

Feronia (November 13). Freedwomen propitiate Feronia in her temple in the Campus Martius; *matronae* sacrifice to Juno Regina.

Bona Dea II (December 3). Feast and ritual in home of a matron of consular or praetorian rank, attended by Vestals, other aristocratic *matronae*, and female musicians; men prohibited to attend. Lower-class women did not attend.

"Private" festivals could be celebrated by ordinary families and individual households, such as the *Ambarvalia*, a spring ritual associated with tilling the fields. These perhaps stood the greatest chance of persistence, such as the *Compitalia*, a holiday for household members that reinforced the status of owners and slaves, or the *Parentalia*, a festival honoring deceased ancestors, discussed in chapter 11. The *Parentalia* was not fearsome like the *Lemuria*, ritual days in which hungry ghosts emerged from the underworld and were repelled by rites involving throwing black beans. A popular festival was the weeklong *Saturnalia*, a riotous holiday dispelling the winter gloom of December, when slaves were allowed to behave as if they were free and people exchanged small presents such as wax candles and *sigillaria* (clay figurines).

The entire traditional Roman festival calendar was probably not celebrated in Italian municipalities and the provinces, as many of its festivals depended on geographical and architectural features of the city of Rome. People who lived outside Rome probably celebrated the private festivals that were not tied to geography, such as the *Parentalia*. Provincial inhabitants also celebrated local festivals that were not Roman or Italian. It was considered proper to revere local deities and shrines, and cults tended to be cumulative, adding to or overlaying but not displacing others. This is seen in Roman Egypt, where Egyptian gods were overlaid with Greco-Roman deities, for example, cow-headed Hathor was assimilated to the Greek goddess Hera and Roman goddess Juno.

The imperial cult also provided many festivals that were not geo-graphically tied to the city of Rome and that helped to unite the Empire through expressing loyalty to the emperor and his family. Such a calendar was discovered on papyrus at Dura-Europos, a city on the eastern frontier of the Roman Empire, where an auxiliary cohort of the Roman army was stationed in the early third century CE. The *Feriale Duranum*, as it is known, records many holidays of the imperial cult, as well as holidays that were peculiar to the Roman army, such as the *Rosalia signorum*, a day when garlands of roses were hung on military standards, probably in commemo-ration of the war dead. The *Feriale Duranum* also shows that the holidays of current emperors and their families were celebrated, not those of their predecessors, so that festivals did not take up the entire year; emperors occasionally purged the holiday calendar of excessive festivals.[16]

WOMEN AND "EMERGENCY" RELIGIOUS ACTIONS

At Trimalchio's lavish dinner for his fellow freedmen, one guest recalled the good old days, when Roman matrons prayed for rain: "women used to go in their *stolae*, barefoot, to the hill, with their hair unbound and their minds pure, and pray to Jupiter for rain. And so just like that it rained buckets, then or never, and they all went home like drowned rats." It was the traditional duty of Roman *matronae* (and related to their repute for *pudicitia*) to take a leader-ship role in religious affairs. In the Roman Republic, women are represented as assisting the state with religious activities in times of emergency, when special devotions were required. This occurred in two major ways: women's provision of expiatory offerings, and women's involvement in the creation or importation of new cults of gods previously not worshipped at Rome.[17]

During the Hannibalic War, after catastrophic defeats, the Repub-lic's state priests and the Senate determined that these disasters required expiatory sacrifices. The entire community made a special effort to appease the wrath of the gods; *matronae* are specifically stated to have offered *lectisternia* and *sellisternia*, ritual offerings of garlands and sacrificial cakes on tables at which empty couches and chairs were placed for the gods. In Livy, women make similar efforts at the time of the Gallic sack of Rome in 390 BCE, melting down their jewelry to help pay for the city's ransom.[18]

Women also led the introduction of new gods (though some of these stories are so distant in time as to be legends). In the early

Republic, when the Roman leader Coriolanus defected to the neighboring Volsci and threatened to besiege Rome, the women of Rome, led by one Valeria and by Coriolanus's wife Volumnia and mother Veturia, persuaded him to desist. In thanks to the gods, Valeria persuaded the Senate to allow the women to build a temple to Fortuna Muliebris, which was funded by the women's own efforts, not the Senate. Also in the early Republic, matrons of the patrician clans established a shrine to *Pudicitia Patricia* (Patrician Chastity). The married women of the plebeian clans were offended and erected a corresponding shrine to *Pudicitia Plebeia* (Plebeian Chastity). In a third example of women's founding new cults, in 214 BCE (historical times), Sulpicia, regarded as the most chaste (*pudicissima*) matron in Rome, founded a shrine of Venus Verticordia (She who turns hearts) to turn aside young women's hearts from lust to chastity. These stories were emphasized by Livy and other Augustan authors, perhaps in support of the Augustan policies emphasizing marriage and repressing adultery, but they show that some matrons were believed to take the initiative in religious affairs.[19]

In 204 BCE, the Roman Senate decided to import the cult of Magna Mater (the Great Mother) also known as Cybele, from Asia Minor (modern Turkey). The statue of Magna Mater, a great uncarved stone, was brought by ship from Asia Minor. When the ship reached the mouth of the Tiber river, Rome's matrons turned out to haul it to the city. One of the Vestals, Claudia Quinta, provided assistance; in the most popular version of this legend, she was of suspect chastity but vowed to let the Great Mother judge her virtue by lending her strength. Miraculously she was able to tow the barge of Magna Mater by herself to the city of Rome. These legends, especially as embellished by the Augustan-era historians Dionysius of Halicarnassus and Livy, reinforce the traditional virtues of Roman women, but still emphasize that women were thought to be influential in religious life.[20]

Other religions that were regarded as "new" introductions were the cults of Dionysus or Bacchus, from Greece; Ceres or Demeter, from Greece; Isis and Osiris, from Egypt; and Mithras, from Persia. The cult of Mithras excluded women, but the other cults were popular with women, as was early Christianity. Modern scholars long argued that women were attracted to these religions because, in contrast with public or state religion, these cults were not closely tied to civic structures or to any one city or state, and thus perhaps appealed to people who were excluded from public life. But, as we have seen, women did hold important state priesthoods; as section "Imperial, Public, and Other Priestesses" shows, they also held municipal priesthoods. Furthermore, these "new" cults were not underground in any sense. Only the cult of Bacchus was suppressed by the Romans in 186 BCE, possibly because it was politically subversive; in a decree of the Senate, large cult events were banned, and meetings of the religion were limited to meetings of two men and three women. Inscriptions show that priestesses of Ceres were respected older women, that many priestesses of Ceres were municipal, and that the worship of Isis included male priests as well as women. Christianity was also long a cult among others, regarded with suspicion by the Roman authorities because its votaries refused to worship the emperors.[21]

WOMEN AND HOUSEHOLD RELIGION

Traditional practices may have persisted as well within the household, where the mother of the family (materfamilias) had the role of carrying out such rituals and maintaining the goodwill of the household gods. The gods of a Roman household were the *Lares familiares* or guardian spirits of the household, usually depicted as two young men in short tunics, poised to dance; the *genius* of the paterfamilias; and the *Penates* or spirits that guarded the household supplies. The hearth itself, sacred to Vesta, was a focus of veneration.[22]

Pompeii and Herculaneum provide the closest archeological look at household religion, showing that it was still practiced in Roman Italy in the late first century CE. At Pompeii and Herculaneum, household shrines might be niches built into the wall, freestanding cupboards, or wall paintings that depicted such niches or cupboards, with painted images of the *Lares* flanking the *genius* of the paterfamilias, a figure wearing a toga with his head veiled for sacrificing at an altar. The *Penates* appear as small statues in household shrines and show that many households venerated an eclectic mix of deities, including Jupiter, Venus, Fortune, Aesculapius (the god of healing), Mercury (a god of commerce), Isis and Osiris, the emperor and his family, and others. Many of the statuettes and other objects in a family's *Penates* were probably handed down from one generation to the next. The physical shrines also have small altars where minor offerings (such as wine, incense, cakes, grain, or flowers) could be made. Interestingly, houses in Pompeii and Herculaneum might have multiple shrines to the *Lares* and *Penates*, some in kitchens and other areas where slaves worked, suggesting that the household slaves also paid cult to the household gods.[23]

How the *Lares* and *Penates* were worshipped is something most ancient authors did not bother to describe, because it was so routine. The practices are attested in Plautus's *Aulularia*, where the household *Lar* of the characters in the play addresses the audience, describing the father of the house as miserly and neglecting to honor him with offerings, unlike his daughter: "She worships me every single day with incense or wine or something else and gives me garlands." Household worship is also attested in Cato's *On Farming*, where the *vilica* (bailiff's wife, a slave woman) has the task of hanging garlands above the hearth and making offerings to the *Lares* on the Kalends, Nones, and Ides of the month and on festival days.

> She must not engage in [non-household] religious activity herself or get others to engage in it for her without the orders of the master or the mistress; let her remember that the master attends to the rituals for the whole household . . . On the Kalends, Ides, and Nones, and whenever a festival comes, she must hang a garland over the hearth, and on those days pray to the household gods as the opportunity offers.

Cato states that the mistress of the household delegated these ritual tasks to the *vilica*, as the master delegated agricultural religious rituals to the *vilicus* in his absence; as long as the rites were performed correctly, it did not matter *who* performed them, a corollary of Roman religion's emphasis on practice rather than belief. However, Cato also instructs the *vilicus* to ensure that the *vilica* does not bring in fortune-tellers or unauthorized cults.[24]

New brides paid cult to their groom's household gods, entering their protection. The bride was brought to her husband's house in a ritual procession. When she reached the crossroads nearest his house, she made an offering of a coin to the *Lares compitales* or Lares of the crossroads, and when she entered his house, she placed a coin on the hearth as an offering to the *Lares familiares* of his family.[25]

Another family-related cult was that of the *Di Manes* or "deified spirits" of deceased ancestors, who received ritual homage at their tombs. Many Roman epitaphs begin with *D(is) M(anibus)*, "to the spirits of" the deceased. Offerings of food and drink might be made to them, poured into stone or terracotta tubes that led into the ground. Worship was paid to the *Di Manes* particularly at the

Parentalia, a private festival held in February. It was a time to remember and mourn lost family members (of which more will be said in chapter 11).[26]

IMPERIAL, PUBLIC, AND OTHER PRIESTESSES

As the first emperor, Augustus presented himself as restoring traditional Roman religion after a period of decline. His greatest innovation, however, was the imperial cult, in which deceased emperors were worshipped as gods and the *genius* or guardian spirit of the living emperor was revered. The concept of divine rulers was familiar to the Romans from the Hellenistic kingdoms, where the Macedonian Greek monarchs of Egypt and Syria had been revered as gods. The Romans had resisted the idea of worshipping a living man as a god. Augustus compromised by deifying only his deceased predecessor, Julius Caesar, as *Divus Iulius*. Augustus promoted the cults of the *Lares Augusti* and *Genius Augusti*, resembling the traditional household cults and worshipped at crossroads in the city of Rome, replacing the *Lares compitales*. He also allowed his *numen* (divine spirit) to be revered, but he himself was not worshipped outright, a policy that most of his successors followed for the next three centuries (the insane Caligula and the arrogant Domitian flirted with godhood during their lives). The living emperor also held many of the traditional state priesthoods simultaneously, as *pontifex maximus*, *flamen Dialis*, augur, and so forth. After his death in 14 CE, Augustus was fully deified, and his widow Livia Augusta became his priestess, modeling her role on the Vestals (she did not remarry). Livia herself was deified by the emperor Claudius (41–54 CE). Other deceased empresses and even women of the imperial family who were not Augustae were also deified.[27]

The imperial cult enabled Romans of relatively low status to hold prestigious positions in imperial society. Freedmen were allowed to hold the priesthoods termed *severi Augustales*, honoring the current emperor's *genius* and the deified emperors. It also gave scope to women to participate in the imperial cult. Many cities and towns had public priestesses, *sacerdotes publicae*, whom we have met already in chapter 9. Other women were priestesses of Bona Dea, Ceres, Isis, Juno, Magna Mater, Minerva, or Venus. Still other women might be greater or lesser functionaries of a cult, its *magistrae* and *ministrae*. Many public priestesses were *flaminicae*, priestesses of the deified empresses and the divine aspect of the present empress. It was possible, but not necessary, for the *flaminica* to be the wife of a *flamen Augusti*, a male priest of the deified emperors and the present emperor's divine aspect. Other *flaminicae* were married to municipal magistrates or other municipal notables. Though expected to be faithful to their husbands, these priestesses did not imitate the absolute chastity of the Vestal Virgins; the municipal priestess Rubria Festa (section "Maternal and Infant Mortality"), died after giving birth to her tenth child. To some degree, these public priestesses also modeled their public images on the empresses, as we have seen in the case of Eumachia as benefactor of Pompeii.[28]

As with the mythology question, we might ask, "Did the Romans really believe that their emperors were gods?" It is also probably inappropriate. Rome was a society based on honor and deference toward social superiors. The nimbus of divinity—in art often a literal halo around the emperor's head, as in the famous portrait of Septimius Severus (193–211 CE) and his family—symbolized the emperor's exalted and semidivine status. The early Christians' refusal to honor the imperial cult by sacrificing to the emperor with a pinch of incense and a few drops of wine was regarded as an insult to the emperor, an act of treason.

In general, a public priestess managed the temple of the goddess or the imperial cult, supervising the temple slaves (women *ministrae*) who worked there. She received visitors, accepted dedications, performed (maybe only nonanimal) sacrifices, and organized festivals, which might have many participants, including children whose father and mother were still living. She tended or oversaw the tending of the statues of the goddess or the emperor and empress, the imperial *imagines*, ensuring that they were cleaned, anointed, and garlanded with flowers. She might fund and oversee additions and repairs to the temple.[29]

The duties of a typical *flaminica Augusti* can be reconstructed from the Dura calendar, which records many holidays of the imperial cult: January 3, on which the Empire's vows for the emperor's health were renewed, and the army renewed its oaths of loyalty; the anniversary of the emperor's accession to the throne; the emperor's birthday; depending on how many family members there were, the birthdays of the emperor's wife and of his children, and the anniversary of the emperor's marriage. The calendar also features sacrifices made to deified predecessors. The *flamen Augusti* and *flaminica* tended the portrait images of the emperor and of his family—the hairstyles of the empresses were, as we have seen in chapter 5, imitated by women in the provinces. They cleaned, anointed, and garlanded the images. On holidays with games, the imperial images might be carried from the imperial temple in a procession (which might be elaborate) to the amphitheater and placed in the imperial box, providing the spectators with the symbolic presence of their rulers. Holidays might include public feasts which the *flamen Augusti* and *flaminica* helped to organize for the city; the public priest and priestess might fund these events themselves or be assisted by other benefactors. As said in chapter 9, public priests and priestesses were usually from local wealthy families and were expected to foot the bill for the city's amenities; they also paid very large sums to hold public priesthoods.[30]

A city's elite women who were not themselves priestesses might participate in the elaborate public rites, processions, and festivals in honor of the gods. This tradition of female participation was quite old; in the middle Republic, married women of high social status had held *lectisternia* and *sellisternia*, banquet tables bedecked with garlands and offerings and set with couches and chairs for the gods, intended to propitiate the gods and restore their goodwill toward Rome. The matrons of Rome held these expiatory offerings at the time of the Roman Republic's greatest crisis, the Hannibalic War, and they also participated in bringing the image of the *Magna Mater*, the Great Mother, to Rome in 204 BCE. The Vestal Virgin Claudia was said to have proven her virginity by towing the boat that held the image of the Great Mother. In Augustus's Saecular Games of 17 BCE, 110 Roman matrons, described as "the brides of Roman citizen men," offered prayers for the increase of the Empire and for eternal victory, and 27 boys and 27 girls whose parents were both still living sang Horace's *Carmen Saeculare*. The 110 matrons also offered traditional *sellisternia* to Juno and Diana.[31]

RELIGION AND HEALING

Even if a woman was not a public priestess or a prominent matron, she might make dedications to the emperor or empress; many of these inscriptions survive. Women do not seem to have revered only female deities (traditional goddesses or deified empresses). Inscriptions and archeological finds best attest the religious practices of ordinary people, both in the mid- and late Republic and in the imperial era. A typical religious inscription is a dedication to a god or gods, by a private person, in the hope of some benefit (the god will ensure the health of the dedicator and their family). Ex-voto inscriptions were created in fulfillment of vows, thanking the gods for some benefit.

Archeological finds associated with religious practices include votive objects, precious or non-precious objects that were deposited in temples or in sacred places (often wells and springs), in the hope of or in thanks for divine favor. Often only an inscription records such votives, the precious objects having been pillaged long ago. The deposition of precious votives is self-explanatory; the dedicator gave up some of their wealth in the hope of the gods' favor or to thank the gods. Non-precious votives were symbolic, such as terracotta models of parts of the human body, for example, hands, feet, eyes, and internal organs. These were probably left in the hope that the god(s) would heal these parts of the body. Eye infections (trachoma) appear to have been common in antiquity; hands and feet might be disabled by arthritis and were necessary for work. Women often left votive models of wombs, suggesting their concern for fertility, a safe delivery, or gynecological disorders.[32]

PRIVATE DIVINATION AND MAGIC

Bordering on religion were the practices of private divination, astrology, and magic, some forms of which were not socially sanctioned. Though the state priesthood did not approve of it, many people in Roman Italy used similar methods of private divination, including auspices and haruspicy. Astrology was a different matter, regarded as a foreign import from the Near East. The Senate from time to time expelled astrologers from the city of Rome. In the imperial era, astrology might be exploited by persons hoping to overthrow the emperor. Augustus collected and burned some two thousand books of astrology, keeping only the genuine Sibylline Oracles, which were kept under lock and key. Subsequent emperors repeated the expulsion of astrologers, and "magic panics" swept the capital from time to time, focused on fear of treason.[33]

Astrology, books of dream interpretation, and divinatory texts give some impression of the concerns of the people who used them. One well-known divinatory text was a handbook of questions with a formula for picking answers, the *Sortes Astrampsychi*. The answers were drawn at random by throwing dice, or indicated by numbers generated by a mathematical formula. In a society where women's prestige and actual legal privileges depended on their bearing legitimate children, a woman might ask questions about her fertility. Despite the practice of astrology, divination, and magic by all people, men depicted women as particularly prone to superstition. Plutarch recommended the education of women as a way to discourage this behavior.[34]

Votive offerings in the shape of uteruses (wombs), terra cotta, 6" long, Roman, late Republic or imperial eras. Roman believers deposited such votive offerings in the shape of afflicted parts of the body at temples or sacred springs in thanks for divine healing. These votives show that women often sought divine aid for reproductive issues, whether infertility, miscarriage and stillbirth, or other problems. (Wellcome Collection)

Magic was widely practiced in Roman society, and not only by women, despite the persistence of lurid depictions of witches in literary texts. Philosophically educated elite men regarded magic with disapproval. But Cato the Elder, writing in the early second century CE before the dominance of such education, collected numerous charms and spells that a Roman paterfamilias (head of household) could perform to heal sick or injured members of the *familia* or livestock. The popularity of magic is shown by amulets and beads with supposed protective powers against curses or divine ill-will. Amulets are among the most frequent small items dropped or lost in antiquity that Roman archeologists term "small finds." Most of these were intended to guard the physical health of the wearer, for in a society with no modern concept of disease transmission, fear of disease blurred with fear of magical ill-will, *invidia* or "envy." Other people worked up curses against their enemies, inscribing them on lead tablets or *defixiones* that were often thrown into a sacred well or spring. Many of these lead tablets were excavated from the shrine of Sulis Minerva at Aquae Sulis (Bath) in Roman Britain and show a wide range of people using curse spells to target rivals in love and business, thieves (who stole their clothing from the baths), and other enemies.[35]

Lararium (household shrine) from the House of the Vettii, Pompeii, Italy, first century CE (before CE 79). This fresco depicts the household gods worshipped by a Roman family. Two *Lares* (guardian spirits depicted as dancing young men) flank the Genius (divine spirit) of the paterfamilias (head of the household). The snake also represented a benevolent spirit. Women of the family tended the shrine, making ritual offerings. (Allan T. Kohl/Art Images for College Teaching)

This brings us to the persistent belief in witches: female practitioners of healing or magic, often elderly women, going by many names. The belief in witches seems based on helplessness in the face of infant and child mortality, fear of women's unsanctioned lore and abilities, and the structural position of women in ancient society, which lacked respected roles for elderly low-status women. Some types of witches, *striges* or *lamiae*, were believed to carry off infants or, as serpent-like creatures, to enter and devour infants and children from the inside. Some witches were the spirits of young girls who died after their betrothal but before marriage; these spirits targeted the children they never had. Other witches were elderly widows, past childbearing age, probable widows living alone. Unmarried and widowed women did not fit the socially sanctioned category of wife and mother, so they were regarded as anomalous and dangerous, especially if they were poor and practiced healing or sold spells to survive. Such women were stereotyped as poisoners (*veneficae*), providing love potions and abortifacients. Many Roman magical remedies employed "filthy" substances: animal and human body parts, animal excretions, and menstrual blood, which was regarded as polluting and able to blight growing plants, tarnish metal, and discolor dyes. People's superstitions attributed uncanny powers to these women, especially in the face of premature or unexplained death. In epitaphs, two husbands describe their wives as slain by witches, "struck down by evil spells" and succumbing to *veneficae*, witches and/or poisoners. Such ominous women contrasted with the respected elderly Vestal Virgin, priestess of Ceres, or *univirae*, widowed matrons who did not remarry after their husbands died.[36]

CONCLUSION

To a great extent, women's public life in the Roman world was religious life; in the Roman Republic, the most prominent women were state priestesses such as the Vestals and the legendary founders of new goddess cults. In the imperial era, the empresses were both deified (after their deaths) and the priestesses of deified emperors. Many of the female municipal benefactors seen in chapter 9 were public priestesses.[37]

Evidently, being a priestess or otherwise associating oneself with religious cult enabled women to acquire a "halo effect" (the term is from modern sociology, not religion) that legitimated their participation in public life. Being a priestess was furthermore associated with chastity and purity. Though only the Vestals were required to be celibate virgins, *pudicitia* or "sexual virtue" within marriage was an attribute both of some deities and of the women who served them, seen most blatantly in the cults of *Pudicitia Patricia* and *Pudicitia Plebeia* and in the requirement that some of these priestesses be both matrons and *univirae* (married only once, not divorced or widowed). The *flaminica Dialis* or priestess of Jupiter was prohibited to divorce her husband, and her bridal veil (*flammeum*) made her a symbol of marriage. The public priestesses of municipal towns and cities were probably all married women, though there is not enough evidence to show whether they were also *univirae*.

However, some modern scholars have emphasized the "limits of participation" of women in public life through religious activities.

The Vestals could only advise the Senate upon religious affairs, and the chief authority upon religious affairs remained the male *pontifex maximus*. The *flaminica Dialis* was subordinated to her husband in an obsolete form of marriage with *manus* (alleviated in the imperial era). Except for the prophetic Sibyl of Cumae, women were not allowed to practice divination, which remained the monopoly of the male augurs and haruspices, who gave religious endorsement to the decisions of Rome's leaders. It is not known whether the public priestesses of cities and towns in the Roman world gained any secular power or influence thereby, except the social power to give benefactions. Furthermore, a "halo effect" that depended upon chastity sexualized elite women and rendered them vulnerable at least to slander; the Vestals might pay for such slander with their lives.

Perhaps most of all, these priestesses all belonged to social elites (most so in the case of the state priestesses of Rome, but also at municipal level). Women of the lower social strata also practiced religion, as shown by inscriptions, amulets, and curse tablets, but were not accorded the ideological protection of *pudicitia*. They may not have been included in the rituals reserved for *matronae* and *univirae*; as we will see, marrying only once and not remarrying when widowed presumed a certain level of wealth. In the festival termed the *Matralia*, Roman matrons invited a slave woman (*ancilla*) into the temple of Mater Matuta (a goddess associated with fertility) and drove her out with blows. The festival of Fortuna Muliebris was paired with one for Fortuna Virilis, in which (Ovid claims) women of the lower strata visited the men's baths to "expose themselves to Fortuna Virilis" in order to increase their sexual attractiveness to men. Ovid, author of the *Ars Amatoria*, is perhaps not trustworthy here, but his claim illustrates the sexual vulnerability of lower-class women (see chapter 7, sections "Introduction" and "Conclusion"). In inscriptions, sub-elite women in the commercial port of Ostia who were priestesses of Magna Mater or Bona Dea claimed status through such religious participation, even if they were freedwomen (former slaves).

The religious practices honoring the dead are a special topic and are described in the subsequent chapter. The participation of women in public and religious life is shown also in funerary practices, in which at least women of higher status received public funerary honors, and many women who did not receive them still received elaborate private monuments.

NOTES

1. On Roman religion, Mary Beard, John North, and Simon Price, *Religions of Rome, Volume I: A History; Volume II: A Sourcebook* (Cambridge, 1998); Jörg Rüpke, *Religion of the Romans* (Cambridge, 2007), ed. and tr. Richard Gordon; for a more accessible introduction, see Alexandra Sofroniew, *Household Gods: Private Devotion in Ancient Greece and Rome* (Los Angeles, 2015); and John Scheid, *An Introduction to Roman Religion* (Edinburgh, 2003).

2. On women's religion, general treatments are Sarah B. Pomeroy, *Goddesses, Whores, Wives, and Slaves: Women in Classical Antiquity* (New York, 1975), 205–26; Laura K. McClure, *Women in Classical Antiquity: From Birth to Death* (Hoboken, NJ), 257–64. For more depth, see Amy Richlin, "Carrying water in a sieve: Class and the body in Roman Women's religion," in *Women and Goddess Traditions* (Minneapolis, MN, 1997), ed. Karen King, 330–74 = Amy Richlin, *Arguments with Silence: Writing the History of Roman Women* (Ann Arbor, MI, 2014), 197–240. For the Republic, see Celia E. Schultz, *Women's Religious Activity in the Roman Republic* (Chapel Hill, NC, 2006); Robin Wildfang, *Rome's Vestal Virgins: A Study of Rome's Vestal Priestesses in the Late Republic and Early Empire* (London, 2006); Lora L. Holland, "Women and Roman religion," in *A Companion to Women in the Ancient World* (Malden, MA, 2012), ed. Sharon L. James and Sheila Dillon, 204–14; Meghan J. DiLuzio, *A Place at the Altar: Priestesses in Republican Rome* (Princeton, NJ, 2016). For the imperial era, see Beth Severy, *Augustus and the Family at the Birth of the Roman Empire* (London, 2003), 96–139; Emily A. Hemelrijk, *Hidden Lives, Public Personae: Women and Civic Life in the Roman West* (Oxford, 2015), 37–107. On practices rather than beliefs, see John Bodel, "Cicero's Minerva, *Penates*, and the Mother of the *Lares*: An outline of Roman Domestic religion," in *Household and Family Religion in Antiquity: The Ancient World* (Malden, MA, 2008), ed. John Bodel and Saul M. Olyan, 248–75 at 263. On the *pax deorum*, see Schultz, *Religious Activity*, 1–2.

3. On these differences, Scheid, *Introduction*, 18–20, 30–31, 130–31.

4. On the state priests, Rüpke, *Religion*, 216–21; Scheid, *Introduction*, 132–43.

5. Rüpke, *Religion*, 54; Scheid, *Introduction*, 133, 142–43. On *confarreatio* see section "Marriage with and without *Manus*."

6. Holland, "Women," 206–10. On a list of priestesses, see DiLuzio, *Altar*, 14. On Vestals, see Wildfang, *Rome's Vestal Virgins*; DiLuzio, *Altar*; on selection of Vestals, see DiLuzio, *Altar*, 119–35; Gellius *Noctes Atticae* 1.12.1–11; figures on social status of Vestals, see DiLuzio, *Altar*, 128.

7. DiLuzio, *Altar*, 135–40; on bank, see ibid., 235.

8. On theater, see Suet. *Augustus* 31.3, 44.3. On *ius liberorum*, see Dio 55.10.2; DiLuzio, *Altar*, 140–41; cf. privileges given to Livia, Dio 49.38.1. On coins, see DiLuzio, *Altar*, 168–69.

9. On virginity, see DiLuzio, *Altar*, 142–51. On the case of 114 BCE, see Plut. *Roman Questions* 83 = *Moralia* 283f–284a; of 91 CE, Plin. *Ep.* 4.11; on execution, Plut. *Numa* 9.5–10.7 = *Women's Life*, no. 511; Dion. Hal. *Roman Antiquities* 2.67.4. On sack, Jill Harries, *Law and Crime in the Roman World* (Cambridge, 2007), 15; Cic. *Pro Roscio Amerino* 25–6.

10. Macrobius *Saturnalia* 1.16.30; Holland, "Women," 206–9; DiLuzio, *Altar*, 16–48; Schultz, *Religious Activity*, 79–80; on women's sacrifice, see DiLuzio, *Altar*, 1–4; Schultz, *Religious Activity*, 131–32; James Rives, "Women and animal sacrifice in public life," in *Women and the Roman City in the Latin West* (Leiden, 2013), ed. Emily A. Hemelrijk and Greg Woolf, 129–46.

11. Ovid *Fasti* 3.393–8; Gellius *Noctes Atticae* 10.15.23; 10.15.2–27.

12. On *regina*, see Macrobius *Saturnalia* 1.15.19; DiLuzio, *Altar*, 63–67. On *Saliae*, ibid., 79–80; Festus 439 L. On women dressed as fighters, see Tac. *Histories* 1.48; Juvenal 6.250–64.

13. Tac. *Annals* 4.16.3.

14. On this emphasis, see Richlin, "Carrying water," 222, 225, 231–32.

15. On a list of festivals, see H. H. Scullard, *Festivals and Ceremonies of the Roman Republic* (Ithaca, NY, 1981), 62–201; Scheid, *Introduction*, 50–54; Richlin, "Carrying water," 228–30; Agnes K. Michels, "Roman festivals: January–March," *Classical Outlook* 68.2 (1990–91), 44–48; "Roman festivals: April–June," *Classical Outlook* 67.3 (1990), 76–77; "Roman festivals: July–September," *Classical Outlook* 67.4 (1990), 114–16; "Roman festivals: October–December," *Classical Outlook* 68.1 (1990), 10–12. On not exclusive, see Holland, "Women," 210.

16. Emily A. Hemelrijk, "Local empresses: Priestesses of the imperial cult in the cities of the Latin West," *Phoenix* 61.3/4 (2007), 318–49, 327–28. On Dura calendar, Brian Campbell, *The Roman Army 31 BC - AD 337: A Sourcebook* (London, 1994), no. 207.

17. Petronius *Satyrica* 44.18; Richlin, "Carrying water," 223.

18. Schultz, *Religious Activity*, 29–36, e.g., Livy 5.50.7, 22.6.18, 22.37.5–15, 25.12.15, 26.9.7–8, 26.12.8.

19. On Fortuna Muliebris, see Schultz, *Religious Activity*, 37–41; Dion. Hal. *Roman Antiquities* 8. 39.1–56.4; Livy 2.40.1–13; Plut. *Coriolanus* 33.1–37.3. On the *Pudicitiae*, see Schultz, *Religious Activity*, 41–46; Livy 10.23.1–10. On Venus Verticordia, see Plin. *Natural History* 7.120–1; Valerius Maximus 8.15.2.

20. On Claudia, see Livy 29.14.10–14 = Jo-Ann Shelton, *As the Romans Did: A Source Book in Roman Social History* (Oxford, 1988), no. 389.

21. On these changing views, see Schultz, *Religious Activity*; Holland, "Women"; Bacchanalia, Livy 39.8–18; *CIL* I.2 581 = *ILS* 18 = Shelton, no. 388.

22. Bodel, "Cicero's Minerva"; Marja-Leena Hänninen, "Domestic cult and the construction of an ideal Roman family," in *Religious Participation*

in *Ancient and Medieval Societies: Rituals, Interaction, and Identity* (Rome, 2013), ed. Sari Katajala-Peltomaa and Ville Vuolanto, 39–49; DiLuzio, *Altar*, 45–46; Sofroniew, *Household Gods*, 27–46; Kimberley Bowes, "At home," in *A Companion to the Archaeology of Religion in the Ancient World* (Malden, MA, 2015), ed. Rubina Raja and Jörg Rüpke, 209–19. On *Lares*, Harriet L. Flower, *The Dancing Lares & The Serpent in the Garden: Religion at the Roman Street Corner* (Princeton, NJ, 2017).

23. Bodel, "Cicero's Minerva," 258, 262–63, 265; Sofroniew, *Household Gods*, 31–42; Flower, *Lares*, 46–62.

24. Plautus, *Aulularia*, 23–25; Cato *On Farming* 143; Bodel, "Cicero's Minerva," 265; Hänninen, "Domestic cult," 43; Flower, *Lares*, 31–34, 40–45.

25. Nonius 852L; Arnob. *Adversus Nationes* 2.67; Schultz, *Religious Activity*, 127; Flower, *Lares*, 78–85.

26. Fanny Dolansky, "Honouring the family dead on the *Parentalia*: Ceremony, spectacle, and memory," *Phoenix* 65.1/2 (2011), 125–57.

27. Severy, *Augustus and the Family*, 112–131; Beard, North, and Price, *Religions*, I.184–6, 189, 206–9.

28. Hemelrijk, "Local empresses"; Marja-Leena Hänninen, "Religious agency and civic identity of women in ancient Ostia," in *Gender, Memory, and Identity in the Roman World* (Amsterdam, 2019), ed. Iussi Rantala, 63–88. On Bona Dea to Venus, *magistrae* and *ministrae*, see Richlin, "Carrying water," 207–17 (inscriptions); Emily A. Hemelrijk, *Women and Society in the Roman World: A Sourcebook of Inscriptions from the Roman West* (Cambridge, 2021), nos. 5.1, 4–5, 9–10, 13–14, 20–21, 23–24. On imperial cult, see Hemelrijk, *Women and Society*, nos. 5.31–41; on *magistrae* and *ministrae*, see 5.44, 46–47; Rubria Festa, 5.32.

29. Hemelrijk, *Hidden Lives*, 88–96.

30. Hemelrijk, "Local empresses," 327–28; Hemelrijk, "Priestesses of the imperial cult in the Latin west: Benefactions and public honour," *L'Antiquité Classique* 75 (2006), 85–117; Hänninen, "Religious agency," 71–73.

31. *CIL* VI 877 = 32323 = 32324 = *ILS* 5050 = *L'Année Epigraphique* 2002, 192 = Hemelrijk, *Women and Society*, no. 5.63.

32. Schultz, *Religious Activity*, 95–120; Holland, "Women," 211.

33. On astrology, Rüpke, *Religion*, 229–31; Scheid, *Introduction*, 124–26, contrasted with public divination, 111–123. On Augustus, Suet. *Augustus* 31.1.

34. Ramsay MacMullen, "Social history in astrology," in *Changes in the Roman Empire: Essays in the Ordinary* (Princeton, NJ, 1990), ed. Ramsay MacMullen, 218–40; on women, Plut. *Moralia* 145c.

35. Sofroniew, *Household Gods*, 83–85. Spells: Cato, *On Farming* 160.

36. On a typology of witches, see Maxwell T. Paule, "*Qvae saga, qvis magvs*: On the vocabulary of the Roman witch," *Classical Quarterly* 64.2 (2014), 745–57, focused on imaginative literature, e.g., Apuleius *Metamorphoses* 1.6–19 (Meroe). On examples of spells on papyrus, see Mary R. Lefkowitz and Maureen B., eds., Fant, *Women's Life in Greece and Rome:*

A Source Book in Translation, 4th ed. (Baltimore, MD, 2016), nos. 531–33. On social structure and older women, see Susan P. Mattern, *The Slow Moon Climbs: The Science, History, and Meaning of Menopause* (Princeton, NJ, 2019). On the precarity of widows, see Thomas A. J. McGinn, "Widows, orphans, and social history," *Journal of Roman Archaeology* 12 (1999), 617–32. On epitaphs, see Hemelrijk, *Women and Society*, nos. 1.32 (*CIL* VIII 2756), 2.48 (*CIL* III 2197).

37. On public life, see Hänninen, "Religious agency," 64.

11

DEATH AND REMEMBRANCE

INTRODUCTION

Roman cemeteries were (at least on certain days of the year) not the lifeless places we think of as cemeteries, at best solemn and awe inspiring, at worst evoking the forgotten dead with worn, time-bleached tombstones half-buried in the ground, silent as the grave. On Roman festival days, family members and friends of the dead, who bedecked the lifelike painted statues and tombstone reliefs with flowers, thronged the cemeteries. The living made offerings of food and wine to the spirits of the dead and themselves dined festively beside the tombs in the memory of the dead.

As an expert on Roman wills put it, "Personal immortality was survival in the memory of others," which could be achieved through funeral rites, eulogies, epitaphs and tomb monuments, the deceased person's will, memorial celebrations involving care of the tomb, and perpetual foundations intended to fund such celebrations and care in perpetuity. Though Roman women's status was in many ways lower than men's, women's lives were not forgotten. They too were remembered in these ways. As reiterated from chapter 1, the extent of commemoration was also highly dependent on women's social and economic status. We know the most about relatively well-off women and very little about how the poorest women's bodies were treated after death.[1]

Some marked differences from modern (Anglo-American) funerary practice appear. In Roman burial practices from early times to the second century CE, the corpse was usually disposed of by cremation, which was considered respectful and normal, though burning of corpses took place outside the city walls, as did burial of the remains (ashes and bones). The second century CE saw a transition to inhumation, burial of the intact body; the rich used sarcophagi (stone caskets), often elaborately carved. Nobody knows why this transition took place. It does not seem based on conversion to Christianity, which had not yet spread far in many parts of the Empire. The concept of the literal resurrection of the body (which required keeping it intact) was slower still to develop.[2]

Pre-Christian Roman epitaphs focused on the life of the deceased, rather than the afterlife, resembling in this respect modern death notices published in newspapers, highly compressed biographies that record the deceased's birth and death dates, education, employment, marriage, and surviving family members. They did not focus on the afterlife, in contrast with Christian grave memorials in early modern Europe and America. Roman epitaphs, of course, are less literal than death notices. They present an idealized picture of the deceased, and this is particularly true for women.

Inheritance was discussed in chapter 6, as it affected the economic status of women. This chapter discusses the making and reading of wills as part of the deceased person's memorial, in which elite Roman men were accustomed to praise and reward faithful relatives and friends and censure or pass over enemies. The extent to which women made wills is uncertain, but elite women had every reason to make wills and transmit property to those they left behind. The inheritance rights of husbands from wives and vice versa, and of children from mothers and vice versa, were weak unless they were provided for explicitly by will.

This chapter discusses the religious festivals in the Roman calendar that were particularly concerned with remembering the dead, above all the *Parentalia* in February. Individual birthdays of deceased persons could also be celebrated. Romans' social schedules were probably filled with memorial parties–meals held with relatives and friends at the tombs of deceased relatives and friends. Cemeteries were thus relatively cheerful places, where people socially bonded as well as expressed grief and where the tombs were painted and bedecked with flowers and offerings of food and wine.

In a society where religion did not stress the immortality of the soul, funerary practices were intended to perpetuate the memory of the deceased and keep them, as it were, socially alive among the living; deceased women were not excluded from these practices, which existed up and down the social scale, from the Republic's aristocratic funerals at which relatives appeared in the masks representing their ancestors, to the memorial feasts and adornment of tombs on special occasions. Roman wills and inheritances are discussed here because they were regarded as part of the perpetuation of memory as well as the transmission of property from one generation to another. How women were remembered, as depicted in funerary eulogies and in epitaphs, was dependent on traditional female virtues but not restricted to them.

FUNERAL RITES

Ancient Roman funeral rites in some ways emphasized traditional gender roles, in which women cared for the deceased's body and expressed grief with greater physical and emotional intensity than men. Many of the roles in a funeral ceremony were played by men. However, women of the Roman elite could also receive funerary eulogies and public funerals, carrying on the memory of elite families in a manner similar to men.[3]

The reconstruction of Roman funeral rites depends on Late Republican and imperial antiquarian and literary authors, as well as late antique commentators on those authors. Some of the practices recorded in these works were obscure and may not all have been followed, but the ritual pollution, the laying out of the body, the procession, the eulogy, and the interment are the core elements.

The core of funerary ritual was the ritual pollution surrounding the corpse, which was not based on scientific concepts of disease transmission. This is also why cremation grounds (*ustrina*) and cemeteries were located outside the walls of cities and towns. When a family member died, the household became ritually polluted, termed *funesta* or "ritually obliged to carry out funeral rites." Family members were not permitted to visit others, conduct public business, or conduct other religious rituals until nine days after the funeral was concluded. The family placed a pine branch or cypress branch over the door of the house to warn others that they were polluted. For the time being, they wore mourning clothing, which was drab or "dirty" in appearance (black cloth was ostentatious) and went unwashed and with their hair unkempt. Women in mourning wore their hair unbound.[4]

Women had the role of saying farewell to the dying and cleaning the body. As the family member was dying, a close female relative kissed him or her on the mouth to "catch the last breath." Any last words were recorded. The eyes of the deceased were closed, and the family members ritually called out the person's name. The wife or mother of the deceased person washed the body, which was placed on the ground, reversing the ritual of birth where the infant was raised from the ground.[5]

The body was then formally laid out. It was dressed in clean clothing; a male citizen was dressed in a toga, even if, as was common for lower-class men, he had rarely worn it when alive. In wealthy houses, the body was laid on a funerary couch in the atrium, covered with a white cloth. It was traditional for women of the family to also do these things, though a *pollinctor* (anointer, mortician) might be brought in to rub the body with fragrant oils.[6]

Another traditional role for women was lamentation, though it was criticized and its depiction depends on source genre. In poetic sources, both men and women are depicted as grieving with physical and emotional intensity, clawing their cheeks and hair, beating their breasts, tearing their clothing, falling down, groaning, and weeping. Mourners might go unbathed and wear dirty or dark clothing. But philosophical authors such as Cicero and Seneca the Younger disapproved of extravagant grief, associating it with women and uneducated people. As Seneca praises the matron Marcia for doing, it was believed that philosophically educated members of the elite should show restraint and self-control in grief, distinguishing them from people of lower status. There were, of course, many elite exceptions to this rule. Cicero himself was completely grief-stricken by the death of his adult daughter Tullia.[7]

The upper-status reason for condemning histrionic grief may be because Roman funerals often featured hired female mourners, who wailed, beat their breasts, tore their cheeks and clothing, and sang laments (*neniae*). They, or their chorus leaders, were called *praeficae*. To hire large numbers of such women was an ostentation forbidden in the XII Tables, Rome's first law code ca. 450 BCE. Furthermore, the hired mourners were lower status and probably shared the ritual pollution and social opprobrium of other workers in funerary occupations. This stigma is best attested in an inscription from Puteoli, recording regulations for a guild or caste of corpse-handlers, who were forbidden to dwell within the city and had to wear a distinctive colored cap or red clothing and ring a bell to warn others of their presence (like medieval lepers) when they entered the city to remove unclaimed bodies—or to remove slaves for torture and execution. The Puteoli corpse-handlers thus also had the stigmatized task of being torturers and executioners and do not seem to have conducted actual funerals. But there is evidence that other workers with the dead, such as undertakers, funeral directors (*dissignatores* or "ushers"), *pollinctores*, musicians, grave-diggers, and others were also stigmatized. Termed collectively *libitinarii*, at Rome they had their shops on the edge of the city in the grove of *Libitina*, the goddess of funerals.[8]

The funeral procession accompanied the body to the Forum, for a public eulogy, in the case of distinguished senatorial and equestrian funerals; these funerals and whether women could have them are discussed in section "*Funera Publica* and *Elogia*." In the case of ordinary people, the funeral procession brought the deceased straight outside the city, where a close male relative delivered an eulogy besides the funeral pyre. Funeral processions were lit by torches (even in the daytime) and accompanied by flute players to warn people away from polluting contact with death. In particular, state priests at Rome such as the *flamen Dialis* and his wife the *flaminica* were required never to have any contact with the dead, even witnessing a funeral procession.[9]

At the graveside, the pyre was lit by a man of the family. It took some hours to burn down, during which time the family members were not permitted to leave. The task of collecting the ashes and unburned bones fell to women of the family, who placed them in a burial urn. The urn was then interred in the tomb (or, in group tombs, in a *columbarium* with multiple compartments for urns).[10]

The family then observed a nine-day period in which they continued to be ritually impure. On the ninth day, a funeral feast (*cena novemdialis*) was held at the tomb, typically with very simple food such as lentils and salt. On returning, the house was swept with a ritual broom, and the household members were purified with water and fire, being sprinkled with water from a laurel twig and stepping over coals or a burning twig. The household members were then permitted to resume their normal activities, though widows might observe an extended period of mourning (discussed in section "Mourning Customs").[11]

FUNERA PUBLICA AND ELOGIA

During the Republic, the funerals of the Roman political elite (senators) were dramatic pageants emphasizing family lineages and the glorious heritage of the deceased man. They are described by the Greek historian Polybius, writing in the late second century BCE. Roman aristocrats kept painted masks, *imagines*, of their ancestors on the wall of the atriums of their houses. These masks now were worn by male relatives of the deceased or by hired actors, giving the impression that the great men of the past were walking again among the living and inspiring younger men of the family to imitate the glory of their ancestors in holding high office and winning military victories. The dead man's body was exhibited in state in the Forum; he might ride in a chariot as if alive. A close male relative of the deceased delivered a *laudatio* (eulogy praising the dead) from the Rostra. The *laudatio* praised the dead man's public and military record, his moral qualities, and his fatherhood of a family.[12]

All these aspects of public funerals (*funera publica*) emphasized masculine roles that women, excluded from holding offices or military ranks and unable to exercise legal *potestas* or represent others in court, were unable to fill. It is remarkable, then, that Roman elite women also had public funerals and public eulogies. At Rome itself, these are attested from approximately the first century BCE to early in the first century CE, until they were displaced by an imperial monopoly on public funerals at Rome. In the smaller cities and towns of Italy and Latin-speaking Western Europe, elite women continued to have public funerals sponsored by these cities and towns. *Laudationes* for women had a standard form, but might praise other qualities that went beyond traditional gender roles.

Aristocratic women themselves do not appear to have had *imagines*. However, descriptions of women's public funerals show that the *imagines* of their male ancestors were also displayed at their funerals, suggesting that these masks were transferred (in marriage or in inheritance) to women from their birth families. The *Senatus Consultum de Cn. Pisone Patre*, a decree of the Senate (20 CE) condemning the senator and governor of Syria Gnaeus Calpurnius Piso for conspiracy against the emperor Tiberius, forbade "anyone related by blood or marriage to the Calpurnian family" to display his mask in a funeral. Aristocratic women's funerals thus also kept alive the memory of their male ancestors.[13]

The historian Tacitus dramatizes this traditional funeral display in his depiction of Junia Tertia's funeral in 22 CE. Deceased at age ninety-five, Junia was the wife of Gaius Cassius Longinus and the half-sister of Marcus Junius Brutus, the chief assassins of Julius Caesar (d. 44 BCE), the ancestor of the Julio-Claudian imperial family.

She had lived through the reign of Augustus (27 BCE–14 CE) and well into the reign of the emperor Tiberius (14–37 CE).

> Junia, too, born niece to Cato [the Younger], wife of Gaius Cassius, sister of Marcus Brutus, looked her last on life, sixty-three full years after the field of Philippi. Her will was busily discussed by the crowd; because in disposing of her great wealth she mentioned nearly every patrician of note in complimentary terms, but omitted the emperor. The slur was taken in good part, and [Tiberius] offered no objection to the celebration of her funeral with a panegyric at the Rostra and the rest of the customary ceremonies. The effigies of twenty great houses preceded her to the tomb—members of the Manlian and Quinctian families, and names of equal splendor. But Brutus and Cassius shone brighter than all by the very fact that their portraits were unseen.

Junia's impressive parade of *imagines* suggests that these masks were passed down in families not merely from father to son, but from father to daughter, and thus accumulated. The masks of the tyrannicides were not displayed, but Junia still insulted the emperor Tiberius in her will by passing him over, since it had become routine for senators and other wealthy aristocrats to praise and leave legacies to the emperor in their wills. Perhaps because of such scenes, the imperial family in the first century CE increasingly monopolized public funerals in the city of Rome, for empresses and members of the imperial family as well as emperors. These imperial funerals became elaborate spectacles, resembling triumphal processions and celebrating the late emperor's' deeds and those of his predecessors, and culminating in his apotheosis (conversion into a god). The funeral of a late emperor was in effect the coronation of his successor, a celebration of continuity.[14]

Women of high social status still received public funerals in the smaller cities and towns of Roman Italy and the Western provinces. Fifty-eight such funerals are recorded from the imperial era in surviving inscriptions, of which 60 percent are from Roman Italy, 17 percent from Roman Spain, and 8 percent from Roman North Africa. The women who received such funerals belonged to the decurial order (or higher).[15]

What was said in aristocratic women's *laudationes* or *elogia*? In Thucydides's *History of the Peloponnesian War*, Pericles had said, "A woman's reputation is highest when men say little about her, whether good or evil," and aristocratic Roman women do not appear to have received eulogies before the first century BCE, when Quintus Lutatius Catulus (consul in 102 BCE) gave a eulogy in honor of his mother Popilia. Julius Caesar, as tribune of the plebs in 68 BCE, gave a eulogy to his wife Cornelia and his aunt Julia, the wife of Gaius Marius, in which he emphasized Julia's ancestry:

> The family of my aunt Julia is descended by her mother from the kings, and on her father's side is akin to the immortal Gods; for the Marcii Reges (her mother's family name) go back to Ancus Marcius, and the Julii, the family of which ours is a branch, to Venus. Our stock therefore has at once the sanctity of kings, whose power is supreme among mortal men, and the claim to reverence which attaches to the Gods, who hold sway over kings themselves.

In invoking this ancient and divine ancestry, Julius Caesar used this eulogy to Julia for his own self-advertisement and association with Gaius Marius, displaying images of Marius in his aunt's funeral procession. So it seems likely that in the Late Republic, aristocratic women's funerals were exploited by their male relatives as a way of keeping the family name and fame before the public eye.[16]

The *Laudatio Murdiae*, an epitaph in the form of a eulogy, of Late Republican date, attests the stereotypical content of women's eulogies. The commemorator, Murdia's son, says that

> the funerary speech for all good women is accustomed to be simple and similar because their natural qualities . . . do not require variations of phraseology, and it may be enough for all of them to have done the same good deeds worthy of a good reputation.

So he praises Murdia as "in modesty, honesty, chastity, obedience, woolworking, diligence and trustworthiness she was the equal and the model of other upstanding women." Women thus were apparently praised mainly for their traditional domestic virtues. However, the son of Murdia also praises her, and foremost in the inscription, for intellectual qualities, in particular her prudence in making a sound will (discussed in section "Women's Wills").[17]

The most famous *laudatio* of a woman is the inscription known as the *Laudatio Turiae*, "In Praise of Turia," even though the part of the inscription that named the couple is destroyed. Earlier scholars identified the wife with the Turia who saved her husband in a chronicle of brave deeds during the triumviral purge of their opponents in 42 BCE. This identification is now rejected. According to the eulogy, the parents of "Turia" were killed in the civil war and she cleared their name. She helped bring her back from exile during the proscriptions and even "prostrated" herself before the triumvir Lepidus's feet to beseech him:

> He dragged you along and abused you as though a common slave; your body was all covered with bruises . . . Braving his taunts and suffering the most brutal treatment, you denounced these cruelties publicly, so that Lepidus was branded as the author of all my perils and misfortunes.

Turia also brought up destitute female relatives and offered them dowries; when she proved infertile, she offered to divorce her husband so he could marry another women and have children, whom she promised to treat as her own and leave her inheritance to. Turia's husband indignantly rejected her proposal.

> How could my desire for or need for having children have been so great, that for that reason I would have broken my promise to you, and exchanged what I could count on for uncertainties? There is nothing more to say. You remained in my house; I would not have agreed to your request [to divorce] without disgracing myself or causing us both unhappiness.

The husband emphasizes their mutual loyalty and devotion. Besides the publicly endorsed virtues of women, such loyalty to the point of death was an ideal found also in epitaphs further down the social scale, where couples record that they lived together for many years "without any complaint." "Turia," however, is also remarkable for her stereotypically masculine virtues, displaying courage, physical bravery, and endurance and confronting opponents in public to help her husband. Other wives of exiled husbands, such as Terentia, the wife of Cicero, and the wife of the poet Ovid also exerted themselves heroically on their behalf.[18]

In the Principate, elaborate eulogies at Rome were probably reserved for empresses and women of the imperial family, and Seneca the Younger praises his mother Helvia (who was still alive) for remaining out of the public eye. One of the reasons for this (besides the tradition that women belonged in the home) was the emperors' wariness of the senatorial men who staffed the Empire's provincial governorships and military commands. Such men were considered *capax imperii* (capable of seizing the imperial power for themselves), and for them to promote their families or allow their wives to exercise influence beyond a certain level was self-aggrandizing. But even women of the imperial family might receive traditional eulogies; in a surviving inscription, Hadrian praised Matidia the Elder, the mother of Hadrian's wife Sabina, in traditional terms: "she was of such modesty that she never sought anything from me"[19]

But elite women still received funerary eulogies and public funerals at the level of smaller cities and towns in Roman Italy and the provinces. These cities' councils decreed and paid for public funerals for women of the local elite. The women were usually of decurion rank, the daughters, sisters, and wives of city councilors and city magistrates. In this respect, the pattern of public funerals for aristocratic women of the Republic was repeated: such funerals kept prominent families before the public eye. However, these women had also distinguished themselves in their own right, as seen in chapter 9. Many had been public priestesses (of the imperial cult) and benefactors of their cities. They received the full spectacle of a public funeral—lying in state, the *laudatio* delivered by a male relative from the city tribunal, the procession of their relatives, household, and city inhabitants to the pyre, a lavish tomb monument, and memorial statues decreed by the city council. Such statues, unlike tombs, could be placed inside the city, in the city forum or other public places where they would be seen.[20]

WOMEN'S WILLS

Another way in which women assured their remembrance was through their last wills and testaments (*testamentum*, pl. *testamenta*). The purpose of a Roman will was not simply the legal transfer property from the deceased *testator* (person who made the will) to their heirs and legatees. The Roman *testator* used the will to assure the economic security of his heirs but also to compliment and express gratitude and respect toward people he approved of (his heirs and legatees) and to reproach and censure those he disapproved of. He might express disapproval directly, disinheriting ill-behaved and ungrateful offspring, or pass over the victim of his disapproval, omitting a legacy, as Junia Tertia did with the emperor Tiberius. A will thus was a social and emotional statement that could also be political. The aristocrats opposed to the emperors upbraided them in their wills. Wills even were quoted verbatim in Latin epitaphs, which are an important source for them. "If you wrote a will with such care that it could not be broken [rendered invalid] . . . you were praised by posterity."[21]

A funerary relief of a woman from Palmyra, Syria, late 2nd or early 3rd century CE. Palmyra, Syria, was a wealthy trading city on the edge of the Roman empire. The habit of commemoration thus spread to well-to-do non-Roman peoples. (Metropolitan Museum of Art/Purchase, 1902)

A man's will might be invalidated if his widow was found to be pregnant with a child who had not been mentioned in the will (either as an heir or disinherited). The existing heirs were probably infuriated. The judgment of the husband was put aside, so that any external heirs and legatees he had chosen were discarded. Further-more, the "automatic" heirs (*sui heredes*, usually a man's children) now increased in number by one, diminishing their shares according to Roman partitive inheritance, which in cases of intestacy div-ided estates equally among all children. The pregnant widow was subjected to a humiliating process of inspection and observation of her childbirth to ensure that she gave birth to the actual child of the deceased man and not another infant substituted for it. This extraordinary procedure was spelled out in the section of the Praetor's Edict termed *de inspiciendo ventre*, "on the inspection of the womb." The procedure seemed determined to prove whether the widow had, as with an adulteress (though she is not accused of adultery), substituted a child that was not the husband's. In general, Roman elites disapproved of undeserving persons who benefited from wills.[22]

The focus on the pregnant widow as a breaker of wills contrasts with the male authors' approval of women who made their own wills with masculine judgment. The question has been whether Roman women made wills, which has been answered negatively: a higher rate of female intestacy appears in legal and other sources.[23]

Married women, furthermore, were at a greater disadvantage should their husbands die intestate; if they themselves died intestate, their children were at a disadvantage. The obsolescence of *manus* marriage meant that married women whose fathers were still alive still belonged to their fathers' families, not their husbands', and were not among their husbands' automatic heirs if their husbands died intestate. When possession of the estate was granted on intestacy, the deceased spouse's *sui heredes* came first, then any other blood relatives, then agnate relatives, and husbands and wives came last.

The Augustan marriage legislation also made it harder for husbands and wives to inherit from each other. If they had no children, they could inherit only one-tenth of their estates from each other; if they had a child, they could inherit an additional one-tenth, with another one-tenth for each child; and if they had three children, they could inherit in full. Mothers also had weak inheritance rights with respect to their children, both from a mother to her children (because they were in her husband's *familia*, not hers) and from children to a mother. These legal disabilities were amended in the second century by the *SC Tertullianum* and *SC Orphitianum*.[24]

Women's testation was subject to minor legal hindrances. Before Hadrian, women could not make wills unless they underwent a change in status called *capitis deminutio*, which severed their legal connection with their agnate relatives. This was a legal formality that could be achieved by *coemptio*, a mock sale of the woman (an old way of creating *manus* marriage used the same ritual). Hadrian abolished the need for *capitis deminutio*. However, women still required the authorization of their *tutores* (guardians) to make wills. The *tutor* had no say about the content of the will.

Women's tendency to make wills was probably correlated with social and economic status. Elite women who inherited substantial property from their fathers or husbands were more likely to make wills. Lower-status women, with little property, were less likely to make wills, especially if they and their family members were illiterate. Nerva and Trajan created a special type of will for soldiers, which liberated them from the usual legal formalities because of their lack of education. In the eyes of the jurists, women were often as ignorant of the law, but did not receive similar privileges.[25]

Women's tendency to make wills may have changed with their stages in life. Among the elite, young women whose fathers were still alive were not able to make wills, as they were still under *patria potestas* and as yet owned no property; the mentality may have persisted even after they became *sui iuris*. Since mothers might give birth to and bury many children, this fluctuation in their progeny made will-making cumbersome (as seen with the pregnant widow's husband's will). Women who had given birth to three children attained greater control over their property, dispensing with a *tutor*'s authorization to make a will. When women were past childbearing age and the number of their surviving children had stabilized, they might be more inclined to make wills. A woman who was *sui iuris* and had attained the *ius trium liberorum* and was lucky enough to outlive her husband might have free disposition over her property.

The women's wills that are attested in literary authors are those of older women, who appear to consider the benefit of their progeny as the ideal Roman male testator would. Murdia, the subject of the *Laudatio Murdiae*, is praised for her prudence and justice in making a will that benefited all her descendants, the children of two marriages. The frequency of mortality and divorce meant that many Roman families were blended. The act of making a will was important in Roman culture; a well-made will conveyed the shrewdness, justice, and benevolence of the testator. Though Pliny the Younger criticizes the wealthy widow Ummidia Quadratilla for spending her "womanly idleness" watching pantomime actors—the actors who performed in the theater she had restored or amphitheater that she had built—he nonetheless praises her prudence in bringing up her grandson more strictly (he was not allowed to watch the actors). Pliny praises Ummidia Quadratilla's will as "most respectable" for leaving her property to her grandchildren as heirs.[26]

Women's funerary foundations (discussed in section "Funerary Foundations") may attest wills directly and imply their existence, since a foundation had to be created explicitly as a provision of a will. The number of these (and of epitaphs that mention the testament) is higher than surviving elite references to women's wills.[27]

COMMEMORATION IN THE LOWER STRATA

Funerary commemoration was not restricted to the upper orders. Funerary monuments might be freestanding, part of an altar, a sarcophagus, or urn; tombs were often socially differentiated, dependents of a household having smaller markers or compartments for urns (*columbaria*, pigeonholes) within a larger tomb enclosure. But the largest tombs are not necessarily those of the highest status or most important people (e.g., the tomb of the baker Eurysaces). Most of the hundreds of thousands of Latin epitaphs that survive from Rome, Italy, and the provinces record relatively ordinary people, who were able to afford the cost of a stone inscription but were otherwise not wealthy. The desire to leave some monument to their existence must have been increased by the treatment of the bodies of the poorest inhabitants. Those who could not afford a carved stone inscription may have settled for painted stone or wooden markers; the walls of Pompeii have revealed how much ephemeral writing (election slogans, advertisements, and graffiti) was painted or scratched upon whitewashed walls. Those who could not afford a marker settled for a funeral pyre or modest burial.[28]

John Bodel estimates that the population of the city of Rome in Augustan times was about 750,000, so possibly 40 per thousand died in any one year (comparable with other large premodern cities) or some 30,000 a year or "more than eighty a day." In epidemics, the rate might be much higher. The number who were interred in tombs outside the city was only 1–2 percent of all dead and "probably considerably less." Poor dependents of wealthy households, whether slaves or clients, may have been burned and interred in columbaria.[29]

The bodies of the poorest inhabitants, especially in the overcrowded and disease-infested city of Rome, were probably buried in mass graves. Authors of the Late Republic mention these graves, terming them *puticuli* (foul pits) and suggesting that they were located on the Esquiline hill before the wealthy Maecenas filled in the pits and built gardens over them. The nineteenth-century archeologist Lanciari thought he had found these pits, but later archeologists were skeptical. The bodies may have been burned en masse in the Augustan period and first century CE, but when inhumation replaced cremation, their disposal remains obscure. In the second century CE and later, the Christians of Rome interred their dead in catacombs which they excavated in the soft volcanic rock underneath the city to avoid the need to purchase land for burial plots outside the city. The worst fate, however, was not to be buried at all, the fate of slave victims of crucifixion, of the battle dead in civil wars, or of enemies of the state.[30]

Epitaphs of ordinary women tended to stress their relationship to a family member. Thus daughters who died young were commemorated by parents, wives by husbands, and mothers by children. Single women are met with relatively rarely in inscriptions, reflecting the expectation that all women married; single women were more likely to be widows.[31]

In Latin epitaphs, women are depicted with stereotypical domestic virtues. In one such epitaph, Aurelia Philematium, freedwoman of Lucius, was married to Aurelius Hermia, a freedman of the same owner; their epitaphs are written in the first person, speaking to the passers-by. Aurelius Hermia calls his wife "chaste in body, my one and only wife, who lovingly presided over my soul, throughout her life was a woman faithful to her husband . . . who never shrank from duty through avarice." Aurelia Philematium describes herself as "chaste, modest, ignorant of the ways of the crowd, faithful to my husband." She says that "He took me to his bosom when I was seven years old," probably not referring to marriage as Roman women could not legally marry until age twelve. The relief, from the Late Republic by the spelling, suggests the desire of freedwomen (and their families and tradespeople; Hermia was a butcher) to aspire to the status of *matronae*. A very unusual epitaph commemorating a freedwoman named Allia Potestas, erected by her two male lovers, praises her physical appearance in unabashedly sexual terms, but also commends her domestic virtues, as "the first to get up and the last to go to bed," skilled in working wool.[32]

Individual tombs display conflicts among family members, perhaps most dramatically in the case of the freedwoman Acte (Rome, c. 80 CE). On one side of the stone is a conventional epitaph, the tombstone of Junia Procula, commemorated by her father Marcus Junius Euphrosynus (a freedman) and his wife; the name of the wife and mother has been obliterated. On the other side is a curse! The husband of Acte berates and curses her for abandoning him in

Tomb of Caecilia Metella, Appian Way, outside Rome, Italy, first century BCE. This massive mausoleum commemorated Caecilia Metella, a woman of a wealthy aristocratic family in the late Republic. Caecilia Metella belonged to the social stratum in which women might receive funeral eulogies and public funerals, but her tomb was unusually ostentatious. In the imperial era, high-status women who were not members of the imperial family were honored with tombs outside the vicinity of Rome. (Ridpath, John Clark, *Ridpath's History of the World,* 1901)

his old age. *Damnatio memoriae,* the obliteration of a person's public record, consigning them to oblivion, is best known when it was applied to emperors and aristocrats condemned for treason; their names in inscriptions were effaced, their statues and busts, ubiquitous in the case of emperors, were destroyed. In lesser conflicts, it is apparent that a person built himself a tomb but was interred elsewhere, probably at the wishes of a subsequent spouse, the commemorator.[33]

MOURNING CUSTOMS

Roman widows were expected to observe a period of mourning. The traditional period of mourning, reinforced by religious custom, for women was ten months, within which time any child conceived by the late husband would be born. The *Lex Julia de maritandis ordinibus* (18 BCE) set the period of mourning at two years, after which a woman must remarry. The *Lex Papia Poppaea* (9 CE) extended the mourning period to three years. The remarriage requirement was lifted for women over fifty and for women who had given birth to three children. Divorced women were given less leeway, eighteen months.[34]

Women in mourning may have worn a *ricinium*, a particular style of mantle, and both men and women wore drab clothing (undyed "dark" clothing, black if they were being ostentatious). In the immediate period between the death and the post-funerary purification, both men and women might put ashes on their heads and women might wear their hair unbound, a symbol of emotional distress in Greco-Roman culture. The full costume of ritual grief, with unbound hair, ashes on the head, torn and dirty clothing, wailing, and breast-beating, was performed by hired female mourners in the funeral procession, who may have sung traditional dirges. Such a theatrical performance of grief was not expected of elite women, who were encouraged to adopt a stoic philosophical attitude to death (influenced by Stoic and Epicurean philosophy).[35]

These features of ritual mourning are distinct from the *univira* or "one-man woman," the widow who, having been married once, never remarried, remaining faithful to her late husband's memory. The *univira* was much admired as a symbol of traditional wifely virtue and fidelity. But being an *univira* conflicted with Augustus' marriage legislation and was probably only affordable for women of the upper orders, where some women inherited enough wealth to live independently. Below the elite, few widows could afford to remain unmarried without economic support, and unmarried widows often moved in with other family members in Roman Egypt. Even in the elite, it is likely that all but the wealthiest widows chose to remarry to avoid the Augustan laws' penalties for the unmarried and to maintain an accustomed lifestyle. Though the property of husband and wife remained legally separate in marriage, they were accustomed to sharing resources in practice.[36]

REMEMBRANCE

Tomb monuments were not simply memorials addressed to the living; they were the sites of religious worship addressed to the *Di Manes*, the "divine spirits" or "ancestral spirits" of the dead. These spirits received offerings at their tombs, particularly on certain holidays: the *Parentalia*, a weeklong holiday in February during which families paid cult to and remembered their dead, lesser holidays in spring, and anniversaries. The *Di Manes*, also called *di parentes* or *dei familiae*, occupied a space somewhere between mortals and gods. As with the gods themselves and the emperors, whether the Romans "believed" in the *Di Manes* is to some degree an inappropriate question; practices mattered, not beliefs, and it was considered obligatory to carry out these practices.[37]

The *Parentalia*, from February 13 to 21, termed *dies ferales* or *dies parentales*, was a holiday set apart for grieving for and honoring deceased family members. At Rome the first day was a public festival, on which public business could not be conducted and state priests made sacrifices. On the other days (which were interrupted by several other, more obscure festivals) family members proceeded to the tombs of their loved ones outside the city walls. They placed wreaths of flowers and offerings of food and wine on altars by the tombs, and often poured food and wine directly into tombs by means of libation tubes, lead or terracotta pipes that led into the gravesite. The family held a feast by the tomb, using food that was kept separate from the ritual offerings, which it was impious for mortals to touch. The scope of such celebrations is attested by the seating and dining facilities that were built into large tombs and the gardens (for the flowers), kitchens, and even lodging facilities that adjoined cemeteries.[38]

But the spirit of the *Parentalia* was intended to express piety and simple affection, in the words of Ovid's *Fasti*:

> Placate your fathers' souls,
> Bring tiny tributes to the erected pyres.
> The dead desire little. They want piety,
> Not rich gifts; deep Styx has no greedy gods.
> A tile covered and arranged with wreaths is enough,
> Sprinkled corn and a thrifty grain of salt,
> And Ceres softened in wine and loose violets.
> Leave them lying on a shard in mid-street.
> I do not forbid larger gifts, but these appease wraiths.
> Build hearths and add prayers and ritual words.[39]

The observance of the *Parentalia* features in tombstone inscriptions that beseech or require the living to observe it. Some funerary inscriptions request the pouring of libations on the *Parentalia* (as with the tombstone of Claudia Achilles in Brixia) or libations and garlands. Tombs themselves might be brightly decorated, built from colored brick at Isola Sacra (the cemetery of Rome's port Ostia) or painted in bright colors, as ancient statuary was usually painted, and were brightened further by being decked with flowers, with violets on the *Dies Violae* or "day of violets" on March 22 and with roses on the *Rosalia* on May 21.[40]

FUNERARY FOUNDATIONS

Some female benefactors combined both the act of benefaction, the *testamentum*, the epitaph, and the remembrance celebration by creating endowments that funded annual remembrance celebrations, making their birthday or death day a holiday for a *collegium* or even for an entire municipality. These endowments were probably specified in the deceased woman's will and were recorded in baroque memorial inscriptions. Such foundations were also created by grief-stricken relatives in memory of the deceased person.

As an example, the wealthy freedman Q. Cominius Abascantus (in an epitaph from 148–49 CE) left very elaborate instructions for rites on the *Parentalia*, including handouts of money to various groups of guests and performers, violet garlands for the tomb, nard to be poured into his tomb, funds for a feast for the decurions and for a sacrifice to his memory. He left a legacy of 10,000 sesterces (HS) to fund these memorial celebrations. The tomb of Junia Libertas in Ostia (early second century CE) provided that if her *familia* had no descendants, the people of Ostia should care for her tomb and 100 HS be spent annually for sacrifices and decoration of her tomb on the *Parentalia* (the money was interest from the estate).[41]

In 153 CE, a woman, Salvia Marcellina, established a memorial foundation for the *collegium* of Aesculapius and Hygeia to commemorate her husband. It proclaims "in memory of Flavius Apollonius, *procurator Augusti* in charge of the imperial painting galleries, and Capito, *Augusti libertus*, his assistant, and her most excellent husband, [by] Salvia Marcellina" and records that Salvia Marcellina gave the *collegium* of Aesculapius and Hygeia a shrine with a statue of Aesculapius and a sun-terrace for banquets and 50,000 HS to fund gifts to the members on festival days. The parents of the deceased girl Ursilia Ingenua even specified that a girls' youth group would honor her tomb on the *Parentalia* or be fined.[42]

Exactly how the foundations operated is unclear. The capital sum is not always very large, and it is unknown how long the foundation was expected to last. If the capital sum was spent, it would obviously run out in a few years. In theory, if the initial sum was shrewdly invested (in land rather than in modern stocks and bonds), the return on investment (which might be the harvest itself) could provide the memorial feasts in perpetuity. But the inscriptions rarely specify such details, which economic historians continue to debate. The largest such foundations funded so-called *alimenta* (discussed in section "Girls in Public Life") charity distributions of food or money to the children of municipal citizens. There were numerous such alimentary programs in Roman Italy, mostly dating from the second century CE. Not all the *alimenta* were memorial in nature. The *alimenta* usually provided food or money to both boys and girls, and girls received slightly less of either, probably reflecting their lower value in Roman society. A few alimentary foundations focused on girls. After the death of his empress Faustina the Elder, Antoninus Pius (emperor 138–161 CE) created a foundation termed the *puellae Faustinianae*, which was featured on coin issues. His successor Marcus Aurelius did the same in honor of his own wife, Faustina the Younger, after her death.

CONCLUSION

Though death itself is the "great leveler," how people commemorate death is often highly socially stratified. The most famous ancient memorials, the pyramids of Egypt, were available only to monarchs, the pharaohs of Egypt. In the Roman Empire, memorials to the deceased became more democratic—available not only to the social elite, such as the senatorial and equestrian orders and the emperors, but to lesser elites and to the relatively ordinary people who left behind hundreds of thousands of epitaphs. Though in some ways they were less valued than men, women also ensured that they were remembered.

However, the social stratification of women in Roman society emerged in other funerary practices. Women of the upper orders might receive public funerals and eulogies that resembled those held for their male peers, though elite women's eulogies tended to praise their ideal qualities as *matronae* and mothers. Elite women were also more likely to be remembered through funerary foundations that funded celebrations in their memory. Women and girls from the sub-elite might receive a stone memorial and simple inscription. The very poorest may not have received memorials or even individual interment.

NOTES

1. Edward Champlin, "*Creditur vulgo testamenta hominum speculum esse morum*: Why the Romans made wills," *Classical Philology* 84.3 (1989), 198–215, 213.

2. On cultural shifts in funerary practices, see Thomas W. Laqueur, *The Work of the Dead: A Cultural History of Mortal Remains* (Princeton, NJ, 2015). On Roman cremation, see J. M. C. Toynbee, *Death and Burial in the Roman World* (Baltimore, MD, 1971), 49–50.

3. Darja Sterbenc Erker, "Gender and Roman funeral ritual," in *Memory and Mourning: Studies on Roman Death* (Oxford, 2011), ed. Valerie M. Hope and Janet Huskinson, 40–60 at 57; Amy Richlin, "Emotional work: Lamenting the Roman dead," in *Essays in Honor of Gordon Williams: Twenty-Five Years at Yale* (New Haven, CT, 2001), ed. Elizabeth Tylawsky and Charles Weiss, 229–48 = Amy Richlin, *Arguments with Silence: Writing the History of Roman Women* (Ann Arbor, MI, 2014), 267–88; John Scheid, *Introduction to Roman Religion* (Edinburgh, 2003), 167–69.

4. On *funesta*, see Cic. *Laws* 2.55; Gellius *Noctes Atticae* 4.6.8; Servius comm. on Virgil *Aeneid* 6.8; 11.2. On bough, see Servius comm. on *Aeneid* 3.64; 4.507; Plin. *Natural History* 16.40; 16.139; Servius comm. on *Horace Odes* 2.14.23; Festus 56L. On dark or drab clothing, see Catullus 64.349–51; Virgil *Aeneid* 10.844, 12.611 versus Plut. *Moralia* 270e–f (discussed in Erker, "Gender," 44). On Roman funerary rites, see Toynbee, *Death and Burial*, 45–64; John Bodel, "Dealing with the dead: Undertakers, executioners and potters' fields in ancient Rome," in *Death and Disease in the Ancient City* (London, 2000), ed. Valerie M. Hope and Eireann Marshall, 128–51; Valerie M. Hope, "Contempt and respect: The treatment of the corpse in ancient Rome," in Hope and Marshall, *Death and Disease*, 104–27; Hugh Lindsay, "Death-pollution and funerals in the city of Rome," in Hope and Marshall, *Death and Disease*, 152–73; Valerie M. Hope, *Roman Death: The Dying and the Dead in Ancient Rome* (London, 2009); Erker, "Gender."

5. Servius comm. on Virgil *Aeneid* 6.218; Erker, "Gender," 46; Lindsay, "Death-pollution," 158.

6. On toga, see Juvenal 3.171; Erker, "Gender," 47–48; Lindsay, "Death-pollution," 163; cf. Virgil *Aeneid* 9.486–9.

7. Seneca *Consolatio ad Marciam* 7.3; cf. Seneca *Consolatio ad Polybium* 6.2; Cic. *Tusculan Disputations* 2.55; Erker, "Gender," 44–45; Richlin, "Emotional work," 272, 274–76. Cicero and Tullia: Susan Treggiari, *Roman Marriage: Iusti Coniuges from the Time of Cicero to the Time of Ulpian* (Oxford, 1991), 493, 495–96.

8. On XII Tables, see Cic. *Laws* 2.22. On *praeficae*, see Lucilius 955M; Varro *On the Latin Language* 7.70; Festus 250L; Erker, "Gender," 48–49; Richlin,

"Emotional work," 283–84. On Puteoli, see *L'Année Epigraphique* 1971, 88; Jörg Rüpke, *Religion of the Romans*, trans. Richard Gordon (Malden, MA, 2007), 232–34; Hope, "Contempt," 111; Bodel, "Dealing," 135–43; Lindsay, "Death-pollution," 144–48. On *libitinarii*, see Bodel, "Dealing," 135–39.

9. For a reconstruction of an elite male Roman's funeral procession, see Christopher Johanson, "A walk with the dead: A funerary cityscape of ancient Rome," in *Companion to Families*, 408–30.

10. Lindsay, "Death-pollution," 161; Erker, "Gender," 52. On sacrifice of a sow at the funeral, see Festus 296L. On women collecting ashes, see Ovid *Tristia* 3.65–70. A bone was interred directly in the earth so that the family would be purified from death-pollution; see Varro *On the Latin Language* 5.23; Erker, "Gender," 53.

11. On the funeral feast, see Juvenal 5.85; Tac. *Annals* 6.5; Plut. *Roman Questions* 7; Horace *Sermones* 2.6.63; Plut. *Crassus* 19. On sweeping, see Festus 68L. On water and fire, see Cic. *Laws* 2.22; Festus 3L, 61L, 69L; Lindsay, "Death-pollution," 166–67.

12. Polybius *Histories* 6.53–4. Hope, "Contempt," 108; Lindsay, "Death-pollution," 164; Erker, "Gender," 49–50.

13. Lewis Webb, "Gendering the Roman *Imago*," *Eugesta* 7 (2017), 140–83, https://eugesta-revue.univ-lille3.fr/pdf/2017/5.Webb-Eugesta-7_2017 .pdf.

14. Tac. *Annals* 3.76. On Junia, see Champlin, "*Creditur vulgo*," 204; Webb, "*Imago*," 167. On imperial funerals, see Toynbee, *Death and Burial*, 56–61; Hope, "Contempt," 108–9.

15. Emily A. Hemelrijk, *Hidden Lives, Public Personae: Women and Civic Life in the Roman West* (Oxford, 2015), 327–29; *Women and Society in the Roman World: A Sourcebook of Inscriptions from the Roman West* (Cambridge, 2021), nos. 6.47–48.

16. On Pericles, see Thucydides 2.45.2; Popilia, Cic. *On the Orator* 2.44; Caesar, Suet. *Julius* 6; Plut. *Caesar* 1; 5.1–2. Eulogies, Webb, "*Imago*," 166, 170–71; Hugh Lindsay, "The 'Laudatio Murdiae': Its content and significance," *Latomus* 63.1 (2004), 88–97, 89; Emily A. Hemelrijk, "Masculinity and femininity in the 'Laudatio Turiae,'" *Classical Quarterly* 54 (2004), 185–97, at 186–88; Hemelrijk, *Women and Society*, no. 1.43. On legendary origins of women's eulogies, see Plut. *Camillus* 8; Livy 5.50.7.

17. On *Laudatio Murdiae*, see *CIL* VI 10230 = *ILS* 8394; Judith Evans-Grubbs, *Women and the Law in the Roman Empire: A Sourcebook on Marriage, Divorce, and Widowhood* (London, 2002), 225–26; Mary R. Lefkowitz and Maureen B. Fant, *Women's Life in Greece and Rome: A Sourcebook in Translation* (Baltimore, MD, 2016), no. 52; Hemelrijk, *Women and Society*, no. 1.43; Lindsay, "Laudatio Murdiae."

18. On *Laudatio Turiae*, see ii.14–18, 44–47; *CIL* VI 1527 = 31670 = 37053 = *ILS* 8393 = *CIL* VI 41062. On extracts, see Mary R. Lefkowitz, "Wives and husbands," *Greece & Rome* 30 (1983), 31–47 at 42–43; Jo-Ann Shelton, *As the Romans Did: A Source Book in Roman Social History* (Oxford, 1988), no. 288;

Women's Life, no. 191; Hemelrijk, *Women and Society*, no. 1.3. In general, see Hemelrijk, "Masculinity"; Jo-Ann Shelton, *The Women of Pliny's Letters* (London, 2013), 58–62. On "Turia's" masculine virtues, see Hemelrijk, "Masculinity," 189–90. On the literary Turia, see Dio 54.10; Appian *Civil Wars* 4.44; Valerius Maximus 6.7.2.

19. Sen. *Consolatio ad Helviam* 19.6. On Matidia, see Hemelrijk, *Women and Society*, no. 7.15 (*CIL* XIV 3579).

20. Emily A. Hemelrijk, "Priestesses of the imperial cult in the Latin West: Benefactions and public honour," *L'Antiquité Classique* 75 (2006), 85–117 at 94–95; Hemelrijk, *Hidden Lives*, 320–29.

21. Tac. *Annals* 6.38 (Tiberius); 16.17 (Nero); Champlin, "*Creditur vulgo*," 209; *Final Judgments: Duty and Emotion in Roman Wills, 200 B.C.–A.D. 250* (Berkeley, CA, 1991), 14, 16.

22. Champlin, "*Creditur vulgo*," 211–12. Inspection, Jane F. Gardner, *Women in Roman Law and Society* (London, 1986), 182–83; Evans-Grubbs, *Women*, 200–01, 261–66.

23. Champlin, *Judgments*, 42, 46–49.

24. See this book, sections "The *Lex Julia de maritandis ordinibus*" and "*Ius Liberorum*."

25. On women's wills, Gardner, *Women*, 17–19, 167–68. On soldiers' wills, J. B. Campbell, *The Emperor and the Roman Army, 31 BC–AD 235* (Oxford, 1984), 210–29.

26. Plin. *Ep.* 7.24. Shelton, *Women*, 244–45; cf. will of Sabina, Plin. *Ep.* 4.10; Shelton, *Women*, 334–35.

27. Alison E. Cooley, *Cambridge Manual of Latin Epigraphy* (Cambridge, 2012), 137.

28. Jonathan Edmondson, "Roman family history," in *The Oxford Handbook of Latin Epigraphy* (Oxford, 2014), ed. Christer Bruun and Jonathan Edmondson, 559–82. On the baker Eurysaces, Sandra R. Joshel, *Work, Identity and Legal Status at Rome: A Study of the Occupational Inscriptions* (Norman, OK, 1992), 80–81.

29. Bodel, "Dealing," 128–29.

30. On the *puticuli*, see Varro *On the Latin Language* 5.25; Horace *Satires* 1.8.8–22; Hope, "Contempt," 111; Bodel, "Dealing," 131–32. On burial of the poor, see Hope, "Contempt," 110–11; Bodel, "Dealing," 128–34. On transition to mass cremation, see Bodel, "Dealing," 133–34. On leaving unburied, see Hope, "Contempt," 112–17.

31. On single women, Cooley, *Cambridge Manual*, 52.

32. On Aurelia Philematio, see *CIL* VI 9499 = *ILS* 7472 = Hemelrijk, *Women and Society*, no. 1.15; Eve D'Ambra, *Roman Women* (Cambridge, 2007), 82–83; Edmondson, "Family history," 570–71. On Allia Potestas, see *CIL* VI 37965 = *Women's Life*, no. 57. On attributes in women's epitaphs, see Werner Riess, "*Rari exempli femina*: Female virtues on Roman funerary inscriptions," in *Companion to Women*, 491–501. On the woolworking, see J. Maurin, "*Labor matronalis*: Aspects du travail féminin à Rome," in *La*

femme dans les sociétés antiques (Strasbourg, 1983), ed. Edourd Lévy, 139–54, at 148.

33. Edmondson, "Family history," 571; Hemelrijk, *Women and Society*, no. 1.68.

34. On ten months, see Plut. *Numa* 12.3; Erker, "Gender," 54–55. On laws, Gardner, *Women*, 50–51; Treggiari, *Roman Marriage*, 494; Thomas A. J. McGinn, *Prostitution, Sexuality, and the Law in Ancient Rome* (Oxford, 1998), 74; Evans-Grubbs, *Women*, 84.

35. On *ricinium*. Kelly Olson, *Dress and the Roman Woman: Self-Presentation and Society* (London, 2008), 42.

36. Shelton, *Women*, 40, 51.

37. Mary Beard, John North, and Simon Price, *Religions of Rome, Vol. 1: A History* (Cambridge, 1998), 31; Rüpke, *Religion*, 68–69; Fanny Dolansky, "Honouring the family dead on the *Parentalia*: Ceremony, spectacle, and memory," *Phoenix* 65.1–2 (2011), 125–57; Ramsay MacMullen, "The end of ancestor worship: Affect and class," *Historia* 63.4 (2014), 487–513, 491, and n. 16 (Plut. *Moralia* 267a–f; Ovid *Fasti* 2.22, 618). On the *Di Manes*, Scheid, *Introduction*, 167.

38. Toynbee, *Death and Burial*, 61–64; Cooley, *Cambridge Manual*, 225–26; Dolansky, "Honouring," 130, 133–26; MacMullen, "Ancestor worship," 490–93; Erker, "Gender," 55–58. Ausonius *Parentalia* pr.A.8–9; Ovid *Fasti* 2.533–570.

39. Ovid *Fasti* 2.533–42.

40. On libations, see *CIL* V 4410; *CIL* V 5907; Dolansky, "Honouring," 138.

41. *L'Année Epigraphique* 1940, 94; another, Hemelrijk, *Women and Society*, no. 4.36.

42. *CIL* VI 10234 = *ILS* 7213 = Hemelrijk, *Women and Society*, no. 6.32. On *collegia*, see Rüpke, *Religion*, 206–14; on Salvia Marcellina, see ibid., 209–10. Ursilia Ingenua, *CIL* V 5907.

CONCLUSION

The overall impression is how diverse the experiences of women were in the Roman world, even within the parts of that world that shared an elite and sub-elite cultural identity as Roman citizens and subjects. The most common experience was probably the high infant and child mortality rates of the Roman world, in which approximately a third of all infants died in their first year and nearly half of all children died before age ten, from diseases that were actually promoted by the high level of urbanization and economic growth in the Roman world. The Mediterranean, and particularly Roman Italy, was a realm of small cities and towns besides the megalopolises of Rome itself, Carthage, Antioch, and Alexandria. Diseases were more frequently transmitted in crowded urban living conditions. The economic growth of the Empire brought amenities such as aqueducts, baths, and fountains to cities but no modern hygiene or sanitary sewers (sewers, when built, were intended to drain water). The urban development led to deforested countryside and increased the spread of malaria, which then, as now, in the tropical areas of the world was a major killer of pregnant women, infants, and small children. Social effects of this high infant and child mortality included the raising of children by wet nurses and the lack of attention paid to the deaths of infants and very small children.

If they were fortunate enough to survive into later childhood (ages seven to twelve), the experiences of girls in upper-class families began to diverge from those of their brothers and from girls in the lower social strata, especially slave girls. Girls from the upper orders (senatorial, equestrian, and decurial) were expected to marry at an early age, starting from the legal minimum age of twelve and extending into their mid-teens. They did not receive the same level of education as their brothers, who were prepared for future public life as politicians and legal advocates by training in oratory, rhetoric, and law. It is likely that women of the upper orders received some literary education, as well as training in basic reading, writing, and arithmetic. In the strata below, girls received only a primary education, if at all. They may have attended primary school. Girls in the sub-elite and below may have been expected to help with domestic tasks, the family workshop or business, or agricultural tasks from an early age. Slave girls were considered able to work from age five or seven. Furthermore, the sexual reputation of girls of the elite strata was carefully protected; they were shielded from obscenity (termed *nupta verba*, words that married women were permitted to hear), and wearing the *toga praetexta*, with its border of purple, separated them visually from slave girls. Freeborn girls of the upper strata were expected to be virgins at marriage; the sub-elite may have shared these values, as epitaphs praising sub-elite women for their modesty and chastity survive. Slave girls, in contrast, were sexually vulnerable.

Roman first-time brides married men who were considerably older, on the average ten years older, and in many cases (if the husband was making a second or subsequent marriage) much older. Such marriages were arranged based not on personal preference but on social considerations, including the relative status and wealth of the two families that would be joined by marriage. This age gap between husband and wife produced a disparity in life experience and authority between husband and wife, at least in wives' first marriages. However, other features of Roman marriage produced greater equality than in later European marriage law. By the mid-Republic, Roman husbands and wives married without *manus* managed their own property separately and were even prohibited to give each other substantial gifts (small gifts, such as food items, did not count). Many relatively young women had lost their fathers (who, because of the age gap, died sooner than their own wives) and became *sui iuris*, able to manage their own property independently. Such women were still restricted by *tutela* (guardianship). But divorce was relatively easy. Many Roman marriages were ended early by the death of a partner or by divorce. In such cases, remarriage was the norm; despite Romans' admiration for *univirae*, women who married only once were relatively rare. Few women were wealthy enough to afford not to remarry; in the sub-elite, those widows who did not remarry moved into the households of their children. The first emperor, Augustus, promoted the *Leges Juliae* or laws regulating marriage and punishing adultery, promoting marriage by allowing privileges to the married and to husbands and wives who had children. The punishment of adultery fell more heavily upon adulterous wives and their lovers; a sexual double standard applied, in which a husband's sexual activity outside marriage was not adultery as long as he confined himself to his own slave partners, prostitutes, and other stigmatized individuals. As long as she had children within her marriage and did not commit adultery, Roman law protected an elite woman's property rights in marriage; in contrast, the law gave little or no protection to those women who lacked the legal right to marry.

The intensely hierarchical, status-conscious Roman world is visible in how women in the Roman world were dressed. Status was thought to be displayed immediately and visibly by dress. The *matrona* of the upper orders wore a *stola*, a long sleeveless overdress over her tunic dress, that hid her body and guaranteed her modesty and *pudicitia*; she wore long skirts covering her feet and showing that she did not do physical labor. Women of the lower strata did not wear the *stola* and probably wore shorter skirts, stopping at mid-calf or ankle, to allow them to walk through dirty streets and engage in physical work. Other markers of status, in a period when all cloth was spun and woven by hand, included expensive materials such as silk and fabric dyed with expensive dyes such as scarlet and purple. Cloth made in artisan workshops was of finer quality than homespun cloth, the latter worn by slaves and the free poor. The prestige of *lanificium* (spinning wool; textile work in general) for elite women grew precisely because they did not have to do it.

The economic lives of women of the elite strata versus the lower orders and slave women were also very different. Elite women who were *sui iuris* and who had given birth to three children received the *ius liberorum*, with liberation from guardianship; they could buy, sell, and loan money and property at will. They mainly did so through intermediaries, using slaves or freedmen to complete business transactions, and thus maintained a facade of feminine domesticity while increasing their estates and engaging in long-range trade and commerce. In contrast, women of the lower social strata did not have representatives to act for them. They may have continued to work for or even front a family-run artisan workshop or business when the men of the family were no longer available, but, in keeping with the domestic ideal, they did not record these roles. Freedwomen may have been an exception. Women of the poorest strata carried out agricultural labor or worked in workshops (particularly spinning and weaving). Very little about their lives is recorded.

Slave women in the Roman Empire suffered from the double burden of being slaves and being women. Slavery in the Roman world was not based on race but was a result of misfortune—conquest, defeated communities being enslaved en masse, or slave traders' kidnapping of unfortunate travelers or picking up abandoned infants to raise as slaves. The Romans still regarded slaves as property and as inferior beings and treated them harshly. However, Roman slavery was highly hierarchical, allowing slaves de facto wealth and placing wealthy and skilled slaves in positions of authority over other slaves. In large households, slave women were less likely to attain such positions of authority and more likely to hold "feminine" occupations that catered to the needs of female owners, such as *nutrix* (child's nurse) or *ornatrix* (hairdresser). A slave woman might be freed for reasons of affection or so that her male owner could marry her; she was probably less able to earn money to purchase her own manumission. Slave women were regarded as sexually available and were sexually exploited; many were sold into prostitution while still children. This dismal picture does not rule out the existence of individual resourceful, successful slave women, such as Caenis, the concubine of the emperor Vespasian, or the freedwomen whom the emperor Claudius offered the *ius liberorum* if they entered the shipping industry.

Roman women were excluded from political office and from representing others in the law courts; both roles were important activities of male *patroni*, patrons who used their power and influence to assist relatives, political allies, and lower-status clients. Roman women of the upper orders also were patrons, both sponsoring literary production and becoming the patronesses of *collegia* (voluntary associations) and entire towns. The greatest female patrons were, of course, the Roman empresses. At the level of smaller cities and towns, wealthy women from the decurial order upward also entered public life as benefactors, funding local amenities such as temples, shrines, baths, theaters, amphitheaters, porticoes, markets, and sponsoring public festivals. Some of these female benefactors were also public priestesses of the deified empresses or of other gods. Women who were less well-off could not be benefactors on this scale, but they could establish funerary foundations, leaving part of their property to fund the holding of remembrance feasts at their graves.

As the public priestesses show, religious activity was an area of the public sphere that was open to Roman women at all social levels. At the top, the high priestesses of the state religion of the city of Rome, the Vestal Virgins and the *flaminicae*, held positions of great honor and influence, though the Vestals risked being put to death for alleged unchastity; their *pudicitia* was equated with the safety of Rome, and a military defeat or disaster might mean that they would be assumed unchaste and buried alive. In the early and middle Republic, elite matrons also sponsored the establishment of new gods, such as Fortuna Muliebris, Pudicitia, and the Magna Mater (Cybele, worshipped in Asia Minor). In the Principate, public priestesses served the cults of the deified emperors and empresses. In daily life, at lower social levels, women worshipped the gods of their households, the *Lares* and *Penates*, and took part in Roman festivals that involved the family. Women at all social levels attended major public festivals, including games in the amphitheater and circus. They were also associated with negatively stereotyped aspects of religion—"superstition," private divination, and magic.

Death was also the experience of all women in the Roman world, in a culture that did not place great emphasis on the immortality of the soul. People coped with the prospect of death through commemoration: the ritually observed funeral, eulogies, the construction of funerary monuments, the reverence paid to deceased family members at their tombs, and festivals such as the *Parentalia* that emphasized the remembrance of the dead. Again, the experience of women was stratified. Elite men, particularly those who had held public and military office, received elaborate funerals, with a procession of relatives wearing ancestral masks, a public eulogy, and a publicly funded interment. Elite women had not held such offices, but also (from the late Republic onward) received eulogies and public funerals. These public funerals of women continued during the Principate, though not at Rome itself. Women in the sub-elite did not receive public funerals but might have highly idealized epitaphs that continued to uphold a domestic and chaste ideal. The poorest women of the Roman world were buried without stone inscriptions; they may have had wooden markers or no marker at all.

ABBREVIATIONS

In documentary citations (inscriptions, tablets, and papyri), the surviving document may be fragmentary and may be restored from two or more fragments, indicated by a + symbol. Successive editions and reprints of the same documents are indicated by an = symbol.

COLLECTIONS

Companion to Families
> Rawson, Beryl, ed. *A Companion to Families in the Greek and Roman Worlds*. Malden, MA, 2011.

Companion to Women
> James, Sharon L., and Sheila Dillon, eds. *A Companion to Women in the Ancient World*. Malden, MA, 2012.

Evans-Grubbs, *Women*
> Evans-Grubbs, Judith, ed. *Women and the Law in the Roman Empire: A Sourcebook on Marriage, Divorce, and Widowhood*. London, 2002.

Hemelrijk, *Women and Society*
> Hemelrijk, Emily A., ed. *Women and Society in the Roman World: A Sourcebook of Inscriptions from the Roman West*. Cambridge, 2021.

Parkin, *Roman Social History*
>   Parkin, Tim G., and Arthur J. Pomeroy, eds. *Roman Social History: A Sourcebook*. London, 2007.

Pompeii and Herculaneum
>   Cooley, Alison, and M. G. L. Cooley, eds., *Pompeii and Herculaneum: A Sourcebook*. London, 2013.

Rowlandson
>   Rowlandson, Jane, ed. *Women and Society in Greek and Roman Egypt: A Sourcebook*. Cambridge, 1998.

Shelton
>   Shelton, Jo-Ann, ed. *As the Romans Did: A Source Book in Roman Social History*. Oxford, 1988.

Women's Life
>   Lefkowitz, Mary R., and Maureen B. Fant, eds. *Women's Life in Greece and Rome: A Source Book in Translation*. 4th ed. Baltimore, MD, 2016.

PRIMARY SOURCES

From the *Oxford Classical Dictionary* (4th ed., 2012).

Cic. *Att.*	Cicero, *Letters to Atticus*
Cic. *Fam.*	Cicero, *Letters to His Friends*
CIL	*Corpus Inscriptionum Latinarum*
D.	*Digest of Justinian*
Dio	Cassius Dio, *History of Rome*
Dion. Hal.	Dionysius of Halicarnassus
Festus	Sextus Pompeius Festus, *On the Meaning of Words*
Herodian	Herodian, *History of Rome*
ILS	*Inscriptiones Latinae Selectae*
Juvenal	Juvenal, *Satires*
Livy	Livy, *History of Rome*
Martial	Martial, *Epigrams*
Plin. *Ep.*	Pliny the Younger, *Letters*
Plut.	Plutarch, *Parallel Lives* (cited individually), *Moralia, Roman Questions*

SHA	Scriptores Historiae Augustae
Suet.	Suetonius, *Twelve Caesars* (cited individually)
Tac.	Tacitus, *Annals of Imperial Rome, Histories, Agricola, Dialogue on Oratory*
Valerius Maximus	Valerius Maximus, *Memorable Deeds and Sayings*

JOURNAL TITLES

AJPh	*American Journal of Philology*
AJAH	*American Journal of Ancient History*
AW	*The Ancient World*
BICS	*Bulletin of the Institute of Classical Studies*
CA	*Classical Antiquity*
CO	*Classical Outlook*
CPh	*Classical Philology*
CQ	*Classical Quarterly*
CW	*Classical World*
G&R	*Greece & Rome*
HSCPh	*Harvard Studies in Classical Philology*
JRA	*Journal of Roman Archaeology*
JRS	*Journal of Roman Studies*
PBSR	*Papers of the British School at Rome*
PCPhS	*Proceedings of the Cambridge Philological Society*
TAPA	*Transactions of the American Philological Association*

CITATIONS OF PAPYRI COLLECTIONS

Standard abbreviations are listed in John F. Oates et al., *Checklist of Editions of Greek, Latin, Demotic, and Coptic Papyri, Ostraca, and Tablets* (Oakville, CT, 2001; later editions online at https://library .duke.edu/papyrus/texts/clist.html and at http://papyri.info /docs/checklist#).

BIBLIOGRAPHY

Allason-Jones, Lindsay. *Women in Roman Britain*. London: British Museum, 1989.

Allison, Penelope M. *People and Spaces in Roman Military Bases*. Cambridge: Cambridge University Press, 2013.

Alston, Richard. *Rome's Revolution: Death of the Republic and Birth of the Empire*. Oxford: Oxford University Press, 2015.

Andersson Strand, Eva, and Ulla Mannering. "Textiles." In Harlow, *Cultural History*, 13–35.

Ando, Clifford. *Imperial Ideology and Provincial Loyalty in the Roman Empire*. Berkeley: University of California Press, 2000.

Andreau, Jean. *Banking and Business in the Roman World*. Trans. Janet Lloyd. Cambridge: Cambridge University Press, 1999.

Bagnall, Roger S. *Reading Papyri, Writing Ancient History*. London: Routledge, 1995.

Bagnall, Roger S., and Bruce W. Frier. *The Demography of Roman Egypt*. 2nd ed. Cambridge: Cambridge University Press, 2006.

Beard, Mary. *SPQR: A History of Ancient Rome*. New York: W. W. Norton, 2015.

Beard, Mary, John North, and Simon Price. *Religions of Rome, Volume I: A History; Volume II: A Sourcebook*. Cambridge: Cambridge University Press, 1998.

Boatwright, Mary T. *Imperial Women of Rome: Power, Gender, Context*. Oxford: Oxford University Press, 2021.

Bodel, John. "Cicero's Minerva, *Penates*, and the Mother of the *Lares*: An outline of Roman domestic religion." In *Household and Family Religion in Antiquity: The Ancient World, Comparative Histories*, ed. John Bodel and Saul M. Olyan, 248–75. Malden, MA: Wiley, 2008.

Bodel, John. "Dealing with the dead: Undertakers, executioners, and potters' fields in ancient Rome." In Hope and Marshall, *Death and Disease*, 128–51.

Bodel, John. "Minicia Marcella: Taken before her time." *AJPh* 116.3 (1995), 453–60.

Borca, F. "Towns and marshes in the ancient world." In Hope and Marshall, *Death and Disease*, 74–84.

Bowes, Kimberly. "At home." In *A Companion to the Archaeology of Religion in the Ancient World*, ed. Rubina Raja and Jörg Rüpke, 209–19. Malden, MA: Wiley-Blackwell, 2015.

Bowman, Alan K. *Life and Letters on the Roman Frontier: Vindolanda and Its People*. London: Routledge, 1994.

Bradley, Keith. *Slavery and Society at Rome*. Cambridge: Cambridge University Press, 1994.

Bradley, Mark, ed. *Rome: Pollution and Propriety: Dirt, Disease, and Hygiene in the Eternal City from Antiquity to Modernity*. Cambridge: Cambridge University Press, 2012.

Brice, L. L., and Elizabeth M. Greene, eds. *Present But Not Accounted for: Women and the Roman Army*. Cambridge, forthcoming.

Brunt, P. A. *Italian Manpower, 225 B.C.–A.D. 14*. 2nd ed. Oxford: Oxford University Press, 1987.

Campbell, Brian. *The Roman Army, 31 BC–AD 337: A Sourcebook*. London: Routledge, 1994.

Campbell, Brian. "The Roman Empire." In Raaflaub and Rosenstein, *War and Society*, 217–40.

Campbell, J. B. *The Emperor and the Roman Army, 31 BC–AD 235*. Oxford: Oxford University Press, 1984.

Cantarella, Eva. *Pandora's Daughters: The Role and Status of Women in Greek and Roman Antiquity*. Trans. Maureen B. Fant. Baltimore, MD: Johns Hopkins University Press, 1987.

Champlin, Edward. "*Creditur vulgo testamenta hominum speculum esse morum*: Why the Romans made wills." *CPh* 84.3 (1989), 198–215.

Champlin, Edward. *Final Judgments: Duty and Emotion in Roman Wills, 200 B.C.–A.D. 250*. Berkeley: University of California Press, 1991.

Cooley, Alison E. *Cambridge Manual of Latin Epigraphy*. Cambridge: Cambridge University Press, 2012.

Cooley, Alison E., and M. G. L. Cooley, eds. *Pompeii and Herculaneum: A Sourcebook*. London: Routledge, 2013.

Cottica, Daniela. "Spinning in the Roman world: From everyday craft to metaphor of destiny." In Gillis and Nosch, *Ancient Textiles*, 220–28.

Cribiore, Raffaella. *Writing, Teachers, and Students in Graeco-Roman Egypt.* Atlanta, GA: Scholars, 1996.

Crook, John. *Law and Life of Rome, 90 B.C.–A.D. 212.* Ithaca, NY: Cornell University Press, 1967.

Croom, Alexandra. *Roman Clothing and Fashion.* Stroud: Amberley, 2010.

Croom, Alexandra. *Running the Roman Home.* Stroud: Amberley, 2012.

Cunningham, Rebecca M., Maureen A. Walton, and Patrick M. Carter. "The major causes of death in children and adolescents in the United States." *New England Journal of Medicine* 379 (2018), 2468–75.

D'Ambra, Eve. *Roman Women.* Cambridge: Cambridge University Press, 2007.

D'Ambra, Eve. "Women on the Bay of Naples." In James and Dillon, *Companion to Women,* 400–13.

Dasen, Veronique. "Childbirth and infancy in Greek and Roman antiquity." In Rawson, *Companion to Families,* 291–314.

Davies, Glenys. "Honorific vs. funerary statues of women: Essentially the same or fundamentally different?" In Hemelrijk and Woolf, *Women,* 171–99.

Davies, Glenys, and Lloyd Llewellyn-Jones. "The body." In Harlow, *Cultural History,* 49–69.

Davies, Glenys, and Lloyd Llewellyn-Jones. "Gender and sexuality." In Harlow, *Cultural History,* 87–104.

Davis, David Brion. *Inhuman Bondage: The Rise and Fall of Slavery in the New World.* Oxford: Oxford University Press, 2006.

DiLuzio, Meghan J. *A Place at the Altar: Priestesses in Republican Rome.* Princeton, NJ: Princeton University Press, 2016.

Dixon, Suzanne. *Reading Roman Women: Sources, Genres, and Real Life.* London: Duckworth, 2001.

Dolansky, Fanny. "Honouring the family dead on the *Parentalia*: Ceremony, spectacle, and memory." *Phoenix* 65.1/2 (2011), 125–57.

Dolansky, Fanny. "*Togam virilem sumere*: Coming of age in the Roman world." In Edmondson and Keith, *Roman Dress,* 47–70.

Donahue, John F. "Iunia Rustica of Cartima: Female munificence in the Roman west." *Latomus* 63.4 (2004), 873–91.

Dross-Krüpe, Kersten. "Production and distribution." In Harlow, *Cultural History,* 37–48.

Edmondson, Jonathan. "Public dress and social control in late Republican and early imperial Rome." In Edmondson and Keith, *Roman Dress,* 21–46.

Edmondson, Jonathan. "Roman family history." In *The Oxford Handbook of Roman Epigraphy,* ed. Christer Bruun and Jonathan Edmondson, 559–81. Oxford: Oxford University Press, 2015.

Edmondson, Jonathan, and Alison Keith, eds. *Roman Dress and the Fabrics of Roman Culture.* Toronto: University of Toronto Press, 2008.

Edwards, Catherine. "Unspeakable professions: Public performance and prostitution in ancient Rome." In Hallett and Skinner, *Roman Sexualities*, 66–95.

Erker, Darja Sterbenc. "Gender and Roman funeral ritual." In *Memory and Mourning: Studies on Roman Death*, ed. Valerie M. Hope and Janet Huskinson, 40–60. Oxford: Oxford University Press, 2011.

Evans-Grubbs, Judith. "Promoting *pietas* through Roman law." In Rawson, *Companion to Families*, 377–92.

Evans-Grubbs, Judith. *Women and the Law in the Roman Empire: A Sourcebook on Marriage, Divorce, and Widowhood.* London: Routledge, 2002.

Fagan, Garrett G. *Bathing in Public in the Roman World.* Ann Arbor: University of Michigan Press, 1999.

Finley, M. I. *The Ancient Economy.* Berkeley: University of California Press, 1973.

Flemming, Rebecca. "Gendering medical provision in the cities of the Roman west." In Hemelrijk and Woolf, *Women*, 271–93.

Flower, Harriet L. *The Dancing Lares and the Serpent in the Garden: Religion at the Roman Street Corner.* Princeton: Princeton University Press, 2017.

Foxhall, Lin. *Studying Gender in Classical Antiquity.* Cambridge: Cambridge University Press, 2013.

Frier, Bruce W. *A Casebook on the Roman Law of Delict.* Atlanta, GA: Scholars, 1989.

Gallia, Andrew B. "The Vestal habit." *CPh* 109.3 (2014), 222–40.

Gardner, Jane F. *Being a Roman Citizen.* London: Routledge, 1993.

Gardner, Jane F. "Proofs of status in the Roman world." *Bulletin of the Institute of Classical Studies* 33 (1986), 1–14.

Gardner, Jane F. "Roman 'horror' of intestacy?" In Rawson, *Companion to Families*, 361–76.

Gardner, Jane F. *Women in Roman Law and Society.* London: Croom Helm, 1986.

Garnsey, Peter. *Food and Society in Classical Antiquity.* Cambridge: Cambridge University Press, 1999.

Garnsey, Peter. *Social Status and Legal Privilege in the Roman Empire.* Oxford: Oxford University Press, 1970.

Garnsey, Peter, and Richard Saller. *The Roman Empire: Economy, Society, and Culture.* Berkeley: University of California Press, 1987.

George, Michele. "The 'dark side' of the toga." In Edmondson and Keith, *Roman Dress*, 94–112.

Gillis, Carole, and Marie-Louise B. Nosch, eds. *Ancient Textiles: Production, Craft, and Society.* Oxford: Oxbow, 2007.

Gowers, Emily. "The anatomy of Rome: From Capitol to Cloaca." *JRS* 85 (1995), 23–32.

Greene, Elizabeth. "Female networks in military communities in the Roman West: A view from the Vindolanda Tablets." In Hemelrijk and Woolf, *Women*, 369–90.

Grmek, M. *Diseases in the Ancient Greek World*. Baltimore, MD: Johns Hopkins University Press, 1989.

Groen-Vallinga, Miriam J. "'Desperate' housewives? The adaptive family economy and female participation in the Roman urban labour market." In Hemelrijk and Woolf, *Women*, 295–312.

Gunderson, Erik. "The ideology of the arena." *CA* 15.1 (1996), 113–51.

Hallett, Judith P. "'Perusine glandes' and the changing image of Augustus." *AJAH* 2.2 (1977), 151–71.

Hallett, Judith P., and Marilyn B. Skinner, eds. *Roman Sexualities*. Princeton, NJ: Princeton University Press, 1997.

Hänninen, Marja-Leena. "Domestic cult and the construction of an ideal Roman family." In *Religious Participation in Ancient and Medieval Societies: Rituals, Interaction, and Identity*, ed. Sari Katajala-Peltomaa and Ville Vuolanto, 39–49. Rome: Institutum Romanum Finlandiae, 2013.

Hänninen, Marja-Leena. "Religious agency and civic identity of women in ancient Ostia." In *Gender, Memory, and Identity in the Roman World*, ed. Iussi Rantala, 63–88. Amsterdam: Amsterdam University Press, 2019.

Harlow, Mary. "Dressed women on the streets of the ancient city: What to wear?" In Hemelrijk and Woolf, *Women*, 225–41.

Harlow, Mary, ed. *A Cultural History of Dress and Fashion in Antiquity*. London: Bloomsbury, 2017.

Harper, Kyle. *The Fate of Rome: Climate, Disease, and the End of an Empire*. Princeton, NJ: Princeton University Press, 2017.

Harper, Kyle. *From Shame to Sin: The Christian Transformation of Sexual Morality in Late Antiquity*. Cambridge, MA: Harvard University Press, 2013.

Harries, Jill. *Law and Crime in the Roman World*. Cambridge: Cambridge University Press, 2007.

Harris, William V. *Ancient Literacy*. Cambridge, MA: Harvard University Press, 1989.

Harris, William V. "Child-exposure in the Roman empire." *JRS* 84 (1994), 1–22.

Harris, William V. *War and Imperialism in Republican Rome, 327–70 B.C.* Oxford: Oxford University Press, 1979.

Hawley, Richard. "Lords of the rings: Ring-wearing, status, and identity in the age of Pliny the Elder." In *Vita Vigilia Est: Essays in Honour of Barbara Levick*, ed. Edward Bispham and Greg Rowe, 103–11. London: Institute of Classical Studies, University of London, 2007.

Heckett, Elizabeth W. "Clothing patterns as construction of the human mind: Establishment and continuity." In Gillis and Nosch, *Ancient Textiles*, 208–14.

Hemelrijk, Emily A. "Female munificence in the cities of the Latin west." In Hemelrijk and Woolf, *Women*, 65–84.

Hemelrijk, Emily A. *Hidden Lives, Public Personae: Women and Civic Life in the Roman West*. Oxford: Oxford University Press, 2015.

Hemelrijk, Emily A. "Local empresses: Priestesses of the imperial cult in the cities of the Latin West." *Phoenix* 61.3/4 (2007), 318–49.

Hemelrijk, Emily A. "Masculinity and femininity in the 'Laudatio Turiae.'" *CQ* 54 (2004), 185–97.

Hemelrijk, Emily A. *Matrona Docta: Educated Women in the Roman Elite from Cornelia to Julia Domna*. London: Routledge, 1999.

Hemelrijk, Emily A. "Patronesses and 'mothers' of Roman *collegia*." *CA* 27.1 (2008), 115–62.

Hemelrijk, Emily A. "Priestesses of the imperial cult in the Latin West: Benefactions and public honour." *L'Antiquité Classique* 75 (2006), 85–117.

Hemelrijk, Emily A. "Public roles for women in the cities of the Latin West." In James and Dillon, *Companion to Women*, 478–90.

Hemelrijk, Emily A. *Women and Society in the Roman World: A Sourcebook of Inscriptions from the Roman West*. Cambridge: Cambridge University Press, 2021.

Hemelrijk, Emily A., and Greg Woolf, eds. *Women and the Roman City in the Latin West*. Leiden: Brill, 2013.

Hersch, Karen K. *The Roman Wedding: Ritual and Meaning in Antiquity*. Cambridge: Cambridge University Press, 2010.

Hin, Saskia. *The Demography of Roman Italy: Population Dynamics in an Ancient Conquest Society (201 BCE–14 CE)*. Cambridge: Cambridge University Press, 2013.

Holland, Lora L. "Women and Roman religion." In James and Dillon, *Companion to Women*, 204–14.

Holleran, Claire. "Women and retail in Roman Italy." In Hemelrijk and Woolf, *Women*, 313–30.

Hope, Valerie M. "Contempt and respect: The treatment of the corpse in ancient Rome." In Hope and Marshall, *Death and Disease*, 104–27.

Hope, Valerie M. "Fighting for identity: The funerary commemoration of Italian gladiators." In *The Epigraphic Landscape of Roman Italy*, ed. Alison E. Cooley, 93–113. London: Institute of Classical Studies, University of London.

Hope, Valerie M. *Roman Death: The Dying and the Dead in Ancient Rome*. London: Bloomsbury, 2009.

Hope, Valerie M., and Eireann Marshall, eds. *Death and Disease in the Ancient City*. London: Routledge, 2000.

Hopkins, Keith. *Death and Renewal*. Cambridge: Cambridge University Press, 1983.

Hopkins, Keith. "On the probable age structure of the Roman population." *Population Studies* 20.2 (1966), 245–65.

Huebner, Sabine. *The Family in Roman Egypt: A Comparative Approach to Intergenerational Solidarity and Conflict*. Cambridge: Cambridge University Press, 2015.

Hughes, J. D. *Environmental Problems of the Greeks and Romans: Ecology in the Ancient Mediterranean.* 2nd ed. Baltimore, MD: Johns Hopkins University Press, 2014.

Isaac, Benjamin. *The Invention of Racism in Classical Antiquity.* Princeton, NJ: Princeton University Press, 2004.

Jackson, Ralph. *Doctors and Diseases in the Roman Empire.* London: British Museum, 1988.

James, Sharon L., and Sheila Dillon, eds. *A Companion to Women in the Ancient World.* Malden, MA: Wiley-Blackwell, 2012.

Johanson, Christopher. "A walk with the dead: A funerary cityscape of ancient Rome." In Rawson, *Companion to Families,* 408–30.

Johnston, David. *Roman Law in Context.* Cambridge: Cambridge University Press, 1999.

Jones, A. H. M. "The cloth industry under the Roman empire." *Economic History Review* 13 (1960), 183–192.

Jones, C. P. "*Stigma*: Tattooing and branding in Graeco-Roman antiquity." *JRS* 77 (1987), 139–55.

Jongman, Willem. "The early Roman empire: Consumption." In *Cambridge Economic History,* 592–618.

Joshel, Sandra R. *Slavery in the Roman World.* Cambridge: Cambridge University Press, 2010.

Joshel, Sandra R. *Work, Identity, and Legal Status at Rome: A Study of the Occupational Inscriptions.* Norman: University of Oklahoma Press, 1992.

Joshel, Sandra R., and Sheila Murnaghan, eds. *Women and Slaves in Greco-Roman Culture: Differential Equations.* London: Routledge, 1998.

Keaveney, Arthur. *The Army in the Roman Revolution.* London: Routledge, 2007.

King, Helen. *Hippocrates' Woman: Reading the Female Body in Ancient Greece.* London: Routledge, 2002.

King, Helen, ed. *Health in Antiquity.* London: Routledge, 2005.

Koloski-Ostrow, Ann Olga. *The Archaeology of Sanitation in Roman Italy: Toilets, Sewers, and Water Systems.* Chapel Hill: University of North Carolina Press, 2015.

Kwiatkowski, D. P. "How malaria has affected the human genome and what human genetics can tell us about malaria." *American Journal of Human Genetics* 77 (2005), 171–92.

La Follette, Laetitia. "The costume of the Roman bride." In Sebesta and Bonfante, *The World of Roman Costume,* 54–64.

Laes, Christian. *Children in the Roman Empire: Outsiders Within.* Cambridge: Cambridge University Press, 2011.

Langlands, Rebecca. *Sexual Morality in Ancient Rome.* Cambridge: Cambridge University Press, 2006.

Laqueur, Thomas W. *The Work of the Dead: A Cultural History of Mortal Remains.* Princeton, NJ: Princeton University Press, 2015.

Larsson Lovén, Lena. "Wool work as a gender symbol in ancient Rome. Roman textiles and ancient sources." In Gillis and Nosch, *Ancient Textiles*, 229–36.

Laurence, Ray. "Health and the life course at Herculaneum and Pompeii." In King, *Health in Antiquity*, 83–96.

Lefkowitz, Mary R. "Wives and husbands." *G&R* 30 (1983), 31–47.

Lefkowitz, Mary R., and Maureen B. Fant, eds. *Women's Life in Greece and Rome: A Source Book in Translation*. 4th ed. Baltimore, MD: Johns Hopkins University Press, 2016.

Levick, Barbara. "Women and law." In James and Dillon, *Companion to Women*, 96–106.

Lindsay, Hugh. "Death-pollution and funerals in the city of Rome." In Hope and Marshall, *Death and Disease*, 152–73.

Lindsay, Hugh. "The 'Laudatio Murdiae': Its content and significance." *Latomus* 63.1 (2004), 88–97.

Lintott, Andrew W. *The Constitution of the Roman Republic*. Oxford: Oxford University Press, 1999.

Loudon, I. "Deaths in childbed from the eighteenth century to 1935." *Medical History* 30.1 (1986), 1–41.

MacMullen, Ramsay. *Changes in the Roman Empire: Essays in the Ordinary*. Princeton: Princeton University Press, 1990.

MacMullen, Ramsay. "The end of ancestor worship: Affect and class." *Historia* 63.4 (2014), 487–513.

MacMullen, Ramsay. "Social history in astrology." *Ancient Society* 2 (1971), 105–16. In MacMullen, *Changes*, 218–24.

MacMullen, Ramsay. *Soldier and Civilian in the Later Roman Empire*. Cambridge, MA: Harvard University Press, 1963.

MacMullen, Ramsay. "Women in public in the Roman Empire." *Historia* 29 (1980), 208–18. In MacMullen, *Changes*, 162–68.

MacMullen, Ramsay. "Women's power in the Principate." *Klio* 68 (1986), 434–43. In MacMullen, *Changes*, 169–76.

Mattern, Susan. *The Slow Moon Climbs: The Science, History, and Meaning of Menopause*. Princeton, NJ: Princeton University Press, 2019.

Maurin, J. "*Labor matronalis*: Aspects du travail féminin à Rome." In *La femme dans les sociétés antiques*, ed. Edmond Lévy, 139–54. Strasbourg: Université des sciences humaines de Strasbourg, 1983.

McClure, Laura K. *Women in Classical Antiquity: From Birth to Death*. Hoboken, NJ: Wiley-Blackwell, 2019.

McGinn, Thomas A. J. *The Economy of Prostitution in the Roman World: A Study of Social History & the Brothel*. Ann Arbor: University of Michigan Press, 2004.

McGinn, Thomas A. J. *Prostitution, Sexuality, and the Law in Ancient Rome*. Oxford: Oxford University Press, 1998.

McGinn, Thomas A. J. "Widows, orphans, and social history." *JRA* 12 (1999), 617–32.

Michels, Agnes K. "Roman festivals: April–June." *CO* 67.3 (1990), 76–77.

Michels, Agnes K. "Roman festivals: January–March." *CO* 68.2 (1990–91), 44–48.

Michels, Agnes K. "Roman festivals: July–September." *CO* 67.4 (1990), 114–16.

Michels, Agnes K. "Roman festivals: October–December." *CO* 68.1 (1990), 10–12.

Minter, Adam. *Secondhand: Travels in the New Global Garage Sale*. New York: Bloomsbury, 2019.

Morland, Paul. *The Human Tide: How Population Shaped the Modern World*. New York: Public Affairs, 2019.

Morley, Neville. "The salubriousness of the Roman city." In King, *Health in Antiquity*, 192–204.

Mouritsen, Henrik. "The families of Roman slaves and freedmen." In Rawson, *Companion to Families*, 129–44.

Nicholas, Barry. *An Introduction to Roman Law*. Oxford: Oxford University Press, 1962.

Olson, Kelly. "The appearance of the young Roman girl." In Edmondson and Keith, *Roman Dress*, 139–57.

Olson, Kelly. *Dress and the Roman Woman: Self-Presentation and Society*. London: Routledge, 2008.

Parker, Holt N. "Loyal slaves and loyal wives: The crisis of the outsider-within and Roman *exemplum* literature." In Joshel and Murnaghan, *Women and Slaves*, 152–73.

Parker, Holt N. "The teratogenic grid." In Hallett and Skinner, *Roman Sexualities*, 47–65.

Parker, Holt N. "Why were the Vestals virgins? Or the chastity of women and the safety of the Roman state." *AJPh* 125.4 (2004), 563–601.

Parker, Holt N. "Women and medicine." In James and Dillon, *Companion to Women*, 107–24.

Parkin, Tim G. *Demography and Roman Society*. Baltimore, MD: Johns Hopkins University Press, 1992.

Parkin, Tim G. "The Roman life course and the family." In Rawson, *Companion to Families*, 276–90.

Parkin, Tim G., and Arthur J. Pomeroy, eds. *Roman Social History: A Sourcebook*. London: Routledge, 2007.

Patterson, Orlando. *Slavery and Social Death: A Comparative Study*. Cambridge, MA: Harvard University Press, 1982.

Paule, Maxwell Teitel. "*Qvae saga, qvis magvs*: On the vocabulary of the Roman witch." *CQ* 64.2 (2014), 745–57.

Peachin, Michael, ed. *The Oxford Handbook of Social Relations in the Roman World*. Oxford: Oxford University Press, 2011.

Pearce, J. "Infants, cemeteries, and communities in the Roman provinces." In *Theoretical Roman Archaeology Conference 2000: Proceedings of the Tenth Annual eoretical Roman Archaeology Conference: Held at the*

Institute of Archaeology, University College London 6th–7th April 2000, ed. Gwyn Davies, Andrew Gardner, and Kris Lockyear, 125–42. Oxford: Oxbow, 2001.

Perry, Matthew J. *Gender, Manumission, and the Roman Freedwoman*. Cambridge: Cambridge University Press, 2014.

Phang, Sara Elise. "Elite marriage and adultery in the camp: Plin. *Ep.* 6.31.4–6 and Tac. *Hist.* 1.48." In *Present but Not Accounted For: Women & The Roman Army*, ed. L. L. Brice and E. M. Greene. Forthcoming.

Phang, Sara Elise. "Intimate conquests: Roman soldiers' slave women and freedwomen." *AW* 35.2 (2004), 207–37.

Phang, Sara Elise. *The Marriage of Roman Soldiers (13 B.C.–A.D. 235): Law and Family in the Imperial Army*. Leiden: Brill, 2001.

Pilkington, Nathan. "Growing up Roman: Infant mortality and reproductive development." *Journal of Interdisciplinary History* 44.1 (2013), 1–35.

Pomeroy, Sarah B. *Goddesses, Whores, Wives, and Slaves: Women in Classical Antiquity*. New York: Schocken Books, 1975.

Potter, David S. *Literary Texts and the Roman Historian*. London: Routledge, 1999.

Raaflaub, Kurt, and Nathan Rosenstein, eds. *War and Society in the Ancient and Medieval Worlds: Asia, the Mediterranean, Europe, and Mesoamerica*. Washington, DC: Center for Hellenic Studies, 1999.

Rawson, Beryl. *Children and Childhood in Roman Italy*. Oxford: Oxford University Press, 2003.

Rawson, Beryl, ed. *A Companion to Families in the Greek and Roman Worlds*. Malden, MA: Wiley-Blackwell, 2011.

Rawson, Elizabeth. "*Discrimina ordinum*: The *Lex Julia theatralis*." *PBSR* 55 (1987), 83–114.

Reardon, B. P., ed. *Collected Ancient Greek Novels*. 2nd ed. Berkeley, CA: University of California Press, 2008.

Richlin, Amy. *Arguments with Silence: Writing the History of Roman Women*. Ann Arbor: University of Michigan Press, 2014.

Richlin, Amy. "Carrying water in a sieve: Class and the body in Roman women's religion." In *Women and Goddess Traditions: In Antiquity and Today*, ed. Karen L. King, 330–74. Minneapolis: Fortress Press, 1997.

Richlin, Amy. "Emotional work: Lamenting the Roman dead." In *Essays in Honor of Gordon Williams: Twenty-Five Years at Yale*, ed. Elizabeth Tylawsky and Charles Weiss, 229–48. New Haven, CT: Yale University Press, 2001.

Richlin, Amy. "Gender and rhetoric: Producing manhood in the schools." In *Roman Eloquence: Rhetoric in Society and Literature*, ed. William J. Dominik, 90–110. London: Routledge, 1997.

Riess, Werner. "*Rari exempli femina*: Female virtues on Roman funerary inscriptions." In James and Dillon, *Companion to Women*, 491–501.

Ripat, Pauline. "Expelling misconceptions: Astrologers at Rome." *CPh* 106.2 (2011), 115–54.

Rives, James. "Women and animal sacrifice in public life." In Hemelrijk and Woolf, *Women*, 129–46.

Robinson, O. F. *The Sources of Roman Law: Problems and Methods for Ancient Historians*. London: Routledge, 1997.

Roller, Matthew. "Horizontal women: Posture and sex in the Roman *convivium*." *AJPh* 124.3 (2003), 377–422.

Rosenstein, Nathan S. "Republican Rome." In Raaflaub and Rosenstein, *War and Society*, 193–216.

Rosenstein, Nathan S. *Rome at War: Farms. Families and Death in the Middle Republic*. Chapel Hill: University of North Carolina Press, 2004.

Roth, Ulrike. "Inscribed meaning: The *vilica* and the villa economy." *PBSR* 72 (2004), 101–24.

Roth, Ulrike. *Thinking Tools: Agricultural Slavery between Evidence and Models*. BICS Supplement no. 92. London: Institute of Classical Studies, 2007.

Rowlandson, Jane, ed. *Women and Society in Greek and Roman Egypt: A Sourcebook*. Cambridge: Cambridge University Press, 1998.

Rüpke, Jörg. *Religion of the Romans*. Trans. Richard Gordon. Cambridge: Polity Press, 2007.

Sallares, Robert. "Ecology." In *Cambridge Economic History*, 15–37.

Sallares, Robert. *Malaria and Rome: A History of Malaria in Ancient Italy*. Oxford: Oxford University Press, 2002.

Sallares, Robert, Abigail Bouwman, and Cecilia Anderung. "The spread of malaria to southern Europe in antiquity." *Medical History* 48.3 (2004), 311–28.

Saller, Richard P. "Household and gender." In *Cambridge Economic History*, 87–112.

Saller, Richard P. "*Pater familias, mater familias*, and the gendered semantics of the Roman household." *CPh* 94.2 (1999), 182–97.

Saller, Richard P. *Patriarchy, Property, and Death in the Roman Family*. Cambridge: Cambridge University Press, 1994.

Saller, Richard P. *Personal Patronage under the Early Empire*. Cambridge: Cambridge University Press, 1982.

Saller, Richard P. "The Roman family as productive unit." In Rawson, *Companion to Families*, 116–28.

Saller, Richard P. "Symbols of gender and status hierarchies in the Roman household." In Joshel and Murnaghan, *Women and Slaves*, 85–91.

Saller, Richard P., and Brent D. Shaw. "Tombstones and Roman family relations in the Principate: civilians, soldiers, and slaves." *JRS* 74 (1984), 124–55.

Scheid, John. *An Introduction to Roman Religion*. Bloomington: Indiana University Press, 2003.

Scheidel, Walter. "Demography." In *Cambridge Economic History*, 38–86.

Scheidel, Walter. "The demography of the Roman imperial army." In *Measuring Sex, Age, and Death in the Roman Empire*, ed. Walter Scheidel, 93–138. Portsmouth, RI: Journal of Roman Archaeology, 1996.

Scheidel, Walter. "Emperors, aristocrats, and the Grim Reaper: Towards a demographic profile of the Roman elite." *CQ* 49.1 (1999), 254–81.

Scheidel, Walter. "Libitina's bitter gains: Seasonal mortality and endemic disease in the ancient city of Rome." *Ancient Society* 25 (1994), 151–75.

Scheidel, Walter. "The most silent women of Greece and Rome: Rural labour and women's life in the ancient world (I)." *G&R* 42 (1995), 202–17.

Scheidel, Walter. "The most silent women of Greece and Rome: Rural labour and women's life in the ancient world (II)." *G&R* 43.1 (1996), 1–10.

Scheidel, Walter. "Real slave prices and the relative cost of slave labor in the Greco-Roman world." *Ancient Society* 35 (2005), 1–17.

Scheidel, Walter. "Real wages in Roman Egypt: a contribution to recent work on pre-modern living standards." Princeton, NJ: Princeton/Stanford Working Papers in Classics, 2008. https://www.princeton.edu/~pswpc/pdfs/scheidel/020802.pdf

Schiedel, Walter. "Roman age structure: Evidence and models." *JRS* 91 (2001), 1–26.

Scheidel, Walter, ed. *The Science of Roman History: Biology, Climate, adn the Future of the Past*. Princeton, NJ: Princeton University Press, 2018.

Scheidel, Walter, Ian Morris, and Richard Saller, eds. *The Cambridge Economic History of the Greco-Roman World*. Cambridge: Cambridge University Press, 2007.

Schultz, Celia E. *Women's Religious Activity in the Roman Republic*. Chapel Hill: University of North Carolina Press, 2006.

Scobie, Alex. "Slums, sanitation, and mortality in the Roman world." *Klio* 68 (1986), 399–433.

Scullard, H. H. *Festivals and Ceremonies of the Roman Republic*. Ithaca, NY: Cornell University Press, 1981.

Sebesta, Judith Lynn. "Symbolism in the costume of the Roman woman." In Sebesta and Bonfante, *The World of Roman Costume*, 46–53.

Sebesta, Judith Lynn. "*Tunica ralla, tunica spissa*: The colors and textiles of Roman costume." In Sebesta and Bonfante, *The World of Roman Costume*, 65–76.

Sebesta, Judith Lynn. "Women's costume and feminine civic morality in Augustan Rome." In *Gender and the Body in the Ancient Mediterranean*, ed. Maria Wyke, 105–17. Oxford: Blackwell, 1998.

Sebesta, Judith Lynn, and Larissa Bonfante, eds. *The World of Roman Costume*. Madison: University of Wisconsin Press, 1994.

Severy, Beth. *Augustus and the Family at the Birth of the Roman Empire*. London: Routledge, 2003.

Shaw, Brent D. "Seasons of death: Aspects of mortality in imperial Rome." *JRS* 86 (1996), 100–38.

Shelton, Jo-Ann. *As the Romans Did: A Source Book in Roman Social History.* Oxford: Oxford University Press, 1988.

Shelton, Jo-Ann. *The Women of Pliny's Letters.* London: Routledge, 2013.

Sick, David H. "Ummidia Quadratilla: Cagey businesswoman or lazy pantomime watcher?" *CA* 18.2 (1999), 330–48.

Smallwood, E. Mary. *Documents Illustrating the Principates of Nerva, Trajan, and Hadrian.* Cambridge: Cambridge University Press, 1966.

Snowden, Frank M., Jr. *Before Color Prejudice: The Ancient View of Blacks.* Cambridge, MA: Harvard University Press, 1983.

Sofroniew, Alexandra. *Household Gods: Private Devotion in Ancient Greece and Rome.* Los Angeles: Getty, 2015.

Sperduti, Alessandra, Luca Bondioli, Oliver E. Craig, Tracy Prowse, and Peter Garnsey. "Bones, teeth, and history." In Scheidel, *The Science of Roman History*, 123–73.

St. Clair, Kassia. *The Golden Thread: How Fabric Changed History.* New York: W. W. Norton, 2019.

Stoltzfus, R. J., L. Mullany, and R. E. Black. "Iron deficiency anaemia." In *Comparative Quantification of Health Risks: Global and Regional Burden of Disease Attributable to Selected Major Risk Factors*, ed. M. Ezzati et al., 163–209. Geneva: World Health Organization, 2004.

Stone, Shelley. "The toga: From national to ceremonial costume." In Sebesta and Bonfante, *The World of Roman Costume*, 13–45.

Talbert, Richard J. A. *The Senate of Imperial Rome.* Princeton, NJ: Princeton University Press, 1984.

Temin, Peter. *The Roman Market Economy.* Princeton, NJ: Princeton University Press, 2013.

Toner, J. P. *Leisure and Ancient Rome.* Cambridge: Polity, 1995.

Toynbee, J. M. C. *Death and Burial in the Roman World.* Baltimore, MD: Johns Hopkins University Press, 1971.

Treggiari, Susan. "Jobs in the household of Livia." *PBSR* 43 (1975), 48–77.

Treggiari, Susan. *Roman Marriage: Iusti Coniuges from the Time of Cicero to the Time of Ulpian.* Oxford: Oxford University Press, 1991.

Ward, Roy Bowen. "Women in Roman baths." *Harvard Theological Review* 85.2 (1992), 125–47.

Webb, Lewis. "Gendering the Roman *Imago*." *Eugesta* 7 (2017), 140–83. https://eugesta-revue.univ-lille3.fr/pdf/2017/5.Webb-Eugesta-7_2017.pdf.

Wildfang, Robin Lorsch. *Rome's Vestal Virgins: A Study of Rome's Vestal Priestesses in the Late Republic and Early Empire.* London: Routledge, 2006.

Williams, Craig A. *Roman Homosexuality.* 2nd ed. Oxford: Oxford University Press, 2010.

Williams, Gordon. "Some aspects of Roman marriage ceremonies and ideals." *JRS* 48 (1958), 16–29.

Winegard, Timothy C. *The Mosquito: A Human History of Our Deadliest Predator.* New York: Dutton, 2019.

Zanker, Paul. *The Power of Images in the Age of Augustus.* Trans. Alan Shapiro. Ann Arbor: University of Michigan Press, 1988.

Ziogas, Ioannis. "Stripping the Roman ladies: Ovid's rites and readers." *CQ* 64.2 (2014), 735–44.

INDEX

About the Author

SARA ELISE PHANG, PhD, received a doctorate in Roman history from Columbia University (New York) and is currently employed as a librarian. She is the author of *The Marriage of Roman Soldiers (13 B.C.–A.D. 235): Law and Family in the Imperial Army* (2001), a legal and social history of Roman soldiers' wives and families in the early Empire, which received the Gustave O. Arlt Award in the Humanities in Classical Studies. She is the author of *Roman Military Service: Ideologies of Discipline in the Late Republic and Early Principate* (2008) and coeditor and contributor to *Conflict in Ancient Greece and Rome: The Definitive Political, Social, and Military Encyclopedia* (ABC-CLIO, 2016) and contributor to Lee L. Brice and Elizabeth Greene's forthcoming collection *Present but Not Accounted For: Women and the Roman Army*.